CONT

COVER IMAGE: *Rainbow Serpent* 1992 HJ Wedge—private collection. Image courtesy of Boomalli Aboriginal Artists Co-operative.

Through time he's been travelling to look for a planet to settle down as he makes the sky, the trees, the land and each different group of people—like the Chinese, the English, the Europeans and the Aborigines. Everybody has their own piece of land to live in. Then when he found his resting place he went into a very, very deep sleep. As he slept he started to dream into the future. It showed his people were very very happy living in peace, killing only what they need to live for their food.

As they go along they start to use fire, to cook, to cut shapes out of trees, to carry their water and other objects. Then some of the men started to cut out big parts out of the trees to make boats to go and hunt and they were so in peace until the white people came out here. Destroying the land itself cause their land was over populated. So they sent a lot of the convicts out here to work, so they can start to build the land up, put buildings in, farming and stuff. Then they started to destroy the native people of this land.

Then the Rainbow Serpent started to go into a type of nightmare dream. He sees in his dream how they destroyed a lot of animals we will never see again. As it gets closer to the 19th century they start to turn out cities—they called it the great country, the land of opportunity, for the whites, but not for the dark people of this land. We were thought of as the lowest class in this land of 'theirs'.

As the spirit was still dreaming his nightmare he sees a lot of things that are going to happen soon, like drugs, alcohol, deaths in custody. He likes to see all different personalities living together as one, white going out with dark people, dark people living with whites in harmony and no racism. But the Rainbow Serpent can see this is not going to be because a lot of the people today are still destroying us in devious ways. When the spirit shall have woken you shall have a lot to answer for what you have done to us. Then you had better watch out because he is your judge and he will destroy you all in a very evil way.

HJ Wedge
12 February 1993

CONTESTED GROUND

Australian Aborigines under the British Crown

Edited by Ann McGrath

ALLEN & UNWIN

> *In memory of Kitty McGrath,*
> *my loving grandmother, who taught me so much,*
> *including the piano she could not hear.*

© this collection, Ann McGrath 1995
© in individual chapters remains with their authors

This book is copyright under the Berne Convention.
No reproduction without permission. All rights reserved.

First published in 1995.

Allen & Unwin Pty Ltd
9 Atchison Street, St Leonards, NSW 2065 Australia

National Library of Australia
Cataloguing-in-Publication entry:

Contested ground: Australian Aborigines under
   the British crown.

   Bibliography.
   Includes index.
   ISBN 1 86373 646 8.

   1. Aborigines, Australian—History. 2. Aborigines,
   Australian—Treatment. I. McGrath, Ann (Ann Margaret).

994.0049915

Set in 11/12.5 pt Bembo by DOCUPRO, Sydney
Printed by SRM Production Services Sdn Bhd, Malaysia

10 9 8 7 6 5 4 3 2 1

Contents

Maps		vi
Illustrations		vii
Acknowledgements		ix
Contributors		xii
Preface	Paul Behrendt	xv
Introduction	Ann McGrath	xxii
1 A national story	Ann McGrath	1
2 New South Wales	Heather Goodall	55
3 Victoria	Richard Broome	121
4 Queensland	Henry Reynolds and Dawn May	168
5 South Australia	Peggy Brock	208
6 Western Australia	Sandy Toussaint	240
7 Northern Territory	Peter Read	269
8 Tasmania: 1	Ann McGrath	306
9 Tasmania: 2	Maykutenner (Vicki Matson-Green)	338
10 Contested ground: what is 'Aboriginal history'?	Ann McGrath	359
Select bibliography		398
Index		402

Maps

Australia: significant Aboriginal sites	xviii
Australia: Aboriginal population, 1991	xx
New South Wales	56
New South Wales: Aboriginal Reserve Lands, 1911	79
Victoria	122
Victoria: distribution of Aboriginal population, 1877	135
Victoria: distribution of Aborigines and Torres Strait Islanders, 1986	157
Queensland	169
South Australia	209
Western Australia	241
Northern Territory	270
Tasmania	307

Illustrations

Inspection by Aboriginal Welfare Board, Dubbo, 1965	7
Aborigines Day, Martin Place, 1964	8
Patricia Kemp and Jenny, South Australia	26
Trial of Aborigines for murder, Franklin Harbour, 1855	28
Aboriginal men in neck chains, c 1920	36
Baby Clinic and Mothercraft Centre, Delissaville	42
Boys Brigade, Ooldea	44
Margaret Tucker, 1974	47
Aboriginal lambmarkers, Welltown, 1900	69
Tribal elders, Tallwood, 1895	69
Aboriginal man on Hawkesbury River	73
Aboriginal nanny and white child	78
Lulu and Clara, Rolland's Plains, 1925	81
Sketch of early violence	128
Going to work, by S.T. Gill	133
Aboriginal cricket team, Sydney, 1867	138
Aboriginal camper, Mallee, 1944	146
Frank Clarke's children, c 1915	147
Pastor Doug Nicholls	148
Land Rights March, Melbourne, 1976	158
Wooroora station Aborigines, c 1900	179
Aboriginal residents, Queensland mission	184
Aborigines sent to Palm Island, 1924	187

Aboriginal workers, Charters Towers, Christmas time	193
'King George and his consort'	197
The Kuri Dance, George French Angas	213
Receiving rations, Oodnadatta, c 1908	216
Two girls carrying buckets, Ooldea	219
School children, Ooldea, 1940s	226
Aboriginal men, Murray River, c 1930	229
Blackwood natives, c 1870–80	246
Schoolgirls, Mt Margaret Mission, 1950	250
Rations day, Kalumburu, 1963	258
Aboriginal hospital orderly, 1942	282
School children, Northern Territory, c 1950	286
'Shanty camp', Northern Territory	290
'No grog past this point'	294
Charles Perkins at Aboriginal demonstration, 1974	298
Truganini, c 1833–40	308
Governor Davey's Proclamation, 1816	318
'Woureddy', c 1833	324
The Conciliation, Duterrau	326
Hobart Aborigines sent to Great Island, 1832	333
Arthur and Alma West	348
Morton Clare Green and Bernard Maynard	349
Granny Mary and Uncle Vern Maynard	352
Morton and Ruby Green	353
Aboriginal Protest, Sydney, 1988	360
Galarrwuy Yunupingu	360
Anita Heiss	375
Land Commissioner Kearney and Pharlap Dixon	378

Acknowledgements

I WISH to thank the contributing historians Heather Goodall, Richard Broome, Henry Reynolds, Dawn May, Peggy Brock, Peter Read, Sandy Toussaint and Vicki Matson-Green; they are an outstanding team. All have been wonderfully committed, conscientious and *mostly* patient throughout the long ordeal. I am extremely grateful for their encouragement to get this book off the ground in its early stages, and their later friendship, support and advice, across the length and breadth of Australia. I hope they are pleased with the final product housing their efforts.

My original publisher, Mark Tredinnick, has been exceptionally encouraging. He has regularly offered a ready ear and plenty of useful advice. I especially appreciate his generous support and legal insights during the protracted copyright negotiations which often drove me crazy. I thank Bernadette Foley and Jo Jarrah for their sympathetic editorial work.

For their friendly and careful efforts in preparing the maps I thank Arthur Fisk and Saha Chaudhury of the University of New South Wales (UNSW) Technical Drawing Office of the Faculty of Materials Science. The School of History, UNSW, has contributed terrific support in many ways, but especially via its Research and Publications Fund, initiated by Martyn Lyons. The Aboriginal Resource Centre, UNSW, has been a great asset, so I thank the generous staff there, especially Paul Behrendt and

Barbara Nicholson. The Australian Research Council has also assisted via its Large Grants scheme, especially with research for Chapter 10.

A number of libraries, galleries and government agencies have kindly co-operated with our requests for photographic and art reproduction. We thank the Mitchell Library, especially Jennifer Broomhead; the Battye Library of Western Australian History; the Office of Aboriginal Affairs, NSW, especially Millie Ingram; the LaTrobe Library, Melbourne; Queen Victoria Museum and Art Gallery, Tasmania; the Australian War Memorial; the National Library of Australia; John Fairfax Pty Ltd; the *Courier Mail*, Queensland; the Art Gallery of South Australia; the State Department of Aboriginal Affairs, South Australia; the Mortlock Library; and the University of New South Wales Publications Unit, especially Tony Potter. Every effort has been made to contact owners of copyright, and if any oversights have been made, we would be grateful if such people would contact us. I hope that none of the photos pose problems to Aboriginal people because of recent deaths or other reasons; please notify me or the publishers if this is the case.

The History Project of the Royal Commission into Aboriginal Deaths in Custody, where this project started, was supported by outstandingly energetic and incisive people like the Commissioners Elliott Johnston, Pat Dodson, Hal Wootten, D. O'Dea and L. Wyvill. Geoff Eames not only got things moving, but provided rock-solid advice and incisive critique and support throughout. Marcia Langton, Mick Dodson and many others from the regionally based Aboriginal Issues Units and Underlying Issues Units offered some useful suggestions which helped shape the project. Errol West, who joined the History Project and greatly assisted the Commissioner, is absent from this book because he did not write a formal paper, but his input was greatly appreciated.

I appreciate finally being granted permission to reproduce work originating from papers prepared for the Royal Commission into Aboriginal Deaths in Custody, including revised versions and ideas contained in E. Johnston, *Royal Commission into Aboriginal Deaths in Custody. National Report into Underlying Issues*, AGPS, Canberra, 1991; P. Dodson, *Royal Commission into Aboriginal*

ACKNOWLEDGEMENTS

Deaths in Custody. Regional Report into Underlying Issues, AGPS, Canberra, 1991; J.H. Wootten, *Royal Commission into Aboriginal Deaths in Custody. Report of the Inquiry in NSW, Victoria and Tasmania*, AGPS, Canberra, 1991; L. Wyvill, *Royal Commission into Aboriginal Deaths in Custody. Report of the Inquiry in Queensland*, AGPS, Canberra, 1991. Commonwealth of Australia copyright reproduced by permission. Thanks are due to the editorial board of *Le Mouvement Social*, who put no obstacles in the way of including a revised English version of an article originally published in French as 'Un domaine de controverse: Qu'est-ce que l'histoire aborigène?', no 167, avril–juin 1994.

For permission to reproduce extracts from poems, I am grateful to Jack Davis and Jimmy Everett; full citations of their work are included in the relevant endnotes.

It has been very important for me to know that colleagues supported my scholarship in various ways. Those who have offered various kinds of assistance, including advice, research tidbits and criticism over the years include Ann Curthoys, Bain Attwood, Julia Horne, Patricia Grimshaw, Graeme Davison, Beverley Kingston, Donna Reeman, Lucy Taksa, Alison Holland, Inara Waldren, Kay Saunders, Jackie Huggins, Marian Quartly, David Walker, John Hirst, Marilyn Lake, Lyndall Ryan, Henry Reynolds, Stephen Garton and Mark Finnane. All those other people who are not named but helped in a number of areas, I thank you too.

My parents Betty and Brian, brothers Paul, John and sister Mary, always support me in a number of ways. Everyone seems to thank the spouse and kids last and I won't deviate here. I hate to think what sort of creature I'd be without my husband Milton and little daughters Venetia and Naomi being there for me.

Ann McGrath

Contributors

Peggy Brock lectures at Edith Cowan University in Aboriginal and Intercultural Studies. In the 1980s she worked as Historian for the Aboriginal Heritage Unit of the Department of Environment and Planning in South Australia, researching Aboriginal community histories. Dr Brock has written several books and articles on Aboriginal history, including *Outback Ghettos: A history of Aboriginal institutionalisation and survival* (1993), and *Women, Rites and Sites: Aboriginal women's cultural knowledge* (editor) (1989).

Richard Broome has researched and taught Aboriginal history at La Trobe University since 1977, with a stint of six years as a commissioned historian during this time. He has published articles on Aboriginal boxers, written commissioned dictionary entries and pamphlets on Aborigines, and *Aboriginal Australians* (1982) reprinted ten times (second edition 1994). His commissioned works *Arriving* (1984) and *Coburg Between Two Creeks* (1987) contained significant Aboriginal material.

Heather Goodall lectures at the University of Technology, Sydney, where she teaches public history and heritage. Her historical publications focus on issues including memory, law and ethics and she also writes on current political issues and media representations. She was joint winner of the John Barrett Prize for Australian Studies. She is working on a history of Aborigines and land in New South Wales, has advised various Land Councils and was a consultant to the Maralinga Royal Commission into Atomic Testing.

Ann McGrath is Associate Professor of History at the University of New South Wales. She wrote *'Born in the Cattle': Aborigines in Cattle Country*, the inaugural Hancock Prize-winner, and a number of articles on Australian cultural history and Aboriginal–white relations, including an essay on citizenship which jointly won the John Barrett Prize. She worked on several land claims in the Northern Territory, led the History Project of the Royal Commission into Aboriginal Deaths in Custody and advised on issues relating to the *Native Title Act 1993*. *Creating a Nation*, which she co-authored with three feminist historians, won the Human Rights Award for non-fiction, 1994.

Dawn May is a Senior Lecturer at the Cairns Campus of James Cook University where she teaches Australian History and Politics. Her research interests have focused on Aboriginal labour in the Queensland cattle industry with a number of books and journal articles being published on the topic.

Maykutenner (English name: **Vicki Matson-Green**) is married to Chris and has a son, Jason, and a daughter, Tarni. She grew up on Flinders Island as a member of the Pallawah community. Vicki has worked for her people for fifteen years. She has served on local Pallawah, State and Federal committees dealing with various Aboriginal political and social issues. During the last five years Vicki has been undertaking a Bachelor of Arts Degree at the University of Tasmania. She hopes to become a lecturer in Aboriginal Studies in the future. Vicki hopes, in her lifetime, to witness the recognition of Aboriginal and Torres Strait Islander sovereignty by the international and Australian communities and the granting of national land rights.

Peter Read is an Australian Research Fellow, and a Visiting Fellow, Department of History, at the Australian National University. He has published several books on Aboriginal history, including, with J.M. Read, *Long Time Olden Time: Aboriginal Accounts of Northern Territory History*. (CD-Rom, Firmware, 1993).

He is a co-founder of Link-up (NSW) Aboriginal Corporation, and is currently the Chair of the journal *Aboriginal History*.

Henry Reynolds has taught for many years at James Cook University and is currently an Australian Research Council Senior Fellow. He is one of Australia's foremost scholars of Aboriginal history with numerous books and articles to his credit. The highly acclaimed *The Other Side of the Frontier* won the Ernest Scott Prize for history and his *The Law of the Land* anticipated many of the findings of the Mabo High Court judgement. He has had considerable input in the public debate over Mabo.

Sandy Toussaint is an Associate Lecturer in Anthropology at the University of Western Australia and was formerly a Senior Research Officer on the Royal Commission into Aboriginal Deaths in Custody. She has worked with Aboriginal people in many settings in Western Australia (for example, the Aboriginal Land Inquiry, the Kimberley Language Resource Centre, the Marra Worra Worra Aboriginal Corporation, the Aboriginal Legal Service, Aboriginal Education). Publications include articles in *Aboriginal History, Alternative Law Journal, Arena, Australian Journal of Social Issues and Social Analysis*.

Preface

UNTIL quite recently almost everything written about the Aborigines of this country was written by non-Aboriginal Australians. With this in mind, and considering the fact that most contributors are not Aboriginal, it would not be surprising if many indigenous Australians initially viewed this book not so much with a sense of *deja vu*, but more an emphatic 'Here we go again'. This would be grossly unfair on several counts.

First, unlike some self-proclaimed 'experts' of other disciplines, whose self-interest was (and in some cases still is) served by projecting Aborigines as a dependent people who require someone to speak on their behalf, most historians of my acquaintance recognise the necessity for Aboriginal people to repossess their own history. In this volume's introduction, Ann McGrath states specifically that most of the contributions were written by non-Aboriginal authors and these do not claim to be 'Aboriginal History'.

Second, the non-Aboriginal authors in this volume played vital roles in propelling the history of Aboriginal Australia to the forefront of national debate. Henry Reynolds' trilogy—*The Other Side of the Frontier*, *Frontier* and *Dispossession*—dilacerated the myth that this country was peacefully settled; Ann McGrath's *Born in the Cattle*, a poignant account of interaction between Aboriginal women and European society, is now indelibly written into the country's history; while Peter Read and Heather Goodall did much to publicly expose the inhumane policies and actions of the Aborigines Protection Board of New South Wales. Read, in particular, has shown an assiduous commitment to Aboriginal Australians. As well as his non-intrusive oral history transcriptions such as *Down with me on the Old Cowra Mission* and *Lost Children*, in 1982 he, in association with Coral Edwards, established 'Link-Up', an organisation that reunites families whose members were separated under the provision of the 'removal' policies of the Aborigines Protection Board.

Third, accounts such as these are a vital part of the history of the relationship between Aboriginal and non-Aboriginal Australians. By understanding the environment and atmosphere within which this relationship was established, we can make better sense of its legacies. Both indigenous and non-indigenous Australians have a lot to learn about each other before reconciliation between the two peoples can be realised. This book will go a long way towards achieving that end.

Paul Behrendt
Director
Aboriginal Research and Resource Centre
University of New South Wales

Following page: Australia showing some significant sites of Aboriginal history. BASED ON INFORMATION CONTAINED IN DAVID HORTON (ED.), *THE ENCYCLOPAEDIA OF ABORIGINAL AUSTRALIA*, ABORIGINAL STUDIES PRESS, CANBERRA, 1994

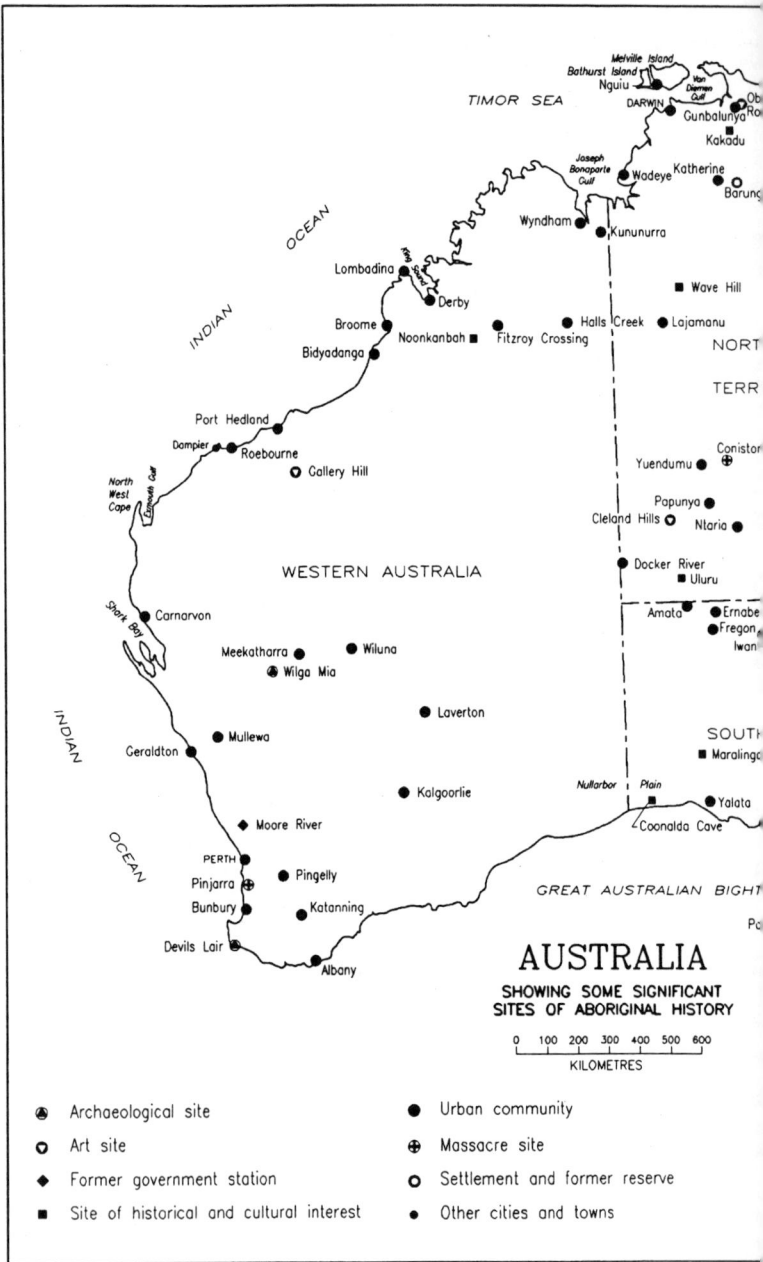

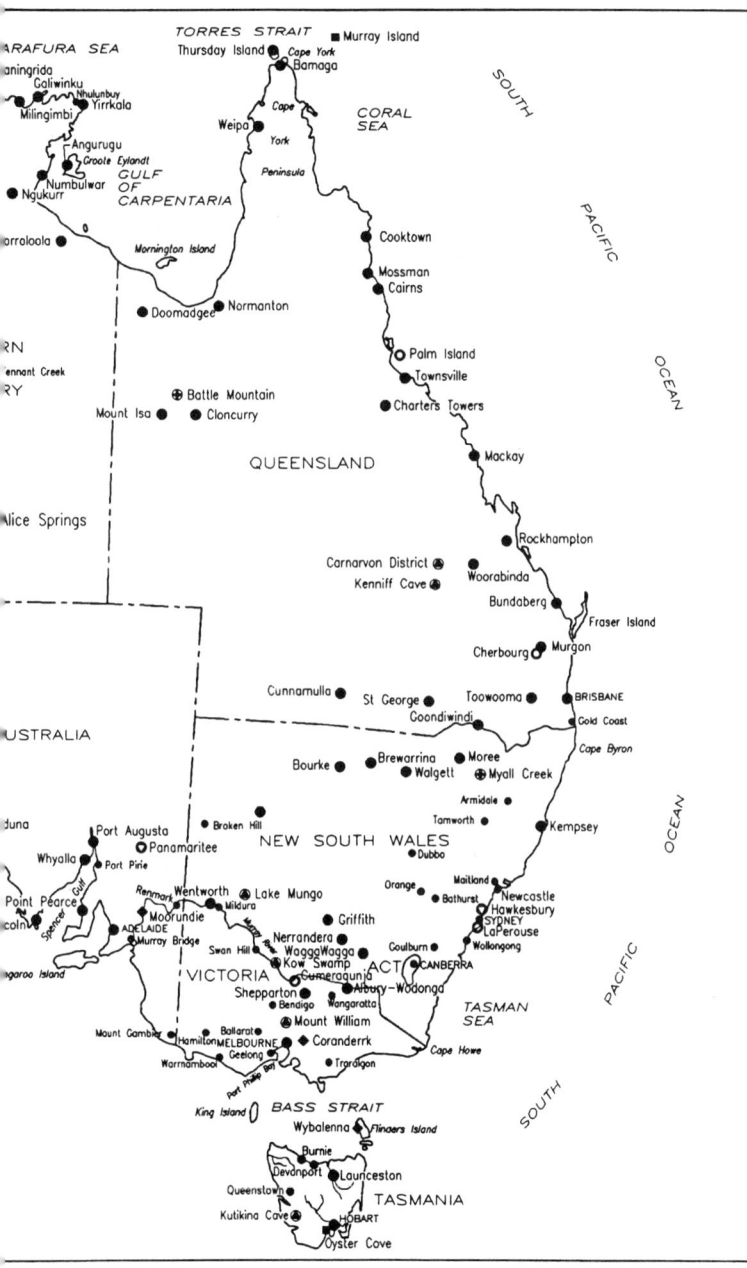

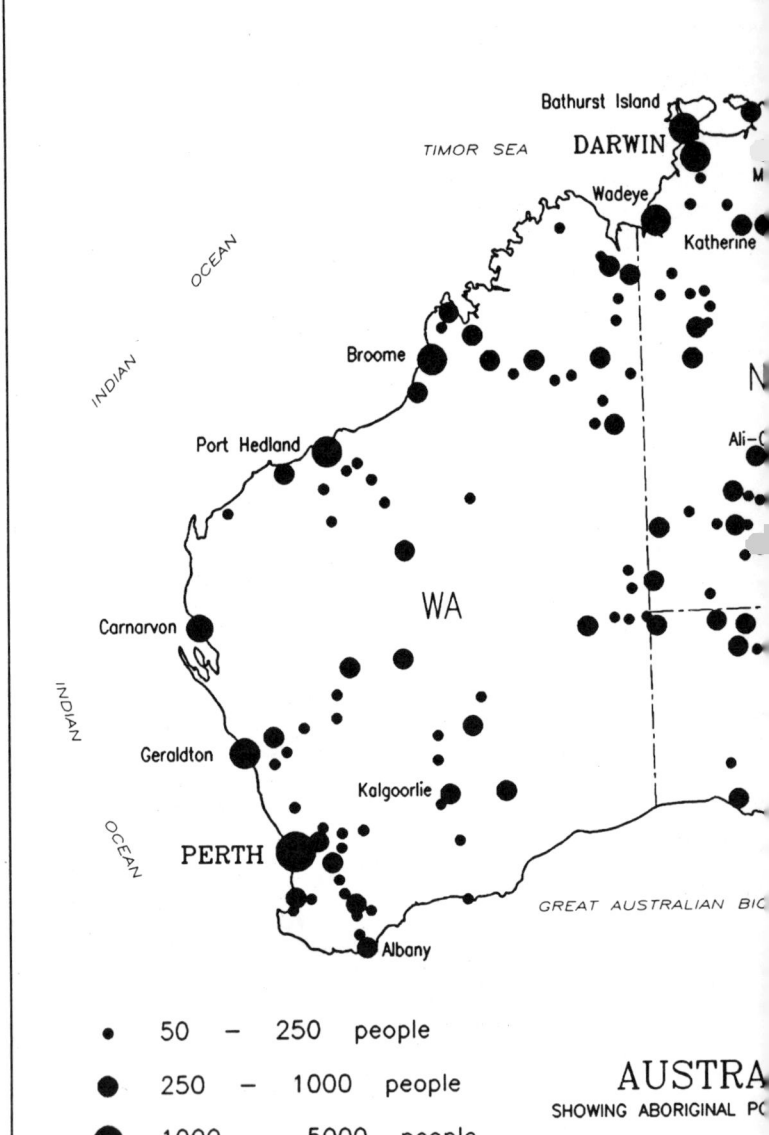

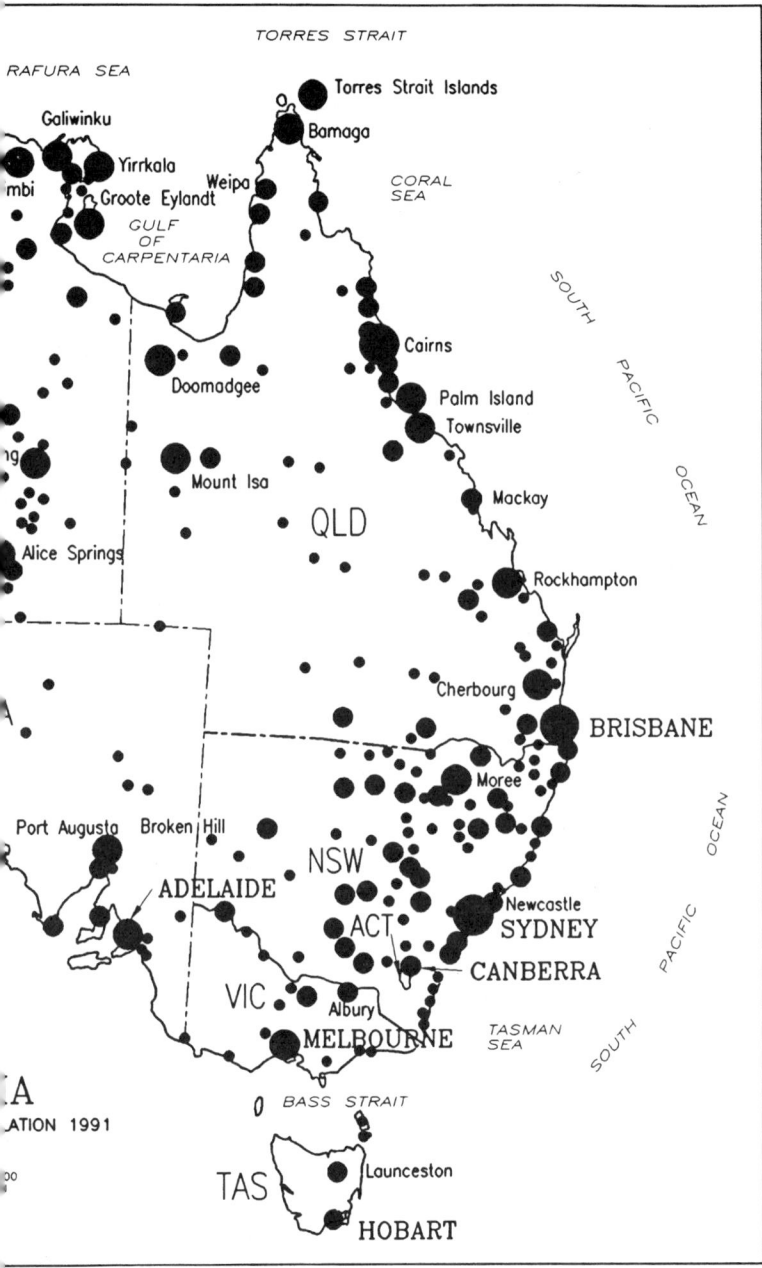

Introduction

IN 1980 I had a home in Darwin with a delightful, though sometimes pea-green, swimming pool. The property was a steal because it was right next door to an Aboriginal community. On my first real estate inspection, all the beige curtains along that side of the house were drawn closed, although it was still daytime. On my second visit, the vendor demonstrated how, if the dogs barked too much, I could simply fire a few rifle shots into the 'reserve'.

Unlike all the other houses in my street, Bagot's large Aboriginal population had no pool and no telephone, so the new non-hostile neighbours came in handy. After growing up in Brisbane (where the Aboriginal family across the road was one of the few I knew) and having also lived in Melbourne, I was gratified to see so many Aboriginal survivors all around me, and relieved they walked that ground with such dignity. Their speech, singing, the occasional bouts of all-night chanting, the campfire cooking smells, the goannas and bush turkeys who used my backyard as a safe haven; it was all fascinating. But I got annoyed

---

Preceding page: Australia showing the Aboriginal population in 1991. BASED UPON INFORMATION CONTAINED IN DAVID HORTON (ED.), *THE ENCYCLOPAEDIA OF ABORIGINAL AUSTRALIA*, ABORIGINAL STUDIES PRESS, CANBERRA, 1994

INTRODUCTION

when I woke to see little faces peering out from inside my mango tree or came home to find shiny kids jumping out of the pool. More disturbing were the number of emergency calls required for police and ambulance.

With a sense of high purpose, I went to a special neighbourhood meeting to argue for more facilities on Bagot. It was attended by a local Member of Parliament, a man who had grown up alongside Aboriginal people. Many Bagot residents viewed him as family but I had seen him ignore them when they waved. At this meeting, the MP proclaimed 'border tensions' in a style evoking cowboy films. One Aboriginal man sat at the back of the group but did not speak. My suggestion that Aborigines should have a swimming pool received raucous laughter; similarly public phones, everyone agreed, would only be vandalised. Neighbours suggesting the construction of a higher fence and the closure of all gates which allowed pedestrian access to the 'white' streets gained enthusiastic support. Angry and sickened, I continued with my swimming pool campaign elsewhere, until politely told by a Bagot community Councillor that they didn't want one in case somebody drowned. Exactly my problem but additionally, they feared payback against the swimming-pool supporters.

Around the same time, Shiela, a Malak Malak woman from Daly River, told me a story about the visit of some young Tasmanians. 'They said they were blackfellers but they weren't black!' she remembered.

> They had white skin, red hair, they talked like white people. We couldn't believe them at first. But then they told us what had happened to their people, how they had lost their land, language, business. They had come a long, long way to see how us mob lived. We came to understand them a little bit. We felt really sad for them people, they were good young people and they were Aboriginal.

Boundaries, property rights, skin colour: Australia's history, like the land itself, remains contested ground. The fuller, Australia-wide story is new to both Aborigines and non-Aborigines. It is that story which this book is about. *Contested Ground* argues that after British colonialism took hold in Australia, the people now known as the Aborigines began to share a common past. But they also had many different pasts. As well as differing clan traditions, they were subject to particular conditions in the different colonies and states.

'Australians' and 'Aborigines' are not mutually exclusive categories. All Australians, black and white, are bound together by a collective past as well as a present; this past lives on today, moulding and reinforcing national life. Australia's history helps explain the deep sense of injustice and the strong sense of common historical experience shared by Aboriginal people. It helps explain the economic, social and residential status of Aboriginal people and their attitudes to white Australians and the nation. Aboriginal Australians do not forget their past; the story of their dispossession lives within them and the memories are handed on to future generations.

Irrespective of where their ancestors were born, all Australians enjoy the spoils and suffer the consequences of the British invasion. Yet as Pat Dodson, Chair of the Aboriginal Council for Reconciliation, has stated: 'So much of the injustice and inequity is related to the lack of knowledge non-Aboriginal people have about our history . . .'[1] More white Australians are finding an increasingly urgent desire to study that past. Perhaps in doing so, they will relinquish some of their fear and denial. To date Aboriginal dispossession has led the colonising class to adopt various stances, to develop a distinctive series of national mythologies. Aboriginal people too, have developed interpretations of the past, of colonial takeover. The peoples have long compared and depicted themselves, favourably and unfavourably, against the other. The history of Australia has thus involved not only two centuries of conflict and collaboration but also a prolonged period of invention, of legend-making, on the part of both Aboriginal and non-Aboriginal Australians.

This book provides a general history of Aboriginal–white relations in Australian history. The national history chapter offers a broad overview which stresses selected themes, especially Aborigines and the State, colonial authority, surveillance, crime and punishment. A series of separate general histories then cover each state and the Northern Territory. We start with New South Wales as the place of the first British occupation, followed by its early offshoots, which became Victoria and Queensland. Western Aus-

INTRODUCTION

tralia, South Australia and the Northern Territory follow. All had larger areas of undeveloped Crown land which have now become, or have the potential to be returned as, Aboriginal territory. South Australia and the Northern Territory have been placed consecutively because of their close association. Tasmania, which receives two chapters, has been placed last because of its unusual legacy of denying Aboriginal existence.

The presence of two Tasmanian chapters came about because the Pallawah author, Vicki Matson-Green, originally down to write the Tasmanian chapter, had to withdraw from the project unexpectedly. When eventually sent my substitute chapter for comments, Vicki objected to its white authorship and tone and was then in a position to write her chapter, so the deadline was extended. Matson-Green's chapter, chapter 9, emphasises the twentieth century while chapter 8 focuses on the nineteenth. Matson-Green's chapter is placed at the end of the state histories because it represents and serves as a fitting conclusion. It demonstrates how, for Aboriginal Australians, regaining pride of identity has been closely tied up with reclaiming the past as well as the present. Matson-Green's chapter highlights the distinctive vision and insights Aboriginal people bring to writing their own history and the inclusion of two different versions of one state's history also exemplifies the contested nature of all writing about Aboriginal–white relations.

The final chapter, chapter 10, presents a survey of history writing about Aboriginal topics, expanding on the controversies of its politics and practice. It also contextualises the historical background to the study of Aboriginal history from which these chapters emerge. Readers interested in gaining more insight into historiography, bibliographical clues or the editor's scholarly and political perspective might find this the best place to start reading.

Contested Ground is the first colony by colony, state by state history of white–Aboriginal relations. Given the fact that Aboriginal matters were in the hands of the colonies and later states, and still remain so to an extent, this approach would seem not only practical but appropriate. The various authors have drawn out some of the differences and similarities between the states but this book highlights the need for further comparative analysis.

Indeed, many authors were reluctant to make sweeping comparisons between their focus state and others. This was partly due to lack of existing studies along these lines but also due to a belief that other regional factors were equally significant. This being a general history, however, it was essential that authors gave special prominence to the common threads, the shared experiences.

Important variables affecting Aboriginal communities nonetheless deserve attention.[2] These include the date of first contact, speed and intensity of settlement or invasion, the population of intruders, type of land use, (for example: mining, pastoralism, agriculture, urban) weapons and transport technology used, government policy, mission policy, contemporary frontier outlook, including racial ideology, demand for labour or converts, demand for sexual services of Aboriginal women. On the Aboriginal side, factors included the ruggedness and extent of their land area, its inaccessibility to horses, the existing Aboriginal ecology and level of vital resource depletion, population density and mobility, ability to hide out, impact of or immunity to diseases, gender imbalances in their populations, clan philosophy, prior intelligence of invaders, resistance strategies, including weaponry and guerilla resistance, desire to fight or co-operate, whether they had enemy clans collaborating with white police and settlers. Such factors, and many more, led to myriad regional variations.

Over and above these, however, each colony, barring Tasmania, had its own legislation governing Aboriginal inhabitants. On Federation, each state continued to enact specific policies for these people, over whom the Commonwealth had no powers until the late 1960s. All Aboriginal people in the respective states and the Northern Territory thus shared a common experience of being under 'the Ordinance' or 'the Act'. While there were many different histories around Australia, there were also many commonalities.

A number of Aboriginal authors were approached to write general state histories for the Royal Commission into Aboriginal Deaths in Custody (RCIADIC) from which this book emanates. These included Jackie Huggins, Noel Pearson, Marcia Langton and Errol West. Regrettably, with the exception of West, they were unable to join the Commission's History Project, though

INTRODUCTION

most contributed significantly in other ways. Nonetheless, I am pleased that this is the first national history to reflect significant consultation with Aboriginal people. All chapters are written by leading historians in their fields, originating as reports written for the Royal Commission. But they have been substantially rewritten to inform a wider readership. In order of appearance, the chapter authors are myself, Heather Goodall, Richard Broome, Henry Reynolds and Dawn May, Peggy Brock, Peter Read, Sandy Toussaint and Maykutenner (Vicki Matson-Green). As well as expertise in their respective regions, the historians were selected because they had past records of engagement in Aboriginal political issues and of working with Aboriginal communities and organisations. They and myself as editor (previously as National Co-ordinator of the History Project of the RCIADIC) were required to liaise with the Aboriginal Issues Units in each regional office of the Royal Commission. Consequently, the contents of the papers were discussed with numerous representatives of regional Aboriginal communities. Aboriginal leaders also advised during the History Project, especially Pat Dodson, the first Aboriginal Royal Commissioner, Marcia Langton, who headed the Northern Territory Aboriginal Issues Unit, lawyer and now Social Justice Commissioner, Mick Dodson and Errol West, then a lecturer at the Riawunna Aboriginal Centre at the University of Tasmania.

Although we generally attempted to use a common terminology, there remain many difficulties in choosing the correct words. The question of whether Australia was invaded or settled, which is, after all, the fundamental premise of the nation's establishment, remains controversial and for many, an extremely disturbing issue. 'Invasion' and 'settlement' have become powerful signifiers for political understandings and agendas. There are many different ways of approaching the problem. Some historians argue that it is a question of perspective; if you are Aboriginal, then it was invasion but if you are white, it was settlement. But can it be totally relative like this; is it only a question of what was going on in people's minds? Furthermore, are we more interested in past participants' mentalities or today's minds reflecting upon history? If we are concerned with contemporary understandings, we would find that amongst the British in the early nineteenth century, opinions differed sharply, with humanitarians concerned about the usurpation of land from Aborigines. By the same token, few of the British—convicts or officers—saw themselves as permanent settlers, let alone nation builders. Those men who first ventured onto frontiers all over Australia were often prisoners, military men with temporary postings, or travelling miners or pastoral speculators looking for quick money. Aboriginal reactions were also mixed and they did not always conceive of the strangers as enemies; they had particular local words and concepts to explain what we now know to be the beginnings of Australia's 'colonisation'. It would seem, therefore, that rather than being interested in describing the 'authentic historical moment', it is more imperative to find words to explain the long-term and ongoing process and its impact.

A growing number of people believe a clear question of justice is at stake, and that because Aboriginal people were killed and lands stolen, it must have been invasion. With the High Court Mabo case of 1992, the law was called upon to adjudicate the premises of British takeover. The law can be rather complicated in its interpretation of legal principle. Yet a complex reading is probably more accurate than a simple dichotomy. And after all, why is it always posited as invasion *or* settlement? Why not invasion *and* settlement? Or settlement *and* invasion? In trying desperately to achieve 'political correctness', there is a danger that some aspects might be exaggerated at the expense of others.

This book therefore adopts a range of terms where they seem most appropriate but it always stresses the intrinsically *colonial* nature of power relations. The paradigm of race relations provides an inadequate tool to explain the peculiar tensions between indigenes and colonisers. Colonialism has wider explanatory potential, for the conflict between Aboriginal and non-Aboriginal people was not premised only on 'race' notions but upon the wider power relations implicit in a colonial past. In this light, the relationship of Aborigines to the nation also requires close examination. Important questions which all Australians must address include the extent to which Aborigines were seen as outside the white nation, by what means this was enforced and reinforced,

INTRODUCTION

and indeed why they were excluded so long from Australian citizenship. The term 'post-colonial' is favoured by some but I do not think it altogether appropriate; Aborigines have not gained full independence. Since the British invasion, and even after Federation, Australia's history is still 'colonial' not only because Aborigines continue to be colonised but because the country is still subservient to an imperial power and at the time of writing does not have its own head of state. Aborigines and non-Aborigines alike remain subjects of the British Crown.

Today the term 'Aboriginal' is another topic of intense debate among indigenous people and academics. Previously, it was state legislation which defined who fitted the category 'Aboriginal', according to skin colour, 'caste' and lifestyle, whereas today, identity depends upon self-definition or community acceptance. In this book the authors have most often used 'Aboriginal people' or 'Aborigines' for people of Aboriginal descent. 'Aboriginal' means people of the soil or indigenes but in Australia it identifies a particular people. Many Aborigines, however, still have land associations which provide a strong sense of belonging and a specific identity. The terms Kooris or Murris are becoming common currency in south-eastern Australia, as is Pallawah in parts of Tasmania. For many other people their nationality, their allegiances, are defined by their Aboriginality. A sense of a common history is primary to that definition but so is a common present, and something of an essential way of experiencing and thinking about the world or 'thinking black'. But this is complicated by the inevitable cultural fusion which has taken place due to exposure to the broader community and government assimilationist policies. Some people are now claiming a dual identity, for example 'Aboriginal–Irish'. But generally, identity is a prime example of the intersection of the personal, the political and the history of both; it sometimes includes a process of self-discovery and a public declaration, often symbolised by an empowering switch of voice to that of the colonised. (See chapter 10 for more on this issue.)

Herein non-Aborigines are distinguished as 'whites' or 'Whites' and sometimes, where it seems appropriate, as 'British' or 'Europeans', terms denoting either cultural or 'racial' origins.

The term 'white' is not so much a description of skin colour as a label given by others; no one is really coloured white, red or black. In New Zealand, the categories Maori and Pakeha are in popular usage. In the Australian case, the hundreds of Aboriginal dialects make a common term problematic. In the Kimberleys it is 'gadia'. In Arnhem Land the whites are called 'balanda', a Dutch derived word adopted from the Macassarese.

Most of the history contained in this book is not claiming to be 'Aboriginal history', that is, to tell the story from an Aboriginal perspective. It is predominantly written by members of the colonising class and it is about the relations between two peoples entwined in the process of colonialism. Any study of Australian colonialism is inevitably a product of the very subject it seeks to write about. Acknowledging that most of the authors are inevitably implicated, we nonetheless share a strong concern for justice. Our work as historians attempts to fight ignorance and hopefully will contribute towards redressing some of the wrongs of the past. But we are still influenced, enriched and entrapped, by culture-bound and often insensitive traditions such as humanitarianism, liberal philosophy, New-Left scholarship and feminism. We believe, however, that greater knowledge brings greater understanding and hopefully this will bring change.

The Mabo debate led Australians, with or without mango trees, to fear the symbolic sanctity of their backyards. *Contested Ground* tells a story which is essential to Australia's history, one which is much more than just a struggle for real estate. As the Aboriginal leader Galarrwuy Yunupingu stated, 'when you take away someone's land, you take away part of their insides'.[3] The contested nature of Australian history and of its soil and sea has flavoured the questioning of our national identity; of what we should celebrate, of who can celebrate. It has raised many questions relating to symbols like the flag, the anthem and more fundamentally, the monarchy and our Constitution. In considering what we hope to achieve for the centenary of Federation in 2001, the issue of Aboriginal reconciliation has become the most important issue of all.

NOTES

1 *The Weekend Australian*, 30–31 July 1994, p.7.
2 A. Markus considers a framework for these in 'Through the Past Darkly', *Aboriginal History*, vol.1, no.1, which informs the proceeding discussion.
3 Personal communication to author, 1986.

1
A national story

TERRA *nullius*, or unoccupied land, was the legally endorsed premise of the British occupation of Australia. This convenient imperial fantasy has long shaped Australia's past, and history writing and teaching has provided it longevity in both law and the popular imagination. Dissenting voices were heard; humanitarians and experts in jurisprudence worried that the Australian colonies were out of step with other 'new world' countries such as North America and neighbouring New Zealand.[1] Nonetheless, *terra nullius* remained firm, being only one of many hypocrisies implicit in colonialism. In Australia a collective consciousness of denial emerged. Unlike the 'dark continent' of Africa, full of its 'conquered' peoples, twentieth century Australia became the 'empty continent'. Its history books attempted to fill Australia's vast spaces with stories of male discovery, exploration and above all, with 'settlement', which became, in the Australian context, a euphemistic term for conquering by force and outnumbering the indigenous population.

Australian history can be summarised as the story of how Aboriginal peoples lost a continent and how the invaders gained one. While opponents of Aboriginal rights argue that land rights or native title will divide the nation, any study of the past reveals that from the earliest times, the British set about creating boundaries and social divisions; the land and its riches were divided up in increasingly uneven portions between the newcomers and the Aboriginal people.

It is deceptive to assume that 'colonial Australia' ended with the coming of the twentieth century, or that successful British settlement meant the end of 'colonial' relations between Aborigines and non-Aborigines. For the first three decades after Federation, the conflict over land, river and sea was still proceeding. Forced relocation and dispossession continued during the decades which followed. Since the British invasion, colonial relations were entrenched not only by land takeover but also by a wide variety of ideas and beliefs, and by the economic, legal, political and social structures which institutionalised and perpetuated them.[2]

Some areas have been more effectively colonised than others, and it is in the less populated regions such as the Kimberley, the Pilbara and Kakadu where Aboriginal traditional ties with the land are strongest. The success of colonialism therefore became a direct gauge of Aboriginal dislocation. First meetings between old and new residents were coloured by the forces and languages of imperialism and colonialism, although these encounters were sometimes the most open-hearted and hopeful moments of all: times of potential diplomacy before the use of capture or force.

In the short and long term, colonialism drastically jeopardised the personal liberty of Aborigines. They immediately lost choices over movement and residence, which was especially devastating for a people for whom travel was a necessity. Their lifestyle was frequently dictated by governments and Christian missionaries who wanted them to become sedentary, or remain under control on their 'settlements'. Aboriginal families also suffered the extreme trauma of having their children taken away to dormitories or distant towns. Association with their own Aboriginal parents and kin was said to be degrading or subjecting them to neglect. Girls and boys were segregated and taught to conform to sex roles approved by an outside culture.

The carve-up of Australia was thus not only about land and property. It separated Aboriginal families, and broke the hearts and minds of individuals—variously Aboriginal children, men and women. Kidnappings of both adults and children were frequent. Crippling changes to Aboriginal lifestyle and land-use patterns were imposed. Individual colonisers were horrifyingly brutal, but blame cannot rest solely on their shoulders, for Australia's colonisation originated in and was implemented by the State with popular endorsement.

It is a truism that colonial intrusions initially polarised those in Australia into two camps: the coloniser and the colonised. Yet paradoxically, the two camps could not remain totally divided physically or mentally; it was the very nature of colonialism that coloniser and colonised came together. In many such meetings, murder, rape, pillage, deceit occurred, but there was also co-operation, affection, generosity, loyalty, even love.

As well as a history of conflict and domination, there was also a history of negotiation, compromise and exchange between Aboriginal people and colonisers. Alliances were formed. Aboriginal midwives delivered white women's babies and Aboriginal women nurtured, even suckled, these children. Lonely white men relied upon Aboriginal women as lovers and de facto wives. Aboriginal women had children by white men. Bodies, words, culture, art, aesthetics, ideas, images became entwined in a complex physical and mental dialogue which continues today, and is most evident in human reproduction and cultural exchange.[3] Children of mixed Aboriginal and European descent were born and grew up in varied contexts, but amidst the environment of Australian colonialism which generally defined them as illegitimate, partially or fully excluding them from the nation and full citizenship.

As well as creative exchanges and possibilities of cultural convergence, colonialism was delimiting. All Australians inevitably become prisoners of such forces. Aboriginal people recognise this, portraying their people, in literature and art, as prisoners in their own country. Their high imprisonment rates make this more than a metaphor, yet the image is particularly appropriate for a nation which commenced as a prison colony. When the imported convicts were freed, the indigenous people became their captives. The history of colonial and State authority over Aborigines—of institutionalisation, law enforcement, detention, imprisonment, and the role of police—have been fundamental in shaping their lives. Aboriginal individuals and communities interacted with these systems of policing and control, co-operating with and resisting them according to their respective goals. Yet the confining power of government policies and practices often made it difficult for Aboriginal people to escape.

The overarching power relations of colonialism meant that the colonisers would win over the colonised. Yet, like all colonisers, there remained a nagging doubt about the tenure of their victory.[4] Many Australians still feel an emotional need to protect their spoils, refusing to share the country with Aborigines. Others listen to pangs of conscience and yearn for a fairer country. The Mabo decision of the High Court in 1992 overruled the legality of *terra nullius*, but it has not yet erased its legacy from the present. Nor has it overturned non-Aboriginal understandings of Australian history, and these in turn shape present public opinion. As is discussed more fully in chapter 10, from Federation in 1901 until the 1970s, Aborigines hardly appeared in national history books except as a backward people easily 'pushed aside' by virile colonisers. The act of history writing has always been political, and Australian historians had and still have a special role in nation building.

Australia's past cannot be truly understood unless it is analysed as a *colonial* history, and as the founding premise of Australian colonialism, *terra nullius* shaped the way this history unfolded. It dictated the basis of property ownership, and influenced the structures of fundamental Australian institutions, including its government. Following British takeover of their land, Aboriginal peoples lost their sovereignty, or their dominion and authority over the land. Consequently, Australian colonialism made Aborigines foreigners in their own land, intruders in their own dwellings. To exemplify this, early governors such as Macquarie in New South Wales required Aborigines to carry passports in order to travel in their own lands. Otherwise they would be treated as enemy aliens. Significantly, these passports were conditional upon Aborigines agreeing to give up their hunting implements, their bush economy and to stop associating with their families. Governor Arthur had the same idea for Tasmanian Aborigines; he planned to capture Aborigines living near the settled districts, and compliant 'chiefs' were to be issued with 'a general passport' signed and sealed by the governor.[5]

In the next century, with national Federation, white Australians remained deeply insecure about their hold on the large continent, by then based not only upon *terra nullius* but upon a belief in racial superiority and an understanding that the land be fully colonised and developed. One of the first Bills passed became known as the 'White Australia Policy' and one of the earliest Royal Commissions which followed was into the white birthrate.[6] Racial exclusion became central not just to the takeover of the land but to the self-image of the new nation. Although Aborigines were excluded from citizenship in this nation, white Australians saw fit to appropriate Aboriginal words, bushcraft skills and local knowledge and later their traditional art and symbolism. But the Aboriginal people were excluded from an active role in culture-making. Aborigines were literally a 'captive audience' forced to look on as white Australians narcissistically admired themselves, constructing and defining the nation as a young country, as superior, as blessed.

When the new nation celebrated its unblemished whiteness amidst Asian seas, Aborigines became an annoying anomaly. In the nineteenth century it had been thought that Aborigines would eventually go away. Either they would follow Tasmania's lead and virtually disappear or they would eventually be 'bred out' through intermarriage. Whites and colonial governments often helped the process along. Against the tide of colonialism, Aborigines, defined as 'primitive', were the doomed race. In some areas, programmes were attempted to 'civilise' the women so they would be eligible for 'nice white men', eventually breeding out 'the colour'. In the 1950s, assimilation promised to destroy Aboriginality by enforcing social conformity. But Aborigines refused to go away. Indeed, there was virtually nowhere for them to go, and like many other indigenous people, they faced a long struggle for their rights.

Terra nullius provided a powerful rationale and became part of Australian nationalism. The all-white Australian Natives Association adopted the term 'natives' for themselves and from the 1880s wanted to define the non-Aboriginal Australian-born as Australia's only 'aborigines'.[7] Even the bushman legend, with its image of the 'typical Australian man' grew out of such denial. Features of

Aboriginality were borrowed so that white men could feel or prove themselves better Aborigines than the Aborigines themselves. The essence of Australian manhood, according to the working man's legend, was to be 'a rolling stone', a traveller, practical, laconic, collectivist, matey, the very image of 'the Aboriginal other' as perceived by white Australians. This white primitive, superior to Aborigines in the ever-threatening bush, was the Tarzan-like 'noble savage' recently metamorphised as Crocodile Dundee.[8]

In line with such national ideals, Aboriginal mothers were excluded from the maternity bonus and their elderly from the pension. The well-being of the Aboriginal people, considered a dying race anyway, was thus best kept low on the national agenda, if not forgotten altogether. The states, rather than the nation, were given responsibility for Aboriginal policy, and Aboriginal people were not even counted in the National Census. Until 1967 Aborigines were excluded from Australian egalitarianism and from democracy; it was only with the referendum of that year that all Aborigines were officially enumerated and learnt of their right to vote in Commonwealth elections.[9] Wage and other struggles followed.

Government policies frequently separated Aborigines from the wider community, and forced them to live on islands or reserves. Many of these were run like internment camps, quarantine stations or prisons. Like foreigners, Aboriginal school children fortunate enough to get into public schools were constantly asked 'where do you come from?' In the 1950s and 60s, some Aborigines were required to carry official documents which classified the owner according to 'caste'. Called 'certificates of exemption' because they exempted the holder from Aboriginal legal status, they had to be carried at all times. These passports to White Australia entitled the holder to enter public places like hotels and to receive other entitlements such as pensions or mainstream education for their children. Like the earlier passport, rights were conditional upon holders giving up an 'Aboriginal lifestyle' and relinquishing contacts with Aboriginal kin and friends. If noticed disobeying these strictures, certificates could be confiscated by police. Like enemy aliens, Aborigines were often singled out and detained by police. Their

Inspection by members of the Aboriginal Welfare Board, Dubbo area, 1965. The State held great power over Aboriginal families. Four authoritative yet uncomfortable-looking men in suits and ties inspect the humble home of a woman caring for her children.
GOVERNMENT PRINTING OFFICE COLLECTION, STATE LIBRARY OF NEW SOUTH WALES

disproportionate representation in gaols suggests they were, and perhaps still are, being punished for their ethnicity and their colonised status rather than merely for their crime.

The various colonial and later State and Commonwealth governments introduced numerous Aboriginal policies which led to intrusions into most aspects of Aborigines' everyday lives. These included inspections of camp sites and other residences, and limitations upon their mode of living, work, financial and leisure activities. Institutionalisation became a dominant theme in Aboriginal lives. Non-Aboriginal people discriminated against Aborigines in many ways, which affected their education, housing, employment, income and, worst of all, their self-esteem.

White Australia's era of nationhood has been a confusing and destructive time for Aborigines. Many Aborigines are bitter and

A white woman with two Aboriginal children at Aborigines Day, Martin Place, 1964. GOVERNMENT PRINTING OFFICE COLLECTION, STATE LIBRARY OF NEW SOUTH WALES

angry—totally fed up with the impositions of white society. They consider it has robbed and cheated them, not just of land, resources, and fair wages, but also of their Aboriginal families, love and identity. Along with the positive struggles come attempts to smother Aboriginal identity, anger and aggression expressed in domestic or other violence, and the self-destructive resistance of alcohol abuse. It is mistaken to say that no Aborigines have given up.

While successive governments attempted to curb distinctive Aboriginal behaviour through policies of 'civilisation' and 'assimilation', many Aborigines resisted total domination by continuing to maintain culturally distinct goals. Against a backdrop of racism and Eurocentrism, Aborigines struggled for land and residential rights, and recognition as equal human beings. From the 1960s, Aborigines and supporters conducted struggles for land rights, civil rights and equal wages. They had many successes, though Aboriginal activists are still struggling for national land rights, compensation and greater control of their own affairs. Since the 1970s, a large number of Aborigines have let go of the shame they were taught and have spoken out more openly about what it means to be Aboriginal. A cultural renaissance has occurred throughout Australia as Aborigines previously denied access to their past culture have sought to gain as much knowledge as they can. Across the country much sharing and exchange have followed, accompanied by an increasing pride in Aboriginal and Torres Strait Islander identity.

Pan-Aboriginal pride was epitomised by the huge gathering at the anti-Bicentennial march in Sydney in 1988. While many other Australians celebrated national 'beginnings', Aborigines from throughout Australia and their supporters drew attention to tens of thousands of years of occupation and, since colonialism, to great injustice. Above all they celebrated their survival as a people.

AN ABORIGINAL WORLD

Aboriginal people have an ancient history of owning the land we now call Australia. It is only since the 1992 Mabo decision that this seemingly obvious fact was acknowledged in an Australian court of law. In the 1980s, attempts to officially recognise prior Aboriginal occupation or ownership in state legislation met nervous reactions. Even at the time of writing, it is not recognised in the national Constitution. Yet Aboriginal history proceeded autonomously from Europeans for longer than we can imagine.

The Australian continent's little-known history of Aboriginal civilisation dates back somewhere between 50 000 and 100 000 years. Archaeological investigations and improved dating techniques promise further breakthroughs. Regional dating variations are not particularly significant, because they reflect the limited nature of archaeological research. Aboriginal people had to adapt to dramatic climatic changes, which affected not only food resources but the very divisions between land and ocean.[10] Aboriginal people share and continue to share important historical knowledge through Dreaming stories, clan sagas, song cycles, dance and art. For them, history is written in the landscape itself;

the land is not just a text book for history, it *is* history and history is the foundation of their present-day lives.

Aboriginal people may have occupied the same area for longer than any other people in world history. They cannot be cast as another minority ethnic group as an immigration which occurred so long ago cannot be compared with one which commenced little more than 200 years ago. While migration is undeniably a central part of white Australian experience, it is not a significant part of Aboriginal history or consciousness. Indeed, Aboriginal art of an extremely sophisticated kind predates the earliest examples of European art.[11]

Many Australians have mistakenly imagined there were few Aboriginal people and that they only lived in the middle of the desert. They have no idea that Aboriginal people once lived in what are now their backyards. Population figures in 1788 are estimated at 750 000, with the densest populations in New South Wales and Victoria, along the coast and rich water courses.[12] The diversity of Aboriginal land-use patterns, food sources, technology, clothing, and shelter is not widely known. For example, Aboriginal people in western Victoria wore fur cloaks and lived in relatively permanent villages with stone housing. In warmer resource-rich areas, Aboriginal people stayed for months at a time. Careful land management techniques were applied to harvest food resources and sensitive and skilful methods were used to hunt game. Hunting and gathering required great physical agility, dexterity and a detailed knowledge of animals and land. Aboriginal people enjoyed a balanced diet and good health, having been naturally quarantined from many of the diseases which affected Europeans.

The social and economic organisation of Aboriginal groups varied greatly throughout Australia, but some general observations can be made.[13] Torres Strait Islanders had a distinctive culture, with close links to Melanesian peoples. They had a more village-oriented lifestyle with market gardens and different traditions of dance, art and belief. Mainland and Tasmanian Aboriginal people had a relatively egalitarian social structure where age, gender and totemic and land affiliations were important demarcations. Women usually provided the staple food supply, owned and had special responsibilities towards sites in the landscape, associated song cycles and what became known in English as 'Dreaming stories'. Women exclusively controlled the secret ceremonies of reproduction, and their maternal function as child-rearers was highly valued. Men also played an important role in nurturing and teaching children, and a wide network of kin had special responsibilities towards each child. When a baby was born, she or he immediately had a niche in a complex cosmology defined by Dreaming songs and stories. Identity was secure, and the child had a variety of land relationships via its conception Dreaming, and via inheritance through father and mother. The child would gradually be introduced to responsibilities towards land and kin and the strict marriage rules. Values taught included sharing, respecting the wisdom of age, protecting the young, gentle treatment and close observation of plants and animals, respect for the dangerous spirits, avoidance of prohibited sacred places and the fulfilment of kinship obligations.

Families and clans travelled the land during the year, harvesting resources when the opportunity was available, and looking after special sites to which they had responsibility. Men and women separately facilitated the reproduction of resources through ritual nurturing. They also spent much time working or negotiating business in the company of their own gender. Decision-making and law enforcement were divided between men and women, and ultimate power was often accorded on the basis of custodial obligations towards relevant land or kin. As with history, the tablet of the law was the landscape itself, explained through Dreaming stories as people travelled. Dancing and singing, story-telling, drawing, painting and sculpture took place all year round, and were an entertaining means of education.

While women were in charge of their own business, sacred and secular, men's power was generally more highly valued in matters of law and punishment concerning the larger group. In some areas, however, women's law was extremely powerful and older women held high status.[14] Large gatherings of many clans took place from time to time to conduct marriage, funerals and religious business, including the male initiation ceremonies. Ritual confrontations were also staged to avenge wrongdoing, and other transgressions could be punished by death, spearings or sorcery. For various reasons, usually to protect them from a lingering death or a poor quality of life, babies were sometimes killed at birth. As untimely deaths and transgressions against the laws of the land had to be punished, revenge killing and terrifying sorcery were fairly common.

DISPOSSESSION

Aboriginal groups encountered other outsiders before the British arrived. In the Northern Territory and parts of northern Queensland, Macassan trepang gatherers had been interacting with Aboriginal people off the coast since at least 1700. Relatively harmonious relations existed, with trading and employment of local Aboriginal men and women. Such items as glass were incorporated into Aboriginal tool-making, and Macassan words became part of their language. Some intermixing occurred, and the all-male crews engaged in sexual associations with the local women, but they were temporary visitors and not interested in land take-over.

The history of Aboriginal dispossession is central to understanding contemporary white–black relations. Colonial takeover was premised on the assumption that European culture was superior to all others and that its bearers could define the world in their terms. According to European conventions, a colony could be established:

> by persuading the indigenous inhabitants to submit themselves to its overlordship;
> by purchasing from those inhabitants the right to settle part or parts of it;
> by unilateral possession, on the basis of first discovery and effective occupation.[15]

British possession of Australia was declared according to the third option; and the land was thus defined as *terra nullius*. In 1770 Captain James Cook and Joseph Banks considered there were few 'natives' along the coast. They deduced that Aborigines had no property rights because they had not laboured to 'subdue' the land by agricultural cultivation. Their observations were later proven incorrect, with the governors of the first settlements soon finding that Aboriginal people lived inland, and had special territories and associations with land on the basis of inheritance and spiritual affiliations. Nonetheless, the terms of British occupation were not amended.

In the first hundred years of settlement there was not consensus about the basis of British sovereignty. Governor King commented in 1807 that Aboriginal people were the 'real Proprietors of the Soil', and lively debate over the issue continued from the 1820s to the 1850s.[16] The justice of the British takeover was far from clear, for what happened in the Australian colonies was out of step with international trends. At the same time, however, the nature of Aboriginal land-use did not fit western definitions of ownership or occupation. In response to Nabalco mining plans, the Yirrkala people of the Northern Territory presented a bark Petition to the Federal Parliament in 1963; after a Supreme Court Hearing, Justice Blackburn stated in his 1971 judgement that all rights to the land were extinguished after 1788, and that because native title had not been legislated by the British, it was not part of the Australian law.[17] This was overruled by the Mabo judgement of the High Court of 1992. The majority rejected the legality of *terra nullius*, arguing that native title existed to traditional lands 'where it has not been extinguished'.[18]

The absence of a treaty was regretted by Governor Arthur after his Van Diemen's Land (later Tasmania) experience. In a letter to the Select Committee on Aborigines which reported to the British House of Commons in 1837 he wrote: 'On the first occupation of the colony it was a great oversight that a treaty was not, at that time, made with the natives, and such compensation given to the chiefs as would have deemed a fair equivalent for what they surrendered.' Had this happened, he considered 'that feeling of injustice which I am persuaded they have always entertained, would have no existence'.[19] His advice may have influenced the signing of the Treaty of Waitangi.[20]

Earlier misinterpretations of Aboriginal population, land-use and style of occupation have ramifications today in popular assumptions and in Australian law.[21] Past Aboriginal negotiations, for example, have been largely omitted from our history, with Aboriginal people portrayed as powerless victims. Even where diplomacy occurred, it is dismissed in a derogatory fashion. Some pastoralists said Aboriginal people 'gave away' their land in return for flour and sugar, or they 'gave away' their children. They failed to acknowlege that loaning children was one of the only ways the Aboriginal people could obtain the right to camp on traditional lands. Rather than being seen as diplomatic efforts, successful adaptations by Aboriginal people have been trivialised as confirming the attractions of civilisation.

The Batman-Kulin treaty of 1835[22] (discussed further in chapter 3 on Victoria) is significant as it was perhaps the only formal treaty negotiated with a group of Australian Aborigines.[23] The Kulin were active agents who negotiated and permitted temporary access to their land in exchange for reciprocal rights to European resources. Batman's treaty was declared invalid by Governor Bourke, not because it was deemed Aboriginal people were not entitled to it but because it was carried out by a private citizen rather than the Crown.[24] George Augustus Robinson, who was employed to conduct a conciliatory process with Tasmanian Aboriginal people, negotiated an unwritten treaty in the 1830s, resulting in their move to Flinders Island.[25] The Tasmanian Aboriginal people demanded special conditions, including regular trips back to their traditional land and the right to pursue their own culture, but these promises were broken.[26] Throughout Australia, Aboriginal people attempted to negotiate with those who first occupied their respective lands and although mutual compromises were sometimes reached, these had no legal standing.

Influenced by the 1830s peak of the British humanitarian movement, the South Australian Colonisation Commission included a preamble in its Act that South Australia was classed as 'waste and unoccupied lands', the Colonial Office was concerned that this conflicted with their policy. They introduced amendments which allowed for a Protector to ensure 'occupation and enjoyment of the natives', requiring their agreement or voluntary sale of land before occupation. The Commissioners ignored these clauses in the Letters Patent by conveniently claiming that Aboriginal people did not 'occupy' the land.[27] Such lobbying, however, did achieve acknowledgement of the Aboriginal people's right to travel over, to hunt, gather and reside upon pastoral leases.

Racial ideas went hand in hand with British imperialism, from the Christian notion of 'the chain of being' where blacks were ranked as inferior and white Christians at the summit, to the rise of anthropology, which turned such ideas into a sustaining 'science'. Their findings were later applied in Africa, Australia and other colonial contexts, providing justification and information to facilitate the implementation of colonialism. Theories like Social Darwinism, popularised by Herbert Spencer in the 1870s and beyond, predicted that the extinction of 'inferior races' in the wake of 'colonial progress' was inevitable. The disease and ill-health Australian Aboriginal people faced in the late nineteenth and early twentieth century only reinforced belief in their inevitable disappearance.[28] Despite the efforts of missionaries like J.B. Gribble in Western Australia and humanitarians in other colonies, the general public was relatively complacent about Aboriginal suffering, and subsequent government policies took on a short-term palliative nature.

Government policies and racial theories were intertwined, but anomalies and conflicts occurred between theory and practice. As suggested in the introduction, approaches taken within various colonies and states also reflected the peculiar demographic and other circumstances in each. Such factors as the impact of the military, the convict population, free settler agriculturalists and pastoralists, miners, the density of the settlement, the time at which it was settled, the state of British and other western technology, especially weaponry were influential.

FRONTIERS

The physical dispossession of Aboriginal people from their land was quite a different phenomenom to their legal dispossession. In the face to face contact, the process of colonial takeover featured both conflict and co-operation. Many Australian colonisers, especially its men, personally implemented the usurpation of land. The story often became violent as Aboriginal people and whites battled for land and other resources.

The Royal Commission into Aboriginal Deaths in Custody, which reported in 1991, was in part prompted by a belief that foul play or murder was responsible for those recent deaths. Aboriginal people's suspicions can be explained by their historical experiences, as well as by police behaviour after the deaths. Passed down through the generations, frontier violence created a distinctive 'popular memory' or historical consciousness. A certain patterning in these stories, a logic of events, explains the predicament of the individual and the group. Past lessons create a basis upon which to assess the present, and contemporary events reinforce them. That Aboriginal people and others often believe that police or gaolers have killed those who died is a serious indictment of Australia's colonial past, as well as proof that the present society has in no way reassured them that that past is over.

Aboriginal elders still ponder the injustices of colonial warfare as they narrate stories of past generations. The late Phillip Pepper, a Kurnai man of eastern Victoria, wrote: 'The white come here and took it by force with a lotta blood bein' shed by the Aborigines, they really died for their own country and got nothin' in return.'[29]

Amy Laurie, a Gurindji woman, spoke of how her grandchildren could not understand why the past generations had not fought back harder when attacked. The elders explained:

> 'You know why we bin let 'em shoot we. Why? We frightened? No, we never gotim rifle.' And we didn't care, they reckon, 'We can die in our own country.'[30]

Aboriginal perceptions of threat by various forces in white society have been perpetuated by a long heritage of control with often harsh means of enforcement. The theft of their land has made them sceptical of white justice. Frontier periods throughout Australia were the shaping times of colonial authority. Early violence against Aboriginal people was an expected 'price' of colonial expansion. What was not bargained for was that the cost to the indigenous people would be so difficult to redress, and that they would not only survive as a people but refuse to give up their struggle for forms of compensation.

A NATIONAL STORY

Amidst the peaceful sounding 'settling' we read about in earlier history books, a lot of 'conquering' of the original landowners took place. In order to make way for British rule and its law to take effect, flagrant disregard of this same law was generally accepted. There were also implicit contradictions in imposing such rule in a 'new' land, for British justice had not been designed to cater equally for people of other cultures, let alone those in the relationship of the colonised. Edicts on paper which required humane treatment of Aboriginal people were not carried out by frontiersmen. Often they were window-dressing to appease the powerful British anti-slavery movement. Furthermore, British statements that Aboriginal people came under the 'protection of the Crown' were inappropriate when they had not chosen to be invaded and taken over as 'subjects'.

The frontier period thus set the tone of 'law and order' to be imposed on Aboriginal people. Tragically, force or its threat became the key means of establishing British justice. Australia has many unrecorded battlefields, and the number of Aboriginal people killed by the newcomers during the frontier era probably exceeds 20 000.[31] Forcibly dispossessed of their land and traditional livelihood, retreat, starvation and migrations to the fringes of white occupied areas or reserves became inevitable. Through its legacy of fear, violence had a lasting impact on Aboriginal people, as was intended. Once they had come within such influence, they would be more likely to obey not just British laws but any instructions given to them by any white person.

Many white frontiersmen literally took the law into their own hands; as colonisers they felt empowered to 'do their job' by participating in conquest. Ordinary citizens thus remained closely involved in 'keeping the blacks in their place'. Community acceptance of violence was so widespread that those who objected were branded fanatics.[32] The legal authorities seldom intervened, providing tacit approval of such actions.

Different styles of violence and techniques of subduing Aboriginal people were employed. This applied even in the earliest, more conciliatory contacts. In 1788, the Eora people who met the first British arrivals at Botany Bay were given displays of musket fire in order to instil a sense of fear of British weaponry.[33]

17

The British wanted to be respected and to dominate; to leave no doubt as to who was in charge.

A series of kidnappings was another stragegy used to command authority, the most famous being of Bennelong, forcibly kept in British custody with chains, bolts and guards. Hostage-taking was practised to acquire intelligence of the original occupants and to force the establishment of diplomatic ties. After Bennelong was returned his freedom, some promising co-operation and co-existence eventuated at Port Jackson and northwards. Conflict intensified, however, as pastoral settlement expanded on the Hawkesbury in the 1790s, then later on the Bathurst plains and along the Hunter in the 1820s. It grew worse during the 1830s and early 1840s along the Macintyre, Gwydir and Namoi, with the famous Myall Creek massacre of 28 Aboriginal men, women and children in 1838. Aboriginal spokespeople repeatedly appealed to have their best hunting areas protected from intruders, but to no avail.[34]

Western Australia was invaded by the British in 1829 and competition for land and resources led to violent struggles. Overt cruelty is remembered in many Aboriginal oral histories, and in 1835 Governor Stirling led a punitive raid in Pinjarra where an estimated eleven Aboriginal people were killed. In 1833 an Aboriginal man from the south-west, Yagan, was shot and killed, and his smoked head placed on public exhibition in Britain.[35]

From the 1840s in Queensland, frontier violence was used to ruthlessly dispossess Aboriginal people. The later occupation of the state, especially in the north, brought advanced rifle and revolver technology, plus the accumulated experience of past conflict in the southern colonies. The strong humanitarian lobby of Sydney and Melbourne was absent and the Native Police Force were brutally effective. The graziers' parliamentary power enabled them to clear and 'settle' the land unimpeded, which meant quelling all Aboriginal opposition. Queensland's vastness and the isolation of many pastoral and mining outposts caused a more protracted frontier struggle than in south-eastern Australia. By the 1880s and 1890s, the era of frontier violence was largely over and colonial 'order' had been imposed.

Queensland frontiersmen, like others, consistently carried guns in case they encountered 'hostile' Aboriginal people; they were in 'enemy territory'. Deaths of Europeans met calls for vengeance. It was indeed doubtful Aboriginal people were being 'protected as subjects of British law'.[36] In Queensland possibly 10 000 Aboriginal people and at least 1000 Europeans died as a result of frontier conflict. The chronic anxiety induced by this situation affected both sides. As the Chief Protector of North Queensland, Archibald Meston stated, Aboriginal people had lived for years 'in a state of absolute terror' and consequently behaved 'like hunted wild beasts'.[37] Such a fearful people were likely to put up less resistance when rounded up onto reserves.

In the Northern Territory the Aboriginal people's first encounter with outsiders was often with Macassarese trepangers or Chinese goldminers. It was the last area to be continuously occupied by the British, though with limited economic success. The British soon abandoned outposts such as Fort Dundas (1826), Raffles Bay (1828)[38] and Port Essington (1838), leaving a legacy of disease,[39] violence and introduced animals. For decades afterwards, the non-Aboriginal population remained very low until the building of the Overland Telegraph Line in the 1870s. As elsewhere, pastoral expansion was accompanied by heightened conflicts, the massacres continuing up to the 1920s and 1930s in Central, north and Western Australia.

Atrocities against the indigenes were often hidden from the public records. The British knew well the implications of committing deeds to paper which, although publicly condoned, did not conform to the 'letter of the law'. The frontiersmen clothed violence in euphemisms such as 'dispersing', 'breaking up', 'shaking up', 'giving a fright' and 'teaching them a lesson'. While frontier warfare was considered men's business, white women sometimes participated.[40]

The violence was certainly not one-sided; Aboriginal people often used force against the strangers, posing a serious danger. Australia-wide, at least 3000 Europeans were killed and another 3000 wounded by Aboriginal people attempting to impose their law on Europeans.[41] Their opposition to the newcomers has often been portrayed as a pan-Aboriginal desire to rid the country of whites, but this is a misinterpretation of Aboriginal culture.[42]

Individual Aboriginal people fought for a variety of reasons. They were generally carrying out their own law, and defending their land from intruders. The British had come uninvited; they had not followed the required protocol of introductions by elders to the land's spirits and contemporary custodians.

Disease also left a shocking legacy of death and fear. Introduced diseases such as smallpox, and malaria in the north, had devastating effects on many Aboriginal groups, even before they came into actual physical contact with Europeans. Populations were halved or virtually obliterated; the severe depopulation caused personal suffering and community crises, placing survivors in a weakened position. Noel Butlin labelled disease as 'our original aggression'[43], and although there is no strong evidence that it was intentionally used in Australia as a means of subduing Aboriginal people, closing off access to land and food resources and poor medical assistance constituted neglect if not malice. By the late nineteenth century and until the 1950s, white health experts were largely motivated by the perceived threat of contagious diseases to their own people.[44]

While in many areas, disease proved to be the main factor responsible for Aboriginal deaths, susceptability was enhanced by the trauma of dispossession, unavailability of traditional food and water supplies, bans on traditional weapons, the unhygienic results of being required to wear European-style clothing, and the lack of immunity to introduced diseases. Alcohol and tobacco also played destructive roles.

Colonies differed in their scale of depopulation. The southeastern peoples were badly hit by smallpox whilst the northerners' contact with Asia gave them greater immunity.[45] A speedy decline was suffered by the Eora of New South Wales, the Port Phillip peoples and the Tasmanian Aboriginal people, several of their clans being rapidly destroyed. The intruders, principally made up of convicts shipped out against their will, stole food, weapons, and raped Aboriginal women. The desperation of the hungry whites to establish self-supporting industries, especially sheep-grazing, led to a push for land and disregard for the original inhabitants. Van Diemen's Land settlers and the ex-convict population was little interested in humanitarian concerns. The death toll of Aboriginal people from violence and disease was shocking, and continued to worsen after they were exiled to smaller islands.[46] Of the three or four thousand inhabitants in Van Diemen's Land prior to the 1790s, only a couple of hundred people survived the 1830s. However, the islanders of Bass Strait, who had formed a community with men of the sealing industry, managed to survive as a distinct and defiant people.

Where there was less competition for resources and land, Aboriginal people had more chance to pursue their traditional economies. Furthermore, the hotter, northern and desert regions and areas without ports or reliable water supplies were less desirable to the newcomers, giving indigenes more time to develop survival strategies. There were fewer intruders, and maritime industries such as trepanging, pearling and fishing often relied upon Aboriginal labour and even company. A proportionally higher non-Aboriginal population also led to greater inter-mixing and mergence of the peoples. Generally the less successful the enterprises, and the less land-intensive the industries, the greater the chances for Aboriginal survival and relative independence.

LAND AND LABOUR

Aboriginal people as a whole have been especially vulnerable to fluctuations in the labour market. While some were attracted by the lure of tobacco, tea and rations, many lost their traditional economy and were subsequently forced into exploitative labour arrangements. A large proportion of Aboriginal people continued to support themselves independently in the late nineteenth and early twentieth century, but government policies often curbed Aboriginal entrepreneurism, such as bartering, selling fish and skins.

The desire of the British to establish their own economic security led to the dismantling of Aboriginal self-sufficiency. Foraging was considered an inferior pursuit, and more significantly, it clashed with British land-use requirements. Although Governor Macquarie, like Phillip, respected individual Aboriginal people, good intentions were outweighed by other colonial imperatives. Macquarie was aware of the many Aboriginal protests from the Daruk regarding the takeover of too much of their choice riverbank land. He broke promises of no further expansion, and classified violent Aboriginal protests and crop destruction as unruly behaviour. Macquarie's desire to change the Eora and other groups became especially pronounced after continuing violence on the Hawkesbury and interior. In 1816, he issued a proclamation prohibiting Aboriginal people from practising their hunting and customary law; they could not carry traditional weapons near town or conduct ritual fights. Gatherings of more than six people near a farm would result in 'enemy' status.[47] Macquarie's 'passport system' offered protection only for those who surrendered. In reward for 'disarming' and presumably giving up hunting with spears, they would be provided with land to 'obtain an honest and Comfortable Subsistence by their own Labour and Industry'. Also supplied were six months' food, a hut, tools, wheat, maize, potatoes, clothes, and 'one Colonial Blanket'. They were thus exhorted to 'relinquish their wandering idle predatory Habits of Life'. Any truce was to be conditional upon Aboriginal acceptance of British rules, including adoption of British cultural mores, and the rejection of Aboriginal political, legal, work and family structures.

From the earliest decades of white settlement at Port Jackson, Aboriginal people were encouraged to become farmers. Some Eora took up land at Elizabeth Bay and Blacktown, with male elders selecting areas near traditional estates. Aboriginal people may have hoped to prevent the land's destruction by outsiders, but a convict was appointed to establish a market garden and British aesthetics were also imposed, with convicts building a 'romantic road'.[48] Before long the Aboriginal people deserted the farms.

Later they saw farming as a means to family independence and established successful farms in Victoria, New South Wales, South Australia and Western Australia. The Cumeragunja people's fight for their farms is narrated in the film *Lousy Little Sixpence*. The Lake Tyers people of Victoria also mounted a protracted struggle to retain their own land. South Australian Aborigines' demands for farming land were supported by a superintendent of the Aboriginal mission at Point Pearce. F. Garnet believed that the granting of land for farms was a means of keeping them from becoming 'outcasts of society' who ended up in gaols.[49] Nevertheless, governments remained insensitive to Aboriginal needs and successes at self-sufficiency, favouring the white farmers who demanded that good land be handed over to them. All types of land allocated for Aboriginal use was frequently resumed. Insecurity of Aboriginal tenure reflected that key tenet of colonialism, to 'colonise' with their own people, to take over Aboriginal land. If Aborigines occupied land, it must by definition be wasted or wasteland. Throughout Australia, Aborigines thus suffered not one, but many dispossessions.[50]

Strong demand for Aboriginal labour sometimes led employers to accommodate Aboriginal cultural priorities. This was especially true in the more remote areas where insufficient white or imported coloured labour was available, and Aboriginal people became indispensable.[51] In inland New South Wales, Queensland, Western Australia, the Northern Territory and parts of South Australia, skilled Aborigines could shape the terms of their employment. Oversupply of Aboriginal labour, however, often lowered financial rewards.[52]

Nonetheless, labour market demand probably influenced levels of anti-Aboriginal violence and it also dictated the location of Aboriginal reserves. Many stories are told of northern pastoral employers hiding suspected murderers from the police because they were good stockmen.[53] Here economic interests, and perhaps also mutual respect, had primacy over white solidarity. When not required for employment, there was not the same need to keep workers healthy, in the habit of employment, and out of gaol. During the Great Depression of the 1930s, Aborigines were not entitled to the same welfare as other Australians. Later rural recessions similarly hit Aborigines hard, and, it seems in some New South Wales towns in the 1970s their imprisonment rates simultaneously rose. (See chapter 2 on New South Wales.)

World War I and II provided Aborigines with an opportunity to enlist as soldiers and be paid and treated on a more equal footing. Elsewhere Aboriginal labour was greatly underpaid, and only in the 1940s and 1960s did the struggles for equal wages receive support from the wider community. Prior to the 1960s, in the Northern Territory and Western Australia, Aboriginal people were often only paid in rations and some work clothing, with no proper housing provided. In Queensland, a cash wage was required from the 1900s, but a proportion of this was held in trust by the State. The government wanted to subvert the Aboriginal people's sharing ethic and encourage thrift and savings, which the Aborigines saw as shameful greed. Although a small cash wage was introduced after the 1940s, many Aboriginal people in Queensland, the Northern Territory, New South Wales and Western Australia[54] were never paid their due wages and their lifetime earnings were returned to consolidated revenue. In the 1930s the Northern Territory (excluding Central Australia) account was balanced at 3000 pounds but little attempt was made to distribute it to its rightful owners. Northern Aborigines were forbidden from purchasing cars or other prestigious items as these were considered too good or too frivolous for an Aborigine.[55] In 1934 the Western Australian Aborigines Department held 2400 pounds in trust[56] and Queensland trust money totalled a startling 293 549 pounds.[57] The Northern Territory Chief Protector had set up the Aboriginal Medical Benefits Fund to urge employers to take responsibility for work accidents and employees' health. The Federal Government confiscated most of this money for consolidated revenue and would not even permit its expenditure on 'Christmas cheer' for the children in the 'half-caste home'.[58] Aboriginal people were thus deprived not only of fair wages, but workers' compensation, medical treatment and the right to freely spend their money.

Wage discrimination meant Aboriginal people lacked 'the family wage' available to other Australians, and bank loans were out of reach. In many states Aboriginal people were prohibited from buying land. They were not entitled to the maternity bonus introduced in 1912, to the dole, to various forms of welfare, including old-age pensions, to the same health or educational facilities as Europeans. Their camps rarely had the basic facilities of running water, power or sewerage.

Little money was spent on providing facilities for Aboriginal education. Public education was designed for white children who spoke English as their first language. Aboriginal knowledge and learning styles were ignored. Mission teachers were often untrained, and inferior facilities for state teachers in Aboriginal schools also ensured sub-standard education. Hoping to maintain their cheap labour force, pastoralists were generally opposed to schooling resident Aborigines. During the 1930s some unions such as the IWW (Industrial Workers of the World) attempted to educate Aboriginal people about their rights, though others protested against their employment, seeing Aboriginal labour as a threat to their conditions. Eventually some Aboriginal labourers found union allies who supported their mobilisation for better conditions, as in the 1946 Pilbara strike and the Wave Hill walkoffs in 1966 and in the Victoria River district 1972-73.

Although Aboriginal people showed outstanding ability at prestigious occupations such as exploration, detective work, stockwork, and army work during the wars, state training schemes invariably placed them at the bottom rung of the labour hierarchy. From Macquarie's time through to the 1960s, any training schemes for Aboriginal girls stressed domestic service, a job disliked in a society with egalitarian aspirations, while the boys were to be trained as 'rural apprentices'. Aboriginal girls and boys taken from their parents were required to perform the most menial and poorly paid occupations and had no choice about employers. If they left employment, they were punished, sometimes in homes for juveniles, while their exploitation as cheap labour was justified as 'uplift' and 'civilisation'. In reality it meant no education other than domestic training, and a lonely life as virtual orphans. Many lost all contact with their real families. During their service in other people's homes, girls who became pregnant were sent to unmarried mothers' institutions, where they were given little choice but to consent to their babies' adoption by white families.

Aboriginal people were expected to fit in with a western-style labour system but they were not entitled to its privileges. Although excluded from many types of work, they excelled and were highly sought after at rural work such as horse breaking, mustering, fruit planting and picking. Outdoor and seasonal work appealed, as they often enabled greater flexibility and travel to visit distant kin. In many cases they allowed people to be based

Patricia Kemp, aged 2 years, with Jenny, South Australia. White station children were often cared for, if not reared by, Aboriginal nannies. NATIONAL LIBRARY OF AUSTRALIA

near or on their traditional land and range area. Aboriginal people often demanded more flexible work arrangements where they could leave jobs to visit people or places, or conduct ceremonies. In many places this included continuing their traditional bush economy.

In rural towns, where so many Aboriginal people still reside, employment networks are family-based and often totally exclude Aboriginal people. The same applied to urban centres. As Mum Shirl, who grew up in Sydney's inner suburbs, stated in her biography, she had little to do with whites 'except that we shopped at their shops, and always had to go to them for jobs and work, but mostly we seemed to be with each other'.[59]

THE LAW

Since colonisation, Aboriginal people experienced an anomalous position in relation to British and Australian law. Prior to and after contact, Aboriginal communities had their legal system, with its internal logic and rationale emanating from the holistic philosophy of the Dreaming. Rather than abstract principles of justice, their laws were evoked more directly and on a more personal basis to maintain or regain community harmony.[60] Theoretically, Australian courts have held that British laws applied to Aboriginal people and whites alike 'except to the extent that the legislature had seen fit to make differences or to allow exceptions'.[61] Tribal law was to an extent accommodated by the Western Australian Native Courts between 1936 and 1954. Yet whereas 'tribal custom' was taken into account in mitigation of a sentence, it could not be a complete defence.[62]

Usually Aboriginal people were subject to British and later Australian law, and additionally to a range of special laws which prohibited and restricted Aboriginal movements and associations. While theoretically they were to be treated as British subjects, they suffered 'severe disabilities in the courts'.[63] They were not given equality of legal status, yet were perceived as law-breakers. In many colonies, legislation entitled police and justices of the peace to extraordinary powers over Aboriginal people. Pastoralists, miners and other employers of Aboriginal labour were often appointed as justices of the peace and magistrates. They tried cases relating to their own or their neighbours' employees, and sent out their station's employees to assist in police efforts to quell Aboriginal actions.[64] In Western Australia, for example, Aboriginal Protectors had special duties to 'minimise the annoyance caused by the Aboriginal people' which included their nudity and begging. In 1849, Aboriginal people could be tried summarily for criminal offences (excluding murder, arson, rape) by two or more justices of the peace and sentenced with up to six months imprisonment plus corporal punishment for male offenders.[65]

This court room scene depicts a trial of Aborigines for murder at Franklin Harbour in December 1855. Three men were subsequently hanged in January 1856. The man standing near the seated witness is a native interpreter. Admittedly the artist has trouble with faces, but the Aboriginal figures look less than human.
MITCHELL LIBRARY, STATE LIBRARY OF NEW SOUTH WALES

Many legal impediments affected Aboriginal people.[66] In some colonies they could not press charges, were held corporately guilty for the crimes of others, and were not permitted to give evidence because they were pagans. But even the lifting of restrictions on giving evidence meant little. The justice system was especially alienating for people who were not familiar with western culture. Aboriginal people often understood little English, and thought they were to provide required answers rather than the 'objective truth'.[67] Juries were almost exclusively white, and rarely sympathised with the Aboriginal defendant or believed Aboriginal witnesses. Even if a white man had provoked the attack, the lesson had to be taught that Aboriginal retaliation was unacceptable. In the 1920s and 30s, numerous cases which Charles Rowley described as 'spectacular injustice' occurred through the courts. These highlighted the conflicts between traditional Aboriginal and British style law. But even more, they drew attention to the fact that Aboriginal people were not receiving justice under the Australian system. Race had long been a crucial factor in administering justice, as demonstrated by studies of the 1888 rape case of a Victorian Aboriginal woman and of rape cases concerning Aboriginal men.[68] Except in the most blatant cases, it was a tradition for whites to be acquitted for the murders of Aboriginal people. In a survey of the North Queensland circuit court between 1882–94, only a quarter of Europeans charged with violent offences against Aboriginal people were found guilty, and none were to be executed, despite the high proportion of murder cases.[69]

In Northern Territory murder trials from 1884 to 1911 all nine Aboriginal people charged with murder of whites were found guilty, and three were executed. In the cases where whites were charged, they were very rarely found guilty, and the murderer was released after a short term. In 1913 Judge Bevan wrote to the Administrator:

> Juries will not convict a white man for an offence against a black, certainly if the evidence is that of blacks, whereas on black evidence there is no difficulty in the way of securing a conviction against a black . . . The jury system may have worked well where the population is all one colour, but the introduction of racial antipathies goes far to undermine the principles of trial by Jury.[70]

Some of the scandals which occurred in the 1920s and 1930s in the far north related to police actions against Aboriginal people (for example, the Coniston and Forrest River massacres[71]). Others involved suspicious deaths in police custody, such as that of Dolly of the Borroloola district. Constable G. Stott was charged with her assault but acquitted. The Supreme Court Judge stated that all the Aboriginal witnesses were 'liars'. Aboriginal witnesses had their images tarnished by being treated as criminals; in frontier areas, they were often chained and imprisoned until the hearing. In 1934 an Aboriginal man, Tuckiar, was charged with the murder of Constable McColl, and Judge Wells found him guilty, despite corroborated evidence of provocation. Aborigines alleged that McColl engaged in intercourse with Tuckiar's wife and refused to compensate the husband. The High Court overruled

Wells' decision, unanimously ruling that Tuckiar should be released into the custody of the Chief Protector. However, Tuckiar mysteriously disappeared the next day without trace. Another man, Willaberta Jack, who was charged with the shooting murder of a white pastoralist (1929), was found dead soon after his acquittal—officially due to 'influenza'.[72] Humanitarians agitated for the establishment of Native Courts as in the Mandated Territory of Papua New Guinea, but their calls were largely unsuccessful.

DETENTION PATTERNS

Aboriginal detention rates have not always been as high as they are today; indeed their escalation is a relatively recent phenomenom. In the nineteenth century, Aboriginal 'crime' was more likely to be punished by frontiersmen than police. For most of the twentieth century, missionaries, government reserve superintendents and employers exercised discipline over Aboriginal people. The greatest increase in official Aboriginal detention has occurred since the 1950s, when increasing numbers of Aboriginal people moved into towns, and the government encouraged their incorporation into the wider community.

Prior to the Assimilation Policy, a separate system of justice operated for Aboriginal people living on reserves. In Queensland and Western Australia, reserves had their own courts, prisons and punishments. Aboriginal people charged and held in their lock-ups do not appear in state or Territory police or prison records. Segregation policies therefore meant not only separate living places but special sets of regulations and an insular, subjective judicial system. In a survey of courts presided over by Queensland reserve superintendents from 1959 to 1962, Colin Tatz found that almost every defendant pleaded guilty, and virtually all were found guilty. He pointed out how trivial behaviours from 'untidyness' to 'immoral conduct' were punishable with incarceration and argued that the judicial system contravened key principles of natural justice. The superintendent or missionary knew the personalities involved, there was no court of appeal, no legal assistance offered, and the accused could be banished for an unlimited time.[73]

Greater association with police meant not only greater surveillance but a tendency for Aborigines to be perceived as law-breakers and undesirables.[74] Special state legislation placed Aboriginal people under a set of discriminatory prohibitions between 1900 and 1960. Furthermore, Aboriginal people's loss of land and lifestyle factors made them especially susceptible to charges of loitering, vagrancy and petty theft.[75] The charge of 'vagrancy' assumes 'respectability' is linked to a fixed residence, and the carrying of a certain amount of cash or savings. These notions were inimical to an Aboriginal travelling lifestyle with reciprocal sharing principles.

Cattle spearing was one of the most common crimes in pastoral districts until the 1930s. Aboriginal people felt justified in taking animals for food off their traditional lands but this conflicted with western property principles. Europeans had freely taken Aboriginal foodstuffs, killing their game foods, and even abducting women and children. Absence of native title made Aboriginal use of open space trespass. In the 1990s, Aboriginal cultural factors relating to use of 'public space' and white perceptions of their residential areas as public similarly led to disproportionate arrest rates.[76]

Discriminatory legislation banned alcohol to people classed as Aborigines until the 1960s or thereabouts. Legalisation of alcohol consumption for Aboriginal people is often cited as the chief cause of increased detention rates. Available figures show, however, that the trend towards higher rates of incarceration had commenced some years before the legalisation of alcohol consumption. Increased rates of incarceration in police cells and prisons coincided with the time that other types of Aboriginal institutionalisation were phased out. The Assimilation Policy of the 1950s led more Aboriginal people to move into towns, resulting in greater visibility than when 'locked' away on reserves and missions. In the 1960s and 70s, greater mechanisation, rural recession, and to a lesser extent, the introduction of equal wages in the pastoral industry, led to higher unemployment rates. Less employer control and the disbandment (sometimes enforced by employers) of supervised work-related camps had a similar effect to shifting Aborigines off the reserves.

Only scattered historical statistics exist on Aboriginal detention rates and incarceration, as separate records for Aboriginal people were rarely kept, but the South Australian statistics provide a spiralling example. The rates of South Australian Aboriginal people in the prison population during the nineteenth century were fairly low—varying between 2 and 7 per cent. From 1905–30 'black and coloured' represented 2.4 per cent admissions, or less than 1 per cent of the Aboriginal population of South Australia. In the years 1956–69, the proportion of admissions steadily rose to 25 per cent of the total. Until the late 1940s, Queensland's Aboriginal people represented only a small though not insignificant percentage of the prison population. Reflecting the tightening reign on reserve dwellers, from 1901 numbers held in prisons decreased, with 6.7 per cent of the prison population in 1902 and 1.4 per cent in 1931. In Western Australia during the 1950–58 period, the rates of convictions for Aboriginal people were climbing steadily, with a more rapid jump between 1955 and 1960. By 1965, Aboriginal people in Western Australia represented 30 per cent of the prison population, compared with an estimated 2–3 per cent of the overall population.

Of Aboriginal people who were charged, most offences were relatively minor, against 'good order'. Drunkenness and obscene language were amongst the most common charges. In her study of Aboriginal people charged in Western Australia, Eggleston found that sentences discriminated against Aboriginal people, with prison sentences much more likely for Aboriginal offenders. Minor convictions soon led to long criminal records.[77] C.D. Rowley's 1965 survey of Victoria, New South Wales and South Australia found that Aboriginal people were subjected to disproportionately high charge rates. In common with wider patterns, very few women were charged. Men were thought to require this type of discipline and had a greater interest in alcohol.

Poverty cannot be overlooked as a factor which precipitates crime. In biographies by now 'respectable' Aboriginal people, they reminisce with some amusement about theft as a necessary means to acquire things other people took for granted. Ruby Langford

Ginibi thus appreciated the stolen money she was given for groceries when all her children were hungry, or the thoughtful present of turf for her backyard from a prison renegade. On her wedding day Mum Shirl's complete bridal outfit was 'hot'.[78] No sense of wrongdoing emerges in recalling these events, but rather a recognition of occasional theft as a worthwhile survival strategy. The hard work required to survive as an Aborigine—tough, often tragic lives combined with police harrassment—led Langford to consider it unsurprising and not particularly 'serious' that one of her sons would have more than one conviction for firing guns at police cars.[79]

The police, legal institutions and the media have often conceptualised Aboriginal groups as criminal classes, leading to increased detentions. Relations are seen as consorting with 'criminals' and despite the minor nature of their offences, the reputations of others are tarnished accordingly. The criminalisation experience is sometimes passed down through generations, to become a seemingly 'normal' way of life. Incarcerations in the family thus become a common experience for many Aboriginal families.

The wide array of other institutions to control Aboriginal people involved high degrees of confinement and isolation. Children's institutions were not only rigidly disciplined but punitive. At Carrolup Settlement in Western Australia, young children were confined in a lock-up known as the 'Boob'. The case of a girl punished for over 60 days because she tried to return to her family was not uncommon.[80] Reserve managers in Western Australia exerted control over marriage, diet, child-rearing, employment, and greatly restricted movement off reserves. Queensland reserves had similar policies: Aboriginal people who rocked the boat by requesting their own earnings, which were held in trust funds, could be banished to Palm Island. New South Wales reserve dwellers who complained about unfair withholding of rations were punished by their own or their children's banishment.[81] Exile on another reserve far from kin and community was a way of keeping Aboriginal people subservient to the wishes of the Board and deterring political activism. Aboriginal people had virtually no recourse to appeal such decisions.

Once Aboriginal people moved nearer to centres of white

settlement, any non-conforming behaviour became more visible and likely to meet opposition. Rising tensions between Aboriginal people and local communities were fuelled by many factors, and during the 1970s and 80s some local councils in New South Wales colluded with police and other authorities to improve their 'tidy town' image.[82] Arrest rates rose rapidly, and media reports of 'race riots' further exaggerated the tensions.

The rhetoric and rationales for earlier protectionist policies were premised on paternalistic notions which defined Aboriginal people as a 'child race' requiring the sort of 'supervision' (the word 'surveillance' was thus not used), the 'gentle hand to guide' that children required. They were therefore to be controlled and punished in a different way to other adults. Assumed too mentally immature for responsibility for their actions, the prison system was not necessarily seen as the logical place for them, or at least not the first point of recourse. But after the 1950s, international opinion pushed Australia closer towards granting equal rights to Aboriginal people. A process of 'exemptions' in various states gave Aborigines the right to drink alcohol, though to gain a certificate, one had to reject links with Aboriginal lifestyle and kin. Without 'good behaviour', most certificates could be cancelled.[83] In many towns, Aborigines were still excluded from public areas such as swimming pools and shops, prompting Charles Perkins to organise the Freedom Rides of 1965.

If Aborigines did not conform to the cultural strictures of the colonisers' society or fulfil their expectations as amenable servile workers, they were categorised as 'bad types' who needed policing. Incarceration through the gaol system was the updated method of control, exclusion, and discipline. That prison could become a key normative institution to teach 'civilisation' to the indigenous people is one of the implicit contradictions of colonialism.

PUNISHMENT AND SURVEILLANCE[84]

Aboriginal people as a group have been the target of various forms of discipline and surveillance—starting often through the barrel of a gun during the 'frontier' eras, then changing into the restrictions affecting mobility and personal liberty policed by mission and reserve authorities.

Changing attitudes to crime and punishment accompanied the social sciences of psychology, psychiatry, criminal anthropology and criminology.[85] In the nineteenth century, alcohol and the vices of civilisation were considered factors which led Aboriginal people to gaol. In an 1887 report on the management of Queensland prisons, imprisonment was considered to have no meaning for Aboriginal people and no deterrent effect. Recommended instead was solitary confinement, of which Aboriginal people were terrified. Although they were to receive the same diet as white prisoners, they were segregated from them.[86] After the experience of Van Diemen's Land, and imprisonment elsewhere, it was found that Aboriginal people did not survive when confined. This was noted in a medical report on Aboriginal people detained for mental health reasons. Imprisonment on an island was considered preferable to 'close confinement' which was 'prejudicial to their health' 'though tempered by many unaccustomed comforts' it was 'the great factor in shortening life'.[87]

Physical punishment of Aboriginal people continued, despite its rejection as brutal in nineteenth century Europe.[88] In frontier regions, physical punishment was even more common. Settler folklore included the belief that Aboriginal people had especially thick skulls and it was almost impossible to strike hard enough to kill them.[89] In Western Australia, justices of the peace could legally lash male offenders 24 times in a row.[90] Native Police were flogged, and troopers, missionaries, employers and reserve managers all considered this an acceptable means of punishing Aboriginal people. One New South Wales reserve manager carried around a rifle, firing occasionally for effect, while another belted people with a baton.[91] Reverend James Watson of Milingimbi admitted in 1925 to using the stockwhip on Aboriginal men, allegedly to punish them for assaulting their wives.[92] Judge Wells of the Supreme Court of the Northern Territory stated in 1938 that 'the only punishment aboriginals appreciate, is a flogging. This has been suggested as the proper punishment for aboriginals by many who know them.' For more serious

Men being brought into a police station in neck chains, c 1920. Dozens of photographs of Aborigines in chains provide evocative evidence of the style of white justice against Aborigines. BATTYE LIBRARY, LIBRARY BOARD OF WESTERN AUSTRALIA, 68174P

offences, he recommended execution, and was angered when the government commuted death sentences to life imprisonment.[93]

Neck and leg chains were used on arrested Aboriginal prisoners in the Centre, north and parts of Western Australia until the 1930s, even though the nearest police lock-up was miles away. Aboriginal chain gangs also conducted road works. H.D. Moseley, who headed a 1934 Royal Commission to consider the 'Aboriginal problem', determined that neck chains were humane.[94] On the one hand, the need for chains implied great success as escapists, but the symbolism of such entrapment and the discomfort it brought was a powerful demonstration of colonial authority.

A continuing Australian tradition of differential treatment in enforcing 'justice' reflects the deeper conflicts ensuing between coloniser and colonised. Vengeance policies were commonplace and remained so into the twentieth century. In the 1930s, when Aboriginal people murdered a white man or Japanese men, as in the Caledon Bay murders, the government sent out police-led 'punitive expeditions'. A Board of Enquiry was set up in 1935 to investigate cases of 'ill-treatment' by Constable McKinnon and others in Central Australia. It was revealed that police whipped and thrashed station Aboriginal people. The Board recommended that the managers report any cases of ill-treatment of Aboriginal people, but it is doubtful this was put into practice. In response to humanitarian pressure from the south, the Superintendent of Police, A.V. Stretton, advised police the following year that they should be 'carefully guarded' in their actions towards Aboriginal prisoners. Stretton advised 'discretion with firearms and recommended the use of lighter chains; he banned punitive patrols and the use of violence in interrogations'.[95]

As traditional forms of Aboriginal justice and punishment were not recognised, Aboriginal people were sometimes charged and/or punished for enforcing their laws. Punishment might entail a spearing in the leg or an execution.[96] An 1887 Report on Queensland prisons lamented the injustice of Aboriginal people being punished twice 'by the law of the race which has dispossessed him of his hunting grounds and taught him the vices of civilisation'. In many cases, however, unless they concerned a non-Aboriginal person or were carried out in the eyes of the law, government authorities ignored intra-Aboriginal violence.

When the 'civilisers', especially missionaries, wanted to curb the violent traditional punishment they commonly did so by using violence themselves. Aboriginal people's supposed closeness to brutes was justification for corporal punishment. Physical suffering was imposed to make Aboriginal people less of a threat to whites. For good colonising motives other contemporary values could be suspended. Yet it is a strange paradox that such punishment, then considered uncivilised in western societies, was condoned as a means of 'civilising' the Aboriginal people.[97]

While the aim of a gaol punishment for non-Aboriginal people was to deprive the offender of individual liberty, this was not considered enough to bring home any message to Aboriginal people. Colonial conquest had already deprived Aboriginal people of their past liberty, including the sites at which they could drink water, hunt, camp and meet their kin. They were denied citizenship rights and the reserve system did not permit them to make decisions about their own lives; its rigid social order was supposed to be a crash course in civilisation but it meant Aboriginal people were often cut off from the outside world and were not allowed to manage their own affairs.[98]

Thousands of Aboriginal families were thus kept in a form of custody on segregated reserves. Custody has been defined as 'safe keeping, protection, charge, care, guardianship' as well as the more judicial 'the keeping of an officer of justice; confinement, imprisonment, durance'.[99] Supervised missions and reserves were highly regimented. While the Northern Territory had more of a laissez faire policy than the states, from the 1930s, systematic records listed data relating to names, tribe, spouse, offspring, medical history, employment record, and police convictions. In 1932, the Chief Protector of Aborigines ordered each Aborigine in the Darwin district to be issued with a bronze numbered disk after a medical inspection and taking of fingerprints. Aborigines were supposed to wear the disks around their necks on red tape provided, but they refused to do so, labelling them 'dog tags' after another recently introduced government initiative. Aboriginal people of mixed-descent were subject to greater scrutiny, taken from their parents at a young age and forced to live in sub-standard accommodation which was both overcrowded and a fire hazard.

The New South Wales managers of government reserves were ill-trained and unpredictable. Backgrounds in management or experience with Aboriginal people were not required, but rather 'firmness', and a head for paperwork and figures. Former policemen, colonial administrators, regimental sergeant-majors and prison warders were welcome.[100] A manager's duties included teaching children and maintaining school records, writing daily, weekly, monthly and annual reports, inspecting and repairing the houses and equipment, entertaining official visitors, collecting rent, supervising work gangs, distributing rations, and enforcing an array of mostly petty regulations.[101] Some managers were decent but there were no real curbs on managerial conduct, and with co-operative police and magistrates, the place could become a 'concentration camp'. Aboriginal people recall tyrannical managers constantly calling in the police to remove people from the mission—as Les Coe explained, they 'treated you like bloody mongrel dogs'.[102] While prisons might be seen as the most extreme example of institutionalisation, their structure and motives were not entirely dissimilar to Aboriginal reserves; as such they were part of a cultural continuum of discipline and socialisation.

Aborigines, however, did not, and today do not, see imprisonment as shameful. The mother of one young man who was found hanged in gaol stated that he was not afraid of prison, as though this was proof of masculinity or personal strength. It was certainly something well within the realms of personal or family experience. Past institutionalisation of self or parents on a regimented mission or reserve could even make it seem like 'home'. These formative experiences were probably interpreted as punishment or discipline anyway although children could be detained in delinquents homes on the basis of their colour alone. Although Aboriginal people at first feared gaol it later become a challenge, a test of one's ability to cope with this white controlled environment. Fear of possible death could add a further edge to this 'trial by ordeal'.

The elderly Gurindji woman, Amy Laurie described her lifestyle during the 1960s and early 70s:

> When I was a drunken woman the police got me for drunk-an'-run-around, and that's why I left the grog. I used to end up in gaol all the time—three months. They didn't think about me, an old woman, but I spent three months down Broome. Five times I went there. Oh, I used to have a good ride too—down and back! I reckon gaol is alright. They feed you really well, and pay you, so you come back with your own money when you work around. They used to ask me, 'How come you come back in gaol again?' 'Why? Because you have everything here.' Oh, I don't like it now.[103]

Amy had alternative explanations of why she gave up drinking. Gaol may have had an element of travel and adventure, and although the living conditions were comfortable compared with what she was used to, she hinted at the loneliness and isolation. Aboriginal attitudes to gaol highlight the material inequalities in Australian society and even the ludicrousness of punishing people whose ordinary lives would be considered punishment by those belonging to most other groups.

But material ease is not everything. Socially, gaols were of course lonely and threatening, and it was difficult to get away from the tensions associated with white people and strange Aborigines. There is also evidence, however, of Aboriginal solidarity in gaols, exchanges of song cycles and ritual business between clans.[104] Then there are the possibilities of an evolving Aboriginal 'gaol culture'. Unfortunately suicide by hanging has become an option within this cultural framework.

Aboriginal spokespersons have stated that membership of the colonised class makes them feel confined and imprisoned, and so to be actually locked up in a gaol is the last straw. This is a telling reflection of Aboriginal consciousness about their position in Australian society. Aboriginal perceptions of and reactions to custody are closely linked with the intricacies of colonial power relations. Aboriginal people are perceived and perceive themselves as 'losers' in a conflict where white Australians were victorious, having celebrated this for many years in works of history and nationalistic ceremonies such as Australia Day. Colonialism did not start and end on a specific date. If we accept that it is the story of one group's attempt to gain and maintain hegemony over another group, then it never ends because domination can never be total. The exception is when the group subject to colonialism is totally obliterated.

RESISTANCE TO COLONIALISM

Aboriginal people have occupied an ambiguous place in the Australian nation. After 1942, under Japanese attack, Australia faced its greatest outside threat. Thousands of Aborigines rallied to defend the land against the enemy but others revealed their understanding to be quite different. The Australian Government was nervous about their loyalty, fearing a fifth column amongst their ranks, especially in remote areas. Waddi Boyoi wanted to negotiate peace in the north-west without anyone getting killed; he reasoned, why not let the whites have one bit of his land and the Japanese the other bit; the local Aborigines would have some left too and they could all share his traditional land.[105] Many Aborigines thus continued to see themselves as the real landowners, and indeed in the north, they had only recently been usurped by what became White Australia.

The tragic heritage of colonialism poses a huge problem for Australian society. Until recently even 'sympathetic' and well-informed white Australians described the situation of Aboriginal people as the 'Aboriginal problem'.[106] Popular conceptions continue to frame the issue this way, asking 'What is the solution?' as though it will be 'solved' by non-Aboriginal people. Earlier administrators such as C.E. Cook, Chief Protector of Aboriginal people in the Northern Territory in the 1920s, perceived 'the Aboriginal problem' as a 'half-caste problem' because the 'full-bloods' would die out. Aboriginal survival was therefore the 'problem', as it made things rather messy. Only in Tasmania did colonists believe the colonising process was complete. The quest for 'real Aborigines' still appeals to many Europeans today as a means of excluding less physically identifiable people of Aboriginal descent. Lowering the numbers is one way of lessening the 'problem'. This extinction myth, perhaps convenient for white residents, is repeatedly challenged by Tasmania's Aboriginal population. It is no coincidence that a spokesperson like Michael Mansell reacts to past non-recognition by making himself and his people's survival so visible.

As we have seen, the surveillance of personal lives, sexual relations, hygiene, child-rearing and general housekeeping became very intrusive in the 'welfare' era. Aboriginal women and men were not given the chance of self-policing but had to put up with inspectors and police with great powers over their financial security and family life. Heavy surveillance of Aboriginal families led to greater institutionalisation and police and prison detention rates. As an easily identifiable and disadvantaged social group, they continue to be greatly over-represented in charge and detention rates. Western Australia has the worst record of 29 times the rates for non-Aborigines. In a depressing irony, the State thus ensured that many of the Aboriginal people have become a type of convict class in contemporary society.

Aborigines' relationship to the nation has remained ambiguous, leading many to argue that they now wish to be recognised as an indigenous nation, or nations within the nation. Aboriginal people have long suffered a protracted campaign of exclusion from the public sphere; until the late 1960s and early 1970s they could

Government policies emphasised health issues and targeted Aboriginal parenting practices. Mothers such as these Delissaville women were told to care for their babies in the 1950s fashion of regimented routines and western hygiene products. Yet basic infrastructure such as running water was often unavailable to complement the lessons. The official caption to this photograph reads: 'The Baby Clinic and Mothercraft Centre is a greatly valued amenity enjoyed by the residents of the Delissaville government settlement, in the Northern Territory. Aboriginal mothers have taken to the system with enthusiasm; and with great benefit to themselves and their families.' AUSTRALIAN NEWS AND INFORMATION BUREAU, PHOTOGRAPH BY J. TANNER, L25349

be officially excluded from main streets, parks, public swimming pools, public bars, the census and the vote. Exclusions now continue surreptitiously and police are sometimes used to implement them. It is hardly surprising then, that Aboriginal resistance to white authority is often specifically directed against the police.

As earlier discussed, the history of Aboriginal groups has varied a great deal regionally, with some clans suffering devastating depopulation. Others retained more autonomy, language, cultural knowledge, and land associations. In the case of the Torres Strait Islands, a relatively independent employment history, geographic separation and cultural differences also set them apart. In northern Australia, a later frontier, a history of economic failures and a small non-Aboriginal population enabled Aboriginal people to maintain a certain autonomy over their lives and to a relatively large extent, maintain traditional land associations and spiritual lives. The *Northern Territory Land Rights Act 1976* helped lead to cultural revitalisation and provided a power base as well as many side benefits such as negotiation, legal and employment experience. Sometimes reserves or pastoral stations formed a basis for community organisation. The largest reserves were in Queensland, Western Australia and the Northern Territory. Earlier State education on the Queensland reserves has had spin-offs in Aboriginal people who are better educated than those in many other regions. Smaller reserves, such as Lake Tyers in Victoria, have also enabled Aboriginal communities to use these bases for mobilisation. But the more repressive the regime, the more likely it was that those who left the reserves would rebel and angrily assert their rights.

The reserves system has, however, also created a legacy of helplessness and inadequacy. While a strong sense of shared identity emerged from such institutionalisation, 'inmates', as they were often called[107], were deprived of decision-making powers over their lives and that of their families. They were denied management of many aspects of their own affairs, including their bank accounts, their children's schooling, whether they exercised their democratic rights. During the 1980s, governments in these states persistently blocked or limited land rights and have not encouraged Aboriginal studies education.

Racism and colonialism were far more powerful forces than sexism in the lives of Aboriginal people, however, Aboriginal men's historical experiences certainly differed from women's. In the colonial context, women were expected to centre their lives on the family, which in the twentieth century came to mean the nuclear family in a suburban house, while the male was expected to be the breadwinner. The gender-power relations of colonialism

A group of boys wearing Boys Brigade uniform, Ooldea, salute the British flag. Here the potent symbols of uniforms, flag and militaristic regimentation suggest that 'civilisation' was being taught to Aboriginal boys amidst desert dunes and spinifex. SOUTH AUSTRALIAN ABORIGINAL HERITAGE PHOTOGRAPHIC COLLECTION, DEPARTMENT OF STATE ABORIGINAL AFFAIRS

meant that Aboriginal women were in demand by colonial men but relationships between Aboriginal men and white women were taboo.

Both men and women suffered conflicting pressures from their own communities and white authorities.[108] They often resisted European pressures, preferring extended family arrangements even though they might break housing rules, and more flexible working arrangements which left them more vulnerable in the labour market. But the loss of independent means of production, virtually no land or chance to accumulate capital, and their confined lives on reserves severely curbed opportunities. Whenever the job market shrank, Aboriginal men found themselves unemployed and they were also excluded from white male focal points. While they were not permitted into public bars in many states until the 1960s, alcohol, obtained illegally, offered an escape from humiliation, and, as in many countries, it continues to be more popular amongst men than women. In some communities there are few other means by which men can prove their manliness and worth. The old rituals have gone and new initiations are sought. Puberty, a desire to prove manliness, drinking and gaol are not uncommonly linked amongst Aboriginal men. Girls and women suffer drug abuse, alcohol-related domestic violence and high rates of early death. The sorts of pressures they face are little understood.[109]

Earlier Aboriginal heroes like Pemulwuy in New South Wales, Nemarluk in the Northern Territory and Pigeon or Jandamarra of Western Australia, made amazing escapes from police and prison confinement. Similarly Aboriginal bushrangers or warriors such as Rebel, Mosquito and Murdering Tommy were admired for their defiance of the white military and police. That Aboriginal people are not ashamed of having been in gaol also expresses their defiance towards the white legal system. Aboriginal people continue to daringly escape today, though the long periods of imprisonment that result make it a rather tragic form of resistance.

Throughout Australia, Aboriginal individuals and families were engaged in more positive struggles. To maintain as much independence and family unity as possible has been difficult but for those who succeeded, worthwhile. Many battled to stay off reserves, while others just kept to themselves, avoiding police or other authorities and bureaucratic control. Less is known about these people than those who were under constant surveillance. Amongst those who came under rigorous control were many who struggled to retain personal space. Some did so through the forbidden pleasures of gambling, petty theft, swearing or drinking.

The political struggles of Aboriginal people had a profound impact. Spokespersons like William Cooper waged patient and ingenious battles through lobbying politicians for human rights and political representation, while the Cumerangunja people staged strikes to protest against infringement of their rights and attracted union and community support. Struggling for decent living conditions and pay, Aboriginal pastoral workers went on strike in the Pilbara in the 1940s, and in the Northern Territory in the 1960s and 70s. Land rights were also fundamental to their protests. The people of Noonkanbah and Mapoon staged lengthy campaigns to protect their land and community from desecration and displacement by mining. The Day of Mourning staged on Australia Day, 1938, was a national meeting of Aborigines which demanded citizenship and human rights. The persistent lobbying by the Federal Council for Aboriginal and Torres Strait Islander Advancement (FCAATSI) and the footwork of activists like Kath Walker (later Oodgeroo Noonuccal) that achieved the successful result of the 1967 Referendum. Henceforth Aborigines would be counted in the national Census for the first time and the Commonwealth could override state powers in regard to Aborigines.[110] More recently, Aboriginal leaders like Pat Dodson have done outstanding work towards national reconciliation, while highly skilled advocates and negotiators such as Noel Pearson, Mick Dodson, Marcia Langton and Lois O'Donaghue helped achieve the historic victory of national land rights under the *Native Title Act 1993*.

Throughout Australia, Aboriginal people have resisted the total domination of the newcomers over their land, bodies and minds. But they have also lent their trust to the newcomers, and openly shared these things with them. The history of negotiation, interaction and co-operation between Aboriginal people and Europeans still needs to be told. Aboriginal people worked for the white people, they married and cohabited with them, especially the women, and raised families. Aboriginal people shared their knowledge of the landscape and their bush expertise, as well as their Dreaming stories, their art, their ritual songs and dances. Aboriginal people have often reached out with hope and trust to forge a better future for themselves and for white people in this country. The only way a better future can happen is if both sides are willing to cross that colonising divide and talk about making amends for the past. Land rights are a priority but this must also happen in regard to education, health, employment, in changing attitudes, and above all in Australians opening themselves to the stories of the tragedies as well as the stories of healing, of co-operation, of negotiation and reconciliation.

The case reports of deaths in custody are revealing examples of how the history of colonialism and especially State intrusion have tragically affected Aboriginal families and individuals. Biographies and autobiographies of people like Margaret Tucker,

Margaret Tucker at Aboriginal demonstrations at the opening of Parliament by Queen Elizabeth, 6 March 1974. COURIER MAIL

Charles Perkins, Grant Ngabidj, Jack Sullivan, Ruby Langford Ginibi and Ida West tell stories of struggle and survival, often humourously, and often with much hope for the future. It is important that all Australians take urgent heed of both the tragedies and the stories with happier endings. As the acclaimed writer and artist Sally Morgan eloquently wrote:

> In the telling we assert the validity of our own experiences and we call the silence of two hundred years a lie. And it is important for you, the listener, because like it or not, we are part of you. We have to find a way of living together in this country, and that will only come when our hearts, minds and wills are set towards reconciliation. It will only come when thousands of stories have been spoken and listened to with understanding.[111]

NOTES

1 See A. Frost, 'New South Wales as *Terra Nullius:* The British Denial of Aboriginal land rights', in S. Janson and S. Macintyre (eds), *Through White Eyes*, Allen & Unwin, Sydney, 1990, originally in *Historical Studies,* vol.19, no.77.

2 For a more detailed study of various periods of Aboriginal–white relations, with a special emphasis on the gender relations, see A. McGrath, Chapters 1, 6 and 12 in P. Grimshaw, M. Lake, A. McGrath, M. Quartly, *Creating a Nation*, McPhee Gribble/Penguin, Ringwood, 1994.
3 For more on these themes, see ibid, pp.87, 91; H. Reynolds, *With the White People*, Penguin, Ringwood, 1990 and in my other forthcoming work on gender, Aborigines and colonialism.
4 A. Memmi, *The Colonizer and The Colonized*, Beacon, Boston, 1965.
5 See chapter 8.
6 While this was a New South Wales Royal Commission it was concerned with national issues.
7 M. Quartly, unpublished paper delivered at Symposium in Honour of Catherine Hall, LaTrobe University, Sept. 1993; also M. Quartly, 'Mothers and Fathers and Brothers and Sisters: The AWA and the ANA and Gendered Citizenship', in R. Howe (ed), *Women and the State*, Latrobe University, Bundoora, 1993.
8 See A. McGrath, 'Aboriginal and Australian Culture' in N. Meaney (ed.) *Under New Heavens*, Heinemann, Melbourne, 1989.
9 See A. McGrath, ' "Beneath the Skin" Australian Citizenship, Rights and Aboriginal Women' in R. Howe (ed).
10 See D.J. Mulvaney and J. Peter White (eds), *Australians to 1788*, Fairfax, Syme, Weldon, Sydney, 1987, part 1, chapters by various authors. See also D.J. Mulvaney, *The Prehistory of Australia*, Penguin, Ringwood, 1975; J. Flood, *Archaeology of the Dreamtime*, Collins, Sydney, 1983; D. Horton, *Recovering the Tracks*, Aboriginal Studies Press, Canberra, 1991.
11 P. Sutton, *Dreamings: the art of Aboriginal Australia*, Penguin, Ringwood, 1988.
12 J. White and D.J. Mulvaney, 'How Many People?', in D.J. Mulvaney and J. White (eds), p.117.
13 See T. Swain, *A Place for Strangers*, Cambridge University Press, Cambridge, 1993. For standard general anthropological accounts see R. and C. Berndt, *The World of the First Australians*, Ure Smith, Sydney, [1964] 1977, and various editions. A. P. Elkin, *The Australian Aborigines*, Angus & Robertson, Sydney, 1938, and various revised versions.
14 See D. Bell, *Daughters of the Dreaming*, McPhee Gribble, Melbourne, 1983. See P. Daylight and M. Johnstone (eds), *Women's Business*, AGPS, Canberra, 1986.

15 A. Frost, *Historical Studies*, vol.19, no.77, p.514.
16 H. Reynolds, *Frontier*, Allen & Unwin, Sydney, 1987, p.133.
17 ibid, p.134. See also H. Reynolds, *The Law of the Land*, Penguin, Ringwood, 1987.
18 The High Court of Australia, *Mabo vs Queensland*, 1992.
19 Select Committee on Aborigines, 1837, *British Parliamentary Papers, (BPP)*, p.17. Before we applaud him as a far-sighted humanitarian, we should note that he was not concerned about its being an exploitative arrangement, believing 'a mere trifle' would be satisfactory. The British obviously regarded treaties expediently.
20 H. Reynolds at AHA Conference, 1990. Reynolds developed the above theme in more detail in his unpublished paper on 'Did Robinson negotiate a treaty with the Tasmanian Aborigines?'
21 H. Reynolds, *The Law of the Land*. Frost *Historical Studies*, vol.19, no.77.
22 See chapter 3.
23 A.H. Campbell, *John Batman and the Aborigines*, Kibble, Melbourne, 1987, part 2 cast shadows on its validity; this view is disputed by Richard Broome in chapter 3.
24 P. Bayne, 'Politics, the law and Aborigines' in J. Jupp (ed.) *An Encyclopaedia of the Australian people*, Angus & Robertson, Sydney, 1988, p.213.
25 H. Reynolds, *Fate of a Free People*, Penguin, Ringwood, 1995, chapter 5.
26 See L. Ryan, *The Aboriginal Tasmanians*, University of Queensland Press, St Lucia, 1982, chapters 9 and 12.
27 Reynolds, *The Law of the Land*, pp.103–18.
28 See discussion of racial ideas in Victorian paper, pp.14–15. Reynolds' Queensland paper, passim and especially pp.9–10, 16.
29 P. Pepper, *You Are What you Make Yourself to Be: The Story of a Victorian Aboriginal Family 1842–1980*, Hyland House, Melbourne, 1980, p.50.
30 A. Laurie and A. McGrath, 'I was a drover once myself' in I. White, D. Barwick, B. Meehan (eds), *Fighters and Singers*, George Allen & Unwin, Sydney, 1985, p.89.
31 Reynolds, *Frontier*, p.53.
32 E. Thorn, 'A White Australia—the Other Side', *United Australia*, 25 Oct 1901; Anti-Slavery Papers, s22/697, Rhodes House, Oxford and cited in Reynolds paper, p.8.
33 *Historical Records of NSW*, 2.

34 A. Atkinson and M. Aveling (eds), *Australians, 1838*, Fairfax, Syme & Weldon, Sydney, 1987, pp.38–63.
35 See P. Dodson report on Western Australia, RCIADIC, p.12 and Historical Chronology. For further information see B. Reece and T. Stannage (eds), *European–Aboriginal Relations in Western Australian History*, University of Western Australia, Perth, 1984.
36 *Moreton Bay Courier*, 6 Nov. 1861. See also chapter 4.
37 Report on the Aborigines of North Queensland, *Queensland Votes and Proceedings (V&P)*, vol.4 no.85, 1896, p.3.
38 See A. Markus, *Governing Savages*, Allen & Unwin, Sydney, 1990. A. Powell, *Far Country*, MUP, Melbourne, 1982, pp.52–61. The Northern Territory report omits reference to Aborigines murdered in these outposts.
39 Malaria and bronchial disease spread rapidly and killed many.
40 See P. Sharp, 'A study of the relationships between colonial women and black Australians', unpublished MA thesis, Deakin University, 1991. A. Gunn, *We of the Never Never*, Hutchinson, London, 1908.
41 Reynolds, *Frontier*, p.30.
42 B. York and F. Robinson, *The Black Resistance*, Widescope, Camberwell, 1977.
43 N. Butlin, *Our Original Aggression*, Allen & Unwin, Sydney, 1983.
44 For example, see C. Cook, 'The Native in Relation to the Public health', in *The Medical Journal of Australia*, 1, 1949, pp.570–1. C. Cook, 'The native Problem—Why is it unsolved?', *Australian Quarterly*, vol.xxii, no.4, p.22.
45 N.G. Butlin 'Macassans and Aboriginal smallpox: the 1789 and 1829 epidemics' and J. Campbell, 'Smallpox in Aboriginal Australia, the early 1830s', *Historical Studies*, vol.21, no.84, April 1985.
46 L. Ryan, pp.124, 160.
47 *Historical Records of Australia* (hereafter *HRA*) 2, pp.142–43.
48 *HRA*, 144, 8 June 1816.
49 See chapter 5.
50 Goodall, A history of Aboriginal communities in NSW, PhD thesis, University of Sydney, 1982, passim. See also A. Haebich, *For Their Own Good*, University of Western Australia, Nedlands, 1988.
51 See A. McGrath, *Born in the Cattle*, Allen & Unwin, Sydney, 1987; H. Reynolds, *With the White People*, Penguin, Ringwood, 1990.
52 See Markus, *Governing Savages*.

53 See for example, Grant Njabidj, *My Country of the Pelican Dreaming: The life of an Australian Aborigine of the Gadjerong, Grant Ngabidg, C. 1904–1977 as told to Bruce Shaw*, AIAS, Canberra, 1981, passim.
54 See for example Haebich, pp.213–15.
55 L.H Giles memo for Government Resident, 7 March 1927, AA (Australian Archives) CRS A659 45/1/1544; C. Cook to Administrator, 11 Nov. 1931, AA, CRS A659, item 45/1/1544; G. Easey to Secretary NT Pastoral Lessees' Association, 30 Nov. 1936, NTPLA records, Aborgines file.
56 Haebich, p.251.
57 Annual Report Chief Protector of Aboriginals, *Queensland Parliamentary Papers*, (QPP) 1936, vol.1, p.1025. See chapter 4.
58 Interview by A. McGrath with C.E. Cook, Darwin, 1982, and various letters, 1936, NTPLA files.
59 B. Sykes and S. Smith, *Mum Shirl*, Heinemann Education, Melbourne, 1981, see pp.20–23. See also J. Jupp (ed.), pp.240–55.
60 See N. Williams, 'Studies in Australian Aboriginal Law 1961–1986' in R.M. Berndt and R. Tonkinson (eds), *Social Anthropology and Australian Aboriginal Studies*, AIAS, Canberra, 1988.
61 P. Biskup, *Not Slaves, not Citizens*, UQP, St Lucia, 1973, p.12.
62 E. Eggleston, *Fear, Favour or Affection*, ANU, Canberra, 1976, chapter 9.
63 M. Sturma in M. Finnane (ed.) *Policing in Australia*, UNSW Press, Kensington, 1987, p.27.
64 Wilson to Administrator, 12 Nov. 1925, AA, CRS A1, 17/124. Cited in McGrath, *Born in the Cattle*, Allen & Unwin, Sydney, 1987, p.119.
65 Biskup, p.9.
66 J. McCorquordale, 'Aborigines: A History of Law and Injustice, 1829–1985', unpublished Doctoral thesis, University of New England, 1985. See also S. Davies, 'Aborigines, Murder and the Criminal Law', *Historical Studies*, vol.22, no.88, April 1987, pp.313–16 and M. Christie, *Aborigines in Colonial Victoria*, Sydney University Press, Sydney, 1979.
67 *Herald* (Melbourne), 11 May 1934.
68 D. Phillips, 'Sex, Race, Violence and the Criminal Law in Victoria: Anatomy of a Rape Case in 1888', *Labour History*, 52, 1987, pp.30–49. C. Harris, 'The Terror of the Law As Applied to Black Rapists in Colonial Queensland', *Hecate*, vol.8, no.2, 1982, pp.22–48. See also S. Davies, 'Aborigines, Murder and the

Criminal Law in Early Port Phillip, 1841–51', *Historical Studies*, vol.22 no.88, April 1987, pp.313–16.
69 G. Highland, 'Race, Justice and the Law in Colonial North Queensland', paper given to History 90 Conference, Brisbane.
70 Cited in A. Markus, p.110.
71 See C.D. Rowley, *The Destruction of Aboriginal Society*, ANU, Canberra, 1970, and B. Fitzgerald, 'Blood on the Saddle: the Forrest River Massacres' in B. Reece and T. Stannage (eds), 1984.
72 Markus, pp.117–19.
73 C. Tatz, 'Queensland's Aborigines: Natural Justice and the Rule of Law', *The Australian Quarterly*, Sept. 1963, pp.33–49.
74 A. Haebich, pp.92–93.
75 See G. Cowlishaw, *Black, White or Brindle*, Cambridge University Press, Cambridge, 1988, chapter 2.
76 K. Carrington, 'Aboriginal Girls and Juvenile Justice: What Justice? White Justice' in B. Morris and G. Cowlishaw (eds), *Contemporary Race Relations in Australia*, Centre for Social Justice, Mitchell, 1990, pp.1–18.
77 Eggleston, pp.176–77.
78 R. Langford, *Don't Take Your Love to Town*, Penguin, Ringwood, 1988. B. Sykes and S. Smith, *Mum Shirl*.
79 Langford, chapter 21.
80 Haebich, p.182.
81 Markus, p.178.
82 See NSW chapter in this volume.
83 For more detail on exemptions and citizenship rights see ' "Beneath the Skin", Australian Citizenship, Rights and Aboriginal Women' in R. Howe (ed.).
84 For further discussion of this topic, see A. McGrath, 'Colonialism, Crime, Civilisation', in *Australian Cultural History*, 12, 1993. Some of the material herein, originating in RCIADIC papers, was earlier published in modified form in this article.
85 M. Foucault, *Discipline and Punish*, Allen Lane, London, 1977 [1975]. M. Poster, *Foucault, Marxism and History*, Polity Press, Cambridge, 1984 and others provide summaries of its critiques. See for example P. O'Brien, *The Promise of Punishment*, Princeton University, Princeton, 1982.
86 The Management of the Gaols, Penal Establishments and lockups of the colony of Queensland, QPP, 1887, p.xxvi.
87 *Transactions of Intercolonial Medical Congress of Australasia*, second

session, Melbourne, Jan. 1889, p.860. An Act to constitute the island of Rottnest a legal prison 1841, WA.
88 It should be stated that convicts received corporal punishment, though not as often as was previously held, and that this system was being phased out by the 1820s in Australia. This was before the beginning of most Australian frontiers.
89 R. Evans, K. Cronin, K. Saunders, *Race Relations in Colonial Queensland*, UQP, St Lucia, [1975] 1988.
90 Biskup, p.9.
91 Markus, p.178.
92 M. Dewar, 'Strange Bedfellows: Europeans and Aborigines in Arnhem Land before World War II', unpublished MA (Hons) thesis, History, University of New England, 1989, p.102.
93 *Northern Standard*, 13 April 1938. Cited Markus, p.119.
94 Rowley, p.300.
95 Board of inquiry into alleged ill-treatment of Aborigines by Constable McKinnon and others, and recommendations, 1935 in AA, CRS A1. 35/1613, also Treatment and handling of Aboriginal prisoners, A.V. Strettton, AA, CRSA1, 36/4477; also McGrath, *Born in the Cattle*, p.120.
96 See Shaw, *My Country of the Pelican Dreaming*.
97 Of course the humanitarian lobby objected. See Reynolds, *Frontier* and C. Rowley, (1970).
98 C. Tatz, 'Queensland's Aborigines: Natural Justice and the Rule of Law', *The Australian Quarterly*, Sept. 1963, p.39.
99 *Shorter Oxford*, 1, 1973, p.477.
100 P. Read, *A Hundred Years War*, ANU, Canberra, 1988, p.89.
101 Read, p.89.
102 Les Coe, cited in Read, p.91.
103 Amy Laurie and Ann McGrath, 'I was a drover once myself' in White, Barwick, Meehan (eds).
104 N.T. personal communication to A. McGrath.
105 See B. Shaw, *Bush Time, Station Time*, Aboriginal Studies and Teacher Education, Adelaide, 1990.
106 For example, see Biskup, 1973.
107 For example, Queensland's Annual Report on Aborigines for 1926 included the statement that 'The conduct of the inmates on each settlement has, on the whole, been satisfactory, only three serious cases arising which needed Police Court proceedings.' p.8, 1926, 1. See also Haebich.
108 For a study of gender and Aboriginal relations see P. Grimshaw,

M. Lake, A. McGrath and M. Quartly, *Creating a Nation*, McPhee Gribble, Ringwood, 1994.

109 The author intends to analyse this in a larger work on gender, Aborigines and colonialism, a project which has been generously supported by the Australian Research Council.

110 See B. Sykes *Black majority*, Hudson, Melbourne, 1989.

111 C. Edwards and P. Read (eds), *The Lost Children*, Doubleday, Sydney, 1989, p.vii.

2
New South Wales

THE relations between Aboriginal people and their invaders on the lands which became New South Wales share many themes with the histories of other states within Australia. Yet there are also unique elements. It was here that the first and therefore the most unpredictable encounters occurred between Aboriginal land owners and invaders. These initial meetings took place without the burden of precedents and betrayals. The unique nature of relations stems also from the length and intensity of colonisation in this first Australian state. Here history has moved far beyond a violent but simple frontier battle into a long and complex interchange between coloniser and colonised. Progress has not been easy or inevitable and each change has had to be fought over in what seems at times an endless series of conflicts.

Yet New South Wales, despite its lengthy colonisation, has also seen some extraordinary flowerings in Aboriginal society, as its members have developed innovative strategies for creating a future in the very changed conditions they face. This chapter will chart the complex interactions of Aboriginal and non-Aboriginal people in New South Wales, from those brutal but sometimes ambiguous frontiers of the eighteenth and nineteenth centuries, to the complex shifts and challenges of the twentieth.

Out of the dense web of the past two hundred years, this chapter will have a special focus on the twentieth century. The

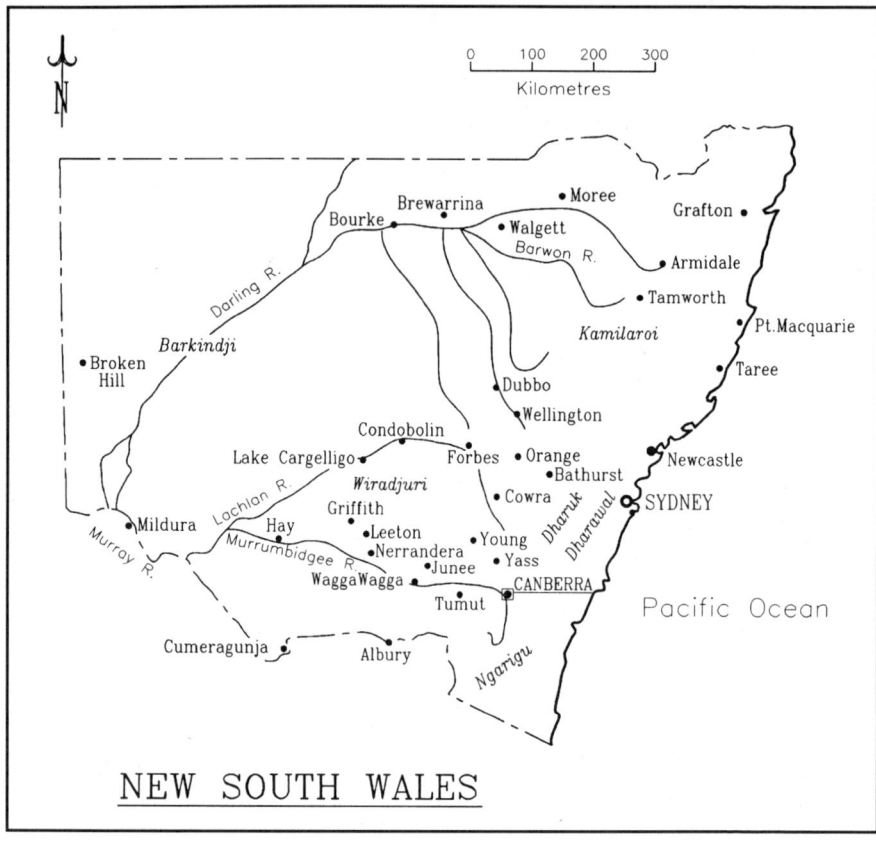

state's twentieth century history, especially the post World War II decades, has been less well explored in historical analyses. The course of events in the long colonised and densely settled eastern states were by then influenced by very different forces from the harsh frontier conditions which predominated in the tropical north and west.

The histories of each state have not, of course, been isolated. During the early twentieth century, the emerging, sophisticated Aboriginal political organisations of the south-east, in particular in New South Wales and Victoria, were to become actively involved in the political campaigns around the conduct of the invasion as it proceeded in the more remote areas from the 1920s.

At the same time, the cultural and social concerns which Aboriginal people in both remote and long settled areas shared, have resonated with and stimulated each other's strategies and organisational directions from at least the 1930s. The politics and perceptions of white Australians in each state have also interacted, but have never been identical. The twentieth century has been the time when 'policy' in relation to Aboriginal people reached its greatest expansion, and the contrasts as well as the similarities in each state's policies can expose a great deal about the internal relations between Aboriginal people and whites at that time. For all these reasons, the twentieth century is important as a rich focus in any study of the basis of current conditions.

Race relations in New South Wales have often appeared in public manifestations to be simple, two-sided conflicts between black and white. When events are examined in detail, however, it becomes clear that each side was made up of different interest groups, sometimes in uneasy alliances but often in outright conflict themselves. Continual tensions arose, for example, between groups within the colonising society. Rural whites have often sought to remove or to incarcerate Aboriginal people. The metropolitan bureaucracies of London and later Sydney have frequently aimed to assimilate Aborigines, reluctantly or not, into those very same rural white populations. So policies have been marked by inconsistencies in conception or implementation, and some have been quite openly sabotaged by white interest groups at the local level. Aboriginal resistance too has altered the course of many policies; some were abandoned as unworkable in the face of Aboriginal intransigence and others transformed to obscure their intent. There have been tensions within Aboriginal activist organisations, some reflecting differences in regional conditions, and others exposing differing strategies in coming to terms with colonisation. Finally, there have been tensions, too, between Aboriginal groups and the white groups with whom they have formed alliances, suggesting the divergent cultural and philosophical bases from which they developed their politics.

This chapter will explore some of those complexities, tensions and ambiguities in the interactions between Aboriginal and non-Aboriginal people. While there are many facets to such complex relations, there are some ongoing themes which can be traced through this history. One is the persistence with which Aboriginal people have developed strategies for surviving and developing within the constraints of the colonial situation. The priority given to particular demands by Aboriginal political movements has varied with time, however, and this chapter will examine the conditions which sometimes thrust land rights to the front of the agenda and at other times saw civil rights emerge as the most urgent demand.

Another theme traced in this chapter will be the increasing control which the government has tried to exercise over Aboriginal people. The conventional interpretation of colonial race relations has been that the greatest restrictions on Aboriginal people were exercised during the late nineteenth century, and that they were then steadily eased as a result of growing enlightenment among whites over the twentieth century. This view of the past has tended to rely on the titles of policies, such as 'Protection', 'Welfare', and 'Self-determination', as if these really did define the goals and practices of government. It has been assumed that the passage from one policy to another marked a reduction in control and an improvement in general conditions. There has also been a tendency to view policy as the most important element in determining the course of events, an independent element created and then carried out on the basis of considered decisions of government.

The New South Wales record shows a very different story. Shifts in economic conditions, particularly the depressions of the 1890s and 1930s, and also the rural recession of the 1960s, were the catalysts of each major increase in the controls over Aborigines, regardless of whether the name of the current policy changed. The policies themselves were implemented unevenly according to the different economic conditions in each region of the state, and the degree of local white hostility to the government's intentions.

The goals of Aboriginal people themselves have been just as important as policy in determining the direction of change. They persistently tried to regain land, to sustain social relations within communities with distinctive cultural characteristics, and to gain recognition as citizens with a right to equality of opportunity. Their attempts to pursue such goals were entwined with efforts to defend themselves from the interventions of government policy or the attacks of local white townspeople. Aboriginal resistance affected the implementation of government policies. The local conflicts which arose when Aborigines refused to accept discrimination generated new policies in turn. This chapter takes as its mainspring the attempt to trace the interactions of these three forces: the economy and its social outcomes, government policy and Aboriginal interests.

OVERVIEW

A relatively high proportion of the Aboriginal population survived the initial severe violence of the invasion in New South Wales and began to rebuild their communities. In many areas Aboriginal people had struck a tenuous economic and social balance with local whites by the 1860s. In farming areas, Aborigines had frequently regained a portion of their traditional lands, as a residential and sometimes economic base. In pastoral areas, they had established an apparently secure economic role in the pastoral industry and lived in camps with access to their traditional lands. These mutual but fragile accommodations began to break down as a result of the 1890s' depression and the rise of cultural and biological chauvinism during the early 1900s. A series of major losses of civil rights followed, such as expulsion from public schooling, exclusion from the Federal franchise, and denial of State benefits, including unemployment relief. State intervention into their family and cultural life was intensified after 1909 by a 'Protection' policy which aimed to 'disperse' them. Aboriginal people faced a renewed loss of their lands through the 1920s, a loss they fought by developing an organised political campaign to restore their land rights.

Then during the 1930s' Depression, the 'Protection' policy changed its fundamental goal as the government capitulated to the demands of rural whites for segregation. 'Protection' now came to mean enforced concentration of the Aboriginal population on a few central reserves, stripping them of any choice in where they would live. This shift in policy fundamentally attacked all Aboriginal peoples' previous attempts to live in some continuing association with their traditional lands.

These assaults on their rights were opposed by Aboriginal political organisations in the 1920s and 1930s, and they advanced a positive platform of reforms demanding land and civil rights. The pace of discriminatory and restrictive control slowed as a result of the successful Aboriginal recruitment of white support but also because of the manpower needs of the war economy in the early 1940s. The postwar 'Welfare' administration, however, simply shifted the approach in Aboriginal policy to one of intrusive monitoring and attempted behaviour control. The Welfare Board's 'Assimilation Policy' retained many of the most destructive 'Protection' legislative powers over Aboriginal families. Aboriginal organisations developed a sustained campaign to restore civil rights and called again for secure Aboriginal land. Yet just as victories in the struggle to protect Aboriginal civil rights appeared to have been won during the late 1960s, another expansion of bureaucratic surveillance occurred as the rural economy began to decline.

A dismantling of the 'Welfare' apparatus led to a proliferation of the sites of control to state housing and social welfare bureaucracies. At the same time, the loss of formal 'Welfare' management over Aboriginal people led local white rural and urban authorities to call increasingly on police to impose 'law and order' by restricting and controlling, by violence if necessary, the area's Aboriginal community. Aboriginal political responses were to draw on new federal funding to challenge successfully the rural residential segregation which had propped up racial discrimination, to take control over providing legal services to Aboriginal people increasingly under pressure by the police and to link their land demands in New South Wales with those of Aboriginal people in other states.

The 1960s and 1970s also, however, saw a rising degree of frustration expressed by Aboriginal people. The strengthening of the Aboriginal voice in politics, increased access to education and a broadening of white support were countered by the recognition of how deeply entrenched was institutional racism in both rural and urban situations. The heightened expectations generated by increasing Federal Government funding were undermined by the loss of most avenues of economic independence as employment was lost when the rural and industrial sectors contracted. These decades generated innovative formulations of Aboriginal aspirations, including self-determination and then sovereignty but many fundamental tensions remained unresolved.

In tracing the history of colonised New South Wales, however, it is important to recognise as a starting point that this history is the result of conflict between two complex societies. Some understanding is needed of the dense, rich Aboriginal populations who owned and managed the land in the south-east of the continent before the British invasion began.

ABORIGINAL AUSTRALIA

The Aboriginal societies of south-eastern Australia had developed a range of patterns of land management and cultural organisation. The language groups which belonged to the fertile coastal lands, like the Dharuk, Gandangara and Kuringgai around what became Sydney, and the Bundjalung on the far northern rivers, were living almost sedentary lives on relatively small, closely settled holdings. From there, they harvested the rich resources of the sea as well as the estuaries and inland wooded areas. Those groups who lived to the west of the mountain ranges were the custodians of far larger tracts of land. They harvested the broad grasslands of the inland plains; pastures they had created by firestick farming. They moved over their lands in established patterns, collecting and storing the grass-seed for their own baking, and hunting the kangaroo, emu and the other game which were also sustained by the grass pasture.

The inland plains populations were particularly densely settled around the large river systems. In the south, along the banks of what became the Murray, the fishing resources were so plentiful that the Jota-Jota and other related language groups had built stone villages for their virtually sedentary lifestyles. In the north, at the junction of the lands of the Ngiyaamba, Yualiai and Murawari peoples where Brewarrina now stands, the largest of the Darling River fish traps was built. This was a complex engineering endeavour, built from stone over many hundreds of metres at a point of rapid fall in the river bed, to allow the owners to harvest fish in any season, no matter how low or high the waters were running.[1] These harvesting techniques supported a far higher Aboriginal population than Europeans have supposed. Many demographers now believe that a conservative estimate of the overall Aboriginal population of Australia just prior to invasion is 750 000 people, with others suggesting three million may have been possible. A large proportion of the population lived in the fertile south-east.[2]

These Aboriginal societies had a complex land tenure, in which association with land might be inherited from both parents or by birthplace, and which gave an individual highest authority only in relation to the land to which he or she held the heaviest custodial obligations. Yet despite the local focus of individual power, everyone in each language group was linked with many others in great cultural, social and trading networks which spanned wide areas, far beyond what are now the borders of New South Wales. These networks were channels of dynamic cultural and economic exchange, displayed most spectacularly in regular, large ceremonial meetings. There are archaeological analyses which now suggest that this dynamism involved competitive exchange cycles and expansion of territorial range and influence in some areas. Significantly, there is no evidence of widespread or endemic warfare among these societies, suggesting effective strategies for the resolution of conflicting interests.[3]

THE INVASION BEGINS

The British invasion began in 1788 around what was to become Sydney. The legal basis for this was confused at the time, with no clear British claim as to the grounds on which they were acquiring the land. There were also many misapprehensions held about the Aboriginal inhabitants, with the British believing initially that there were very few Aborigines living in Australia, that those few were clustered around the coast and that they had no sense of property or ownership in land or in anything else.[4]

The first personal contacts between the land-owning Eora group of the Dharuk people and the English and Irish invaders were exploratory on both sides. Cook's journals indicate that Aboriginal land owners tried to prevent the Europeans' landing in 1770, and during the first months of the Port Jackson settlement, the Eora made it clear that they deeply opposed the clearing of their land.[5] Yet there were also examples of Aboriginal interest in Europeans and their practices, as well as of their attempts to teach the newcomers both language and proper social behaviour.[6] The Europeans brought with them not only expectations about the Aborigines but assumptions about what was 'natural' and 'proper' and 'good'. Images of austere but noble 'savages', such as reported by James Cook in 1770, were hopelessly entangled with old concepts of the 'Great Chain of Being', in which 'hunters and gatherers' were placed on the lowest order in creation. The rising Christian Revivalists brought conflicting dimensions to this body of popularly held knowledge. While the Reformers' concern for humanity played a major role in the ending of slavery and the later interest in the rights of colonised indigenous people, the evangelist wing of the revival held a crude contempt for heathens.[7]

Yet there was still a period of possibilities for experimentation in relations, for hope as well as fear. There were many ambiguities in the recorded contacts between Governor Phillip and Bennelong, for example, the Dharuk man kidnapped by Phillip in order to be 'civilised', or between Aboriginal women like Bennelong's partner, Barangaroo, and the British men such as Watkin Tench. Each brought to the encounter not only vastly unequal power but also different culturally created expectations on which they drew to try to interpret the other socially and sexually.[8] Only later did plague, hunger, greed and violence close down those possibilities to a narrow range of bitter and degrading stereotypes.

The birthing of Warreweer's baby in Sydney in 1791 offers a glimpse of the ambivalence present in early contacts. The birth took place in the presence of Eora midwives but with a group of white women watching as well, suggesting a degree of mutual trust and frequent contact. Yet the events also demonstrated the distance between the world views of the two groups of women, and the white women's insistence on cutting the cord with scissors and on washing the baby, against the conventions and beliefs of the Eora midwives, demonstrated both the technology and the arrogance which would contribute to later mistrust and anger.[9] The intimacy of these early contacts continued to occur as many Aboriginal women became, willingly or unwillingly, servants or sexual partners to whites. Yet the hostility of war and colonial repression were to force wide social distances between Aborigines and whites and there has been little public acknowledgement of such close relationships and the knowledge which must have flowed between both groups of people.

The British had brought their own, convict, labour force, so they did not initially need much Aboriginal labour. There was little real pressure to cultivate peaceful relations with the indigenous land owners, and a series of incidents of conflict had already taken place to sour relations by late in 1789, leading to an ominous gathering of Aboriginal people around the British camp. Then a tragedy of proportions barely grasped by whites began: smallpox, along with other infectious diseases such as influenza and measles, took hold in epidemic form throughout the Aboriginal groups. Disease wiped out or decimated many clans among the Kooris around Sydney but then extended its devastation far beyond the range of white settlement, spreading along the densely populated coastal and inland river valleys. Most of the Aboriginal groups met by white explorers in the following decades had already been savaged by terrifying new illnesses.[10]

The invaders were soon engulfed in a lesser crisis of their own as their initial farming attempts failed in the unfamiliar land. Starving and with no interest in the needs of Aboriginal owners, the colonisers pushed out to take over the fertile river banks of the Hawkesbury and Nepean Rivers west of Sydney. These lands were the main source of yam cropping for the Dharuk owners, who were forced to take up arms despite their weakened state in the wake of the epidemics. The Dharuk sustained their guerilla-style resistance fighting along these river lands from 1790, in the face of a series of engagements with troopers, until a major leader, Pemulwuy, was shot and killed in 1802. To the south-west, the neighbouring Gandangara were offered some respite when Governor King promised in 1804 that they would be undisturbed on the upper reaches of the Nepean if they left the white farmers alone further downstream. This promise was broken by uncontrolled white expansion, and soon the Gandangara too faced 'punitive expeditions' and an apparently final massacre at Appin in 1816.[11]

This relentless military 'pacification' was to be repeated but the outcome of the invasion was always more complicated than the invaders might have hoped. As the Kooris, Murris and Wiimpatjas of the rest of what became New South Wales were to do, the Gandangara demonstrated a breathtaking resilience. Despite the onslaught, they retained the resourcefulness to regroup. By 1876, they had successfully regained some of their own country in the Burragorang Valley through negotiations with the local Catholic church, and on this land they developed a farming base which they worked independently until the 1920s.[12] Ravaged by disease and violence, they nevertheless retained not only the will to resist the invasion of their lands but flexibility in the methods they chose and the outcomes they sought in negotiating with their invaders.

The invasion continued, taking many forms over time and distance. The international demand for Australian wool in the 1820s and 1830s meant that the invasion of the central grasslands was the most rapid and brutal. Aboriginal game and harvesting resources were devastated as thousands of sheep were herded across the Great Dividing Range within a few years. Driven by the profits to be made on world markets, invading stock owners had high motivations for demanding rapid security on the inland grassland pastures. A terrible toll in Aboriginal lives was taken by both military and private massacre parties engaged in the relentless 'pacification' of the western plains. Conversely, Aboriginal armed resistance was the most urgent on these grasslands in response to the scale and pace of the invasion.

Some of the fiercest fighting and the most ruthless massacres took place on the grasslands countries of the Gamalarai and Ngiyamba in the north-west, where Myall Creek, Waterloo Creek and Hospital Creek are the best known but not the only slaughter grounds.[13] Although both sheep and cattle owners initiated violence against Aboriginal land owners, the cattle runs developed the most sustained arguments against Aboriginal presence, insisting that cattle were frightened by the mere sight or smell of Aborigines. The levels of violence in these north-western areas showed a pattern of greatest ferocity where cattle were being run, compared to sheep runs.[14] Another grassland people to suffer intensely were the Wiradjuri in the south-west, where Windradyne led the eastern clans in a campaign of guerilla resistance which caused the declaration of Martial Law at Bathurst in 1824.[15] The Paakantji, seed harvesters of the western Darling, also resisted militarily and succeeded in driving stockholders off their river lands for a decade during the 1850s.[16]

Differences had begun to open up between the colonial British in Australia and their metropolitan superiors. The rising influence of the evangelical reformers and anti-slavery organisations forced the British Colonial Office to demand that administrations in all the Australian colonies recognise native title and usage rights over pastoral lands. It was widely acknowledged in both New South Wales and in Britain by the 1830s that Aboriginal people did have a well defined sense of property in land. The reformers did not believe that the British settlement of colonies should not go ahead but they believed that it should be done on a just basis. For them, surrounded by the nineteenth century success of capitalist expansion, a just colonisation meant one in which indigenous people's property rights were recognised and a fair 'equivalent' was paid to them in return for their lands.[17]

During the 1830s the reformers held power in London and directed their efforts to securing a recognition of Aboriginal property rights in the newer Australian colonies such as South Australia, where the avoidance of convict transportation seemed to allow hopes of a more equitable society being established. Although failing in this goal, the Reformers during the 1840s attempted to include the recognition of native title rights to Crown lease land in the legislation of 1842 and 1847 which regulated the pastoral expansion of New South Wales. Earl Grey, the Colonial Secretary of State for Colonies and sympathetic to the Reformers, instructed New South Wales Governor Fitzroy in 1849 to enforce an interpretation of the Land Acts which guaranteed Aboriginal access to their traditional lands in a form of dual occupancy with pastoralists, in which Aborigines and squatters had 'mutual rights'. Grey's instructions called for further steps, including the establishment of small, agricultural reserves as allowed for in the 1842 Act, and the provision of medical and other assistance to Aborigines.[18]

The pastoral lobby was powerful in New South Wales at the time and continued to defend squatters and their employers who participated in widely known massacres of Aboriginal land owners. A restriction on Crown pastoral leases was anathema to them, and their opposition defeated the implementation of the instruction, although it did not invalidate Grey's interpretation of the 1842 Act.[19] Fitzroy proceeded, however, to act on the recommendations of his Commissioners for Crown Lands, the officials charged with administering the far extents of the squatters' runs. These Commissioners had been uniformly supportive of Grey's proposals to restrict the rights of Crown lessees but as a less favoured option, a number of them suggested areas within their jurisdictions to be set aside as reserves. These were each about a square mile and were suggested because Aborigines already used them as camping or ceremonial sites.[20]

In 1850, around 40 of these areas were approved as reserves across the new pastoral districts, which were outside the longer-settled 'Nineteen Counties' around Sydney. Some were no more than police paddocks but others were important havesting sites, such as the Brewarrina Fisheries, and carried the force of police protection to stop whites fishing there or interfering with the structure, a protection which was still being actively enforced in 1906. Others, such as the site at Boobra lagoon on the MacIntyre River, recognised the great significance of the lagoon as a Rainbow Serpent site to the Bigambul people and was chosen because they insisted on camping there despite continuing violence from squatters aimed at driving them away from their country.[21] The British Colonial Secretary of State saw these areas of land as recognitions of Aboriginal people's ownership of land. The New South Wales Governor spoke of them as 'privileges' rather than as rights but their very existence was an acknowledgement of the widespread awareness in the colony as well as in Britain of the need to make some 'recompense' for the enormous loss sustained by Aboriginal land owners.[22]

Aboriginal owners made little additional use of these reserves at the time they were notified, for two reasons. One was that they were still struggling to maintain their ownership rights and access to the whole of their language and clan areas of land. They had resisted invasion violence and moved away from threats when they had to but they had tended to move around to safer places within their own land, rather than migrating away from it altogether. As long as some access remained to the rest of their lands, any acceptance of the small reserves might be seen to suggest that Aboriginal owners were withdrawing their claim to the whole of their land.[23] The other reason for Aboriginal disinterest in asserting particular association with these early reserves was that the state of the economy and the political climate changed dramatically in 1851.

The relentless pace of the invasion had already been slowed by the collapse of world markets for wool in 1840, affecting particularly the north coast and the far west. In these areas, the level of violence was reduced and opportunities were created for more varied and innovative forms of resistance, including abducting stock and sabotaging agriculture.[24] It allowed, too, for Aboriginal people to develop negotiation and survival strategies to take advantage of the situations where employers, particularly sheep owners, were coming to value Aboriginal labour. Then, the gold rushes which began in 1851 rapidly drew most white workers away from the pastoral runs. Suddenly, squatters were desperately seeking labour and they turned to Aborigines.

Within two years, Commissioners for Crown Lands all over the state were effusive in their praise for Aboriginal stock workers for both sheep and cattle. Many Commissioners reported that the pastoral industry in their area could not survive now without Aboriginal labour and stock owners frequently stated that Aboriginal workers were to be preferred to whites, being more careful, more reliable and less cruel to the animals.[25] Violence against Aboriginal people virtually ceased on any large scale and Aboriginal land owners had largely undisputed access to their land once

Workers and elders: Aboriginal lambmarkers, Welltown, 1900, and tribal elders at Bora Ceremony, Tallwood, 1895. These photographs depict the same group of men, from the Aboriginal community at Tallwood, on the Queensland–New South Wales border. They were able to fulfil their ceremonial obligations as traditional men at the same time as they took part in the specialised work of European pastoralism. BICENTENNIAL COPYING PROJECT, STATE LIBRARY OF NEW SOUTH WALES again. Small reserves were irrelevant to Aboriginal people in this context. By the 1870s, however, these reserved areas and the ideas embodied in the reserves were to be taken up again by Aboriginal land owners.

The employment which Aboriginal people took up in the 1850s ranged across the unskilled and semi-skilled work of developing rural capitalism. Many men and women were employed as stock workers, shepherds and shearers, with little early evidence of employers making the gender assumptions which limited such work among Europeans to men. Although some of this work was for rations only, and much of it was in exploitative conditions, there were some Aboriginal workers receiving cash wages equal to whites, particularly in the shearing sheds.[26] In the agricultural areas, Aboriginal workers were also employed in the various stages of farming and harvesting, and in some areas they took up specialised areas of manufacture, notably in the Macleay and Nambucca River valleys, where Aboriginal men began to learn the crafts of boat building.

In all these regions Aboriginal women became domestic workers as well as outdoor labourers. From as early as 1849 they were being employed in the trusted positions of nannies to station managers' children in the north-western areas.[27] They did both this intimate domestic work and the heavier work of laundering and cleaning for countless pastoral concerns, a role which continued until the mid-twentieth century in many western areas. When the gold rushes abated, the numbers of white labourers rose in most areas but Aboriginal people had forged a distinctive place for themselves in the rural workforce. Aboriginal women were often the only available domestic labour, and Aboriginal men continued both to fill skilled jobs as shearers and to be recruited as seasonal labour for the busy times like mustering, lambmarking and harvesting.

By the 1860s, however, a process had become evident which would be repeated for all rural labourers, Aboriginal and white. A whole category of work was eliminated by changing technology. In this first case it was shepherding which was made redundant by the introduction of fencing.

REGAINING LAND

A wave of intensification of European land use was made possible by fencing and other technological changes, and pushed along by the rising white population after the discovery of gold. Closer settlement legislation in 1861 was just the first of a series of government responses to populist demands to settle more whites on the land. Disputes between whites over land increased and in the process of settling one of these, the Privy Council in 1889 was forced to make a determination on just what the legal basis for the colony's foundation had been.

The Reformers' 1830s recognition of native property rights no longer attracted support in a Britain embittered by rebellions in Jamaica and by the rising popular attraction to biological determinism and 'Social Darwinism'. The Privy Council decided that the most convenient basis for the holding of real property was the legal fiction that Australia in 1788 had been *terra nullius*, a land 'desert and uncultivated', with a population which had no political structure with which to negotiate and no property rights.[28] It is ironic that this 1889 decision should have been made at the very time when Aboriginal people in New South Wales were being most successful in reasserting their rights to their traditional lands.

The pressure of intensifying white land settlement after 1860 began to disrupt the fragile truces which had been achieved between Aborigines and settlers in some areas. As south coast pastoral properties were broken up for farming to feed the gold fields, and then south-western runs fenced and reduced in size, then converted to wheat farms, Aboriginal land owners found their camps once more unwelcome and their access to their lands again obstructed. The Aboriginal response was to begin to use new strategies to regain control over at least some of their own country. The idea of a small piece of land now seemed much more attractive, offering Aborigines secure residence within their own lands and forming an acknowledgement of their interests in the whole of their traditional country. Petitions, deputations and alliance with local whites replaced guerilla tactics now, as Aborigines in the south-west and along the coast in the 1870s made the State Government aware that they were seeking farming land. Some Aboriginal groups were impatient with such methods and simply moved onto vacant land within their traditional country and began planting crops, either without legal recognition or with only the tenuous hold of a permissive occupancy.

Many Aboriginal people did put their demands for land on paper, and they made three points consistently. First, they said they wanted the land for economic independence by hunting or farming, often using terms like 'selection' to emphasise their interest in economic independence as well as in a refuge from the harassment of white invaders. Second, they were adamant that they did not want the power to sell the land but wished to secure it in perpetuity, for their children and all their later descendants. Thirdly, they wanted land within their own country, their traditional lands. William Cooper was a young man petitioning government for some of his family's lands around Cumeragunja on the Murray in 1887 when he made this point in language he hoped white politicians would understand, saying he wanted to secure 'this small portion of a vast territory which is ours by Divine Right'.[29]

Some of these reassertions of land holding were finally acknowledged by the government in the 1880s, when it began again to gazette small portions of Crown land as 'Reserved for the use of Aborigines'. Of the 114 reserves gazetted by 1895, 72 (63 per cent) were declared over land already independently settled and under crop to Aboriginal farmers or with Aboriginal owners ready to take up the land immediately. In most cases, Aboriginal families continued to live on and farm these lands for decades, entirely without British intervention or control.[30]

There were some regions where British land-use was changing so fast that Aborigines were pushed entirely out of employment and away from any access to their country for traditional social activity or subsistence harvesting. In the south-western wheat belt and on the south coast there was clear evidence of Aboriginal poverty and distress by the 1870s. Aborigines from these areas moved to towns where they demanded boats for fishing and other compensation for loss of livelihood. When south coast Kooris moved to Circular Quay, the government found their poverty as

An Aboriginal man on the Hawkesbury River with his garden. Corn was a common crop on all the coastal Aboriginal farming areas. Undated, but before 1930. MITCHELL LIBRARY SMALL PICTURE FILE

---

well as their lifestyle too embarrassing to be ignored, and it finally responded to missionary pleas to allow them to control and evangelise those groups.[31]

The State Government set up the Aborigines Protection Board in 1883 to monitor the church activity and to give out rations. The Board had, however, very few other clear-cut duties, no legislation and very little power, other than that which was already vested in the police officers who were its agents across the state. In fact from the 1880s to the early 1900s the Board took action only in response to pressures applied to it. It responded to missionary and philanthropic calls for supervised aid to Aborigines in some areas but it also responded to Aboriginal calls for independent control over land by gazetting and handing over, free of any supervision, the independent reserves. Yet again, it responded to white employer calls—this time on the northern slopes—to subsidise their Aboriginal pastoral workforce with rations in the off-season. Reserved areas were proclaimed to secure their residence close to the properties which were being divided by 'closer settlement' but which retained high labour needs.[32]

Aborigines experienced mixed conditions from the 1860s to 1890s. In some areas they were working for rations only, in others they were employed for wages, and elsewhere were living by a combination of seasonal employment and traditional subsistence harvesting. Women were widely employed in domestic positions, sometimes casual and often for food rather than for wages but their work formed an important securing link with white populations. Like working class children in rural areas, Aboriginal children were also employed by whites as servants, baby-sitters and labourers, in totally unregulated and often exploited situations. The outcome of this involvement was that in the 1880s, despite some regional poverty, Aborigines were 82 per cent self-sufficient due to some combination of these activities.[33] Although there was a significant degree of exploitation, there were very few Aborigines living on white 'charity' at that time and the development of the Aboriginal farming base in the 1880s enhanced their economic conditions.

Not all the independent farming was self-sustaining. The family wheat blocks on Cumeragunja on the Murray, for example, were farmed so skilfully that they yielded at or above the regions' average each year but they were very small. In this region 500 acres was regarded as a 'living area' but the Aboriginal family blocks were only 27.5 acres, which could never support a family, and so Kooris there remained dependent on seasonal labouring. In the Burragorang Valley, however, and on the north coast from the Hunter Valley to the Bellinger River, Kooris had been able to secure small areas of highly fertile land, which by the mid 1880s were supporting around one hundred extended families by mixed farming and some dairying. Aboriginal farmers, like the Drews at Kinchela and many others, took up material aspects of British rural life, acquiring sulkies, comfortable home furnishings and pianos. Yet they retained an active ceremonial life and taught their children Gumbainggirr and Dhangadi as first languages, using their modest economic and land security to sustain their rich traditions.[34]

'FREE, SECULAR, PUBLIC' AND SEGREGATED

At the same time, Aborigines were seeking access to the institutions of white Australian public life, in particular the new 'free, secular and public' state schools. This occurred first in the areas where farming had given an added economic confidence, the south-west and the north coast but during the 1890s, Murri pastoral workers too began calling for schools to be set up on the remote properties on which they formed the major workforce, such as Goondabluie north of Walgett. They all met with resistance from local white citizens, whose complaints were eventually and somewhat reluctantly supported by the State Department of Public Instruction. One by one between 1880 and 1902, the public schools of New South Wales were closed to Aboriginal children.

This was not an impersonal decision by Sydney-based administrators but a series of bitter local struggles, in which white citizens opposed Aboriginal parents face to face and forced their children out of the schools. The reasons they offered were usually that Aboriginal children posed a threat to the health of whites but whenever these claims were investigated they were found to be baseless. The major health problems cited were always nits and lice, conditions from which all working class children suffered throughout the state. The real anxieties held by white parents appear to have been that school would encourage close social and perhaps later sexual relationships between their children and Aboriginal children, an outcome which had ramifications for local status and power.

Eventually, the constant white protests wore down the central administration, and in 1902 the Director of Public Instruction issued a regulation which allowed a public school to be racially segregated if there was any complaint by any white parent. Aboriginal parents in many towns repeatedly challenged these bans but the racial segregation of New South Wales public schools was maintained officially for over 40 years, and in reality until the 1960s. Until 1973, all Aboriginal children could still be temporarily excluded from a public school if one Aboriginal child was believed to be suffering an infectious disease.[35]

DEPRESSION, DISPOSSESSION AND DISPERSAL: 1890s–1920s

The Depression of the 1890s was extremely difficult for Aborigines and many were forced out of work. As there was no general dole, these unemployed Aborigines sought temporary aid on the Aboriginal ration lists, which suddenly increased the economic demand on the Protection Board. It was concerned that this would be a permanent drain on state resources but, of more significance, the Board's members were alarmed at what they took to be a rapid increase in the numbers of non 'full-blood' Aborigines which the unemployment lists revealed. At this time, there was widespread alarm at the declining birthrate among the white population. State parliamentarians were afraid that the Board was fostering the increase of a group with different cultural values to Anglo-Australians. In those years of Federation and 'White Australia' sentiment, such fears were a powerful motive to change direction, and by 1904 the Protection Board had begun to seek strong new legislation to break up Aboriginal communities.

The Board most frequently referred to its new policy as 'dispersal' and this accurately conveys its aims, if not the real effects of the policy. It is, therefore, a more appropriate description of the policy than the conventional assumptions that the Protection Board sought to 'segregate' Aborigines. Its first legislative base, gained in 1909, gave no powers to confine, nor did the Board seek such powers. Instead, it empowered the Board to expel Aborigines from reserves and managed stations and to force them to move away from any town or reserve. The Board believed it was necessary to push adult Aborigines into the white working class as isolated labourers, and aimed to make them live independently of government and separate from any other Aborigines.[36]

The most intense Board activity was focussed on children, over whom it gained powers *in loco parentis* in 1915. The Board took over an already existing system of managing working class children, which had been in existence for decades under the State Children's Relief Department and had functioned to police working class families and turn their children into domestic servants and labourers. The Protection Board, however, added its own aim, expressed many times in its annual reports, which was to 'save' as many children as possible by removing them from the Aboriginal community to be trained and indentured as domestics and labourers, and, most importantly, to be taught to forget their families. The children were never to be allowed to return to their homes. The Board's goal was the eventual 'withering away' of Aboriginal communities altogether.

The impact of this policy fell most heavily on girls, as racist dogma encouraged fears about their sexuality and whose fertility was seen as a great threat to the goal of reducing the Aboriginal population. The Girls' Home at Cootamundra was established first in 1912, reflecting the Board's aim to cut the Aboriginal birthrate by taking away girls at puberty. They were to be indentured from there as domestics, unfree labour to meet the demand from middle class homes, which in Sydney were increasingly deprived of servants by the movement of white working class girls into higher paid factory work.[37]

As the economy began to improve after 1904, the closer settlement movement, which aimed to establish more small-scale white farmers on the land, was renewed. Whites began to view the continuing success of the independent Aboriginal farms with acquisitive interest. From 1905, the Protection Board came under increasing pressure to revoke these reserves in favour of white settlers. This pressure intensified and local Lands Department officers frequently demonstrated sympathy with the white claimant. By 1914, Lands Department action had forced a number of bitterly-protesting north coast Aboriginal farmers off their land. The First World War added the emotive pressure of the Returned Servicemen's Resettlement schemes, and by 1917 the Protection Board had ceased its earlier defences of Aboriginal tenure and agreed to revoke as many of the small reserves as the Lands Department should request.

Percy Mosely's case at Ballengarra was just one example of what this meant for Aboriginal farmers. In 1917 Mosely and his family were forcibly evicted from his farm in mid crop because the Local Lands Board had given a white man a lease over the reserve lands. Mosely travelled to Sydney to protest and received some sympathy from the Protection Board, who offered him

Aboriginal women took on the role of nanny or nurse to white children from early days. Only in 1912 did the Aborigines Protection Board institutionalise their job by sending young Aboriginal indentured servants to be nannies, thus making it synonymous with the hated 'apprenticeship'.
BICENTENNIAL COPYING PROJECT, STATE LIBRARY OF NEW SOUTH WALES

money in compensation for his lost harvest. Mosely refused the money and returned to badger the Local Lands Board for the restoration of his occupancy. He was repeatedly overlooked when the lease renewals were made but he persisted in demanding access to the lands, and in 1924 he was still there. He had negotiated a private sharecropping arrangement with the current white lessee, who allowed Mosely to crop some of the land in return for the use of Mosely's pair of Clydesdale draught horses.[38]

This pressure for revocation led to the loss of 13 000 acres of Aboriginal reserve between 1911 and 1927, half of the total Aboriginal reserve land in the state. Of the land lost, 75 per cent was from the north coast, and all of it was fertile, independently settled Aboriginal farming land.[39] Bellbrook and Burnt Bridge on the upper Macleay were two of the very few such reserves which survived the 1920s, saved from alienation only by their relative remoteness and lower fertility.[40] One of the most productive farms had been the Kinchela lands settled by the Drew families at the mouth of the Macleay. These were lost not to white farmers but to the Protection Board itself, to set up more of the machinery

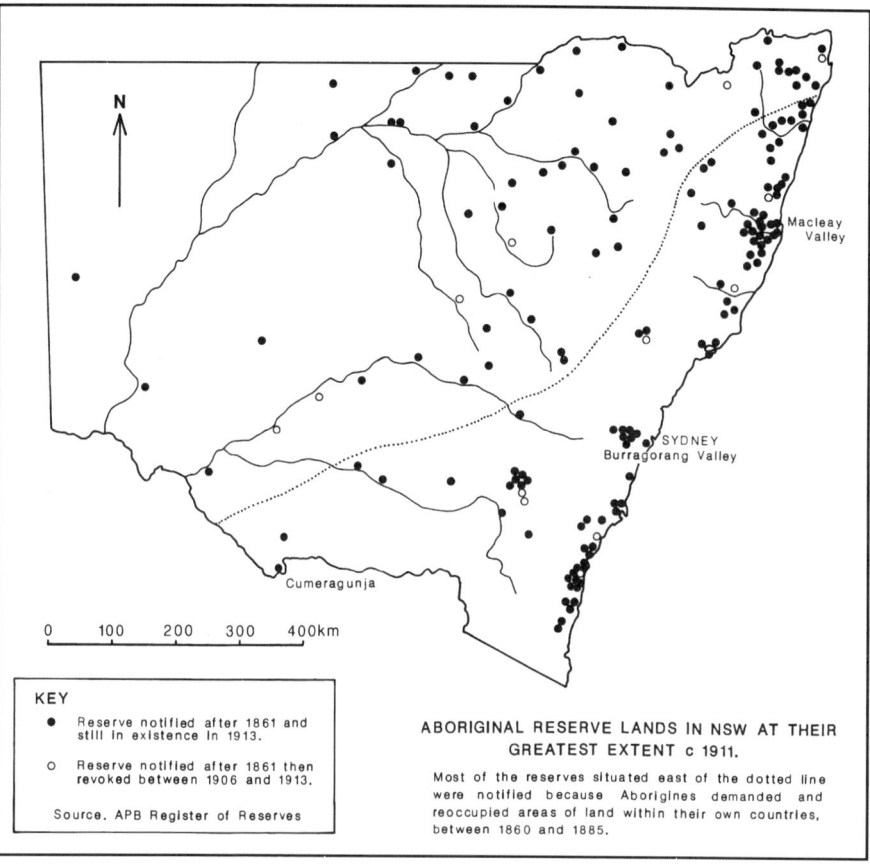

ABORIGINAL RESERVE LANDS IN NSW AT THEIR GREATEST EXTENT c 1911.

Most of the reserves situated east of the dotted line were notified because Aborigines demanded and reoccupied areas of land within their own countries, between 1860 and 1885.

KEY
● Reserve notified after 1861 and still in existence in 1913.
○ Reserve notified after 1861 then revoked between 1906 and 1913.

Source. APB Register of Reserves

for the most destructive aspect of its dispersal policy, the removal of children. Kinchela farm, which had been a flourishing symbol of independent Aboriginal survival strategies, became Kinchela Boys' Home, a feared place where boys removed from their families were kept in loneliness and often abuse, in order to teach them to forget their Aboriginality.

The Board's dispersal policy generated turmoil among New South Wales Aborigines as they were expelled or forced off reserves or as they escaped to protect their children from 'removal'. The loss of the self-supporting farms was devastating, especially on the north coast but the improved employment conditions of the 1920s allowed Aborigines some flexibility to move to new areas away from Board threats to their children. There were never more than 15 per cent of the Aboriginal population under Board managerial control over these years. The Board had created an illusory dispersal, reducing its ration lists from the inflated numbers of the Depression but generating large population increases in town camps beyond its control. There Aborigines continued to regard themselves as Aboriginal, maintained their extended family relationships and obligations, and were most definitely regarded by whites as Aboriginal.

The Board did, however, succeed in reaping a bitter harvest of children. More than 1500 Aboriginal children were taken from their families between 1912 and 1938, at a time when the total known Aboriginal population of the state was only between 6000 and 10 000. As it was young women whom the Board most wished to control, the majority of the children taken were girls between ten and fourteen, who made up over 80 per cent in the first decade and then around 70 per cent by the 1930s.[41] These children were interned in the Board's 'Homes' for training then 'apprenticed' as indentured domestic servants. Most of them faced hard, exploited work, extreme isolation and, for both girls and boys, the frequent terrors of sexual abuse. Margaret Tucker and Jimmie Barker were the first Aboriginal 'apprentices' to write about these experiences but now other equally painful personal accounts have been recorded, confirming the abundant official documentation of their harrowing experiences.[42]

For many other Aboriginal children there are few accessible records. Those whose skin colouring was fair were channelled into the Child Welfare system, where their Aboriginality was officially denied. The racism which flourished in these institutions was no less destructive for being covert.[43]

These young people seldom acquiesced in their treatment, whichever the network into which they were sent. Despite attempts to obstruct them, one in five of the children taken by the Board absconded and around three-quarters of them returned eventually to their own or another Aboriginal community. Margaret Tucker and Jimmie Barker are both examples of the way this brutal process actually galvanised their determination to fight back politically throughout their lives. Even for them, however,

Aboriginal women also worked as domestics, casual and permanent, on properties and in towns in the agricultural areas of New South Wales. This photo of Lulu and Clara, taken at Rolland's Plains near Kempsey in 1925, documents the seldom-recorded work done by Aboriginal women of all ages. Such work often created a fragile economic link with towns which aided Aborigines in their struggle against forced removal. BICENTENNIAL COPYING PROJECT, STATE LIBRARY OF NEW SOUTH WALES

the cost was terribly high. The emotional scars borne both by the children and their families form a stark and enduring monument to racism.[44]

The Board had not expected white resistance to its dispersal policy, which had been formulated to appease Treasury and parliamentary fears. The policy had led, however, to great increases in the Aboriginal populations camping close to country towns, which meant more Aboriginal demands for school access for their children, more competition between white and Aboriginal workers and greater visible Aboriginal presence on the town streets. This was also a time when the general concepts of the eugenics movement were widely circulating among whites, a movement seen as 'scientific' and 'respectable'. This gave weight to its proposals for confinement and sterilisation as a 'solution' to the 'problems' of poverty, delinquency, 'unregulated' sexual activity and chronic poor health, as well as to the then incurable venereal diseases. Demands to confine Aboriginal people appeared to be totally consistent with such widely held and authoritative beliefs.[45]

Local councils began to hector the Protection Board in the early 1920s, demanding that it acquire for the first time the power to round up and confine Aborigines, which of course was precisely the opposite of the Board's own goals. Bitter struggles developed over the decade, with Moree a typical example, where the Aboriginal population had increased due to the Board's closure of its station at Terry Hie Hie.

Throughout the 1920s, the Moree Municipal Council systematically used denial of services, then evictions, demolitions, mass gaolings and disenfranchisement to try to move the Murris of the town's 'Top camp' to a new reserve two miles away from the town boundaries. The Council favoured this site because it was close enough to recruit Aboriginal workers but far enough away to be out of sight. When Murris still refused to move, and gained the support of the local Methodist minister in their determination to hold their ground, the Council initiated the segregation of the local school. It then succeeded in calling in the Child Welfare Department on the pretext that the Aboriginal children were not going to school. The children of the most vocal protesters were indeed removed and so everyone else was under threat. Even then, only the families with young children were finally coerced into moving to the new reserve, where an unfurnished shed had been set up to serve as a 'special' Aboriginal school.[46]

More informal means of control became widespread: police harassment to enforce illegal curfews and vigilante gangs to discourage Aborigines from town streets.[47] Aborigines resisted such pressure in a number of ways, sometimes organising petitions, as did the Kooris at La Perouse and Batemans Bay, or taking legal action, like the Roberts families at Lismore. Yet their great vulnerability lay in the Board's power over their children, particularly if the local school closed its doors and the parents could be accused of failing to secure an education for their children.

Not only in Moree but in Yass, Walgett and many other towns, Aboriginal parents found that to protest a school segregation or to try to live in the town of one's choice, meant losing one's children to the Aborigines Protection Board or the Child Welfare.[48]

FIGHTING BACK: 1920s

The strength of Aboriginal resistance to the dispersal policies was just as much a shock to the Board as white opposition had been. The families of children under threat opposed the removals, confronting Board and police officers who tried to steal children, or fleeing to safer places. Communities like Cumeragunja opposed the seizure of their family farms and the expulsions of individuals from the station with a series of law suits and then with sustained civil disobedience in the early 1920s. The Kooris of the north coast, hardest hit by land losses and, later, by the removal of children, formed a public and organised movement in 1924, the Australian Aboriginal Progressive Association (AAPA).

Soon linked with south coast and Sydney communities, the AAPA strongly protested the loss of the lands and of children. The organisation held rallies of up to 500 people in towns along the coast from 1925 to 1927, where speeches were made by senior men in their own languages, ceremonial leaders who had until recently also been farmers. They called on the government to restore their traditional lands, their farms and their children. The AAPA petitioned Parliament and press, bitterly condemning the Board for tolerating the sexual exploitation of the young girls who were 'apprenticed out' and then sent home pregnant. Beyond this, the organisation organised secret support networks for girls abused in this way. Fred Maynard, the Hunter Valley Koori who was a major spokesperson for the AAPA, demanded the acknowledgement of the achievements of Aboriginal civilisation which had developed the social egalitarianism for which so many trade unionists and other Australians were striving. He called for enough land for self-sufficiency for each New South Wales Aboriginal family and for recognition of cultural difference, with

Aborigines allowed free access to public schools but, like Catholic and other religious groups, also able to run their own schools.[49]

This organisation gained considerable public support from white nationalist groups like the Australian Natives' Association. While it could not stem the loss of lands, the AAPA caused enough public embarrassment to force the Protection Board to modify the child removal policy. Children were thereafter allowed to return home at the end of their indentures. However, as most of them were girls, the Board still felt it could interfere in their lives and it instructed its managers to ensure that ex-apprentices married rapidly and lived 'respectable' lives. These young women continued to bear the brunt of the Board's attempt to culturally indoctrinate Aborigines. They found themselves hurried into these 'respectable' but often inappropriate marriages, then had their homes constantly under intrusive scrutiny, and knew that their children were always vulnerable to removal if they did not satisfy the Board's inspectors.

A NEW DEPRESSION LEADS TO SEGREGATION: THE 1930s

The 1930s' Depression interrupted the Aboriginal political movement by closing off the few economic options they had had in the 1920s. The Protection Board, in a bid to meet the shortfall in its budget in the first lean year of 1929, appealed to the government to allow it to take control of the recently granted child endowment payments to Aboriginal families. It argued that Aborigines could not handle the cash but the only complaints the administering body had made was that some Aborigines were underspending their grants. Nevertheless, the Board was granted control over all Aboriginal families' child endowment and used the additional funds to cover the cost of its increasing ration lists as Aborigines were thrown out of work.

Aborigines faced heavy job losses but were systematically refused the new State unemployment benefits in New South Wales. In Victoria, Aborigines were eligible for the dole like any other workers but the Department of Labour in New South Wales decided that Aborigines would first have to prove they had 'performed a white man's work' before they would be given any relief. This was a test which no one ever defined. In practice it became an excuse for the issuing officers, who were the local police, to exclude most unemployed Aborigines. Despite protests by both Aboriginal workers and the Protection Board, Aborigines were forced to turn to Board rations, which were equivalent to only half of the meagre unemployment food relief available to white unemployed. Aborigines were also usually excluded from work relief, which was administered by local government, unless there was some particularly heavy or unpleasant work to be done.

Increasing numbers of Aboriginal people were forced onto the Protection Board's resources. By 1935, over 30 per cent of the known Aboriginal population was under the direct and dictatorial control of Protection managers and many more were on reserves under the surveillance of the police. The Board was forced to admit the failure of dispersal. Aborigines had not disappeared or 'merged' with the white working class. Now more people than ever, over 10 000, were identified as Aboriginal by collectors of the census, who, as it happened, were also the police.[50]

The Board's limited finances were unable to meet the sudden demand. No new housing or services could be provided between 1929 and 1935 for the massive increases in station and reserve population, which were often carrying twice the population who had lived there only a year before. The poverty and sudden overcrowding caused major epidemics of respiratory and eye disease which swept the managed stations in 1934 and 1936. The Board responded by finally giving in to town demands for segregation. In addition, the Board believed that it could only fund improved living conditions on a reduced number of large, centralised, managed stations. So in 1934 it formulated a policy to 'concentrate' all Aborigines on these newly expanded stations from which they would not be free to leave until they had been 'educated' or 'trained' to live in ways acceptable to whites. The policy of resocialisation, previously only applied to the children removed from their communities, was now extended to all adult Aborigines as well.

Under the resulting 1936 amendment to the Protection Act, all Aborigines, including those of 'light caste' who had previously been told they were not Aborigines at all, were to be confined for as long as it took to reshape their lives. For the Board, this was a programme with an end in sight, 'assimilation' into the white community, a delayed but eventually more effective 'dispersal'. For local government councils and rural white communities, the end was the confinement itself, which they fully expected to be permanent. This was consistent with the continuing dominance of eugenics-inspired beliefs that permanent confinement was the answer to both social and health 'problems'.

Enforced concentration began in 1934 and continued until 1939, although it was implemented unevenly across the state. Aborigines called it the 'Dog Act' because it meant they could be carted around and penned up like animals. The most dramatically affected were Aborigines living where the rural economy appeared to be undergoing the greatest restructuring, in the western and north coast pastoral industry areas where the largest properties were again being broken up. Whole communities of Aborigines were moved hundreds of miles by cattle truck and dumped on Protection Board stations at Menindee, Brewarrina, Toomelah and Burnt Bridge. Aborigines protested bitterly but they had been made even more vulnerable by the legislative changes of 1936, which brought anyone 'deemed' by a magistrate to be 'Aboriginal' under the power of the 'Dog Act'. Particularly if they had young children, Aborigines had few real choices. Even so, many only acquiesced in the transportation after threats at gunpoint, like the Murris moved from Angledool to Brewarrina in 1936. Others stayed in the new 'concentration' stations only so long as economic conditions forced them into dependence on Board rations, like the Wangkumarra of Tibooburra in the Corner Country, who were dumped 200 hundred miles away at Brewarrina in 1938. They were still 80 strong in 1940, despite the deaths of many of their old people, and with the first hint of improved job chances, they chose to defy Protection Board threats and to walk the 190 miles back to their country.[51]

COALITION FOR CITIZEN'S RIGHTS: 1930s

The massive loss of economic and civil rights suffered by Aborigines in the 1930s meant that when their political movement reemerged, its focus had shifted. This time a coalition of regional movements was formed. The Cumeragunja community had linked with others in south-western New South Wales and Victoria in 1934 to form the Australian Aboriginal League (AAL). This was led by William Cooper, now an elderly man who had farmed the land he had petitioned for in 1887 but had been driven away early in the 1930s by poverty and Protection Board persecution. He wrote the AAL letters which protested the New South Wales economic discrimination which excluded Aboriginal workers from the dole. The broader AAL policy drew on long-held Cumeragunja aspirations for restoration of their land. In a decade when irrigated farming was widely regarded among the white community as a panacea for unemployment, the AAL proposed a realistic plan for the redevelopment of the family farms programme all over New South Wales. Its focus was on the Riverina, where Cumeragunja would be the pilot project using a well-researched irrigation scheme.[52]

The west and north-western communities of New South Wales developed the Aborigines' Progressive Association (APA), led by Bill Ferguson, Pearl Gibbs and Bert Groves, which protested not only economic discrimination but also the enforced movements which were throwing the western communities into turmoil, and led to the appalling conditions on the Protection Board managed stations. Their demands were for immediate equal civil rights, an end to the Protection Board and for a long-term plan of land settlement. Both the AAL and the APA drew on a somewhat uneasy mixture of Christian and Left-wing supporters.[53] On the north and south coasts, the AAPA was reactivated with Jack Patten as spokesperson, opposing Protection Board control and calling for restoration of Aboriginal lands, including the reserves taken in the 1920s. This organisation, although now renamed the Aborigines' Progressive Association like the western organisation, still drew on white support from the nationalist groups which had backed the AAPA in the 1920s. Some like the Australia First Movement had moved far to the right during the Depression and now advocated a virulent anti-Semitism and support for a White Australia. However, the Movement hated

British control over Australia and so did not wish to make biological race the essential foundation of its nationalism. It placed a high value on Aboriginal culture as this seemed to offer a rich body of symbols and traditions for a distinctive sense of Australian identity. This cultural interest led the Australia First Movement into active support for the Aboriginal political movement.

For each of the Aboriginal movements, the deterioration in access to civil rights had made this issue the most urgent demand, with land issues shifting to a long-term goal. These movements called for 'Full Citizen's Rights', a demand which was immediately recognisable to the growing numbers of white supporters in Christian and Left-wing organisations, who believed that Aborigines had adopted the liberal platform of equal civil rights for all. One of the most successful and symbolically significant Aboriginal protests was the declaration of a Day of Mourning in 1938 to mark the Sesquicentenary of Australian settlement.

The strong increase in white support for the Aboriginal movement pushed the government into reorganising and renaming the Protection Board as the Aborigines Welfare Board in 1939. The new Board included anthropologists and later a token Aboriginal position but the old 'Dog Act' legislation was retained and real power never left white hands. Aborigines bitterly rejected the new bureaucracy, insisting: 'We are not savages, sinners or criminals. We do not need anthropologists, clergymen or policemen to look after us.'[54]

The most moving demonstration of Aboriginal distress occurred at Cumeragunja in 1939. Despite William Cooper's long and patient correspondence, the Board contemptuously rejected the AAL's irrigated farm proposals. Then mismanagement and victimisation by the Board manager pushed Kooris there to such a state of outrage that they walked off the land they had been fighting to regain for 50 years. The Cumeragunja people set up a protest strike camp on the Victorian side of the Murray River at Barmah. They stayed for nine months, despite arrests, harassment and a freezing winter. Supported by Melbourne-based activists like Margaret Tucker, they mobilised press cover and trade union support to demand the restoration of their farms and an end to Board rule. While they achieved the dismissal of the manager, they did not regain their independent lands, and many moved to Victorian fruit towns like Shepparton or to Melbourne, where they formed the nucleus of later political activity.[55]

ASSIMILATION BY SURVEILLANCE: 1940s TO 1960s

The war generated such a change in the economy that Aborigines found themselves suddenly freed from economic dependence on the Board. By 1948, only 21 per cent of the Aboriginal population remained under managerial control on stations and 96 per cent of Aboriginal men were employed.[56] Aborigines had moved to areas where the Welfare Board had little means of control and where new work opportunities had arisen. The Welfare Board was forced to admit the failure of its 'confine and educate' plan, yet it was plagued by new and rising protests from white townspeople about the increased presence of Aborigines in towns like Moree, Coffs Harbour and Griffith.

In 1948 the Board formulated a new version of its re-education policy. In the aftermath of Nazism, general public opinion had become less sympathetic to eugenics-inspired confinement plans, at the same time as changing economic conditions made it less practical. So the Board set aside plans to concentrate Aborigines by active relocation, and began to construct a system of surveillance, which was aimed at monitoring those Aborigines who had succeeded in extricating themselves from Board control. The Aborigines' Welfare Board appointed District Welfare Officers (DWOs) to the towns where large populations of Aborigines had recently settled, and told the officers to observe and report on all Aborigines in the area. The means of control and social change was to be the newly developed 'Exemption Certificates' which would be awarded to 'deserving Aborigines', those who pleased the AWB and so were said to be of 'a superior intellectual type'. These certificates were supposed to allow access to public education, housing, services and facilities on the same basis as white citizens.[57]

Aborigines had to apply and be recommended to achieve an exemption, which meant proving to the DWO that they were willing to live separately from other Aboriginal people, to work in approved 'regular' jobs and save for 'approved' purchases. Home furnishings would be 'approved', for example but sharing of wages with kinfolk or spending money for travel to maintain extended family relationships would be definitely 'disapproved'. Denial or revocation of exemption certificates meant families were more vulnerable to school segregations and to loss of their children, were far less likely to receive Federal unemployment benefits or old age pensions, and were denied access to hotels and alcohol, which meant exclusion from the labour exchange of many country towns as well as from the social network of the rural male workforce.

Despite the high cost of not participating in the 'exemption' process, many Aborigines refused to be humiliated into applying for what they called a 'Dog Licence'. Between 1943 and 1964, when the system lapsed, there were only 1500 applications for exemption certificates out of a vulnerable population of 14 000.[58] Yet even without co-operating, Aborigines faced increasing interference and surveillance as the widening network of DWOs relentlessly inspected and judged rented homes and riverbank shacks as vigilantly as any managed station hut.[59]

The old system of 'apprenticing' children was said to have been dismantled in 1939 but the power to remove children had not been diminished, merely transferred to the Child Welfare Department. The Welfare Board's managers and DWOs (a number of whom were ex-managers) continued to act as 'friends of the court', advising police and Child Welfare officers on Aboriginal home conditions and the desire of parents to 'rehabilitate' and 'assimilate'. Increasing numbers of Aboriginal children appear to have been taken in the 1950s and 1960s. Although this is difficult to trace in the Child Welfare system, the Aborigines' Welfare Board homes demonstrated the increase: there were only 170 children in the homes in 1951 but by 1961 there were 300. Fewer children were employed as domestics after the war, although this continued to occur into the 1960s. More often, children were fostered. First they were sent to 'suitable' Aboriginal families but after 1956 the Board began advertising, successfully in its view, for white families to foster Aboriginal wards, thus increasing cultural and social alienation. Aboriginal families were warned repeatedly in Welfare Board reports that if they did not demonstrate a willingness to live like white people their children would be taken.[60]

NO BOOM FOR ABORIGINES: THE 1950s AND 1960s

The extension of Welfare Board interference in Aboriginal lives occurred during the 1950s and 1960s at the same time as economic opportunities again contracted. Once more, whole categories of jobs were lost as technology and industry structures changed. Mechanised harvesters, for example, eliminated the need for many workers in the inland wheat and coastal corn industries, while wheat silos eliminated the need for bag sewers. Trucks and motor bikes reduced the need for horsemen and other stock workers in both sheep and cattle industries, while road trains eventually eliminated droving jobs. Irrigated agriculture offered many seasonal harvesting jobs but Aborigines faced severe competition in the Riverina from postwar European migration. Job losses forced white rural working class families to move to urban industrial areas but Aboriginal affiliations to land and kin meant that many Aboriginal workers tried to stay on their lands despite the economic changes.

In the 1960s, only one new crop generated many jobs: cotton farming demanded chipping weeds out from between the young crop plants. This was hard labour in poor conditions but at least it offered some work for Aborigines who made up the majority of the seasonal workers. In this industry, however, the increasing use of herbicides and pesticides diminished the need for chippers at the same time as it endangered them, and caused deterioration of the land and riverine environment. This had implications for continuing subsistence harvesting. Aboriginal fishing, for example, was undermined in the 1960s when inedible introduced species and intensive chemical-based agriculture damaged the native fish supplies in the Darling and other rivers. This coincided with a time when cash work decreased.[61]. Ironically, the one introduced species on which Aborigines had come to rely for food and cash income, the rabbit, was at this same time being decimated by myxomatosis.

On the coast, the spread of white residential, leisure and tourist development began to eat away at Aboriginal residence and access to the coast for subsistence. Two targets of this pressure were the Gumbaingirr people's scenic home on Stuarts Island at Nambucca, in 1955 and the Bundjalung lands at Yamba, in 1958. The Welfare Board was prepared to accede to white demand by revoking these and other remaining Aboriginal reserves. On the south coast there was similar pressure. Jerinja Kooris, knowing about their Dangadi relations' loss of farming lands in the 1920s, were deeply alarmed when the Nowra Council divided their reserve at Roseby Park in the late 1950s with a road to facilitate tourist access. Loss of reserve lands because of these pressures was most intense in 1955 to 1965, precipitating reluctant Aboriginal migration and reactivating the land issue as a major platform of New South Wales Aboriginal politics by 1960.[62]

The Welfare Board had never wanted to abandon the goal of active concentration of the Aboriginal population. In the weakening economic conditions, it could allow this process to occur by attrition. Read[63] has described the Board's refusal to maintain accommodation and facilities on smaller reserves on the Wiradjuri lands of the south-west, its bulldozing of houses while families were unavoidably away on the ever lengthening seasonal work tracks, and the revocation of the reserves themselves to force people on to the few remaining managed stations. In other areas, such as the Macleay Valley, Morris[64] has described a differing situation, where newly appointed managers were imposed on the people of previously independent reserves like Burnt Bridge and Bellbrook. Although this latter strategy generated less population movement, both processes marked an intensification of Welfare Board scrutiny into and control over Aboriginal lives.

FAILED PROMISES TO DESEGREGATE: 1948–1969

The Board held out promises of improved conditions for Aborigines when it began constructing its postwar system. The most attractive had been access to housing and education. The Board believed that when it offered houses it was offering the status and improved health and material conditions of a 'proper', 'respectable' dwelling. The Board's aim was to use such houses as behaviour modification tools in themselves, to be inspected constantly to ensure the Aboriginal residents had paid an adequate level of attention and expenditure, made a proper commitment to the material appearances of 'stability'.[65] The houses were to be 'pepperpotted', an arrangement by which the Aboriginal house would be surrounded on all sides by white residents, guaranteeing that there would be no Aboriginal neighbours. So 'assimilating' families faced constant scrutiny and judgement from their all-white neighbours as well as from the DWO.[66]

For Aborigines, the offer was intensely attractive but for different reasons. They were desperate for security of residence in the area of their choice. Every shift in the economy and every decision of the Protection Board since the turn of the century had made it harder for Aboriginal people to stay in the town or on the land where they had previously reached some equilibrium, however tenuous, with the settler colony. The dispossessions and dispersals of the 1920s, the constant threats to children, the enforced concentrations of the 1930s, and the eviction orders and bulldozers of the 1950s had caused a turmoil of forced migrations.

Even when people moved to the next town, seeking asylum within their own country, they usually found only temporary residence, in even less secure conditions than those which they had been forced to leave. A few rural Aborigines had managed to buy a block of land in town but many were lost to local councils to pay for rates in years of unemployment. Most Aboriginal families were looking to rent but were confronted with an informal and unspoken alliance between landlords, real estate agents and local councils. There were sometimes slums on offer but much of the time there was a strange absence of any rental accommodation whenever Aboriginal people inquired.[67]

So the Welfare Board had a powerful attraction indeed when it announced that if Aboriginal families could demonstrate that they would live in 'conformity to the standards of white people' the Board would secure a house for them in town.[68] Yet the Board failed to fulfil this most central of its promises. The

Aboriginal need for housing was acute: in 1949, the Board estimated that 600 to 700 houses were required simply to meet the current demand. In the following year alone, the Board built 60 houses on managed stations. But from 1946 to 1960, only 39 houses were built for Aborigines inside municipal boundaries. The towns simply would not admit Aborigines and their usual weapon was control over the sale of land. Suddenly no land could be found for Board acquisition, or vendors of potentially suitable land would inexplicably take their blocks off the market, as at Nambucca Heads in 1958. On the few occasions in which the Board did succeed in buying land, as in Cowra in 1951, the tradesmen who had been engaged to build the houses would be intimidated by their fellow townsmen until they withdrew their tender or the Board would be flooded by deputations and petitions from local government and white residents.[69]

The Welfare Board had failed to appreciate the depth of rural commitment to segregation. This was an edifice which had been built up from at least the 1880s, when Aboriginal people had begun in numbers to demand access to the services and institutions of the new liberal democracy being established. 'Public' schools had been only the most formal of the closures. Over the years, hospitals had been closed down to Aborigines and in particular women had been made aware of this medical segregation. The Protection Board attempted to intervene in Aboriginal health as well as culture by sending increasing numbers of Aboriginal women to hospital to have their babies. In response, white townspeople demanded that labour wards must be denied to them. Many Aboriginal women remember the discomfort and humiliation of birthing on the hospital verandah or in a makeshift area at the rear of the main buildings.

Leisure was strictly segregated, with picture shows, swimming pools and tennis courts usually closed to Aborigines, and Aboriginal football teams denied a place in the local competition, all on the grounds of fictitious 'health risks'. The limits of this 'petty apartheid' were bizarre. White residents in Lake Cargelligo spent the 1950s trying to preserve their 'Whites only' public toilet. They demanded that the manager of nearby Murrin Bridge Station bring the Aboriginal residents of the station into town for shopping for no more than two hours, so that they would not use the town's 'amenities'. Otherwise, the town demanded, the Welfare Board must build a separate, 'Blacks only' toilet block, which was to be surrounded by seating, so that Aboriginal shoppers would only be allowed to rest in the same strictly limited area.[70]

The keystone of this whole system was the segregation of residential areas. Exclusion of Aboriginal people from the 'real' town meant they could always be defined as 'outsiders', like the Murrin Bridge shoppers in Lake Cargelligo, and always denied the access accorded to 'real' citizens. When the Welfare Board boasted to Aborigines that it could provide them with 'a house in town', they hoped to breach this fundamental core of the rural structure of racial hierachy and power relations.

There were a number of factors operating during the Welfare Board's period which exacerbated white rural tensions and increasingly hardened the resolve to defend the colour bar. The Board's reserve revocations had generated further population movements which intensified town alarm where Aboriginal populations were already rising in pursuit of seasonal work. Perhaps just as significant were shifting economic conditions, with employment declining sharply in 1958-60 in the Riverina and north coast regions, and in 1966-69 in the western pastoral areas, in both cases because of changing technology, mechanisation and drought.[71] This meant unemployment for white workers as well as Aboriginal and led to a loss of white population to the cities in these periods. This increased the insecurity of the whites who remained, particularly those in areas of greatest economic decline. Significant too was Aboriginal political pressure to desegregate the towns, which had been mounting since 1956.

Certainly not all rural whites were opposed to Aboriginal presence in towns. There was a small but growing body of white rural support for desegregation, an oddly assorted network in which some participants were Christian, some trade unionists, some Labor or Communist Party members. The Board had fostered 'assimilation committees' in the 1940s but by the late 1950s many had come to criticise the Board itself for caving in to town opposition to desegregation.[72] Some members of these committees formed effective lobbies inside local government ranks. At 'Australia's Little

Rock', Coonamble in 1960, an alliance of Aborigines and a few townspeople succeeded where the Welfare Board had failed, by acting in secret to buy a number of house blocks within the town. A few of these white supporters went beyond the demand for access to town services, and began to join with Aborigines to criticise the whole basis of 'assimilation', recognising the cultural and social costs imposed on families forced away from contact with their communities to live in 'pepperpotted' houses.[73]

Yet overall the entrenched resistance to residential desegregation was so powerful that the Welfare Board, in one situation after another, failed to penetrate rural residential segregation. As a result, the Board became the legitimator of that segregation. The Board consistently resolved disputes by succumbing to town opposition. It then either created reserves just outside municipal limits and built houses on them, as at Gulargambone and Coffs Harbour, or placed new houses on existing managed stations, as it did at Cowra. As late as 1967 the Board was being forced to acquire land by reservation on the outskirts of town boundaries.[74] Rural whites found that the Welfare Board could be relied upon to keep Aborigines out of town.

The Board failed too in its promise to desegregate public schooling, despite its claims in 1955 to be rapidly closing the 'special' poorly resourced 'Aboriginal schools'. The frequent result, documented well by Fletcher for Collarenebri[75], was a covert but no less powerful form of segregation. Aboriginal children were allowed into the public school but then placed all in one class, with no white students, and at times even allocated separate playing areas fenced off from white children. By 1961, such internal segregation had contributed to the disproportionately low numbers of Aboriginal children who stayed on till the later years of schooling.[76]

It was apparent from very early in the 1950s that the Board was being obstructed and failing in its goals. The Board admitted that there was 'strenuous local opposition' in Cowra in 1951 and 'fierce prejudice' in Moree in 1952.[77] Yet it was not prepared to challenge local power structures openly and instead began to blame Aboriginal people for its own failures. In education, the Board 'blamed the victim', arguing that the poor retention rates exposed in 1961 were caused by the 'fact' that: 'Aboriginal children, as a whole, do not possess an intelligence quotient comparable to that of their white counterparts.' It later retracted this crude racist view in order to try to lay blame for the low retention rate, just as inappropriately, on Aboriginal parents.[78] In housing, the Board's reports from 1955 carried stern criticisms of the 'many' Aborigines 'who are content to live in substandard conditions on the outskirts of towns'. Indeed, the Board now pronounced that Aborigines themselves were to blame for the prejudice against them: 'The disadvantages under which they labour, are largely attributable to their failure to make the best use of the resources available to them.'[79]

Only in 1967 did the Board admit that the major obstruction to housing Aborigines in towns had been 'local antipathy', the widespread and growing white resident opposition to desegregation.[80]

The Board then, from the 1940s into the mid 1960s, delivered very few of its promises to Aborigines. Instead, it actually acted to *contain* Aborigines, maintaining and even justifying segregated living conditions and using exemptions and threats to children to police Aboriginal behaviour. Like its predecessor the Protection Board, the Welfare Board acted in the interests of the white population.

ABORIGINAL PERCEPTIONS OF RURAL SEGREGATION: HOUSES OR LAND?

Aboriginal views about each of these local struggles were seldom recorded, although their interest was intense. Lismore was one area in which articulate Aboriginal spokespeople and some aldermanic allies ensured an airing of the issues in the local press. Here the Welfare Board in 1957 attempted to acquire a few blocks of land within the town to rehouse the Kooris of Cubawee but the Municipal Council blocked the sale and the debate continued to rage until 1961. The councillors and citizens who supported the Koori right to have access to the town did so because they opposed racial inequality and discrimination, as well as arguing that the dilapidated housing and low-lying swampy grounds of

Cubawee posed a health risk to both Aborigines and whites.[81] The Aboriginal statements suggested that they had differences with their supporters as well as their opponents, and most importantly that simple equality was not the fundamental issue to them.

In 1959 Pastor Frank Roberts, Senior, a Bundjalung lay preacher, attacked the allegations that Kooris all suffered from hookworm and other health problems. He characterised the attempts to move people away from Cubawee as another shirking of the responsibility to provide decent services to the land which his family and other Bundjalung people had been fighting to keep for decades. Roberts demanded government action to resume compulsorily any additional land required for Aboriginal housing, irrespective of local government wishes, and summed up the whole dispute with the sentence: 'We have been robbed of our heritage.'[82] When Bert Groves spoke a few months later in Lismore, he further clarified the issues from an Aboriginal perspective when he debated with local Church of Christ pastor, A. Caldicott, who was seen as a moderate supporter of Aboriginal rights. Groves demanded that:

> pressure should be brought to bear on the Government to force it to resume land for the aborigines, who were the rightful owners of the land in the first place.
> Pastor Caldicott: Do you think it just and right to resume land belonging to others?
> Mr Groves: The land belongs to the aborigines.[83]

Such statements suggest Aboriginal people saw these conflicts as being about more than the right for all citizens to have equal access to the nation's resources. Beyond this, they saw the issue to be one of their heritage, which they presented as consisting of prior and continuing rights in land, and they located this in the historical context of the repeated attempts to make them move away from their chosen living areas within their country. Like the earlier statements of William Cooper in 1887 and Fred Maynard in 1927, the language of liberal rights carried additional meanings about the traditionally-sanctioned rights of original owners. This is how Pastor Frank Roberts expressed it: 'We are members of a democratic people and therefore have a perfect right to live in a place suitable for us.'[84]

RESISTANCE AND ASSERTION: ABORIGINAL POLITICS, 1950s AND 1960s

Rather than the long boom experienced by many white Australians, the 1950s and 1960s were decades when New South Wales rural Aborigines faced constriction of the job market, an increase in bureaucratic surveillance and interference, the loss of more of their reserve lands, and continued residential and educational segregation. Aboriginal individuals and communities resisted these processes in varied ways; for example, many refused to engage in the exemption system, attempting to maintain their wide family obligations despite obstruction and disapproval by managers and DWOs.

Informal protest could widen to a broad and well-organised mobilisation. Although residential segregation was often impenetrable, local Aboriginal protests against town colour bars were widespread. Aborigines could challenge the petty apartheid of the towns, but always at the risk of being branded 'troublemakers' and becoming the target of police and bureaucratic interference. Barbara Flick has written movingly about the way her mother and aunt in Collarenebri became outraged that their children were being humiliatingly penned up behind rope barriers so far down the front of the picture show hall that they were almost under the screen. These two women confronted the picture show owner in public, defied him by taking seats outside the barriers and shamed him into taking down the ropes.[85]

Such local acts of courage were supported by the continuing work of Aboriginal political activists Pearl Gibbs and Bert Groves. They campaigned through the Council for Aboriginal Rights (CAR), based in Dubbo and with some Sydney trade union support, although the white support of the 1930s had been eroded by the Welfare Board's early liberal rhetoric. Their protest meetings gained some press attention for the appalling conditions Aborigines were facing in north-western New South Wales, with no town housing to rent because of white racism, no services to town camps because of local government reluctance to encourage Aboriginal presence and no freedom under Welfare Board control on the managed stations.[86]

This organisation assisted contacts between Aboriginal communities protesting at local segregation and the increasing use of the bulldozer, whether by local councils against the camps or by the Welfare Board against reserve housing.[87] By 1956 the Aboriginal activists had gained some urban support with the formation of the Australian Aboriginal Fellowship (AAF) in Sydney. The AAF served as a focal point for re-emerging white support and in 1957 sent union representatives on a fact-finding tour to Walgett to publicise rural segregation and tension.[88] The Board still controlled entry to reserved land but by this time Bert Groves had been elected to the Aboriginal position on the Welfare Board, and used his freedom as a Board member to enter reserves so he could research and speak on behalf of both the CAR and the AAF. This allowed him to make important contributions to local struggles like that at Lismore in 1959.

Rent strikes are another example of the way local, informal protest could widen into broader actions, this time in relation to opposition to the Welfare Board. It had demanded rent from its tenants, often for miserable unserviced huts, as a tool for educating Aborigines to 'accept responsibility'. Although these rents were nominal, many people resented paying for poor quality housing under conditions of intense scrutiny on their own land. Their informal lack of co-operation already threatened to make the system unworkable when in 1960, a group of residents on Purfleet Station at Taree organised a formal rent strike. Led by Horace Saunders, a fisherman with six children, a total of twenty Koori families faced Board prosecution and eviction to demand changes. They attracted the interest of sympathetic local whites, a number of whom were active in either the Labor Party or the Communist Party, and gained support from the powerful Newcastle Trades and Labour Council. Eventually, in 1961, even the Board had to admit that what it faced at Purfleet and elsewhere was not financial irresponsibility but widespread civil disobedience in protest, the Board conceded, 'for dispossessing them of their lands'.[89]

Other forms of resistance to the repression of the postwar years also occurred—resistances which were more ambiguous and destructive. For some Aborigines, public expressions of defiance were made by adopting forbidden behaviour, such as drinking, despite (or perhaps because of) the continued illegality of supply of alcohol to them. Chronic alcohol abuse was a constant factor in Aboriginal life over these years but it was mainly confined to mature men, and while debilitating, had not escalated to the scale of later years. Again, for women, gambling on cards and bingo were unquestionably seen as resistance to Welfare officers and police but for some this resistance toppled over into uncontrollable and self-destructive addiction.[90]

Through the 1950s, Aboriginal political challenges to town segregation and to increasing Welfare Board surveillance could be seen as being within the framework of a civil rights campaign for the equality of citizen's rights, even though the housing and rent issues for Aborigines were strongly linked to their assertion of prior rights to land. By 1960, the issue of land itself had re-emerged as an immediate and fundamental element of New South Wales Aboriginal political agendas. As had been the case in the 1920s, the initiative for this reassertion of the land issue arose from Aboriginal people in the region where land was coming under renewed and intensifying threat.

In the late 1950s, this was the Bundjalung area of the far north coast. Their rights to their lands were threatened during the 1950s because of the final restructuring of the beef cattle industry in the upper reaches of the rivers, around Woodenbong, Tabulum and Baryulgil, and the extension of urbanisation and tourism on the coast, as at Lismore and Yamba. The Bundjalung were, however, in a strong position to articulate their growing concerns about economic threats, reserve revocations and enforced urban movements. They had an established network of Aboriginal-controlled fundamentalist Christian churches operating throughout the Bundjalung lands, led by lay preachers like Frank Roberts, Snr, and his son Frank Roberts, Jnr, who was ordained as a pastor in the Church of Christ in 1956. These forms of Christianity recognised their people's Aboriginal cultural values, encouraged confidence in rights to land and endorsed the hierarchical authority held by older Aboriginal people. The meetings held by the churches allowed opportunities to share common concerns about land and political repression.

Another element in the strength of the Bundjalung were their links with the Aboriginal people of the Armidale area, who were encountering a supportive interest among academics at the University of New England. Finally, they developed contacts with advocates of co-operatives, like the 'red' Anglican bush brother, Alf Clint from Tranby College in Sydney, who argued that this form of organisation was consistent with Aboriginal modes of community management and would allow independent economic development of Aboriginal lands.

Cabbage Tree Island, home of many branches of the Roberts family, began its sugar farming co-operative in 1960, followed by other Bundjalung communities.[91] In that year, Alex Vesper, a Bundjalung man from Woodenbong, rose to his feet at the annual conference of the newly established national organisation to support Aboriginal political action, the Federal Council for Aboriginal and Torres Straits Islanders (FCAATSI). Vesper moved for the agenda to be laid aside and then demanded that the conference begin to pay immediate attention to land issues, calling for security of tenure for Aboriginal people, support for their rights to own land and compensation for all lands taken away.[92]

Despite Koori protests, the pressure on land intensified: from 1957 to 1964, the major loss of reserves and land area was from the Bundjalung lands. In 1964, six out of the nine reserves revoked were on the north coast and five of these were high country Bundjalung.[93] These communities persisted with their co-operatives but they were all badly undercapitalised, and so could not yet meet the community's hopes for economic independence.[94] The Bundjalung representatives on state and national Aboriginal political organisations continued to demand that land become the first item on any political agenda. They were not alone. Kooris on the south coast added their voices to the demand to reorient the Aboriginal political platform from equality and civil rights only to one which made land a priority. The Jerinja from Roseby Park in 1960, for example, called on the South Coast Trades and Labour Council to support their campaign for farming and residential lands to protect them from urban residential expansion and tourist development.⁹⁵ Their combined and increasingly urgent demands for recognition of rights and needs over traditional lands arose from the growing pressures within New South Wales, and this south-eastern demand had forced a shift in the FCAATSI platform before the Northern Territory Yirrkala and Gurindji calls for land in 1963 and 1966.⁹⁶ By the mid-1960s, the coastal concerns about land loss were to be matched by those of Murris in western New South Wales, who were faced with loss of both reserves and access to land as the pastoral industry again restructured and the Welfare Board closed down remote reserves in favour of new, cramped 'town settlements'.

URBANISATION: VOLUNTARY AND FORCED

By the late 1950s some Aborigines had decided that the industrial areas of the cities offered better economic, educational and political conditions than the suffocating small rural towns. Their migration was along paths trodden already by kinsfolk, so that chain migration occurred to Sydney suburbs where some Aboriginal families had been living for decades. Redfern and Alexandria were the most publicised destinations but Aboriginal communities were also well established on the old Gandangara and Dharuk lands of western Sydney. Conditions were poor, with many Aboriginal migrants able to afford no more than crowded slums. They met intense racism from real estate agents and local governments at any signs of increasing Aboriginal population. What was not present was Welfare Board control: the Board had never developed a strong urban surveillance structure and it appeared to find the task of monitoring complex and dense urban communities just too difficult. Without the Welfare Board to contain Aborigines, local government and white residents called on police to control their presence and behaviour. By the early 1960s Aboriginal concern about police harassment was becoming more public as they were able to document the increasing raids on hotels and homes.

The growing Sydney Aboriginal population formed supportive networks which offered social and then later political organisation.

The 'Redfern All-Blacks' football club was one such body, which provided a vehicle for strengthening community links and also a base for negotiating with predominantly white support groups like the AAF. Ken Brindle, an activist involved in the 'All-Blacks' was central in mobilising and directing the Australian Aboriginal Fellowship to address the pressing issues for urban communities, notably accommodation and police harassment. Brindle himself was savagely bashed by Redfern police when he tried to assist the family of Patrick Wedge, a Wiradjuri man shot by police in 1963. The Council for Civil Liberties' involvement in Brindle's defence and damages claim laid the foundation for later alliances between urban lawyers and Aboriginal activists.[97]

The Welfare Board had begun to recognise its own failure to break into rural residential segregation by the early 1960s, and it attempted to intervene in the stalemated conflicts between towns and Aborigines by pushing Aborigines towards the industrial workforce of the coast. While some Aborigines clearly chose migration, at least temporarily, many others had continued to assert their rights to live in the area of their choice, which was often related to their traditional country and always to their extended family relationships. From 1960, however, the Welfare Board began to argue that young people and their families should 'pull up roots' and seek housing and training in the cities. In 1962 it threatened those Aborigines who failed to respond that they would be forced off reserves and stations. In 1963, the Board began to use the Housing Commission to acquire houses in urban areas rather than in the rural towns with highest Aboriginal populations and highest demand for houses.[98] The intention was made very plain to Aborigines: if you wanted a house at all, you would have to move to Sydney or Newcastle.

At the same time, as the conditions under which Aborigines were living had become more public due to agitation by Aboriginal and white groups, the Board made a final attempt to minimise the isolation of some Aboriginal reserves and to be seen to be addressing the health and housing crisis. Some large and remote stations were closed and a series of housing settlements were rapidly built on small pieces of reserve land at the edge of towns like Brewarrina, Bourke, Kempsey and Moree from 1964 to 1966.

All cheap and jerry built, this makeshift housing at least allowed the Board to call them 'town settlements' rather than reserves.[99] These white towns had all won their battles to keep Aboriginal families outside municipal boundaries but the Welfare Board then simply dumped large Aboriginal populations in overcrowded and poorly-built houses on the very edges of the towns, exacerbating anxieties and tensions.

For Aboriginal people, this often seemed like a further entrapment. For those at Brewarrina, for example, the move to West Brewarrina meant the loss of access to hundreds of acres of reserve around the old Mission, one of the worst losses of Aboriginal reserve lands in the west. The new 'town settlement' was a slum, poorly built on a treeless hill, and soon referred to by all as 'Dodge City'. Fences and locked gates increasingly confronted these Murris as access to pastoral lands closed down too with loss of employment, and their growing sense of frustration was expressed in the early 1970s in the political lament 'we are landless and landlocked'.[100]

CHANGING THE LAWS

The Aboriginal movements had been openly condemning the cultural destruction sought by the 'Assimilation Policy' since 1958, when Bert Groves reasserted, for the first time since 1927, the cultural distinctiveness and values of Aboriginal societies.[101] Aboriginal involvement in the AAF and the early meetings of FCAATSI had encouraged the national, pan-Aboriginal perspective which had been so evident in the Aboriginal Progressive Association of the 1930s. Since 1957, there had been strong New South Wales Aboriginal support for the AAF campaign to change the Federal Constitution to make the Commonwealth Government responsible for Aboriginal Affairs, the fulfilment of another platform of the 1930s movements. In the early 1960s, however, the focus of political organising returned to New South Wales, and the Aboriginal movements campaigned strongly during 1962 for the abolition of the Welfare Board and the dismantling of the Assimilation Policy. They generated a debate about the relative merits of 'assimilation' and 'integration' which continued in the press in the following years.[102] Major changes had already occurred when the Commonwealth Government agreed in 1960 to grant pensions to any aged Aborigine, regardless of 'caste', place of residence or 'exemption'. The powers of the 'Dog Licence' were now greatly diminished, and with them, the power of the New South Wales Board to threaten and intimidate Aborigines.

The remaining legal restriction was Section 9, the ban on the supply of alcohol to Aborigines. After an effective Aboriginal and AAF campaign, this too was removed in March 1963, taking with it the final power of the Exemption Certificate. Regardless of whether their abuse of the drug arose from despair or from a form of resistance, given the destructive effects which alcohol had had on some Aboriginal people in the past, this was an ambiguous victory.[103] Yet the level of Aboriginal drinking appears to have been little affected. According to police reports to the Welfare Board, those Aborigines who wanted alcohol before had been able to obtain it at an inflated 'black-market' price from publicans, and storekeepers sold methylated spirits to alcoholics.[104] This avenue of abuse at least was closed off by legalisation, although there were many towns where Aboriginal access to the normal venues for social drinking has never been achieved, with Aboriginal drinkers instead confined to the least comfortable back bars of many country pubs.

There are some figures available on arrests of Aborigines for public drunkenness over the 1960s and early 1970s in New South Wales. These suggest that there was not an increase in Aboriginal drinking associated with legalisation of supply in 1963. Instead, the substantial increase in alcohol abuse occurred in the early 1970s when Aboriginal employment in many areas had dried up altogether and the level of confrontation between local government and Aborigines had risen still further.[105] Economic and political issues were thus far more significant in exacerbating alcohol abuse than legalisation of supply.

Through the early 1960s, there was growing urban support for rural activism which challenged the segregation in picture shows, swimming pools and pubs, all symptomatic of the fundamental residential segregation. The New South Wales Labour

Council delegation to Walgett in 1964, for example, was widely covered in the metropolitan press. It was not until 1965, however, that there was major attention given to the issue. This was generated by the Freedom Ride, a bus convoy organised by Sydney University students and led by Charles Perkins. While this event took its name from the civil rights activism occurring at the time in the United States, Perkins' bus travelled to the sites of longest standing conflict between Aboriginal people and white townspeople. In doing so it mapped out decades of Aboriginal resistance to rural segregation. The students' tape recordings and photographs of ugly confrontations in Walgett, Moree and other towns over attempts to break the colour bar produced chilling evidence for urban audiences of the racism in rural New South Wales. It was also a very public announcement of a new alliance between Aborigines in both urban and rural areas and white students, who were later to become the lawyers and other professionals staffing the 1970s Aboriginal-controlled organisations. It contributed far more than the Welfare Board had ever done to public awareness of the problem, and to the breaking down of the petty but infuriating segregation of rural public spaces. Residential segregation, however, was to be far more persistent.

The years of previous campaigning, which culminated in the direct action and high publicity of the Freedom Ride, forced the New South Wales Government to hold a Select Committee Inquiry into the Welfare Board in 1966. Its Report condemned the Board but largely because it had not been assimilationist enough, as it continued to foster Aboriginal communities by allowing reserves to persist, when it should have been actively 'pepperpotting' families all over the state. The Report's underlying directions to the bureaucracy were therefore to continue and indeed accelerate many of the very policies opposed by Aborigines. Nevertheless, it spelt the end of the Welfare Board as an entity. Its functions were dismembered and transferred to relevant departments, such as the Housing Commission and Child Welfare Department. The demise of the Welfare Board appeared a positive step, and a new rhetoric of 'integration' replaced the earlier 'assimilation' terminology. It seemed that political activism had made a major impact.

Just as dramatic were the results of the long-awaited Federal Referendum, which in 1967 won overwhelming support for the proposals to recognise Aboriginal people symbolically by including them in the general census count and to transfer responsibility for Aboriginal Affairs to the Federal Government. Close analysis of the voting returns showed, however, that the areas with the lowest 'yes' votes were those rural areas with large Aboriginal populations, which had usually manifested the most entrenched discrimination and segregation.[106] In New South Wales, the racial conservatism of rural areas was being fanned into the open by the political challenges of Aboriginal reassertion and by the growing sense of insecurity as the Welfare Board was dismantled. This body which had effectively managed and contained Aborigines for white townspeople was now going. In reality, the diffusion of the sites of control and surveillance to a number of other departments made those powers greater and more difficult to fight. The large bureaucracy of the Housing Commission, for example, could much more effectively force Aborigines to conform to 'normal' standards in house use, rent and location than the smaller and more personalised Welfare Board had been able to do. Yet for rural local government, particularly in those towns with newly constructed and adjacent 'town settlements', the situation looked far less controlled than in previous years. From the early 1970s rural media in western areas began to call for more police, more control of Aborigines and more 'law and order'.[107]

THREATS TO SECURE RESIDENCE CONTINUE: 1970s

The Aboriginal political movement also expressed grave concerns about the directions of New South Wales policy. Aborigines had little real input into the new administration, the Directorate of Aboriginal Affairs under the Ministry of Social Welfare. Although an elected Aboriginal Advisory Council first sat in 1970, it had no powers independent of the Minister, and in one of its earliest acts agreed to the revocation of Kinchela Reserve. The pressure on Aborigines to conform to Housing Commission expectations of nuclear family and urban living was intensifying, and the new Directorate was found to be even more openly committed to urban relocation than had been the Welfare Board. The recommendations from the Directorate to the Housing Commission in 1971 show far more houses being constructed for Aborigines in urban areas than in areas of highest demand like Bourke. Such discrepancies demonstrated the distance between Aboriginal demand and Directorate intentions.[108]

Aboriginal concerns were not allayed when the head of the Directorate, Ian Mitchell, initiated the Aboriginal Family Resettlement Programme, a scheme to assist supposedly voluntarily migrating families. Aboriginal people suspected that substantial pressure was applied to community leaders to attract them with house and job offers in order to stimulate chain migration and that the covert goal was the old Protection Board one of closing down the reserves altogether, leaving atomised, urban families rather than Aboriginal communities. At least 200 families had been moved in this way by 1980 but 25 per cent of them had returned to their rural homes, and more were to do so in the following years as employment opportunities in urban secondary industry disappeared. The programme finally collapsed due to urban unemployment in 1988.[109]

The anxiety generated among Aborigines in the early 1970s by the recognition that they would continue to be under pressure to leave their home countries if they wanted decent housing, was heightened by the continued threats to reserve lands by revocation. The Bundjalung and South Sea Islander communities at Fingal at Tweed Heads had come under sustained pressure for tourist development in 1969, and only major lobbying by Aboriginal activists and wide print and television publicity had saved the land. Other reserves looked even less secure. Some concessions were made to reassure the most politically active communities like Woodenbong that their reserve would not be revoked but the Directorate was clearly not committed to maintaining what little remained of the Aboriginal land base.

WHOSE LAW? WHOSE ORDER?

To these concerns about the direction of policy were added the very immediate concerns generated by increasing police harassment, most noticeably in the inner suburbs of Redfern but also in rural areas. Tensions were rising as local authorities, urban and rural, expressed their insecurities. The alliance between Aborigines and urban professionals, first obvious in 1965, bore fruit in the documentation of police harassment and violence in the early 1970s and then in the formation of the Aboriginal Legal Service in Sydney in 1971, with branches established in rural areas by 1973.[110] This New South Wales attempt to make the legal system more accountable was influenced in many respects by strategies being tried in urban African–American communities by groups like the Panthers. Yet its central impulse and strategies were responses to the realities New South Wales Aborigines were facing in both urban and rural areas as police were being called on more frequently to 'manage' Aborigines in the seeming vacuum left by the Welfare Board.

The use of white professionals working under the direction of Aboriginal people was untried in Australia. It brought immediate results by improving legal representation for Aborigines to the level accessible to the urban working class.[111] To go beyond this to challenge the widespread institutionalised racial discrimination embedded within the legal system, more fundamental political changes were needed. This was the basis in 1975 for the Aboriginal Legal Service (ALS) and the Central Australian Aboriginal Legal Aid Service to call for a wide ranging national Royal Commission to inquire into Police–Aboriginal relations, particularly into the wider role of police as a body interconnected with other institutions such as the state child welfare and health authorities and local government.[112] The fall of the Whitlam government in 1975 ended plans for such an inquiry until the issue of Aboriginal deaths in police cells and gaols pushed the complex matter again into prominence and generated the Royal Commission into Aboriginal Deaths in Custody in 1987.

As well as the problem of immediate interactions with white society through the police, Aboriginal political concerns in the early 1970s had reflected the increasing pressure on land and on the right to live in communities in the area of people's choice. This focus on issues of land and country was demonstrated in the Tent Embassy, a demonstration initiated by New South Wales Aboriginal activists in 1972. With inspired symbolism, the concerns of south-eastern Aboriginal communities were aligned with those of Aborigines from all over Australia. The increased pressure on the incoming Whitlam government to make concessions on Land Rights had effects outside Commonwealth territories too, as the New South Wales Government thus renamed the Aboriginal Advisory Council the 'Lands Trust', although without giving it any more powers and certainly no more land.

CHALLENGING RESIDENTIAL SEGREGATION

Aboriginal communities were using the newly available Commonwealth funds to more effect: the emergence of housing companies in many rural towns reflected the assertion by these communities that they intended to remain on their chosen country *and* have decent houses. As the rural recession deepened in the mid-1970s, many rural areas lost significant numbers of white residents, and the combination of vacant houses and some available funds for Aboriginal housing companies led to the first real breakdown of rural residential segregation. The housing companies were thus able to buy up the empty houses in previously white neighbourhoods.[113] Such a process continues to be partial and incomplete but to the extent that residential segregation has been challenged, it has been Aboriginal housing companies which achieved what gains have been made. Aboriginal goals have not been to have 'pepperpot' housing, however, and they continue to struggle with state housing authorities. These are now more inclined, with federal funds, to build homes in the rural towns where Aboriginal people choose to live but they still seek to separate Aboriginal families and in general refuse to build on Aboriginal reserve land.

CONCLUSION: LAND AND SOVEREIGNTY

Beyond the limited success of the housing companies, Aboriginal political action continued to focus on land issues through the early 1970s. It gained strength from the public awareness of the relative success of the land rights campaign in the Northern Territory but was grounded in 200 years of very local Aboriginal campaigns to regain traditional lands and reestablish an economic base in the south-east. The New South Wales Aboriginal Land Council was formed out of this movement in 1976. It included veteran land rights activists from the coastal movements of the 1920s, people from the west who had experienced the enforced moves of the 1930s as well as younger people involved in these issues for the first time. This body successfully lobbied the New South Wales Government to establish a Select Committee Inquiry into land rights, and out of this came the recommendation for land rights legislation in New South Wales which was eventually passed in 1983.

A related idea was beginning to emerge by the mid-1970s. This was sovereignty, an amorphous but powerful formulation of a number of strands which had been developing in Aboriginal politics. These strands included both criticism of the apparent reforms of the 1970s and a strengthening of the reassertion of Aboriginal culture and values.

Aboriginal mobilisation for equal and non-discriminatory access to education, housing and other public services was increasingly tempered in the 1970s by disillusion with an 'equality' which differed little from 'assimilation'. It still spelled 'the same as whites' and denied Aboriginal aspirations to develop their own cultural directions. The past decades had seen economic pressures continue to erode Aboriginal opportunities for employment, and government policy had in reality increased Aboriginal insecurity about their children and their place of residence. 'Equality' was often invoked in these circumstances only to make disadvantage permanent. With this rising sense of disillusion was a rejection of increased bureaucratic surveillance, well-established under the Welfare Board and expanding ever more rapidly under the diffusion of Federal and State departments with whom Aborigines were dealing after 1972.

This critique occurred at the same time as the developing cultural reassertion of the 1970s which included not only an appreciation of the rich quality of traditionally-based art and knowledge but a recognition of the dynamism of urban-based Aboriginal culture. Linked with the movement to regain lands, the cultural reassertion of the 1970s offered positive alternatives to the old 'assimilation' package still being offered. These trends were accompanied by another with powerful implications. The determination of Aboriginal people to gain access to educational resources finally succeeded, even if slowly at first, and the decade saw a growing number of Aboriginal lawyers and other professionals graduating and taking their places in either Aboriginal-controlled organisations or in mainstream positions.

None of these trends were entirely congruent, and as in the past, they have been refracted through the wide regional differences between Aboriginal community conditions. These were further diversified by the consolidation of large Aboriginal populations in Sydney and regional cities, despite the vulnerability of these urban communities to industrial unemployment. The concept of sovereignty developed influence and depth, as well as ambiguities, from the tensions between all these strands: critique, cultural reassertion and social change. These have continued to interact in complex ways, forming and reforming to shape the public face of Aboriginal political and cultural action throughout the 1980s and 90s.

NOTES

1 J.P.White and J.F.O'Connell, *Prehistory of Australia, New Guinea and Sahul*, Academic Press, Sydney, 1982; J.Flood, *The Archaeology of the Dreamtime*, Collins, Sydney, 1983; D.J.Mulvaney and J.Peter White (eds), *Australians to 1788*, Fairfax, Syme and Weldon, Sydney, 1987.
2 Noel Butlin, *Our Original Aggression*, Allen & Unwin, Sydney, 1983.
3 A.Ross, T.Donnelly and R.Wasson, 'The Peopling of the arid zone' in John Dodson (ed.), *The Naive Lands*, Longman Cheshire,

Melbourne, 1992; H.Lourandos, 'Intensification in Australian Prehistory' in T.D.Price and K.Brown (eds), *Prehistoric Hunters and Gatherers*, Academic Press, Sydney, 1985.
4   H.Reynolds, *The Law of the Land*, Penguin, Ringwood, [1989] 1992.
5   P.Grimshaw, M.Lake, A.McGrath, M.Quartly, *Creating a Nation*, McPhee Gribble/Penguin, Ringwood, 1994, p.22.
6   ibid, pp.10, 11, 22.
7   See Bernard Smith, *European Vision and the South Pacific: 1768–1850*, Oxford University Press, London, 1960.
8   Ann McGrath, 'The White Man's Looking Glass. Aboriginal–Colonial Gender Relations at Port Jackson', *Australian Historical Studies*, vol.24 no.95, 1990.
9   Described by Ann McGrath in *Creating a Nation*, pp.7–9.
10 Butlin, pp.11–41.
11 Keith Willey, *When the Sky Fell Down*, Collins, Sydney, 1979; Eric Willmot, *Pemulwuy: The Rainbow Warrior*, Weldons, Sydney, 1987; L.Brook and J.L.Kohen, *The Parramatta Native Institution and the Black Town: A History*, UNSW Press, Kensington, 1991; *Historical Records of NSW*, vol.5, p.513.
12 H. Goodall, 'Land in our own country', *Aboriginal History*, 13, 1991.
13 J.Mathews (ed.), *Two Worlds of Jimmie Barker*, AIAS, Canberra, 1977; R.H.W.Reece, *Aborigines and Colonists*, University of Sydney Press, Sydney, 1974; Roger Millis, *Waterloo Creek*, McPhee Gribble, Ringwood, 1991.
14 Crown Lands Commissioner for Gwydir, R. Bligh to Chief Commissioner, 8/1/1849, CCL Letters Sent, Gwydir, A-1849–1852, (State Archives, SA, 2/7634).
15 Bill Gammage, 'The Wiradjuri War 1838–40', *Push from the Bush*, 16, Oct. 1983, pp.3–17; Mary Coe, *Windradyne: a Wiradjuri Koorie*, AIAS, Canberra, 1989.
16 B.Hardy, *West of the Darling*, Jacaranda Press, Milton, 1969 and *Lament for the Barkandji*, Rigby, Adelaide, 1976.
17 Reynolds, *The Law of the Land*; H.Reynolds, 'Mabo and Pastoral Leases', *Aboriginal Law Bulletin*, vol.2, no.59, Dec. 1992, pp.8–10.
18 Reynolds, *The Law of the Land*, pp.146–50; and 'Mabo and Pastoral Leases'.
19 Reynolds, *The Law of the Land*, p.150.
20 Colonial Secretary's In-Letters (CSIL) Special Bundle: Aboriginal Reserves, 1849, (SA 4/1141.2).

21 See CSIL Special Bundle: Aboriginal Reserves, 1849, for individual recommendations, then, for decision, see Chief Commissioner of Crown Lands, Circular, 16 Feb. 1850, (CCL Gwydir, Letters Received, 1843 on, SA 2/7627); A.W.Mullen, Surveyor, Report on Brewarrina Fisheries, 8 Sept. 1906, (SA).

22 Earl Grey to Governor Fitzroy, 11 Feb. 1848; and Fitzroy's instructions to Crown Law officials, 18 July 1848. CSIL, Special Bundle: Aboriginal Reserves, 1849.

23 Surveyor General to Colonial Secretary, 27/11/1848, CSIL Special Bundle: Aboriginal Reserves, 1849; CCL Bligh to Chief Commissioner, 24/1/53, Governor's Despatches, vol.74, Mitchell Library, Microfilm CY1949.

24 H.Reynolds, *The Other Side of the Frontier*, Penguin, Ringwood, 1981; Barry Morris, *Domesticating Resistance: The Dhan-gadi Aborigines and the Australian State*, Berg, Oxford, 1990.

25 Commissioners for Crown Lands, Annual Reports on the Conditions of the Aborigines, for 1852 and 1853, collated in the Governor's Despatches, vols 74 and 75, Mitchell Library, Microfilm CY1949 and CY1950; B. Hardy, *Lament for the Barkandji*, Rigby, Adelaide, 1976; H. Goodall, 'A History of Aboriginal Communities in NSW, 1909 to 1939', unpublished PhD thesis, University of Sydney, 1982.

26 Ann Curthoys, 'Race and Ethnicity: a study of the response of British colonists to Aborigines, Chinese and non-British Europeans in New South Wales, 1856–1881', unpublished PhD thesis, Macquarie University, 1973.

27 Crown Lands Commissioner for Gwydir, R. Bligh to Chief Commissioner, 8/1/1849, CCL Letters Sent, Gwydir, A-1849–1852, (State Archives (SA): 2/7634).

28 Reynolds, *Law of the Land*, pp.32–33.

29 H. Goodall, 'Land in our own Country', p.5.

30 Goodall, 'Land in our own Country', p.22.

31 Ann Curthoys, 'Good Christians and useful workers' in Sydney Labour History Group, *What Rough Beast?* Allen & Unwin, Sydney, 1982.

32 Goodall, 'A History of Aboriginal Communities in NSW'.

33 S. Johnson, 'New South Wales Government Policy towards Aborigines, 1880–1909', unpublished MA thesis, University of Sydney, 1970.

34 Goodall, 'Land in our own Country'; Morris, *Domesticating Resistance*.

35 Goodall, 'A History of Aboriginal Communities in NSW'; J.J.Fletcher, *Clean, Clad and Courteous: A History of Aboriginal Education in NSW*, Southwood Press, Sydney, 1989.
36 Goodall, 'A History of Aboriginal Communities in NSW'.
37 Peter Read, *The Stolen Generations*, NSW Govt Printer, Sydney, nd, and Peter Read, *A Hundred Years War: The Wiradjuri and the State*, ANU Press, Canberra, 1988; Goodall, 'A History of Aboriginal Communities in NSW'; Goodall, ' "Saving the Children": Gender and the Colonisation of Aboriginal Children in NSW, 1788 to 1990', *Aboriginal Law Bulletin*, vol.2, no.44, June 1990, pp.6–12.
38 Goodall, 'A History of Aboriginal Communities in NSW'.
39 Goodall, 'Cryin' Out For Land Rights', in Burgmann and Lee (eds), *Staining the Wattle*, Penguin/McPhee Gribble, Ringwood, 1988; Goodall, 'Land in our own Country'.
40 Morris, *Domesticating Resistance*.
41 Goodall, ' "Saving the Children": Gender and the Colonisation of Aboriginal Children', p.7.
42 Margaret Tucker, *If Everyone Cared*, Grosvenor Books, Melbourne, [1977] 1987; J.Mathews (ed.) *The Two Worlds of Jimmie Barker*, AIAS, Canberra, 1977; Peter Read, *The Stolen Generations*; Coral Edwards and Peter Read (eds), *Lost Children*, Doubleday, Sydney, 1989.
43 Monica Clare, *Karobran*, Alternative Publishing Co., Chippendale, 1978; Commissioner J.H.Wootten, *Report into the Death of Malcolm Smith*, RCIADIC, 1989.
44 Coral Edwards, 'Is the Ward Clean?', in B.Gammage and A.Markus (eds), *All That Dirt*, Research School of Social Sciences, Australian National University, Canberra, 1982; Edwards and Read.
45 Ann Curthoys, 'Eugenics, Feminism and Birth Control', *Hecate*, vol.15, no.1 1989; Stephen Garton, 'Psychiatry, Eugenics and Child Welfare in NSW', *Historical Studies*, vol.22, no.86, Apr. 1986.
46 Moree Council recorded its decisions and actions in detail in its Minute Books, 1923 to 1933, and its strategies are confirmed in the APB, Child Welfare and Education Department archives. The long campaign against the town's Murris was recorded from the other side in the letters of the local missionary to his organisations' journal, *Our Aim*, see Goodall, 'A History of Aboriginal Communities in NSW', pp.204–15.

47 Marie Reay, 'A Half-Caste Aboriginal Community in North Western New South Wales', *Oceania*, vol.XV, no.4, June 1945; Goodall, 'A History of Aboriginal Communities in NSW', pp.160–85.
48 ibid, pp.186–215.
49 ibid, pp.216–52.
50 ibid, chapter 6 for a more detailed discussion of these Depression processes of exclusion.
51 ibid, pp.408–409.
52 Many of Cooper's later letters to the Commonwealth Government have been published in Andrew Markus' edited collection, *Blood from a Stone*, Allen & Unwin, Sydney, 1988. The letters to the NSW Premier and some copies of those to the NSW Protection Board are found in the NSW State Archives.
53 J. Horner, *Vote Ferguson for Aboriginal Freedom*, Australian and New Zealand Book Co., Sydney, 1974; Goodall, 'A History of Aboriginal Communities in NSW', pp.353–400.
54 *Australian Abo Call*, 4 July 1938.
55 Goodall, 'A History of Aboriginal Communities in NSW'; Tucker, *If Everyone Cared*; Horner, *Vote Ferguson*.
56 *AWB Annual Report*, 1948 and throughout the period.
57 *AWB Annual Reports*, 1941, 1943, 1945: 3 and 8.
58 *AWB Annual Reports* from 1948 throughout, but particularly 1948: 2, 1949: 4, 1953: 5, 1961: 6; See Read, *The One Hundred Years War*, for a discussion of the Exemption Certificates.
59 *AWB Annual Reports*, particularly 1949: 4, 1951: 4, 1952: 10, 1954: 3, 1958: 4, 1961: 6, 1963: 11.
60 *AWB Annual Reports*, 1948 to 1969, in particular 1957: 4, 1958: 4, 1961: 6, 12, 1963: 11.
61 *Namoi Valley Environmental Report*, NSW Govt Printer, Sydney, 1980.
62 *AWB Annual Reports* for this period; Joe Howe, Helen Hambley, Dick Hunter, Ray Peckham, *Report to the South Coast Trades and Labour Council*, Dec. 1961, p.4, held in SCTLC Archives.
63 Read, *A Hundred Years War*.
64 Morris, *Domesticating Resistance*.
65 *AWB Annual Report*, 1951: 4.
66 *AWB Annual Reports*, 1950: 6; 1951: 4, 1958: 5, 1959: 5, 1967: 10.
67 Goodall, 'A History of Aboriginal Communities in NSW', pp.160–85; *AWB Annual Report*, 1963: 5.

68 *AWB Annual Report* 1951: 4, and most later reports for similar statements, eg 1963: 5.
69 *AWB Annual Reports*, in particular 1949: 4, 1950: 6, 1960: 3&4.
70 Tom Evans, 'A Family History of Murrin Bridge Reserve', 1992, manuscript in author's possession, based on correspondence between the Lake Cargelligo Progress Association and the AWB, recorded in *AWB Minute Books*, 8/2949, 18458, held NSW State Archives.
71 *AWB Annual Reports* for these years.
72 Read, *A Hundred Years War*; Ann Curthoys, work in progress on Freedom Ride.
73 *People*, 26 Oct. 1960; *SMH*, 15 June 1960; Helen Hambley, interviews with author, 1988–89; Faith Bandler and Len Fox, *The Time Was Ripe: The Story of the Aboriginal Australian Fellowship, 1956–1969*, Alternative Publishing Company, Chippendale, 1983, pp.25,132; *AWB Annual Report*, 1961: 5.
74 *AWB Report*, 1963, p.4.
75 J.J.Fletcher, 'Collarenebri: An Attempt to Integrate Aboriginal Children', *Leader*, vol.6, no.1, 1975.
76 *AWB Report*, 1961.
77 *AWB Annual Reports*, 1951, p.4, 1952, p.8.
78 *AWB Reports*, 1961, p.5; 1962.
79 *AWB Annual Reports*, 1956, p.5; 1960, p.9; 1956, p.5.
80 *AWB Annual Report*, 1967, p.10.
81 Bandler and Fox, p.76.
82 Letter to the Editor, *Northern Star*, 9 Feb. 1959.
83 'Aborigines Not Ready For Assimilation', *Northern Star*, nd, 1959 or 1960, in 'Blue Wren' Scrapbook of Pastor Frank Roberts, Junior. Held by Roberts Family.
84 Letter to the Editor, *Northern Star*, 9 Feb. 1959.
85 Barbara Flick, 'Colonization and Decolonization: An Aboriginal Experience' in Sophie Watson (ed.), *Playing the State*, Allen & Unwin, Sydney, 1990.
86 Bandler and Fox, pp.117,133,167; *Sun*, 3 May 1956.
87 Read, *A Hundred Years War*; Margaret Sommerville and Patsy Cohen, *Ingleba and the Five Black Matriarchs*, Allen & Unwin, Sydney, 1990.
88 Bandler and Fox, p.61.
89 B.Fowler, 'Aborigines and the Welfare Board', Letter to the Editor, *SMH*, 6 Sept. 1960; AWB Report 1961, p.5.

90 Goodall, 'A History of Aboriginal Communities in NSW': Aboriginal recollections.
91 *AWB Annual Reports*, 1960, p.8, 1961, p.10, 1962, pp.10–12, 1963, p.12.
92 Faith Bandler, *Turning the Tide*, Aboriginal Studies Press, Canberra, 1989, p.35; Bandler and Fox.
93 NSW *Govt Gazettes*; *AWB Annual Reports* for these years.
94 *AWB Annual Reports*, 1960 to 1963, 1965, 1967.
95 Report of Joe Howe, Helen Hambley, Ray Peckham and Dick Hunter to the South Coast Trades and Labour Council, 1960, p.4. Held in SCTLC Archives.
96 Bandler, *Turning the Tide*, pp.35, 51.
97 Bandler and Fox, pp.81–92.
98 *AWB Annual Reports*, 1960, p.9, 1961, p.12, 1962, pp.4,10, 1963, p.7, 1967, p.5.
99 *AWB Annual Reports*, 1964 to 1968.
100 Phil Ayers, Vocational Officer, Brewarrina, 1971 to 1977: Personal Communication.
101 Bandler and Fox, pp.115–19.
102 See *SMH*, 26 Dec. 1964.
103 See also Ann McGrath, 'Beneath the Skin: Australian Citizenship, Rights and Aboriginal Women' in R. Howe (ed.), *Women and the State*, La Trobe University, Bundoora, 1993, a special edition of the *Journal of Australian Studies*.
104 *AWB Annual Report*, 1964.
105 Sources are scattered, including figures for conviction rates from 1945 in M.Reay, 'A Half-Caste Aboriginal Community'; from 1964 Brewarrina Police Charge Books, reviewed by Cunneen and Robb, in *Criminal Justice in North-West New South Wales*, Bureau of Criminal Statistics and Research (BSCR), Sydney, 1987; 1965 figures from a survey conducted by C.D.Rowley, in *Outcasts in White Australia*, Penguin, Ringwood, 1971; 1969 figures from an ABSCHOL survey in Walgett, reported in Peter Tobin, 'Aborigines and the Political System' in F.Stevens (ed.), *Racism and the Australian Experience*, vol.2, Australian and New Zealand Book Company, Sydney, 1972; 1974 figures from Peter Tobin, *Quarterly Report to the Aboriginal Legal Service* (typescript in author's possession) and from M.Parsons, *Report to the Aboriginal Medical Service*, 1974 (typescript, author's possession); NSW BCSR, 1973, *Minor Offences: City and Country*, Statistical Report 18; NSW BCSR,1974, *Court Statistics*, Statistical Report 6, Series 2; and

1979 and later figures from C. Ronalds et al, *Study of Street Offences by Aborigines*, NSW Anti-Discrimination Board 1982.
106 Scott Bennett, 'The 1967 Referendum', *Australian Aboriginal Studies*, no.2, 1985.
107 See the review of the Bourke *Western Herald* over these years by C.Cunneen and T.Robb, *Criminal Justice in North West NSW*. First 'law and order' calls were in 1971, and they intensified during 1974 and 1975 and thereafter.
108 *Directorate of Aboriginal Affairs Annual Report*, 1971, pp.7–8.
109 I.Mitchell and J.Cawte, 'The Aboriginal Family Voluntary Resettlement Scheme: An approach to Aboriginal adaptation'. *ANZ Journal of Psychiatry*, 1977, vol.11, no.29, A.K. Eckermann, B.Watts and P.Dixon, *From Here to There, Comparative study of Aboriginal rural–urban resettlement*, Qld and NSW. Department of Aboriginal Affairs, AGPS, Canberra, 1984.
110 P.Tobin, 'Aborigines and the Political System' in F.Stevens (ed.), *Racism and the Australian Experience*.
111 NSW Bureau of Criminal Statistics and Research, 1974, *Court Statistics*, Statistical Report 6, Series 2.
112 Minutes, Brewarrina ALS meeting, 16 Mar. 1975; ALS telegram to NSW Premier Lewis, 6 May 1975; *Dubbo Daily Liberal*, 9 May 1975; *SMH*, 8 Sept. 1975; *Australian*, 10 Sept. 1975; *SMH*, 9 Sept. 1975, 22 Sept. 1975; *SMH* 9 Sept. 1975; *Moree Champion*, 9 Sept. 1975.
113 M.Parsons, *Report To the Aboriginal Medical Service*, 1974; Widjeri Housing Co-operative, *Statement on Aboriginal Needs . . . for Bourke and Surrounding Areas*, Sept. 1974 (typescript, author's possession).

3
Victoria

SINCE 1802 when the party from the *Lady Nelson* surveyed Port Phillip Bay for future European settlement, the indigenous peoples who became known as Aboriginal Victorians[1], have suffered from the colonial condition. As the Tunisian scholar of colonialism, Albert Memmi, so clearly explained in the 1960s, the colonial process reshapes both stranger and native into the coloniser and the colonised.[2] The forces of colonialism reshaped Aboriginal Victorians into victims and voyagers.

As victims they were dispersed from their land, had their economy and their traditional world ruptured, and their autonomy severely curtailed. Pride and independence often gave way to dependence and self-doubt. Their world was never the same because of the European presence. They could never again frame their thinking without including the fact of the colonisers' existence and power. However colonialism is never completely victorious, for where there is power there is always resistance to that power. Since 1802 Aboriginal Victorians have maintained significant customary ideas and practices and continued to exercise considerable control over their destiny despite the pressures of colonialism. Colonialism is also strangely creative as well as being destructive. Many Aborigines have been voyagers: to borrow a term first used by W.E.H. Stanner in 1958 to describe Aboriginal agency.[3] Many have voyaged into the new cross-cultural world, exploring the possibilities and flexibilities of the Aboriginal–European interface to create new cultural forms.

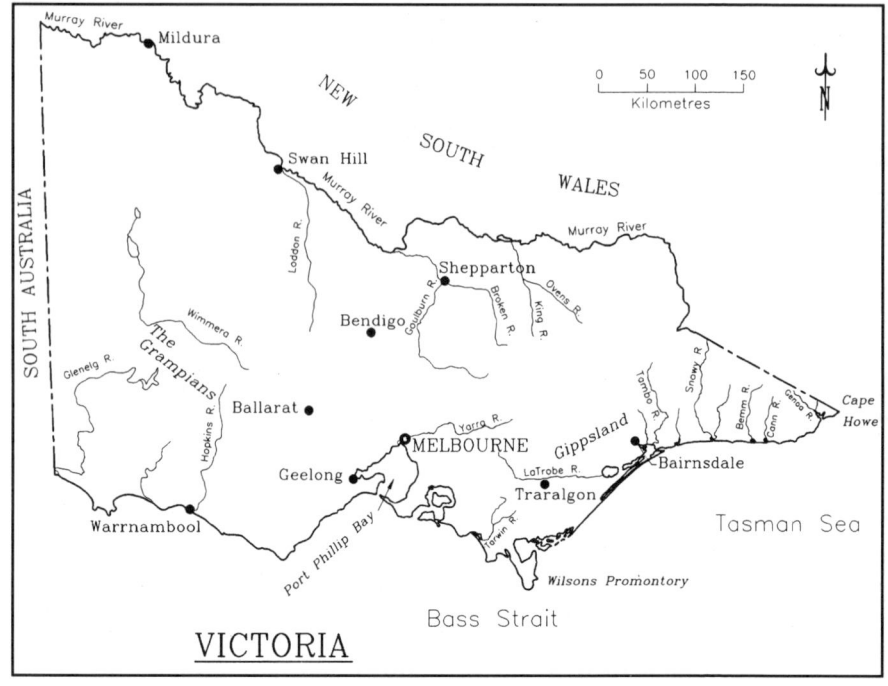

ABORIGINAL COUNTRY LONG TIME AGO

Aboriginal people are no strangers to change, for their world has been in a cycle of creation and recreation since Bunjil and Pallian breathed life into figures of clay and bark to make the first people. They taught these people to hunt and keep the law, before dispersing them across the face of the land now called Victoria.[4] Scientific, as opposed to traditional Aboriginal knowledge, poses not such a creation but an ancient migration from south-east Asia. Archaeologists presently identify a definite continuous Aboriginal occupation of the Keilor River terraces near Melbourne for the past 40 000 years.[5]

For perhaps 50 000 years, possibly much longer, Aboriginal peoples in Victoria have responded to massive environmental changes as significant as any in the last two million years. An ice age with temperatures up to 15 degrees C cooler than today forced them to use possum-skin cloaks, more adequate shelters, and different food sources. A warming climate 20 000 years ago caused the extinction of the megafauna, changed Aboriginal food supplies and caused a shift in totemic ideas. Rising sea levels climaxing 9000 years ago, reduced Victoria's area by a quarter as the coastal plains were flooded forming Bass Strait. Clan lands and boundaries were radically altered over generations. The archaeological record reveals technological change over 40 000 years, from crude to finely-ground stone tools, to the adoption of a bone and wood tool kit 5000 years ago.[6]

Throughout 1500 generations, ten times the gestation of the agricultural mode of production, Aboriginal Victorians shaped their relationship to the land. By 1802 they had formed themselves into about thirty different cultural-linguistic groups. Each linguistic group was composed of land-owning clans responsible for the land and its fertility. Each clan owned particular stories about the journeys and creations of the great ancestral beings. The natural world was shaped by, and still contained, the power of these great ancestors. People, land and ancestral beings were bound together in a oneness through a totemic relationship. Each person through their totem had power and responsibility to care for land and living things.

Clan affiliations attached people to the religious world while membership of bands organised the tasks of daily living. Bands of several families foraged for a rich diversity of animal, marine and vegetable foods with digging sticks, spears and other techniques. When the eels ran at places like Lake Corangamite or myriads of Bogong moths clung to dark crevasses in the High Plains, perhaps 500 people or more from many regional bands gathered to eat, socialise and discuss the weighty business of feud, marriage or ceremony. Others on the plains combined their labour to make massive nets to catch duck, emu or kangaroo.[7]

Theirs was an affluent life—if affluence is taken to mean that the basic needs of food and shelter can be easily met. Early European observations of Aboriginal eeling, fishing, vegetable gathering or possum hunting, reveal that a family could be fed with less than five hours of work. The only penalties were that the people had to maintain their population in balance and also keep on the move lest the law of diminishing returns set in when a group remained in one place for too long.[8] Yet in the Western District some groups about 3000 years ago overcame the problems of sedentary life by developing hydraulic farming. By expending considerable communal labour to build a complex system of stone water channels, some of which were up to 500 metres long and a metre deep, the Jaadwa, Tjapwurong and Gunditjmara peoples of the region became semi-sedentary eel farmers. They built villages of stone-walled, turf-roofed huts. One paddock near Lake Condah contains the ruins of 146 such houses.[9]

The long evolved life on the land was not ideal but it was probably closer to the ideal than achieved by many other human societies. A possum skin cloak and bush shelter were not always a comfortable protection against a Victorian winter, especially as the people had no means of heating water. Food gathering was a constant if not arduous task. Fighting between clans and domestic strife was a reality, and sorcery gave the hint of danger to every life. But kinship and local clever men could reduce such threats.[10] Over-arching all were the bonds of community, ceremony and the land, that gave each person a place in life and a sense of relevance and purpose. Into this tight-knit, autonomous world flowed the tide of European expansionism.

ENCOUNTERING EUROPEANS

The crew of Cook's *Endeavour* spied land off Point Hicks in the dawn light of 20 April 1770. Aborigines no doubt often saw the *Endeavour* as it coasted south-eastern Australia, for Cook recorded seeing their fires. Yet an Aboriginal–European encounter did not eventuate on the Victorian coastline until the wreck of the *Sydney Cove* in 1797 (of which we have few details), followed by a meeting in 1802 when the *Lady Nelson* surveyed Port Phillip. Yet before 1797 Aborigines felt the colonial sting of introduced disease. The weight of evidence suggests that smallpox which killed possibly half of the Eora (Port Jackson) people in 1790 spread southward along the rivers to much of central and western Victoria. Oral evidence records people fleeing before the scourge as scores fell, and sightings of pock-marked survivors by Europeans record the spread of the disease. A further outbreak occurred in 1830. There is of course no certainty because of the absence of an exact diagnosis, and some scholars remain sceptical,[11] but experienced contemporary opinion firmly believed it was smallpox. If smallpox death rates of between 40 to 60 per cent recorded among indigenous peoples overseas are applied to Aboriginal Victoria, it means the pre-contact Aboriginal population might have been not 12 000, as long thought but in excess of 60 000 people.[12]

Once Aborigines encountered Europeans, disaster often followed. Violence flared between the Bunerong and the crew of the British survey brig *Lady Nelson* at Sorrento in 1802. Curiosity, ambivalence and one Aboriginal death, resulted from a meeting at the Werribee River in late 1803 with Lt James Tuckey's party, which was surveying the bay for the abortive first European settlement at Sorrento. When this settlement was abandoned in 1804, William Buckley, a convict runaway, was left behind to make his own way among the Wathaurung near Geelong till 1835. His adventures were later graphically described in a life story.[13] Astonishingly, no further European settlement was attempted until 1826, when Corinella on Westernport became a military outpost for eighteen months. Then private enterprise in the form of the Henty family at Portland in 1834 and Fawkner's and Batman's parties at Melbourne in 1835, formed the first permanent European settlements in Victoria.

In May and June 1835 John Batman surveyed parts of the bay west of Melbourne and purportedly purchased 600 000 acres from the 'chiefs' of the Kulin—the five linguistic-cultural groups of south-central Victoria—on behalf of a Hobart syndicate of capitalists, the Port Phillip Association. Two deeds were drawn up, allegedly signed, and payments of blankets, tomahawks, flour and so forth were made. It was agreed to pay a 'yearly rent of tribute' in goods to the Kulin and their heirs in return for the land. By this purchase the syndicate sought to force the government to allow settlement of the southern coast and to play to the humanitarian lobby in Britain by their gestures of purchase and fair dealing. Governor Bourke moved swiftly to declare the purchase null and void and uphold the Crown's claim to eastern Australia made by Cook in 1770. Any recognition of Batman's parchment would be tantamount to an admission that the Aborigines, not the Crown, owned the land and had the right to alienate it.[14]

The Batman treaty is significant because it was the only purchase ever negotiated between Aboriginal owners and European intruders. However, were the Kulin the victims of a cruel swindle? The land exchanged for a yearly tribute of food and trade goods was worth in European contemporary terms of purchase a massive £150 000—at a time when a shepherd's annual wage was £50. One scholar has recently suggested that Batman even forged the signatures of the Aboriginal 'chiefs'.[15]

However, questions of swindles and hoaxes overlook Aboriginal understandings of the agreement. Certainly the communication of ideas would have been difficult between the parties despite the presence of Batman's Aboriginal guides from Sydney. Certainly the Kulin had no notion of land sales and would have rejected such an idea if they did understand the Europeans' desires. However, research by Diane Barwick reveals there were clan heads of great status among the Kulin. Five of the eight alleged 'chiefly' signatories of the treaty with Batman have been identified as being clan heads.[16] If these 'chiefs' agreed to the compact—even signed the parchment—what did they mean by it?

In the 1840s the Aboriginal Protector, William Thomas, observed the *tanderrum* ceremony by which visitors introduced by brokers were given temporary use of Kulin land.[17] Batman's overtures, complete with Aboriginal negotiators, gifts and conciliatory gestures, fitted into Aboriginal conceptions of negotiations. While they may appear to us as victims of a poor deal, in their terms they were landowners who it seems freely chose to give a small band of strangers access to land in exchange for some tempting items: flour, mirrors, beads and metal hatchets and blades. They recognised the efficiency of the latter instantly. Indeed, a week earlier Batman had peered into a woman's string bag and found a sharpened piece of iron hoop, obviously traded hundreds of kilometres from New South Wales.[18]

The Kulin were victims in this transaction yet voyagers too— meeting strangers, controlling them through negotiation, and gaining access to something novel of value. They were active agents who experimented in a new cross-cultural world. Some have called Derrimut, who warned Fawkner's party of an impending Aboriginal attack in October 1835, a traitor or collaborator.[19] Yet as a Bunerong clan leader he seems to have chosen negotiation over violence as a way of dealing with strangers.[20] Batman, who duly made payments on the first anniversary of the treaty, heightened the Kulin's understandings of the agreement. Reciprocity was their traditional governing principle and Batman fitted their pattern. Gift exchange was continued between the Kulin and Governor Bourke in 1837 and with the Aboriginal Protectors when they arrived in 1839. Aboriginal voyaging can be seen too in Marie Fels' important recent study of the Port Phillip Native Police. She reveals that the initial members of the force were all clan leaders or their sons, who used their role as policemen to enlarge their power and authority within Aboriginal society and at the cultural interface.[21]

Aboriginal accommodation and negotiation with white intruders did not always hold sway on the Port Phillip (after 1851, Victorian) frontier but the earlier historical paradigm of white violence and Aboriginal resistance drawn in the 1970s by some historians is clearly too simplistic. This is not to condemn the very important achievements of the first generation of Aboriginal historiography but only to recognise that our understandings have deepened throughout the 1980s. For instance, Michael Christie's *Aborigines in Colonial Victoria 1835–86* (1979) made important contributions, especially by challenging the stereotype of peaceful European settlement and Aboriginal passivity.[22]

However, by representing Aborigines as resistance fighters in the face of rapacious whites, he created a new and powerful stereotype of a violent frontier. To do this he made a number of questionable interpretations and omissions. First, like other earlier scholars,[23] he exaggerated the Aboriginal resistance by assuming to know Aboriginal motivation: namely a war of resistance against European intruders. This is to suggest a single motivation only, and one set in terms of race and a war for the land—concepts alien to traditional Aboriginal thinking from what we can know. Contemporary evidence suggests that some motivation is unknowable, while other actions were in the traditional

This portrayal of a violent encounter reveals a time when weapons technology on the frontier was more evenly matched. C. MUNDY, OUR ANTIPODES, 1852

mode of feud, and the upholding of Aboriginal law over ritual or social transgressions.[24] Secondly, Christie claims the Aborigines were overwhelmed because 'Aboriginal spears were no match for settler's guns', whereas the facts of pre-1850 weaponry suggest a more even contest.[25] This claim leads onto a third, that 2000 Aboriginal people were killed in Victoria making it a violent encounter. His figure is derived not from careful grassroots calculations but the application of the top end of an 1888 continent-wide 'guesstimate' by Edward Curr that 15–25 per cent of Aborigines died by the rifle. An Aboriginal death count of 2000 with only 59 Europeans killed by Aborigines, attributes to Victoria by far the highest black/white death ratio of any Australian frontier, whereas much evidence suggests it was one of the least violent of frontiers.[26] The Aboriginal death toll in Victoria is probably about half what Christie suggests, although Beverley Nance's calculation of 400 seems too low. Certainly Nance, who explores the role of sorcery and *inter-se* killings in Aboriginal society, shows how Christie has under-emphasised this traditional source of black deaths.[27]

Christie and others are correct to see the role of terror in Aboriginal–European relations—a theme that continued beyond the frontier, albeit in more subtle forms. But he and others of the 'violent frontier' school underestimate the range of frontier relations. Christie devotes only a paragraph to diseases (the greatest killers of Aboriginal people), fails to recognise the role of Aboriginal workers on the pastoral frontier[28], and overlooks the diversity of black–white relations including friendships, sexual liaisons and trade. A recent study of the Western District addresses this diversity and reveals the complexity of frontier encounters to reveal Aborigines as both victims and voyagers.[29]

Far greater than violence was the impact of pastoralism which in four years from 1836 transformed the economies of the Aborigines of central and south-western Victoria. This pastoral expansion—the most rapid in Australia, perhaps even in human history—engulfed most of arable Victoria by 1850.[30] Both hunting and gathering and the pastoral economic mode range widely and so there was direct competition over land and its resources: water and grass. The sheep displaced kangaroos and other herbivorous animals, and ate out the tasty murnong yams in several seasons. Duck, emu and bush turkey retreated before the European advance. While Aboriginal groups in marine and mountain ecologies fared better, those on the plains suffered greatly. William Thomas, an Aboriginal Protector, wrote in 1844: 'I do not think that of the five tribes who visited Melbourne that there is in the whole of the five districts enough food to feed one tribe.'[31]

Here was genocide: not in deliberate killing as others have argued (although this occurred too often) but in the unintended clash of two incompatible economic systems as pastoralism ground over the top of hunter–gatherer society. In wider perspective this was a clash between traditional itinerant land use and modernism. The six million sheep in Port Phillip and the farmers who followed were cogs in the capitalist–industrial system that stretched to the woollen mills of Yorkshire and to the jumpers on the backs and the food on the tables of an expanding world population.[32] Introduced diseases were another unintended consequence of contact. This is not to excuse the many killings but to recognise the process for what it was.

The outcome was swift for the Kulin and other Aboriginal Victorians. In 1835 there were an estimated 10 000 Aboriginal people in what became Victoria, while in 1853 only 1907 remained—a decline of 80 per cent in less than a generation. Violence caused about 10 per cent of the losses, disease, malnutrition and infertility accounted for most of the decline.[33] As this disaster was acted out, the European population grew to 45 000 in 1850 and by the end of the 50s gold-rush decade, to 330 000.[34]

The British authorities did not stand idly watching this destruction,[35] but their efforts to keep the peace on the frontier were often less than effective or even-handed. Cook's act of possession in 1770, without Aboriginal consent, had incorporated Aborigines as British citizens. One of the great colonial rationalisations for dispossession was that Aborigines gained the benefits of British civilisation, Christianity and protection. However, a British House of Commons Select Committee representing humanitarian opinion, claimed in 1837 that 'very little care has since been taken to protect them [the Aborigines] from the violence or the contamination of the dregs of our countrymen'.[36] The humanitarian lobby which captured the British Colonial Office at this time, caused Lord Glenelg, the Secretary of State for the Colonies, to remind Governor Bourke in July 1837 that Aborigines were subjects of the Queen and entitled to the full protection of Her laws.[37] The Port Phillip Aboriginal Protectorate (1839–49) flowed from this concern. The four Protectors under the Chief Protector, George Augustus Robinson, were, without coercion, to settle the Aborigines on reserves and teach them the virtues of a sedentary, Christian life.[38]

However, protection and equality under the law proved impossible in a cross-cultural situation. Language barriers, Aboriginal inexperience with the processes of British law, and the prejudices of European judges, juries and defence counsellors, all subverted the course of justice. Aborigines could not press charges or give evidence because they were pagans, and at times they were held co-operatively guilty for the crimes of others.[39] Only occasionally did the problems of cross-cultural law work to their advantage causing the court to release them from trial.

The administration of the law could be arbitrary. Following

Aboriginal reprisals on settlers in the Goulburn River area in 1840 Governor Gipps was pressured by the settlers to send a party under Major Lettsom to apprehend those responsible. After a raid in October on all the Goulburn people camped by the Yarra River in Melbourne, 400 were marched at sword point to the Melbourne Stockade. Protector William Parker secured the release of all but 30. One of the remainder, Nerruknerbook, was shot while attempting to escape: probably the first Aboriginal death in custody in Victoria. Nine were sentenced to ten years' transportation in a court that did not, could not, hear their evidence. While boarding a ship for Sydney, they dived overboard: leg-irons and all. One man was shot and recaptured, the rest apparently escaped.[40]

Cross-cultural justice was seriously flawed, despite good intentions in London, because it was the law of the colonisers, and this law was administered in a context of ethnocentric and racial ideas. These ideas were rooted in western discourses since the fifteenth century—about colour (given early expression in Shakespeare's *Othello*); about hierarchies and races of people; about diversity of cranial capacity; and about savagery, paganism and primitiveness—all of which constructed dark-skinned peoples as inferior.[41] These ideas which came as 'cultural baggage' to Victoria were compounded by colonial experience as two physically, culturally and economically divergent groups fought over land in an unequal colonial context. The tensions and frustrations led to violence. David Wilsone, a Werribee squatter, deep in debt and losing sheep to Aboriginal raiders, wrote home to Scotland in 1839–40 that the Aborigines were 'one link removed from the orang-outang' and should be exterminated.[42]

Yet these views were contested by those who employed Aborigines, those who had little trouble from them, and those young squatters, like Edward Curr and George McCrae, who counted them as friends. Katherine Kirkland at Trawalla Station was shown by Aboriginal women how to use murnong roots and sling her baby at her side as she worked. Many European men fraternised with Aboriginal women, albeit often in an exploitative way but some lived with Aboriginal women as companions as well as bed-fellows.[43]

European colonialism devastated Aboriginal society and perhaps predictably some fatalism resulted. In 1843 Billibellari, a Woiworung elder and 'signatory' to the Batman treaty, told William Thomas, the Aboriginal Protector, that many of his people say 'that no good have them Pickaninneys now, no country for black fellows like long time ago'. Yet switching from victim to voyager he added: 'if Yarra blackfellows had a country on the Yarra . . . they would stop on it and cultivate the ground'.[44]

The British Government's protective efforts ended with the closure of the Port Phillip Protectorate in 1849 after a colonial Committee of Inquiry deemed it an expensive failure. This committee, completely bereft of ideas, recommended 'that no hasty steps should be taken towards the introduction of a new system until more mature consideration can be given to the subject'.[45] Left to their own devices for the next thirteen years, the Aborigines survived through pastoral and agricultural work, supplemented by their traditional economy.

Although the gold rushes made them an even smaller minority in their own lands, the demand for their labour boosted their social standing. F. Jones, a Lucknow pastoralist, who was suffering the loss of his labourers to the goldfields in 1853, wrote of his Aboriginal workers: 'wanting their services I could neither have worked my sheep or secured my wheat crop this season . . . nor indeed could I have carried on the ordinary work of the station without their assistance'.[46] Jones paid his Aboriginal workers, although not at the European rate.

The Woiworung or Melbourne people made a significant contribution to the labour supply in the Plenty Ranges, weeding, harvesting and washing sheep. It was reported by William Thomas, a former Protector and now sole Guardian of the Aborigines, as being 'of the utmost importance to the community'. The young men in European-fashion scythed a respectable tally of a half-acre a day, while the older men knelt in traditional style to cut the grain. In the off-season they gathered lyrebird feathers and possum skins in the ranges for sale in Melbourne and lived off the land in the traditional way. Thomas often met them on the road, travelling for their master or bringing

Aborigines often worked alongside Europeans on the Port Phillip pastoral frontier. DETAIL FROM *GOING TO WORK* C 1850 BY S.T. GILL (1818–1880) WATERCOLOUR, 24.9 × 33.4 CM, NATIONAL LIBRARY OF AUSTRALIA

their guns to Melbourne for repair. Some owned horses and others were 'genteely dressed'.[47] A small government ration depot existed for their use at Warrandyte. Thomas remarked in 1857 that they rarely used its provisions but if 'the blacks have been at work around, would occasionally call, have a chat, ask for a stick of tobacco, then wind their way to their employment'.[48]

These people seemed to have assimilated to European ways. They certainly worked and dressed like rural labourers, owned horses and guns, and spent their surplus on alcohol and tobacco in the manner of pastoral workers. They were clearly independent like many rural workers of their day in times of labour shortages. However, when they took leave of their employers it was to follow Aboriginal desires—to visit with the Bunerong of Westernport, to travel to a ceremony or just return to their country. In 1853 William Thomas wrote in some despair of these workers:

> the hook, axe, or bridle down, and all further of civilisation for the day is over; off goes apparel and they bask under the canopy of heaven as in their primitive wildness, evidently enjoying their

freedom from encumbrance . . . such is their wandering
propensity, that all the kindness, entreaty or persuasion, cannot
secure them one day beyond their determination; and they have
lately been particularly cautious how they make bargains for
labour on this account.[49]

The Woiworung still corroboreed with the Bunerong and fought with the Gippsland people. In 1856 they even performed for the diggers at the Queen's Theatre, Melbourne, drawing audiences for a week. Yet the shouts, their staccato, angular movements, and the rustle of anklets of leaves at the theatre, came not from several score of dancers as formerly but six men. By 1857 the pressures of colonialism, disease, debilitation, violent death and despair had reduced the Woiworung to seventeen and the Bunerong to eleven people.

It was with a sense of urgency that these people conceived the need (as had Billibellari in 1843) for a place of their own. Seven Kulin men from the Woiworung and Taungerong (Goulburn River) peoples waited on William Thomas in February 1859 to seek his help to gain land on the Acheron River. The men, dressed in the coarse jumpers and fustian trousers of rural labourers, met with Gavin Duffy, the Minister for Lands a fortnight later. The *Argus* reported:

> they were all robust and well-made men, apparently equal in
> physical power to the average of Europeans . . . Their
> countenances were intelligent and animated. Their entrance into
> the boardroom was made in an unembarrassed and quiet manner
> and at a sign from Mr Duffy they seated themselves with an air
> of grave courtesy.[50]

Duffy, a prominent Irish nationalist and land reformer, who appreciated the land hunger in these men's eyes, and who was influenced also by a February 1859 Select Committee report calling for protective reserves, allowed the Kulin to select 4500 acres.[51] The Kulin pioneered the site but were moved off after protests by local European pastoralists. After three such moves the Kulin 'squatted' on a traditional site on the Yarra flats near Healesville in March 1863. They called it Coranderrk, after the white flowering Christmas bush that flourished there.[52]

UNDER THE HAND OF GOVERNMENT

A Central Board of Aborigines, the first of its kind in Australia, was created in 1860 to proclaim Aboriginal reserves, and oversee local protection committees and the distribution of funds. The Board managed reserves at Framlingham (1861), Coranderrk (1863), and indirectly controlled church mission stations at Ebenezer on Lake Hindmarsh (1859), Ramahyuck at Lake Wellington (1861), Lake Tyers (1861) and Lake Condah (1867) (see map below). It also controlled several small reserves and ration depots through a system of local guardians. The Board sought to protect Aboriginal people by segregating them on reserves, by educating and Christianising them, and by teaching them the

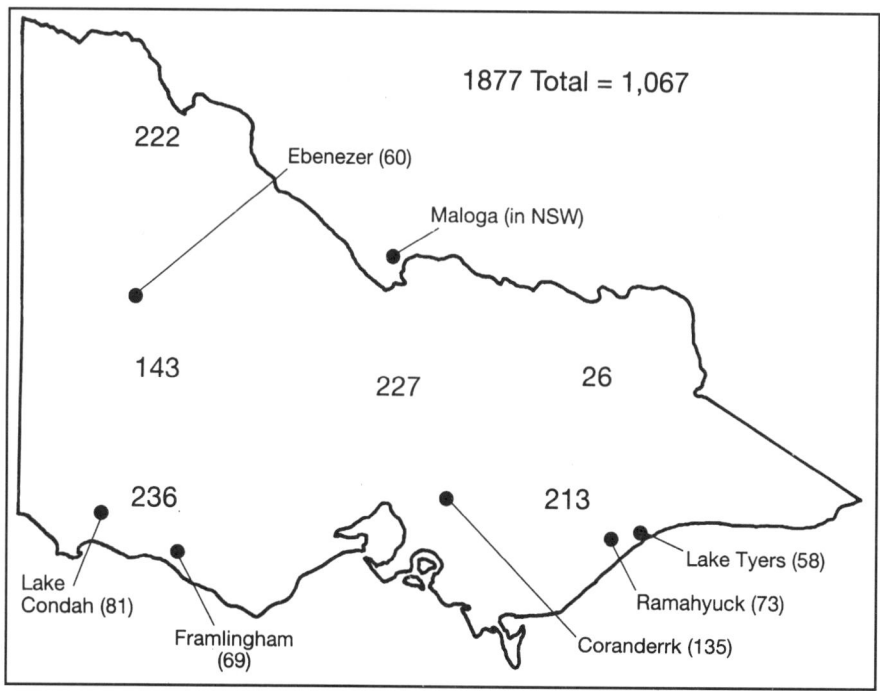

The distribution of the Aboriginal population of Victoria in 1877 by regions, including (in brackets) the various Reserve and Mission populations.

virtues of hard work and agricultural self-sufficiency. The Board's paternal agents tried to coax people onto the reserves, especially children considered 'neglected' or in moral danger. Most refused such suggestions and by 1869 only a quarter of Victorian Aborigines resided on the reserves.[53]

The Board wished to control Aboriginal movement and gained this power under the *Aborigines Act 1869* which reshaped the Central Board into the Board for the Protection of Aborigines. The new Board could prescribe where Aborigines should live, and control their work contracts and their earnings. It could remove Aboriginal children from their parents if they were deemed in need of care, protection and education. The children were removed to a reserve, usually Coranderrk, or an industrial or reformatory school. Later regulations empowered the Board to decide where children could be educated, and to direct children to live in a dormitory. People defined as 'Aborigines' under this 1869 Act included those of full descent, and so-called 'half-castes' and their children who habitually associated with Aborigines.[54]

While those on the reserves became victims of a protective and paternal Act, which paved the way for other such legislation in Australia, Aborigines also explored new ways of living. The people at Coranderrk, favoured by the fertile Yarra flats and the rare benevolent and non-interfering stance of the manager, John Green, formed a model agricultural settlement.[55] Green allowed those at Coranderrk to manage the farm work and their own internal affairs. They soon won acclaim for their pioneering from numerous influential visitors and their hops won first prize at the Melbourne International Exhibition. By the 1870s their houses were said to be superior to many belonging to the surrounding European rural workforce. Diane Barwick argues that the women were important in this cross-cultural voyaging and she reveals how many adopted Christianity and European material culture with zest.[56] On the other reserves there was a more regimented management, and it seems fewer Aboriginal responses to cross-cultural possibilities, as Aboriginal creativity was stifled.

Despite the Board's ability to order Aboriginal people to live on reserves, a police census of 1877 revealed that only 486 out of 1067 Aborigines in the colony did so. However there was a continual flow on and off the reserves but usually they moved only within the broad regions shown in the preceding map. Indeed the people often formed a new identity based on the reserve. They became Condah people, Lake Tyers or Coranderrk people, for as time went on, the reserves were also their birthplace and homes. Once the Moravian Mission at Lake Boga failed in 1857 the people on the Murray River had no local mission. Some drifted to Coranderrk or Ebenezer while others eventually developed a Cummeragunja identity based on the New South Wales reserve which emerged in the 1880s out of Daniel Matthews' settlement at Maloga.[57]

The reserves and their hinterlands formed the beat of the various regional groupings of Aboriginal people. They moved off the reserve to seek paid work, some variety of life or leisure and freedom from control. They went back to find the succour of community and familiar places. As in traditional times their movements were logical and regular. Particular pastoral stations or country towns were frequented. For instance in the 1870s the Kurnai based at Lake Tyers and Ramahyuck missions in Gippsland developed a relationship with hop farmers, Alfred and Liney Howitt of Eastwood. About thirty Kurnai left the missions annually to pick the Howitt's crop. Liney Howitt recorded in 1873 that the Kurnai were the fastest pickers and 'they are certainly the best, not a leaf left in their bins—quite [superior] to the white pickers in that respect'.[58] They earned up to ten shillings a day from the Howitts, equal to what they earned in a week at other rural work. The harvest time, coming as it did in late summer, provided a nice holiday as well as a lucrative interlude for the Kurnai. They felt secure with the Howitts who received them more warmly than farmers in surrounding country towns. Alfred Howitt gained from the visits too, for he discussed traditional life with the Kurnai and produced many papers and several books of lasting value in anthropological literature.[59]

A few Aboriginal men moved further afield. A dozen from the Madimadi and Wotjobaluk people of the Wimmera and the Mallee regions who worked in the pastoral industry played cricket for Edenhope. An Aboriginal team was formed in the district and it played exhibitions in Melbourne. Two players, Cuzens and

Off to beat the English at their own game: the Aboriginal Cricket Team, Sydney, 1867. *Back row, from left:* Tarpot, T.W. Wills (coach), Mullagh; *front row, from left:* King Cole *(foot on chair),* Jellico, Peter, Red Cap, Harry Rose, Bullocky, Cuzens, and Dick-a-Dick *(standing).* MITCHELL LIBRARY, STATE LIBRARY OF NEW SOUTH WALES

Bullocky represented Victoria in intercolonial matches. Promoters sensing their crowd appeal organised an Australian tour and then went to England in 1868, making it the first Australian team to tour the mother country. They played 47 matches in England, winning half, due to the skills of Lawrence, Cuzens and especially Johnny Mullagh. An exhibition of Aboriginal sports followed most matches.[60] After the tour Johnny Mullagh voyaged on in white ways, playing with the Harrow Club in the Western District till 1890. He was once asked by pastoralist Tom Hamilton why he never married and he replied: 'A white woman won't have me, Mr Tom, and I will never have a black one.'[61] Did he mean there were no available Aboriginal women or had he adopted the values of Europeans? Mullagh died in 1891 aged 50 at his camp on Pine Hills Station.

Once the Board gained greater powers after 1869, a struggle

developed between the Board and the Aborigines centred on Coranderrk. The Board sought to break up what it saw as a troublesome and costly reserve, beginning with the forced resignation of John Green. The people responded with letters of protest, petitions, press interviews, deputations and even strikes which occurred intermittently over a decade. They were supported by white sympathisers in Healesville and some radicals in Parliament. The Aboriginal protests invoked a Royal Commission in 1877 and a Parliamentary Inquiry in 1881, both of which recommended Coranderrk's retention and its refurbishment. This unrest at Coranderrk encouraged lesser insubordination on the other reserves.[62]

The Board, under fire from press, Parliament and Aborigines, began to lose faith in its founding ideology—paternal humanitarianism. The 1877 Royal Commission had already considered whether Aborigines should be segregated on reserves or absorbed into the community. There was considerable concern that reserve life pauperised the Aboriginal inmates. The able-bodied should be moved off to support themselves. This accorded with the prevailing middle class philosophy of self-improvement and self-reliance. Such a policy would also reduce the cost of reserves and remove troublemakers. Besides, new Social Darwinist ideas encouraged different policies for those of full and mixed Aboriginal descent, who it was claimed were at different stages of ability and acceptability due to differing degrees of whiteness.[63]

The Board framed the new *Aborigines Act, 1886*—a blend of old segregationist and new inclusionist thinking. Under this Act the reserves were to be retained for those deemed 'full bloods', 'half-castes' over 34, and their 'half-caste' wives and children. 'Half-castes' under 34 could live on reserves only under licence from the Board. Those unlicensed were to move into the general community but they could apply for rations, clothing and blankets for seven years to assist their transition into the wider society.[64] The Governor could make regulations for 'the care and oversight in the management or condition of half-castes, the apprenticeship of children and the removal of orphans to institutions'. Regulations were gazetted on 12 September 1890.[65]

The 1886 Act faced the real problem of what was to become

of reserve communities, especially those which were not economically viable. At that stage only Coranderrk paid its way. However it created a flawed and coercive solution. The artificial categorisation of Aboriginal people into 'full bloods' and 'half-castes' split families. The forced departure of the younger 'half-castes' deprived the communities of their muscle power which condemned them to economic oblivion and eventual closure. For instance the population of Framlingham fell from 94 to 35 after the implementation of the Act, while at Coranderrk it fell from 120 to 60, leaving only 10 able-bodied men.[66]

Those forced off the reserves often squatted nearby in humpies, although some of the Coranderrk exiles moved to the Maloga Mission on the Murray and later settled at Cumeragunja. Just as their rationing ended in 1893, they faced the worst depression in Australia's white history, which threw 30 per cent of Victorian breadwinners out of work, at a time when there was no social welfare except for private charity. Aboriginal people survived on occasional work, bush tucker and with the secret help of those on the reserves. A report in 1909 described those squatting near Framlingham as being in 'a wretched state', although J. Stahle, the manager at Lake Condah, reported that those near that reserve 'make an honest livelihood for themselves and families'.[67] The 1901 Census revealed that others moved further from the main reserves. Of the 652 Aborigines in the state, there were 46 Aboriginal people in Melbourne, 13 in the Colac-Geelong region, 16 about Ararat, 15 near Echuca, 8 in the Ballarat region, and 20 around Rutherglen-Benalla. Some of those off the reserves were successful. William Thorpe at Cunningham (Lakes Entrance) and George Thomas at Orbost raised large families in respectable circumstances.[68] But many others faced tough times. The Protection Board was forced to support distressed 'half-castes', and the Premier John Murray amended the Aborigines Act in 1910 to formally allow the Board to do so. However in practice aid was confined in most cases to the winter months.

Regulations gazetted in 1890 under the 1886 Act enabled the Board to send children, who were not orphans but who were deemed 'neglected', to the care of the Department for Neglected Children. They were sent for training: the boys to the Salvation

Army farm school for wayward boys at Bayswater, and the girls to one of several Homes where they were trained for domestic service. The Aboriginal artist Tommy McRae, a Kwatkwat man who frequented the Wahgunyah region, had his children removed over six years from 1891.[69] In 1900 eight other Aboriginal boys and two girls were taken, trained and sent out to situations. James Bray, the superintendent of the Salvation Army Bayswater farm school, in 1900 reported on the type of young inmates with whom the Aboriginal boys were forced to mix: 'some are unfortunately very vicious, and others are intellectually weak. But we are labouring on, feeling sure that patient perseverance will prevail.'[70] The Protection Board's vice-chairman, D. McLeod, who visited the farm school, thought the Aboriginal boys 'appeared to be very happy and content' and undergoing training sure 'to make them upright and intelligent members of the community'.[71]

The Aboriginal population was under considerable stress in these post-frontier years. Not only did the Board harass them, and after 1886 broke up Aboriginal families but their population levels plummeted. Their numbers declined by more than half in the two decades after 1860: from 1907 in 1863 to 870 in 1882. In 1901 they numbered 652 and their population fell to its lowest level of just 586 in 1921. This decline stemmed largely from high rates of adult and child mortality. Barwick found from details of the deaths of 698 people on the reserves between 1876–1912, that approximately two-thirds died under the age of 40, and 40 per cent died from respiratory diseases: mostly tuberculosis. Women who bore children between 1857–1904 lost half of them, those who bore children between 1885–1925 lost over a third, and women who bore children between 1902–1944 lost a quarter of their offspring. By the 1960s child mortality rates had declined to 5 per cent, still twice that of the white population.[72] These mortality rates were caused by poor housing and hygiene and a meagre standard of living both on and off the reserves. Even the model settlement at Coranderrk was in decline by the 1880s and reserve housing has been inadequate ever since. Of course those forced to live in bag humpies off the reserves generally suffered high levels of ill-health as well.

Population losses and the policy of absorption led to the decline of most reserves. The Board's decision to close them down sealed their fate. Ebenezer was shut in 1902 and the Board closed and sold most of the others by 1923. The residents of Ebenezer and Ramahyuck, and most of those from Lake Condah, Coranderrk and Framlingham were dispersed and the remnants transferred to Lake Tyers in the early 1920s which was enlarged and refurbished. However, a handful of elderly people were permitted to remain at Coranderrk until they died, while a few resisters squatted at Framlingham which remained unsold. Apart from three annual reports in the 1920s, the Board ceased its annual reporting to Parliament in 1912. Thus its management at Lake Tyers remained closed to Victorian eyes.

MAKING A LIFE IN VICTORIA

The removal of Aboriginal people to Lake Tyers in Gippsland where a strict regime operated, increased numbers there from 50 to about 250. The *Aborigines Act 1915* and its regulations, consolidated in 1928, laid down that the manager was 'to supervise the good order and conduct of the stations', their rationing, work on the stations, and the 'moral and social welfare' of the inmates. The matron was to visit dwellings daily and give instructions on cooking, washing, sewing and to oversee the cleanliness of the station. Those wishing to leave the reserve for work or social reasons had to seek the manager's permission. The Board and the manager were instructed to discourage departures, and the granting of travel monies was only made in the most extreme circumstances. People could be removed for misconduct or if considered able, to earn their living off the reserves. 'Half-castes' could live on the reserve under licence but were liable to be expelled for insubordination. Those classed as 'quadroons, octoroons, and half-caste lads' were to leave the station at the age of eighteen and were allowed to visit only at the manager's discretion, and for no more than ten days at a time.[73]

Despite such rigid controls, oral tradition recalls there were good managers at Lake Tyers. Captain J.A. Newman introduced many economic and material improvements and encouraged the people to direct their internal affairs themselves. He only managed Lake Tyers for two years from 1929 but remained in the district and offered work to Aborigines who moved off the reserve. Major Ronald Glenn, who was there from 1931 to 1945 was less well regarded but he encouraged sport which gave the people pride and a chance to leave the reserve temporarily. Also, some regulations came to be administered in a lax way during the 1940s, especially those requiring 'half-caste' residents to be licensed to stay.

Overall, the reserve had a history of controversy. The inmates continually subverted the system and occasionally went on strike. Aboriginal, church, welfare and other interested groups, were outspoken about conditions at Lake Tyers, especially after World War II. From the 1940s the Board was continually on the defensive as the Australian Aborigines' League (see below), then led by Bill Onus, criticised conditions, the lack of freedom and the lack of a future at Lake Tyers.[74] White support groups joined the chorus of criticism. Yet Lake Tyers' oral history recalls many good times at this place they called 'home'.[75]

The 1920s marked the low point of Aboriginal numbers in Victoria, different estimates ranging from 402 to 586 in 1921, a point dangerously close to the extinction of a people. By 1933 estimates ranged between 1034 and 1229, before climbing slowly to between 1796 and 2989 people in 1961.[76]

The large discrepancies in the population estimates reflect the tenuous existence of the Aboriginal community off Lake Tyers and beyond the control and therefore interest of the Aboriginal Protection Board. These people lived in small communities, often in fringe camps, in places traditionally familiar to them across the state. For instance in 1926, families comprising 40 people were living in make-shift housing by the Wimmera River near Antwerp supporting themselves by seasonal work.[77] Aboriginal breadwinners and their families followed the cycle of fruit and vegetable picking with its concomitant poor housing and health care, intermittent wages and interrupted schooling. Those living outside the Aboriginal Acts in Victoria had theoretical rights not enjoyed elsewhere in Australia. They could drink alcohol legally if they chose, their children could attend any state school and they had the franchise. Yet in practice, their itinerancy precluded them from the vote, prejudice and reticence kept some from school, and customary practices saw them refused alcohol at many hotels.

Most white Victorians knew little of the camping, itinerant lifestyles of Aboriginal Victorians, and many of those who did were hostile or indifferent to them. Nineteenth century ideas that Aborigines were primitive and genetically inferior still thrived in the 1930s and beyond. Such flawed thinking was encouraged by scholars. For instance, the eminent Sir Baldwin Spencer, Professor of Biology at Melbourne University, claimed in 1926 that the structural simplicity of the Aboriginal brain meant 'he is like an overgrown child in matters of character and emotional expression' and was ill-suited to higher forms of education.[78]

With the coming of Depression, one Aboriginal community at Framlingham near Warrnambool, became newsworthy. In December 1933 the *Warrnambool Star* exposed the appalling conditions of 70 people who lived in bag huts adjoining the Framlingham reserve. They had no assistance from the Board because of their mixed descent yet did not get help from the Sustenance Department because they were Aboriginal. Nor did they receive child endowment or the old age pension. They survived on dwindling amounts of rural work, rabbiting, and a few dairy cows. Their children rarely attended school. J.A. Rollo, Shire President, remarked that in Warrnambool 'the colour bar is very real. They are half-starved now and they are increasing in numbers. Unless something is done the problem will become acute. They may be forced to steal. It is not possible for them to get work.'

The government and the Protection Board, together with a local citizens committee, provided sustenance, a school was planned, and some land was to be made available for farming.[79] The *Herald* commented in racial terms that the Board must accept responsibility for 'all those persons who had too much aboriginal blood to hope to compete on an equable basis with white men, or it must find some way of ridding the state of the squalid and undesirable settlements which are growing up'.[80]

Others chose material hardship to escape the regimentation of Lake Tyers reserve. For instance a number of families collected at a fringe camp, Jackson's Track, near Jindivick in the Drouin area. There, amidst material difficulties, Lionel Rose, future world bantamweight champion, and others grew up. Euphemia Mullett who raised twelve children there in the 1950s recalled:

> Our house was made from bark, and the roof was made of bark too but it never leaked. When it got older you changed the bark. It was nailed onto wooden poles. The chimney was made of scraps of tin. We used sugar bags, not glass, over the windows and to partition the rooms. In the living quarters, where we had to eat, we had a table made with four posts in the ground. We used to sit on kerosene tins, or a box. We used to have a dirt floor . . . There was no showers, or no running water or anything. We used to get our water from the creek—carry it up in kerosene tins, not buckets.[81]

However, she added that the water was 'better than the water we get now'. Indeed, there was a great happiness at Jackson's Track despite the difficult conditions—for there was plenty of bush to roam in, a school nearby for the children, and a close-knit family life of singalongs, prayer meetings and Christmas parties. Euphemia's son, Russell Mullett, recalled, 'we were free at Jackson's Track. Anybody could come and visit . . . the Manager of Lake Tyers wouldn't hassle us.'[82]

Some lived in materially better circumstances. Percy Pepper and his family farmed a soldier settlement block at Koo-Wee-Rup after his discharge from the First AIF. The family did well until flooding and poor drainage forced them and other returned men off their blocks. One of the sons, Phillip Pepper, who was married on the eve of the Depression, survived it by cutting timber, bean picking and doing 'susso' work on the roads.[83] Joseph Wandin, a Coranderrk descendant, trained as a teacher and was admitted as an Education Department teacher in 1901—staying in the service until 1950.

Despite being on the fringe, some Aboriginal people made an impact on the wider society, notably in sport. The *Herald* football commentator reported in 1929 that 'for speed, dash, untiring energy and spectacular leaping at the ball no player in Association football surpasses Doug Nicholls, who has been one of Northcote's best men in the season's matches'.[84] The reporter also

Unidentified Aboriginal camper on the track in the Mallee, 1944.
HERALD AND WEEKLY TIMES LTD

referred to his athletic prowess. Lynch Cooper from Cumeragunja won various sprint titles, including the prestigious Stawell Gift in 1928 and the World Sprint Championship in 1929. Those at Lake Tyers also excelled. The cricket team were local premiers in 1933–35, and the football team were district finalists from 1934 to 1936.[85] An Aboriginal football team played in a Melbourne competition in the 1940s. Some had more local but equally respected reputations. Pelham Cameron who died at the age of 79 at Dimboola, was reportedly 'highly respected in the district' a prominent local cricketer, footballer and rower.[86] The Clarkes of Framlingham also established reputations as sportsmen.[87] From the 1930s Aboriginal boxers made their presence felt in the boxing tents and in championship circles.[88] Others contributed to other forms of combat through war service.[89]

Aboriginal politicians also emerged in the 1930s. The initial impetus came from Cumeragunja residents who had moved to Melbourne and settled in Fitzroy. The Cumeragunja community had developed a fierce sense of independence fostered by economic success and the influence of Thomas James, a Mauritian of Indian extraction, who married into the community. James was the Cumeragunja school teacher for 40 years to 1921, and he developed a forthrightness in the people and the ability through education to press their case.[90] Their independence was reinforced by a weak Aboriginal administration from distant

The sporting children of Frank Clarke of Framlingham pictured about 1915. From left, Norman, Jessie, Fleetwood and George. The Clarke men would attend country sports meetings for enjoyment and the chance to earn 'a quid' in a foot race or a boxing match. AMY LOWE, WARRNAMBOOL

Sydney. James moved to Fitzroy in the 1920s and was outspoken on Aboriginal affairs. For instance, in June 1929 he publicly criticised discrimination against Aborigines in employment.[91] James' brother-in-law, William Cooper of Cummeragunja, came to Melbourne in 1930. In 1933 when aged 72, he organised a petition to King George V. It called for Federal control of Aboriginal affairs, for an advisory council including an Aboriginal representative to oversee policy, and for an Aboriginal member of Federal Parliament. Over 2000 Aboriginal signatures were collected in all states by 1937 but the petition never left Australia. The Federal Government decided that as the King had no control over constitutional change it was pointless. Besides, the government wished to avoid any embarrassment. Cooper formed the Australian Aborigines' League in 1934. He also conceived the brilliant idea of keeping the 150th anniversary of Australia Day in 1938 as a Day of Mourning which caught the attention of

Pastor Doug (later Sir Doug) Nicholls makes another point for the Aboriginal cause. HERALD AND WEEKLY TIMES LTD

Prime Minister Lyons and inspired Aboriginal protestors 50 years later. In the early 1930s Cooper also enlisted young Doug Nicholls to the struggle. Nicholls became the inspirational force in Victorian Aboriginal affairs for the next 30 years.[92]

Those at Cumeragunja made another coup by striking against the management of the New South Wales Aboriginal Welfare Board in February 1939. The subsequent walk-off from the reserve and the formation of a camp at Barmah received considerable public support in Melbourne, with sympathisers taking car loads of food and clothing to the strikers. Few of the strikers returned to Cumeragunja and most eventually settled in bag and tin humpies on the river bank at Mooroopna.[93] They received no official help as the Victorian Chief Secretary stated in antiquated racial terms, that they were not Aborigines: 'they were quadroons, octoroons and of like colour, and were ordinary citizens, entitled to the benefits and privileges of citizens, also their responsibilities'.[94] Yet he ignored the reality that they defined themselves as Aborigines and were seen and treated as such by white Victorians. These fringe dwellers lived in stigmatised limbo—as Aborigines but not recognised officially as such—until 1957.

Amidst growing criticism, the Bolte government in 1955 appointed Charles McLean, a retired chief stipendiary magistrate, to enquire into the state of Aboriginal Victorians, their administration and their place in the community. McLean reported in early 1957 after visiting Aboriginal communities, interviewing Doug Nicholls, Shadrach James, local and Board administrators, teachers, police and others, and taking written submissions from interested people and organisations.

McLean counted 1346 Aboriginal people living in Victoria: about half the number estimated by anthropologist Diane Barwick several years later.[95] He reported that most rural Aborigines lived in squalid humpy-conditions except for those at Lake Tyers and Framlingham. Those in Melbourne lived in overcrowded slum or condemned housing. McLean rejected any innate mental differences between Aborigines and whites. However, he ascribed their lack of adequate housing, jobs, education and health, partly to their inclination to rove, to drink, to share resources and to act improvidently. He also ascribed it to white prejudice.

McLean, asked to consider 'the absorption' of Aborigines into the general community, recommended new Aboriginal welfare legislation. In respect to Lake Tyers, he called for a 'helpful but firm, policy of assimilation'. There should be a return to the spirit of the 1886 Act 'to encourage or force' the able-bodied off the reserve, and the reserve should be reduced twenty-fold to 200 acres, to be set aside for the care of those unable to fend for themselves. The definition of 'Aborigine' should be widened in the new Act to include 'any person having an admixture of Australian aboriginal blood'. For those not on Lake Tyers, he recommended an 'active policy of assimilation' by a new welfare board and its officers, to counteract the disadvantages these people experienced in housing, education and employment. It was a hopeful policy 'directed to the social and economic uplift of the aborigines throughout the State, to the end that they may take their place in the ordinary life of the community' and it mirrored Hasluck's assimilationist efforts at the Federal level. However, McLean's assimilationist drive meant that

Aboriginal people had to become like ordinary Victorians: like it or not they were to be remade.[96] The Victorian Government quickly passed into law the *Aborigines Act, 1957* along the lines suggested by McLean, ushering in a new era of bureaucratic interventionism.

The new Welfare Board set about assimilating the state's Aboriginal people. Since Aboriginal humpies had been emblazoned in the press as the most evident 'Aboriginal problem', the Board began to rehouse the people. It proudly opened the Rumbulara Housing Settlement near Mooroopna in 1958. The ten prefabricated concrete houses without internal doors, and with slot-machine electricity meters, were to teach Aboriginal campers to live in European houses. When they were deemed suitable they could graduate to a house in town, amidst other Victorians. A similar project opened at Manatunga outside Robinvale in 1960. However, by 1961 the Board abandoned this idea for houses scattered in country towns. Here it met resistance from white residents who objected to having Aboriginal neighbours, for fear of declining standards and property values. The Board finally handed its housing efforts to the State Housing Commission when its own tardy efforts were unable to keep pace with increasing Aboriginal housing needs. The Commission continued the policy of scattering Aboriginal housing in white areas, to increase the chances of breaking Aboriginal kin networks and forcing assimilation. Some of those at Lake Tyers were bribed from the reserve with housing.[97]

The Welfare Board also continued the policy, in place since the 1886 Act, of absorbing the mixed descent population by the removal of children. Albert Mullett recalled how his family kept on the move in the 1930s to avoid the Board's grasp.[98] Aboriginal singer Archie Roach was in and out of foster homes and institutions until he was placed with a Scottish couple who brought stability, if not a clear identity, to his life.[99] Melissa Brickell was taken from her mother by police who plucked them off the street in Fitzroy. Melissa, aged six, allegedly looked 'neglected', and for that 'crime' did the rounds of institutions for a number of years.[100] It is unclear how many Aboriginal Victorians suffered similar fates. Fortunately, the Aboriginal Protection Board of Victoria was moribund and inefficient from the 1930s, which led to fewer Aboriginal children being forced into state care. However, in 1955 there were still 24 Aboriginal children in the Ballarat orphanage alone and Diane Barwick reported there were over 150 Aboriginal children in state children's institutions in 1956–57, about 10 per cent of Victorian Aboriginal children.[101]

The Aborigines Welfare Board continued this policy of removal as part of its aggressive assimilation policy. It is likely that removal of children was a basic reason for the unsettled element within the Aboriginal community. In 1974 Barwick said of the Aboriginal family: 'the majority of adults heading today's problem families, those most likely to lose their children, were themselves reared in institutions and have never known the secure affection of family life or experienced the socialisation processes of their own community.'[102]

Archie Roach, who did not even know he was Aboriginal till he was fourteen, became in his own words 'a hopeless drunk' until he developed an identity with the help of the Fitzroy Aboriginal community. Melissa Brickell felt unloved and angry through her teenage years until found by her mother.

The policy of removal was officially ended in 1968 by the new Ministry for Aboriginal Affairs but the trauma of removals would last for decades.[103] For instance, existing placements continued and some new ones probably occurred because the Victorian Aboriginal Child Care Agency (VACCA) reported that until 1977, 90 per cent of Aboriginal children placed in white homes were eventually returned to institutional care. VACCA was established by concerned Kooris in 1976. By 1978 it became government policy to consult VACCA on all Aboriginal child placements with the aim of keeping them wherever possible in their family or the Aboriginal community.[104] The personal tragedies of removal remained unknown to most white Victorians until the widely publicised case of Russell Moore (James Savage), a Victorian-born Koori, who was convicted for murder in Florida in 1989. After much legal argument about the trauma of his removal from his mother when only four-weeks old and his upbringing by a white family in the United States far from his roots, his death sentence was commuted.[105]

In the early 1960s a ginger group within the Welfare Board, led by a Monash University academic, Colin Tatz, produced a policy document which modified the hard assimilationist line and allowed Aborigines to retain their cultural identity if they so desired. However internal dissension and external criticism of the Board, especially over the fate of Lake Tyers, led to the creation of the Ministry for Aboriginal Affairs in 1967. This Ministry was Federally funded, bulging with staff, including Aborigines, and driven by a belief in social engineering. Its 1974 report boasted: 'the Ministry believes that social engineering principles are as fundamental as any relating to the physical sciences. The programs which have been developed and maintained in this State, based on these principles, are a clear demonstration of the validity of this claim.'[106]

This social engineering was to end with the merging of the Aboriginal and white segments of the population as Aborigines reached full equality and lost their identity. It was still assimilation but with a softer face. However, by the early 1970s, Aboriginal Victorians began to reassert their identity and run their own affairs. The Ministry's reports became increasingly defensive. With relief—and the relief of those it sought to serve—its powers passed to the Federal Department of Aboriginal Affairs in January 1975. A small bureaucracy was later re-established. An inter-departmental committee was established in Victoria in 1979 to co-ordinate Federal Aboriginal programmes in this state. In 1982 the Premier's Department established an Aboriginal-staffed unit to liaise between the government and Victorian Aborigines. The departments of Health and Education also established Aboriginal advisory units.

KOORI RESURGENCE

Until 1974 the Victorian Government sought to make Aboriginal people into 'ordinary Victorians'. However, Aborigines resisted these efforts. Diane Barwick found that by 1960 'probably only a half-dozen elementary families or households now scattered throughout Victoria so completely assimilated or absorbed into the larger society that their earlier identification and association with Aborigines is no longer meaningful to them'.[107] The other 90 per cent (about 3000 people in 1960) continued to see themselves as a distinct people. Many now called themselves 'Kooris'—an imported New South Wales term—as distinct from white Victorians, who they called 'Gubbas'.[108] Yet, despite the development of a pan-Koori feeling, historical regional loyalties persisted to form three broad Koori groupings which remain today: the Yorta-Yorta (Cumeragunja–Shepparton people), the Ganai (Kurnai) from Gippsland, and the Western District people. These groupings reflected family and historical affiliations which in the 1960s created an in-marriage rate of 90 per cent. It is likely that the drift to Melbourne has weakened these affiliations and the regional ideas and suspicions upon which they are based.[109]

Over five generations, colonialism has taken its toll on traditional cultural ideas. Recent investigators found few remnants of language, religious ideas and rituals.[110] Aboriginal genetic heritage was also diluted—Philip Pepper claimed there were only two 'full-bloods' in Victoria in 1985.[111]

However cultures are dynamic. Aboriginal people today are not 'traditional', yet they are no less Aboriginal. They have a strong culture and identity based on elements of their traditional heritage and ideas formed by 150 years of both opposition and accommodation to the European presence. Kooris retain distinct kinship relations and tight family bonds which shape marriage, household structure, family and child-rearing practices, and also their ideas about reciprocity and sharing. Their dances and socials, weddings and funerals, reaffirm their Koori identity. In the 1960s only 11 per cent of married men and 27 per cent of married women had married outside the Koori community, and those who did so sometimes disappointed their fellow Kooris.[112] The people still have a strong affiliation with the land, particularly the reserve or region from which their family derived. Many still believe in bush remedies, magical happenings and spiritual connections with deceased kin. In this Koori world of common understandings, most people put kin and family before self and personal ambition.

This cultural bonding infused Koori political action over the past generation in defence of their heritage. In 1958 some white Victorians, including Doris Blackburn and Stan Davey, together with Doug Nicholls and other Kooris, formed the Victorian Aboriginal Advancement League (VAAL). VAAL soon had an office, a magazine called *Smoke Signals*, and a full-time field officer, Doug Nicholls. Initially it fought Aboriginal inequality and injustice on a wide front but it quickly began to concentrate on Victorian matters. After much struggle the League provided two Melbourne hostels for young people, a holiday programme, and established a network of supporting branches. Its Kew branch fostered a Cumeragunja farm project in 1965.[113] In 1963 the League led a vigorous and successful fight to stop the Welfare Board dismantling Lake Tyers. Indeed, the government gazetted it as a permanent reserve in 1965, and in 1971 the 4000 acre reserve was handed over to about 40 members of the community under communal freehold title. Under such title each member held trust shares that prevented any future sale of the reserve if any one member objected. However this victory was marred by a protest march and petition from 213 other Koori people who also claimed rights to Lake Tyers.[114] The Framlingham community also received communal title to 500 acres of land under the same *Aboriginal Lands Act 1970*—the first hand back of land in Australia.

In 1962 the old Australian Aborigines' League was reformed as a separate Aboriginal branch of VAAL. This Aboriginal branch developed a more political emphasis than VAAL's earlier welfare approach, which eventually led to a split and the Aboriginalisation of the VAAL executive in 1969, amidst controversy and financial pain. This upheaval reflected a growing trend for self-management and calls for land rights by Kooris. In January 1971, the Koori artist Lin Onus and three other Kooris, occupied Sherbrooke Forest. They demanded land rights, the protection of Aboriginal culture and better welfare measures. Those at Framlingham claimed 6000 acres of the forest adjoining the reserve. Following Sydney trends, Aboriginal-run legal, housing and health services emerged in Melbourne after 1972. There has been a continuous creation of Aboriginal community organisations ever since.

All this activity reflected and fostered a resurgence of Aboriginal identity. The word 'Koori', a secret, insider word, was first used publicly in 1969 when a Koori Club was formed in Fitzroy, and the word soon became a badge of pride. Various study programmes arose to foster Koori self-esteem. One Koori high school student from Victoria, Jill Johnson, wrote to the magazine *Identity* in 1972:

> Before the whiteman came to this country our wise men were greater than the world's best scientists, our tribesmen survived in the most harsh conditions . . . but times have changed. We have to show the Europeans that we are as good as they are, even better. I am in a Black Studies Group which studies Aboriginal culture and reveals many astonishing facts about our people . . . Watch out, whiteman, these Aborigines are stepping out.[115]

In 1983 Worawa College, a residential school for Koori children, was opened at Frankston and now operates from Healesville. It provides a standard Victorian education with the addition that for one hour a day the children study Aboriginal culture. After a year the school noted academic improvement and a greater sense of responsibility and independence among most students. One student, Naomi Atkinson, stated: 'I am glad to be with my own people in this school where we learn our culture which is great. I have learnt more about my own people than I have learnt before and I am now proud to be black.'[116] The development of an Aboriginal consciousness was also reflected by the creation in the 1980s of the Koori Information Centre, the Aboriginal Cultural Heritage Unit of the Museum of Victoria, and the Koori Oral History Programme. A group of women in Collingwood founded the Aboriginal History Programme and produced a series of history pamphlets. Kooris are now voyagers in their own history; demonstrating for themselves that their forebears were victims but also active agents in their own making.

In 1991 there were 16 570 Aboriginal and Torres Strait Islander people in Victoria who formed 0.39 per cent of all Victorians. Of these, 12 724 identified as Aborigines and 3846 as Torres Strait Islanders. As no further breakdowns are as yet available from the Australian Bureau of Statistics, regional population distributions must be described from the 1986 Census. In 1986 almost half of the 12 610 Aboriginal and Torres Strait

Islander people in Victoria (termed Kooris below as a shorthand) lived in Melbourne. This proportion showed a marked urban shift from the 1960s, when only one-fifth of Victoria's Kooris lived in Melbourne. In 1986, Kooris were found in all parts of Melbourne but were below their state average in five-sixths of Melbourne's statistical divisions. They were most above their state average concentration in the divisions of Fitzroy, Northcote and Preston where they formed between 0.67 and 0.68 per cent of the population—hardly a heavy cluster. In Healesville they formed 1.82 per cent of the population. Kooris were also spread thinly throughout all country areas but were above their state average of 0.31 per cent in the following centres: Traralgon (0.49 per cent); Warrnambool (0.65 per cent); Mildura (1.55 per cent); Orbost (2.02 per cent); Swan Hill (2.40 per cent); Echuca (2.65 per cent); Bairnsdale (2.68 per cent); Shepparton (2.70 per cent) and Shepparton–Mooroopna (3.40 per cent).[117]

Some indicators in the 1986 Census reveal the social position of Kooris. In 1986 56 per cent of Kooris rented dwellings, compared to 22 per cent of all Victorians, and 39 per cent owned or were purchasing their home, compared to 71 per cent of all Victorians. While 5.7 per cent of Kooris lived in caravans and improvised dwellings only 0.25 per cent of all Victorians did so. Whereas total Victorian unemployment was 5.6 per cent in 1986, that for Kooris was four times as high at 24.1 per cent. In 1987 the 52 Aboriginal prisoners in Victorian places of correction formed 2.7 per cent of the prison population, 8.68 times their proportion of the population.[118] However, while Victoria had the highest prison mortality rate of 4.3 deaths per 1000 prisoner years from 1980–88 there were no Aboriginal prison deaths recorded in Victoria in this period. Between 1980 and 1988 there were three Aboriginal deaths in custody, all of them in police custody.[119] Aboriginal–police relations have often been difficult according to studies in 1965 and 1980.[120] However the appointment of a Koori as a police liaison officer in the 1980s and recent moves since the Royal Commission into Aboriginal Deaths in Custody have laid the basis for better relations.

In the first years of European contact Aborigines had their land taken, their economy undermined, their culture attacked and

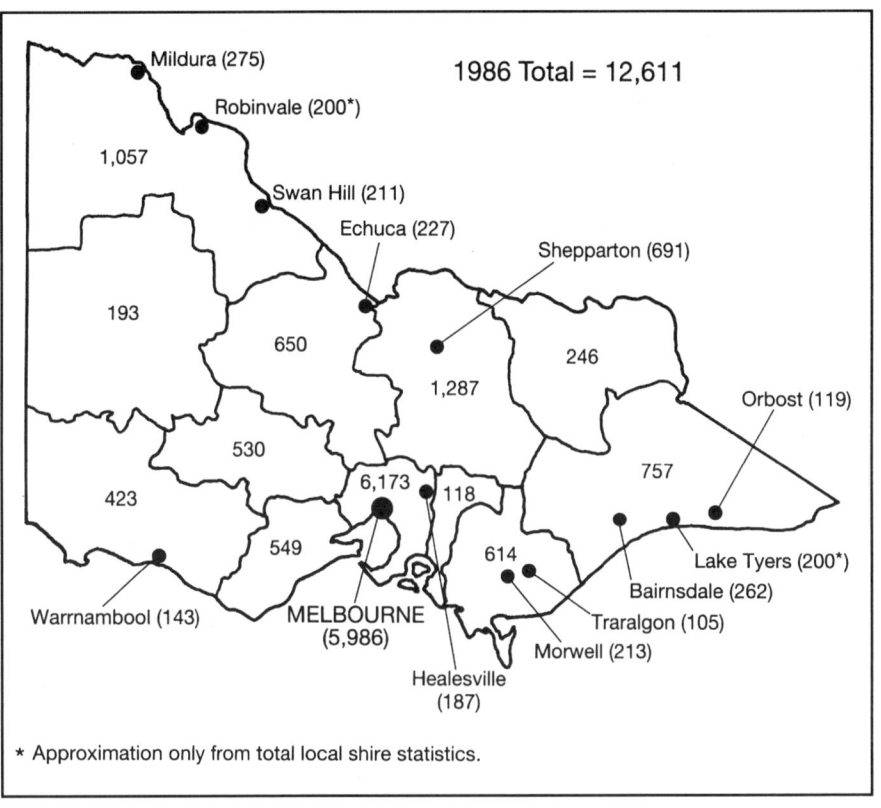

The distribution of Aborigines and Torres Strait Islanders in Victorian statistical divisions in 1986, including (in brackets) those resident in named key statistical local areas.

devalued, and their population literally decimated. The Victorian frontier may not have been as violent as northern frontiers but the cultural and population loss was proportionally greater than almost anywhere else in Aboriginal Australia, due to the pressure of settlement and economic disruption. Aboriginal people lived in the post-frontier world either on reserves under the paternal and close eye of managers, or as fringe dwellers suffering severe disadvantages in housing, employment, education, health, and citizen rights. Between 1886 and 1920 their reserve communities were broken up to absorb the people into the wider society. One

Land Rights marchers, Collins Street, Melbourne, Australia Day 1976. DAVID SYME & CO. LIMITED

benefit was that the people (except those at Lake Tyers) were less under the sway of white bureaucrats than Aborigines elsewhere in Australia at the time, and theoretically had more rights and freedoms than any other Aboriginal people. However, the Aboriginal Protection Board was still a controlling force in their lives like in other parts of Australia. Between 1869 and 1968 Victorian Aboriginal policy encouraged the removal of children from their families to speed assimilation. This amounted to a policy of cultural genocide. At best it was an ignorant, ethnocentric and well-intentioned attempt to lift Aboriginal living standards, and at worst, a racist attempt to end Aboriginal culture and Aboriginal physical traits, through genetic mixing.

Aboriginal people also had to suffer the psychological and social pressure of being a stigmatised fraction of the population—powerless and devalued—and all the while struggling to maintain a sense of who they were. The white colonial adventure made these formerly independent people into victims but they always maintained some control over their lives, their culture, and their sense of identity. They became voyagers in a cross-cultural world. Colonialism has technically ended in Victoria with policies that seek to give Aboriginal Victorians equity and justice, and the right to maintain their distinctive cultural ideas. However, the colonial legacy still remains, and will do so for at least another generation. In 1986 Kooris experienced four times the unemployment rate of other Victorians, eight times the public housing rate, and were twenty times more likely to live in makeshift housing. Their ill-health was greater and their life expectancy was about twenty years below other Victorians.[121] They suffered almost nine times the rate of imprisonment of other Victorians. The colonial mentality still lives in the recesses of many Victorian minds. Until white prejudice and black inferiority is fully eradicated, Aboriginal Victorians will not control their own making which began in this land over 50 000 years ago, and will remain in the custody of white power and at risk.

NOTES

1 I will follow contemporary nomenclature and use 'Koori' for Aboriginal Victorians only when discussing the 1960s onwards, for the reasons set out in R.Broome, 'Should We Call a Koori a "Koori"?', *Australian Historical Association Bulletin*, 68, Sept. 1991, pp.43–46.
2 A.Memmi, *The Colonizer and the Colonized*, Beacon Press, Boston, 1967, p.121.
3 W.E.H.Stanner, 'Continuity and Change Among the Aborigines' in his *White Man Got No Dreaming: Essays 1938–1973*, Australian National University Press, Canberra, 1979, pp.48–49.
4 William Thomas, 'Brief Account of the Aborigines of Australia Felix', in T.F.Bride (ed.), *Letters from Victorian Pioneers*, Heinemann, Melbourne [1898] 1969, pp.422–25.
5 P.J.F.Coutts and R.M.Cochrane, *The Keilor Archaeological Area*, Victorian Archaeological Survey, Melbourne, 1977 and discussion with Paul Ossa, Archaeologist.
6 J.M.Bowler, 'Some Developments in Reconstructing Late Quaternary Environments in Australia', in R.L.Kirk and A.G.Thorne (eds), *The Origins of the Australians,* Australian Institute of Aborig-

inal Studies, Canberra, 1976, pp.55–77; J.Flood, *Archaeology of the Dreamtime: The Story of Prehistoric Australia and Her People*, Collins, Sydney, 1983.

7 B.Gott, 'Ecology of Root Use by the Aborigines of Southern Australia', *Archaeology in Oceania*, vol.17, no.1, 1982, pp.59–67; P.Beveridge, *The Aborigines of Victoria and Riverina*, Hutchinson, Melbourne, 1889, pp.73–75; G.Krefft, 'On the Manners and the Customs of the Aborigines of the Lower Murray and Darling', *Transactions of the Philosophical Society of New South Wales*, 1862–65, pp.368–69.

8 M.Sahlins, *Stone Age Economics*, Aldine-Atherton, Chicago, 1972, chapter 1; T.Dingle, *Aboriginal Economy. Patterns of Experience*, McPhee Gribble/Penguin, Melbourne, 1988.

9 S.Bowdler, 'The Coastal Colonisation of Australia', in J.Allen, J.Golson, R.Jones (eds), *Sunda and Sahul: Prehistoric Studies in Southeast Asia, Melanesia and Australia*, Academic Press, London, 1977, pp.205–46; S.Webb, 'Intensification, Population and Social Change in South-Eastern Australia: the skeletal evidence', *Aboriginal History*, 8, part 2, pp.154–72; H.Lourandos, 'Change or Stability?: hydraulics, hunter-gatherers, and population in temperate Australia', *World Archaeology*, 11, 1980, pp.245–64; Flood, pp.205–206.

10 J.Morgan (ed.), *The Life and Adventures of William Buckley*, Australian National University Press, Canberra, [1852], 1980, chapters 3–6.

11 D.Barwick, 'Mapping the Past: an atlas of Victorian clans 1835–1904', *Aboriginal History*, 8, part 2, 1984, fn.13 and 17; J.Critchett, *'A Distant Field of Murder': Western District Frontiers 1834–1848*, Melbourne University Press, Melbourne, 1990, pp.68–85.

12 N.Butlin, *Our Original Aggression: Aboriginal Populations of South-eastern Australia 1788–1850*, Allen & Unwin, Sydney, 1983; J.Campbell, 'Smallpox in Aboriginal Australia, 1829–31', *Historical Studies*, vol.20, no.81, Oct. 1983, pp.536–56; Judy Campbell, 'Smallpox in Aboriginal Australia, the early 1830s', *Historical Studies*, vol.21, no.84 April, 1985, pp.336–58; N.Butlin, 'Macassans and Aboriginal Smallpox: the "1789" and "1829" epidemics', *Historical Studies*, vol.21, no.84 April 1985, pp.315–35.

13 Morgan (ed.).

14 For Batman's Journal and Report see C.P.Billot, *John Batman: the story of John Batman and the founding of Melbourne*, Hyland House, Melbourne, 1979, chapters 9–10. For government responses see

P.Jones (ed.), *Beginnings of Permanent Government, Historical Records of Victoria (HRV)*, vol.1, Government Printer, Melbourne, 1981, chapter 1.

15 A.H.Campbell, *John Batman and the Aborigines*, Kibble Books, Melbourne, 1987, part 2; R.Harcourt, 'Batman's Treaties', *Victorian Historical Journal*, vol.62, nos3–4, Dec. 1991–March 1992, pp.85–97.

16 Barwick, 'Mapping the Past: an atlas of Victorian clans 1835–1904', pp.100–31.

17 Thomas, 'Brief Account', pp.434–35.

18 Batman's Journal, 31 May 1835, Billot, pp.89–90.

19 M.Christie, *Aborigines in Colonial Victoria 1835–86*, Sydney University Press, Sydney, 1979, p.52.

20 C.P.Billot (ed.), *Melbourne's Missing Chronicle: being the journal of the preparations for departure to and proceedings at Port Phillip by John Pascoe Fawkner*, Quartet Books, Melbourne, 1982.

21 M.Fels, *Good Men and True: The Aboriginal Police of the Port Phillip District 1837–1853*, Melbourne University Press, Melbourne, 1988.

22 Christie, p.1.

23 For the 'violent school' see F.Robinson and B.York, *The Black Resistance*, Widescope, Melbourne, 1977, and P.Gardner, 'Massacres of Aboriginals in Gippsland, 1840–1850', *Historian*, no.27, Oct. 1975, pp.19–24.

24 H.Reynolds, *The Other Side of the Frontier*, Penguin, Melbourne, 1982, especially chapter 3.

25 Christie, p.63. For another view on the match of weapons see R.Broome, 'The Struggle for Australia: Aboriginal–European Warfare, 1770–1930' in M.McKernan and M.Browne (eds), *Australia: Two Centuries of War and Peace*, Allen & Unwin, Sydney, 1988, pp.97–100.

26 Broome, 'The Struggle for Australia', pp.117–18.

27 B.Nance, 'The Level of Violence: Europeans and Aborigines in Port Phillip 1835–1850', *Historical Studies*, vol.19, no.77, Oct, 1981, pp.532–52.

28 R.Broome, 'Aboriginal workers on south-eastern frontiers', *Australian Historical Studies*, vol.26, no.103, pp.202–20.

29 Critchett.

30 J.Powell, *The Public Lands of Australia Felix: Settlement and Land Appraisal in Victoria, 1834–91*, Oxford University Press, Melbourne, 1970, chapter 1.

31 Thomas Journal, 11 Aug. 1844, quoted in H.Sullivan, *An Archaeological Survey of the Mornington Peninsula, Victoria,* Victorian Archaeological Survey, Melbourne, 1981, p.17; J.Penney, 'Murrundi Aborigines and Murray Squatters', *Victorian Historical Journal,* vol.6, no.1, March 1989, pp.42–50.

32 For a development of this argument about genocide see T.Barta, 'Relations of Genocide: Land and Lives in the Colonization of Australia', in I.Walliman and M.Dobkowski, *Genocide and the Modern Age: Etiology and Case Studies of Mass Death,* Greenwood Press, New York, 1987, pp.237–51.

33 B.Blaskett (nee Nance), 'The Aboriginal Response to White Settlement in Port Phillip District 1835–1850', MA thesis, University of Melbourne, 1979, pp.394–95; and Nance, 'The Level of Violence'; Thomas in *HRV,* vol. 2B, pp.603–607; and *Central Board for the Aborigines,* first report 1861, p.29.

34 *Victorian Year Book. Centenary Edition,* 1973, pp.1069, 1090.

35 R.H.W.Reece, *Aborigines and Colonists: Aborigines and Colonial Society in New South Wales in the 1830s and 1840s,* Sydney University Press, Sydney, 1974, chapter 3.

36 Quoted in *HRV,* vol. 2A, p.62.

37 Quoted in *HRV,* vol. 2A, pp.69–70.

38 E.J.B.Foxcroft, *Australian Native Policy,* Melbourne University Press, Melbourne, 1941; Christie, chapter 4.

39 S.Davies, 'Aborigines, Murder and the Criminal Law in Early Port Phillip, 1841–1851', *Historical Studies,* vol.22, no.88, April 1987, pp.313–36; Reece, pp.179–82 and index.

40 Christie, pp.110–12; W.Thomas Report, Sept. 1840–Feb. 1841, Victoria Public Record Series 4410, unit 3.

41 W.D.Jordan, *The White Man's Burden: Historical Origins of Racism in the United States,* Oxford University Press, London, 1974, chapter 1; H.Reynolds, *Frontier,* Allen & Unwin, Sydney, 1987, chapters 4–5.

42 D.Wilsone letters, 12 March and 6 April 1839, 26 June 1840, La Trobe Library, MS 9825.

43 R.Broome, *Arriving,* Fairfax, Syme and Weldon, Sydney, 1984, pp.32–33.

44 Thomas Journal, Sept.–Dec. 1843, VPRS 4410, unit 3.

45 'Report from the Select Committee on the Aborigines and Protectorate', *NSWLC,* 1849, pp.1–2.

46 In Charles Tyers Report, 'Aborigines', *VICLC,* 1853–54, C33, p.21.

47 William Thomas, Reports for 1852–53, 'Aborigines', *VICLC*, 1853–54, C33, pp.5–17.
48 William Thomas, Yearly Report 1856, VPRS 44, unit 639.
49 Thomas, 'Aborigines', *VICLC*, 1853–54, C33, p.11.
50 *Argus*, 5 March 1859.
51 'Report of the Select Committee of the Legislative Council on the Aborigines', *VICLC*, 1858–59, D8, pp.iii-vi.
52 D.Barwick, 'Coranderrk and Cumeroogunga: Pioneers and Policy', in T.Scarlett Epstein and D. and H. Penny, *Opportunity, and Response, Case Studies in Economic Development*, C.Hurst, London, 1972, pp.21–24.
53 Christie, chapter 7.
54 An Act to Provide for the Protection and Management of the Aboriginal Natives of Victoria, 33 Vic. No.349 and further regulations 13 Feb. 1871, 6 March 1876, reprinted in P.Pepper and T.De Araugo, *The Kurnai of Gippsland*, Hyland House, Melbourne, 1985, appendix 2.
55 Barwick, 'Coranderrk and Cumeroogunga: Pioneers and Policy', pp.18–44.
56 D.Barwick, 'And the Lubras are Ladies Now', in F.Gale (ed.) *Woman's Role in Aboriginal Society*, Australian Institute of Aboriginal Studies, Canberra, 1974, pp.51–63. For an account of Ramahyuck Mission see B.Attwood, *The Making of the Aborigines*, Allen & Unwin, Sydney, 1989, chapter 1.
57 For an account of Maloga see N.Cato, *Mr Maloga: Daniel Matthews and his mission, Murray River, 1864–1902*, University of Queensland Press, St Lucia, 1976.
58 B.Attwood, 'Off the Mission Stations: Aborigines in Gippsland 1860–1890', *Aboriginal History*, vol.10, part 2, 1986, pp.145–46.
59 W.E.H.Stanner, 'Alfred William Howitt', in D.Pike (ed.), *Australian Dictionary of Biography*, vol.4, Melbourne University Press, Melbourne, 1972, pp.432–35; D.J.Mulvaney, 'The Ascent of Man: Howitt as anthropologist', in M.Walker Howitt, *Come Wind, Come Weather: A biography of Alfred Howitt*, Melbourne University Press, Melbourne, 1971, pp.285–312.
60 R.Harcourt and J.Mulvaney, *Cricket Walkabout: The Australian Aborigines in England*, Macmillan, Melbourne, 1988.
61 Quoted in J.Hamilton, *Pioneering Days in Western Victoria: A Narrative of Early Station Life*, Warrnambool Institute Press, Warrnambool, [1914] 1981, p.80. See also D.J.Mulvaney, 'Johnny

Mullagh' in Pike, *Australian Dictionary of Biography*, vol.5, pp.308–309.

62 Christie, chapter 8; S.Leitinger, 'The Board, the Parliament and the Aborigines: A Battle for the Aborigines' Right to Self-Determination: Coranderrk, 1863–1884', BA Hons. thesis, La Trobe University, 1991.

63 Attwood, chapter 4.

64 *The Aborigines Act 1886*, 50 Vic. no. 912, is accurately reprinted in Pepper and De Araugo, *The Kurnai of Gippsland*, pp.275–76.

65 The 1890 regulations, *Government Gazette*, 12 Sept. 1890, p.3719 are reprinted in Pepper and De Araugo, pp.281–87.

66 L.Wilkinson, 'Fractured Families, Squatting and Poverty: the impact of the 1886 "Half-caste" Act on the Framlingham Aboriginal Community', *Law and History in Australia*, 2, 1983–84, p.11; Barwick, 'Coranderrk and Cumeroogunga', p.36.

67 Wilkinson, p.15 and J.Stahle, Board for the Protection of the Aborigines, Annual Report, 1912, p.7.

68 Christie, p.202.

69 C.Cooper and J.Urry, 'Art, Aborigines and Chinese: a nineteenth century drawing by the Kwatkwat artist Tommy McRae', *Aboriginal History,* 5, pt.1, pp.82–83.

70 Department of Neglected Children and Reformatory Schools, Annual Report, 1900, *VICPP*, 1901, vol.3, no.30, p.14.

71 D.McLeod to Commandant Booth, 8 Aug. 1900, in Department of Neglected Children and Reformatory Schools, Annual Report, 1900, p.16.

72 D.Barwick, 'Changes in the Aboriginal Population of Victoria, 1863–1966', in D.J.Mulvaney and J.Golson (eds), *Aboriginal Man and Environment in Australia*, Australian National University Press, Canberra, 1971, pp.288–315.

73 *Aborigines Act 1915* (6 George V no.2610) and Regulations, *Victorian Government Gazette*, 13 Sept. 1916, consolidated and virtually reprinted as *Aborigines Act 1928* (19 George V no.3631) and regulations *VGG*, 13 May 1931.

74 *The Age*, 15 May 1947.

75 Pepper, *You Are What You Make Yourself To Be*, chapters 10–13; Pepper and De Araugo, *The Kurnai of Gippsland*, chapters 36–41.

76 Barwick, 'Changes in the Aboriginal Population of Victoria, 1863–1966', pp.298–300.

77 *Victorian Parliamentary Debates* 1913–14, 134, pp.2613–14.

78 *Herald,* 7 Jan. 1926. See also A.Markus, 'After the Outward

Appearance: Scientists, Administrators and Politicians', in B.Gammage and A.Markus (eds), *All That Dirt, Aborigines 1938*, History Project Incorporated, Canberra, 1982, pp.83–106. For racial ideas in the 1960s see L.Lippman, *Words or Blows: Racial Attitudes in Australia*, Penguin, Melbourne, 1973, chapter 12.

79 *Star*, 28 Dec. 1933, 1 Jan., 30 May 1934.
80 *Herald*, May 1934 (exact date indistinguishable in *Herald* clippings fiche series 'Aborigines–General', Borchardt Library, La Trobe University, ML 88–174).
81 Quoted in A.Jackomos and D.Fowell (eds), *Living Aboriginal History of Victoria: Stories in the Oral Tradition*, Cambridge University Press, Melbourne, 1991, p.16.
82 Quoted in Jackomos and Fowell (eds), p.20.
83 Pepper, chapters 8, 11.
84 *Herald*, 18 May 1929.
85 Letter R.Glenn to A.Vroland, 29 Oct. 1936, La Trobe Library MS 9212.
86 *Herald*, 11 Aug. 1932.
87 R.Broome, 'Victoria's Boxing Champs', *Aboriginal News*, 3, no.9, 1980, pp.24–26.
88 R.Broome, 'Professional Aboriginal Boxers in Eastern Australia 1930–1979', *Aboriginal History*, 4, part 1, 1980, pp.49–72.
89 A.Jackomos and D.Fowell (eds), *Forgotten Heroes: Aborigines at War from the Somme to Vietnam*, Victoria Press, Melbourne, 1993.
90 Barwick, 'Coranderrk and Cumeroogunga', pp.44–68; M.Tucker, *If Everyone Cared*, Ure Smith, Sydney, 1977, chapters 1–8; M.T.Clark, *Pastor Doug: The Story of Sir Douglas Nicholls, Aboriginal Leader*, Rigby, Adelaide, 1965, chapter 3.
91 *Herald*, 29 June 1929.
92 A.Markus (ed.), *Blood from a Stone: William Cooper and the Australian Aborigines' League*, Monash Publications in History, Melbourne, 1986; J.Horner, *Vote Ferguson for Aboriginal Freedom*, Australia and New Zealand Book Company, Sydney, 1974, chapters 5–6.
93 Clark, chapter 11.
94 Henry Bailey, *Sun*, 15 May 1941.
95 Barwick, 'Changes in the Aboriginal Population of Victoria, 1863–1966', p.300.
96 'Report Upon the Operation of the Aborigines Act 1928 and the Regulations and Orders made Thereunder', *VPP*, 1956–58, vol.2, no.18, pp.14, 16, 23.

97 G.Lyons, 'Official Policy Towards Victorian Aborigines 1957–1974', *Aboriginal History*, 7, 1983, pp.61–79; Lippman, pp.147–49.
98 A.Mullett, 'Living as a Koori in Victoria', in *La Trobe Library Journal*, vol.11, no.43, Autumn 1989, p.3.
99 Jackomos and Fowell (eds), pp.70–71.
100 Jackomos and Fowell (eds), pp.102–105.
101 *Herald*, 27 April 1964; D.Barwick, ' "A Little More Than Kin": Regional Affiliation and Group Identity Among Aboriginal Migrants in Melbourne', PhD. thesis, Australian National University, 1963, p.293.
102 D.Barwick, 'The Aboriginal Family in south-eastern Australia', in J.Krupinski and A.Stoller (eds), *The Family in Australia*, Pergamon Press, Sydney, 1978, second edition, p.208.
103 *The Age*, 10 June 1968.
104 Victorian Aboriginal Child Care Agency Co-op Ltd. Statement of aims and principles, roneod, nd.
105 For the Savage/Moore case see P.Bone in *The Age*, 21 Sept. 1989.
106 Quoted in Lyons, 'Official Policy', p.75.
107 Barwick, 'A Little More Than Kin', pp.27–28.
108 R.Broome, 'Should We Call a Koori a "Koori"?', *Australian Historical Association Bulletin*, no.68, Sept. 1991, pp.43–46.
109 Barwick, 'A Little More Than Kin', chapters 1, 4.
110 Barwick, 'A Little More Than Kin', p.324; Lippman, p.187.
111 Pepper, p.262.
112 Barwick, 'A Little More Than Kin', chapter 2; Barwick, 'The Aboriginal Family in south-eastern Australia'.
113 Anonymous, *Victims or Victors: The Story of the Victorian Aborigines Advancement League*, Hyland House, Melbourne, 1985.
114 *Sun*, 20 July 1971.
115 *Identity*, Jan. 1972.
116 R.Broome, *Arriving*, pp.244–45.
117 Statistics from Aboriginal Statistics Unit, Australian Bureau of Statistics, Darwin.
118 D.Biles, 'Aboriginal Imprisonment: a Statistical Analysis', Royal Commission into Aboriginal Deaths in Custody, Research Paper no.6, 1989, p.8.
119 D.Biles, D.McDonald and J.Fleming, 'Australian Deaths in Custody 1980–1988: An Analysis of Aboriginal and Non-Aboriginal Deaths in Prison and Police Custody', Royal Commission into Aboriginal Deaths in Custody, Research Paper no.7, 1989, pp.5–6, 30.

120 E.Eggleston, *Fear, Favour or Affection*, Australian National University Press, Canberra, 1976; G.Lyons, 'Aboriginal Perceptions of Courts and Police: a Victorian study', *Australian Aboriginal Studies*, 1983, no.2, pp.45–61.
121 I.Anderson, *Koorie Health in Koorie Hands*, Health Department of Victoria, Melbourne, 1988, p.40.

4
Queensland

RECENT archaeological work in North Queensland has established that Aboriginal occupation goes back at least 30 000 years.[1] Earlier sites are likely to be discovered in the future although many of the most heavily populated areas were probably on or near the ice-age coastline which ran along the outer-edge of the Barrier Reef and were drowned as a result of rising sea levels between 15 000 and 6000 years ago. Over several hundred generations Aboriginal society adapted to and in turn altered its physical environment, creating a way of life responsive to a wide range of habitats: hot, dry savanna, dense tropical rainforest, mangrove, dune and coastal wetland, and cool southern forests.

Along the north coast resident clans had long-term contact with Torres Strait Islanders and traded artefacts and ideas with Papuan society on the far shore of the Strait. Macassan seamen fished the waters of the Gulf of Carpentaria and cured beche-de-mer in camps established on the coast. The date of their first appearance is unknown but it may have coincided with the first visits by Dutch and Spanish expeditions in the seventeenth century. By the early nineteenth century the sea-lane—the so called inner-route—inside the Barrier Reef and through Torres Strait was being regularly used by ships sailing between ports on the eastern seaboard and those in South and East Asia. Clans living on the off-shore islands had frequent contact with passing ships which normally anchored every night while in dangerous reef

waters. Castaways like Eliza Fraser, James Morrell and Barbara Thompson lived with coastal clans for varying periods of time.

The major land expeditions—those of Mitchell, Leichhardt and Gregory—had far less impact on Aboriginal society than the constant maritime traffic along the coast while the influence of convict settlement at Moreton Bay was confined to its immediate hinterland. But once the pastoralists pushed into Queensland from 1840 onwards their occupation of runs was extremely rapid. Between 1840 and 1870 most of the easily accessible grazing land was stocked with sheep or cattle. In the 1880s the Queensland squatters drove their herds across the Northern Territory and took up land in the East Kimberley. The discovery, exploitation and in many cases the abandonment of goldfields took place at an equally frenetic pace. During the 1870s and 1880s diggers, including many Chinese, rushed to the Gilbert, Etheridge, Mulgrave, Palmer and many other lesser known fields. From 1856 this rapid expansion of settlement took place under the aegis of settler-dominated colonial governments (New South Wales until 1859 and then Queensland) which displayed far less concern for the Aborigines than did the Imperial Government during the 1830s and 1840s. What is more, Queensland inherited the harsh racial attitudes which had developed on the expanding southern frontiers during the 1820s and 1830s.[2]

The pioneer pastoralists moved up onto the Darling Downs expecting trouble and ready to use their guns to shoot their way out of it. Many of them had had previous frontier experience and had absorbed its ethos of violence. In letters to their parents the Leslie brothers reported that, on their expedition to the north, they were 'taking plenty of firearms for fear of the blacks'. And they used them. Eighteen months later they explained that they 'never allow them [the Aborigines] to come about the station or hold any communication with them except it be with a gun or a sword'. Three years later the message was even more sinister, with Walter Leslie writing: 'Our shooting here is mostly confined to the rifle and pistol used in defence of our men's lives and property.' Despite their weapons the Leslies were chronically insecure. Patrick Leslie regretted taking his wife to Canning Downs, explaining that, 'I would not take her again into such a situation for the fortune of a Peer. The constant dread of the Blacks and the fearful risks one runs so far from civilised life is enough to deter anyone from such a step.'[3] While reminiscing about the early years of settlement on the Condamine G.S. Lang noted that he and his companions lived with their guns on hand for 'nearly three years'. When they bathed in the river, 'carbines and ammunition had to be on the water's edge'.[4]

In 1848 the distant government responded to the continuing conflict on the northern frontier by establishing a small Native

Police Force under the command of Frederick Walker who recruited fourteen young Aboriginal men from the Riverina and after a brief training period they rode north.[5] They had an immediate effect on conflict along the Condamine and Macintyre. The troopers were particularly suited to the task at hand combining the skills of both white and black—the ability to ride and shoot and the capacity to live off the land, find water and track their opponents even in the most difficult country. Walker saw his role not as a participant in frontier conflict on the side of the Europeans but as the agent of an impartial state who would maintain law and order. He did not intend to carry 'war into an enemy country' but to put the law 'into effect against both white and black without distinction'. The blacks were not to be treated as enemies but as 'British subjects who like armed Bushrangers were defying the law'. But this was certainly not the way that frontier settlers viewed the matter. Walker quickly discovered that they believed that 'a system of warfare ought to be authorised by Government'.[6] It was a conflict of opinion which was resolved decisively in favour of the settlers, a decision enhanced by the grant of responsible government to New South Wales in 1856 and to Queensland on separation three years later. Each shift of power—from Downing Street to Sydney and from Sydney to Brisbane brought government closer to the frontier—politically, intellectually and morally.

In 1859 there were just over 30 000 settlers in the colony. The Aboriginal population cannot be accurately determined but it may have been more than 100 000.[7] The Europeans occupied the south-east corner of the colony—a triangular slice of territory bounded by the coast, the New South Wales border and a line drawn from Rockhampton to St George. In area it was certainly no more than 20 per cent of the total land surface.[8] The existence of such a large area of 'unsettled' land promoted a sense both of boundless opportunity and of mission to engage in 'the great work of reclaiming the wilderness'.[9] The editor of the *North Australian* wrote in 1861: 'Our mission is to populate and develop the resources of the country . . . and that mission *must* be fulfilled.'[10]

A 'Working Man' had written to the same paper a few months earlier, explaining that 'we are as yet but as the pioneers that precede the army in its march, clearing the forest, marking out the roads for the main body of our countrymen to advance'.[11]

The pastoral industry became the backbone of the economy, providing 90 per cent of the colony's exports and many members of the first Parliament were squatters or had direct financial interests in the industry. Unlike the colonists elsewhere in eastern Australia before 1856, and in Western Australia until 1900, the Queenslanders were released from the restraint which had been exercised—albeit fitfully and often ineffectually—by the Imperial Government and its local representatives. Despite many complaints sent to England during the nineteenth century about the treatment of Aboriginal people the Colonial Office regarded the matter as an internal issue. Humanitarian opinion had some influence in Brisbane—a Moreton Bay Aborigines Friendship Society was established in the 1850s—but it was weaker than in the southern cities. The two early attempts at missionary endeavour, the Roman Catholics on Stradbroke Island and the Lutherans on the outskirts of Brisbane, had both failed by 1859. There was little further missionary activity for 30 years. It was rare to find anyone at the time who spoke out in favour of Aboriginal rights to land, even to the usufructuary rights which the Imperial Government had recognised in 1848 and which were incorporated in Queensland pastoral leases after that date.[12]

The violence which accompanied the settlement of the Darling Downs and the Brisbane Valley continued on into the 1850s as settlers pushed into central Queensland. The Aboriginal attacks on Hornet Bank Station in 1857 and on Cullinlaringoe in 1861, resulting in the deaths of 30 white men, women and children shocked and angered the settlers and evoked demands for indiscriminate revenge.[13] The New South Wales Select Committee set up to inquire into the Hornet Bank affair reported that they were satisfied that there was no alternative but to carry matters through with a strong hand, and punish with necessary severity all future outrages upon life and property.[14]

Public opinion was even more inflamed. When news of the deaths at Hornet Bank reached Ipswich 'even those habitually calm and merciful [were] often heard to advocate vengeance and extermination'.[15] A correspondent who wrote to the *Queensland*

Guardian after hearing of the deaths at Cullinlaringoe argued that the tribe must be punished. 'Whether it numbers scores or hundreds . . . the deadly bullet must do the work of the more legitimate executioner—justice must triumph over law.'[16]

When the punitive expeditions, both official and private, traversed large areas of central Queensland with guns blazing, revenge clearly did triumph over law and the legal doctrine—honoured more in the breach than in the observance—that the Aborigines were British subjects protected by the law. The tragic events of 1857–61 ensured the future of the Native Police Force which continued to ride the frontier until the first decade of the twentieth century. When news of the deaths of the Wills family at Cullinlaringoe reached Brisbane, a correspondent writing in the *Queensland Guardian* argued 'and now we can understand and appreciate the value of [the Native Police] we thank Providence for it and commend it to its work'.[17]

Any pretence of strict legality or of even-handedness in the activities of the Native Police was dispensed with. In January 1858 the Commandant E.V. Morrisset issued instructions to the officers of the force which reflected the harsh new outlook. 'It is the duty of the Officers', the tenth paragraph read, 'at all times and opportunities to disperse any large assemblage of blacks; such meetings if not prevented, inevitably lead to depredation or murder . . . '.[18]

The instruction to disperse large gatherings at all times and opportunities was not rescinded until 1896, 38 years later. If there was ever any doubt about what 'to disperse' means it was dispelled by the colony's Attorney-General who told Parliament in 1861 that it was 'idle to dispute' that the term 'meant nothing but firing at them'.[19] The frontier settlers had got the kind of force they had wanted all along. A prominent squatter-member of the 1861 Select Committee on the Native Police declared that 'the natives must be regarded in the same light as inhabitants of a country under martial law'. He believed that 'from the natives knowing no law, [nor] entertaining any fears but those of the carbine, there was no other means of ruling them'.[20]

The activities of the Native Police Force did not obviate the need for individual involvement in frontier conflict or preclude the widespread carrying of guns. On the frontier, men were armed, often with rifle and revolver, while travelling and working, and loaded guns were kept ready in the home.[21] How many individuals were personally involved in frontier violence is hard to say. The use of brutal means both to gain control of the land and when that was done, to 'keep the blacks in their place', was widely accepted. The editor of the *Rockhampton Bulletin* remarked in April 1876 that a 'reckless disregard of the common rights of humanity was far too often exhibited by men whose moral sensibilities' had been blunted 'by too great familiarity with deeds of blood in skirmishes which take place on our frontier settlement'.[22] Following a massacre by Native Police on the outskirts of the mining town of Morinish, a local resident wrote with deep concern to the Rockhampton paper:

> One inevitable effect of these massacres continuing unpunished and unrepressed will be, that the youth of the colony will grow up with a reckless disregard of human life, which, in due time will yield congenial fruit. Already the evil leaven has begun to work. I have frequently felt grieved and indignant at the levity, with which many of the colonial youth speak of those outrages on the blacks.[23]

A high degree of tolerance of violence and atrocity prevailed in colonial Queensland. It often caught the attention of observant visitors, as was the case with the distinguished British colonial official Sir Arthur Gordon who visited the colony in 1883. In a letter to his friend the British Prime Minister William Gladstone, he confided that while in Queensland he had met men of culture and refinement, of the greatest humanity and kindness to their fellow whites, 'and who when you meet them at home you would pronounce to be incapable of such deeds' yet they 'talk, not only of the *wholesale* butchery . . . but of *individual* murder of natives, exactly as they would talk of a day's sport, or of having to kill some troublesome animal'.[24]

One of the most disturbing examples of this callousness is illustrated in the diary of Caroline Creaghe, written during a visit to north-west Queensland in 1883 a month or two before Gordon was writing of his concern to Gladstone. She was 22 at the time and a child of the Australian elite—a daughter of Major General

George Robinson and niece of two colonial governors. She had recently married H.A. Creaghe, a member of the English aristocracy. While staying on frontier cattle stations she made several references in her diary to the local Aborigines. On 8 February 1883 she noted that on Lawn Hill Station the manager had '40 pairs of blacks' ears nailed round the walls, collected during raids after losses of many cattle speared by the blacks'. A fortnight later on Carl Creek station she observed that when the men returned from the run: 'They brought a new black gin with them; she cannot speak a word of English. Mr. Shadforth [the manager] put a rope round the girl's neck and dragged her along on foot. He was riding. This seems to be the usual method.'

The following day she recorded that the woman was chained up to a tree a few yards from the house. She was 'not to be loosed until they think she is tamed'.[25] These incidents are recorded in a matter of fact way without any indication of shock or disapproval.

People who took a stand against racial violence were often decried and abused. The squatter Ernest Thorn attempted to frustrate a party bent on attacking an Aboriginal camp near his property. As a result he got 'a bad name' which followed him for many years and 'rose up in judgement' against him for many years. He was, he recalled, branded as 'a dangerous man'.[26] The journalist A.J. Vogan had a similar experience. Having exposed the activities of the Native Police in a novel called *The Black Police* he found that he had acquired powerful enemies. Writing to the Anti-Slavery Society in London, he explained that as a consequence his profession was closed to him, 'marked man as I now am'.[27] The Catholic priest Duncan McNab informed a Parliamentary Committee that in his experience he had found 'too generally prevailing a certain disposition to regard and treat as a fanatic, anyone who shows an inclination to advocate [the cause] of the Aboriginals or to benefit them'.[28]

Both government policy and individual behaviour towards the Aborigines were shaped by racial ideas which the settlers brought into the colony with them and which in turn were influenced by local developments. Belief in racial equality, which in the early years of Australian settlement had drawn strength from both

Enlightenment philosophy and traditional Christianity, had faltered by the time that Queensland was separated from New South Wales. Assorted schools of 'scientific' racism which flourished in Europe and North America in the first half of the century were finding favour in the Australian colonies in the 1840s and 1850s. The establishment of responsible government in Queensland in 1859 coincided with the publication of Charles Darwin's seminal work *On the Origin of the Species* which, as a consequence of the work of his many followers who adapted the concept of evolution to explain the development of human societies, was ultimately to have a major influence on racial thought.[29]

The common view throughout the second half of the nineteenth century was that Aborigines were 'savages' who shared common characteristics with 'savages' in other parts of the world. This belief was deeply rooted in European thought influencing at one and the same time those who advocated amelioration and those who promoted much harsher policies. Settlers hostile to the Aboriginal cause spoke and wrote of 'the wretched characteristics of our black population—their fearful superstitions, their bestial tastes, their undisguised squalor and filth, their indolent habits and their nomadic disposition'.[30] But the views of the missionary William Ridley, a so-called 'friend' of the blacks, appear to our eyes to be little better. As a leading figure in the short-lived Moreton Bay Aborigines Friendship Society, he wrote in 1856:

> It had been remarked that they [the Aborigines] were the most degraded and lowest race in the world. It must be admitted, so far as he knew, that in some points they were singularly, and also uniquely defective, as if some features of human nature were waning, or else they were much demented.[31]

From the very beginning of settlement it was widely accepted that the Aborigines were doomed to extinction, a view bolstered by experience in New South Wales and Tasmania and by generally available knowledge of earlier demographic disasters which befell the Indian populations in the Americas. A writer in the *Moreton Bay Free Press* argued in 1852 that the whole history of colonisation proved that when a 'country inhabited by savages' was occupied by a 'superior race' the fate of 'its original inhabitants is from that moment sealed'.[32] 'The native race', a correspondent in the *Brisbane Courier* explained in 1865, 'will perish before our advance as does the autumnal grass before a bush fire'.[33]

Darwinian ideas gave strength to many pre-existing racial ideas, linking them with the greatest scientific achievement of the age. The concept of race was further embedded in colonial thought, the various races being equated with the species in the natural world.[34] Increasingly the Aborigines were seen as members of a less evolved, earlier race, a biological and cultural fossil preserved by the isolation of the continent. The laws of evolution, it was confidently assumed, were pushing the race to the brink of extinction. There was little that could be done about it. Conflict attending the expansion of the frontier could be seen, in this light, as a regrettable but inevitable conflict of races out of which the fitter would survive prepared for further evolutionary advance. A settler who professed strong sympathy for the Aborigines told the visiting Norwegian scientist Carl Lumholtz that he would do anything he could to 'ameliorate their present wretched condition' but nothing could be achieved 'for it is an immutable law of nature that the strong will prey upon the weak'.[35] A writer in the *Queenslander* similarly believed that the callousness towards the Aborigines arose not from a lack of sympathy but from a 'firm conviction that their stage of civilisation is too many hundreds and perhaps thousands of years behind our own to allow their race to thrive side by side with ours'.[36] An even more significant statement of Social Darwinism was that of Archibald Meston in a report to the government in 1889, a few years before he was to exert a profound influence on the protectionist policies adopted after 1897. 'The Australian blacks', he insisted,

> are moving rapidly on into eternal darkness in which all savage and inferior races are surely destined to disappear. All effort to preserve them, though creditable to our humanity, is a poor compliment to our knowledge of those inexorable laws whose operations are as apparent as our own existence. Their epoch of time is near its termination, the shadows deepening towards everlasting night. It is a mournful picture, that of the old

inhabitants who for unknown ages have roamed the primeval forests of this mighty continent, now moving off silent and swift-footed into oblivion before the presence of the white strangers.[37]

It is much more difficult to describe what happened on the 'other side of the frontier', given the large number of Aboriginal land-owning groups involved and the general lack of evidence available to us. However a composite picture can be pieced together which conveys the overall situation while not necessarily being true to every clan in the colony.[38] Knowledge of the Europeans undoubtedly preceded the advancing tide of settlement. News about the mysterious powers of guns and the propensity of white men to use them was spread far and wide. Many clans had seen and hunted wild cattle well before the settlers' herds and flocks came over the horizon. Iron, glass and tobacco were often in use well beyond the outer fringe of European settlement. Even so the arrival of the first permanent settlers was an awesome experience. Violence was not instantaneous or even inevitable. Contact often began peacefully and in a few districts that situation was maintained. Many clans attempted to avoid contact as long as possible; others sought to establish amiable relations with the powerful newcomers and absorb them within their networks of obligation. But the situation was fraught with danger. So many things could go wrong. Both white and black were stretched taut with anxiety. Mutual misunderstanding abounded. Conflict over women, access to water, use of land was endemic. Once violence began it usually spiralled out of control and continued for months and in some places for years where the rugged terrain gave the tribesmen the advantage over mounted white stockmen and native troopers. Recurrent skirmishing persisted for 50 years and took many lives. At least 1000 Europeans died and perhaps 10 000 Aborigines although we will never know the true figure. Many were wounded on both sides of the frontier.[39]

The fighting came to an uneasy end everywhere sooner or later. The pressures on tribal society were enormous. People had lived for long periods gripped with chronic anxiety. They had seen their kin gunned down. It became increasingly difficult to sustain the lifestyle of the hunter and gatherer as the Aborigines

Wooroora station Aborigines c 1900 in the process of 'coming in'. JOHN OXLEY LIBRARY

were forced away from the river valleys and other surface water into mountainous, arid or other marginal country. In his official Report on the condition of the Aborigines in North Queensland, Archibald Meston described one group who came to meet him 'like hunted wild beasts, having lived for years in a state of absolute terror'.[40] Individuals and small groups gradually 'went in' and attempted to come to terms with the white men, eventually living more or less permanently in camps on pastoral stations or on the outskirts of the pioneer townships.

The Europeans welcomed the end of hostilities both because they had been costly financially and psychologically and because in most frontier districts there were chronic shortages of labour. Young men and women were soon absorbed into the white economy. In the north and west of the colony, black stockmen and women were the mainstays of the pastoral industry while on the coast Aboriginal workers were of vital importance for the pearling and beche-de-mer industries. Until the government forced the issue in the early twentieth century, Aboriginal workers rarely received wages but were paid in kind with varying quantities of food, clothing, tobacco, alcohol or opium. Their working conditions were usually very poor and the use of violence—of fists, boots and stockwhips—was commonplace and fully supported by public opinion in communities obsessed by the need to 'keep the niggers in their place'. When the local clans were first 'let in' to Bowen the editor of the local paper warned his fellow townspeople:

> we must not cease to be firm and must take especial care to show our black neighbours that whilst we are willing, nay anxious, to hold our hands from slaughter, we are at the same time determined to enforce at all hazards and by any means submission to our laws and that any infraction of them will be met with retribution prompt and severe.[41]

Aborigines living on the fringes of white society were almost completely powerless and received little protection from violence and exploitation. Neither the law nor public opinion shielded them from the ill-disposed, a writer in the *Queenslander* observing in 1883 that 'everyman seems to consider himself as quite justified in carrying out the utmost vigour of the law towards an aboriginal, often for some very trivial and insignificant office'.[42] In all parts of the colony men were bashed, women raped and children stolen from their families.

The fear engendered during Queensland's 'border wars' continued to determine Aboriginal behaviour for a long time after the shooting stopped. The local blacks, a settler noted in 1889, 'have learnt in their terror to submit to anything that the conquering race may choose to do'.[43] While visiting sheep and cattle stations in the south-west, Archibald Meston informed the Colonial Secretary of the situation he found:

> Never before had I seen aboriginal men living under such extraordinary terrorism, many of them fine athletic fellows who could in case of a row have settled with their terrorisers in a very summary fashion. But many of them had long been treated as the dogs are treated and were scared into the belief that their employers wielded the power of life and death.[44]

By the late nineteenth century Aborigines had established fringe camps on the outskirts of practically every town in the colony.

The larger towns had two or three such settlements with a total population of several hundred. The camps were characteristically located a mile or two out of town—beyond the cemetery, the Chinese gardens or the rubbish dump or on the other side of the river. They were composed of clusters of humpies constructed with an assortment of traditional building materials and cast-off European commodities.

Camp dwellers scraped together a precarious living from what could be gained by hunting and gathering in the immediate neighbourhood and with food received from the townspeople in return for work or sexual favours. The camp dwellers performed a wide variety of tasks for townspeople who could not afford or find white servants. Townspeople were always ambivalent about the camps. They benefited from the cheap labour but they were determined to keep the local blacks 'in their place'. Individual and vigilante violence was common, a Brisbane resident explaining that when the occasion demanded 'every private individual takes the liberty . . . [to] administer a sound thrashing for offences against the decency and peace of the neighbourhood'.⁴⁵ It appears that a curfew was imposed in practically every town in the colony. Southern visitors were often shocked when they saw the police driving the local blacks out of town at sunset. Two sisters passing through Maryborough were 'deeply outraged at the way they were driven down the street, like so many sheep or dogs, to the water's edge, when they plunged in and swam to the opposite side [of the river]'.⁴⁶ The practice was, as the Gympie Police Magistrate admitted, 'doubtless illegal in itself' but the government usually turned a blind eye to action which had widespread popular support.⁴⁷ In 1896 the Colonial Secretary Horace Tozer declared his unqualified support for the police when they 'removed' the Aborigines, arguing that 'no law is necessary to justify this save the law of necessity'.⁴⁸

By the 1890s there was mounting humanitarian pressure on the Queensland Government to do something about the plight of the colony's Aboriginal population which had dwindled to less than 25 000.⁴⁹ In 1896 Archibald Meston, considered an authority on the topic, was commissioned to make appropriate recommendations⁵⁰ and some of his suggestions subsequently formed the basis of the *Aboriginals Protection and Restriction of the Sale of Opium Act, 1897*. While the creators of this Act may have seen it as a solution to a short-term problem,[51] the administrators had a different idea and from the beginning used it as a device for social engineering and control. It became the instrument with which Aboriginal people could be stripped of the most basic human rights. The Act was the first measure of separate legal control over the Queensland Aboriginal people,[52] and it was far more restrictive than any legislation operating in New South Wales or Victoria at the time.[53] Administrators were able to gain control over Aboriginal affairs through the extensive use of regulations which were made lawful through proclamation by the Governor-in-Council. In this manner decision-making passed from the politicians to the public servants. Most acquiesced with this arrangement as the welfare of Aborigines was only one small part of a busy minister's portfolio. But not only did public servants have responsibility for a huge amount of delegated legislation, individual Protectors had extensive autonomy in administering the Act and its regulations.

Provision was made in the Act for a system of Protectors who were to inquire into cases of ill-treatment of Aboriginal people and to generally supervise their employment. While this may have appeared commendable at the time, it did provide the foundation for State paternalism. Meston was quite definite about the type of person who should be appointed to the position of Protector; it should be someone who had the ability to instil fear into those being defended.[54] With a penchant for physical fitness and strength,[55] Meston believed that Protectors should possess similar qualities, arguing that no 'white man can command the fear and respect of the Australian black without an unmistakable manifestation of superior physical and intellectual force allied to a liberal disposition and evidence of some importance'.[56]

While Meston did not stipulate that police should act as Protectors, he considered it necessary that the people filling these roles should be invested with the powers of a magistrate. In this manner they could legally deal with the injustices committed against Aborigines. Initially it was decided to appoint police to the position but in presenting the bill to Parliament, the minister made it quite clear that this was to be only a temporary measure and he hoped that his successor would 'make the system more perfect'.[57] In 1898 Police Commissioner Parry-Okeden was made responsible for the general administration of the Act assisted by Walter Roth in the north and Meston in the south. In 1904 a separate administrative sub-department of the Home Secretary's Office was created to look after Aboriginal issues. At the same time Roth was appointed the first Chief Protector of Aborigines in Queensland.[58]

The 1897 legislation made provision for the creation of a series of reserves where Aboriginal people could be 'entirely isolated from contact with other races'.[59] In deciding on the location of these institutions, traditional land areas were ignored. For instance Durundur, 15 miles from Caboolture, catered for coastal Aboriginal people as well as those from the western parts of the state, while the reserve encircling Yarrabah Mission was to be extensive enough to accommodate all North Queensland Aborigines. By 1897 there were already six missions operating; one at Deebing Creek, 5 miles from Ipswich; one at Marie Yamba, 60 miles north of Mackay; Yarrabah near Cairns; one on the Bloomfield River, south of Cooktown; one at Cape Bedford, 14 miles from Cooktown by water; and Mapoon on the mouth of the Batavia River.

In the more remote parts of the state Aborigines continued to share their land with pastoralists, who believed they had paramount right to the land as they would use it more productively. Although Queensland law did allow Aborigines the right to hunt and cross any unfenced leased Crown land, which was the status of almost all cattle properties, it was a right that was rarely acknowledged by pastoralists.[60] Despite their status as Aboriginal Protectors, when there was a conflict of interest between blacks and whites, police favoured the European interests. Station owners frequently received the assistance of police in moving blacks from one location to another. For instance Watson of Gregory Downs station wrote to the Police Commissioner seeking assistance in having a dozen blacks who were 'always prowling about the homestation' removed to the Lawn Hill Reserve.[61] It proved to be almost impossible to reconcile the two types of land-use. Pastoralists particularly objected to Abo-

Aboriginal residents had little chance of avoiding the pervasive influence of religion on Queensland missions. QUEENSLAND PARLIAMENTARY PAPERS, 1909, VOL. 2

rigines camping on waterholes as it prevented cattle from drinking.[62] Protector Galbraith of Normanton was adamant that Aborigines should have access to waterholes: 'To deprive them of this right simply means wiping them out or driving them into the smaller towns, where women must prostitute themselves in order to enable the men and children to live.'[63]

In the eyes of the Northern Protector and his contemporaries, the only practical solution was the creation of more reserves for Aborigines in the remote areas. It was argued that in 'the extreme North, for instance, the formation of one large aboriginal reserve of the whole of the Peninsula north of the Coleman and Morehead Rivers . . . would answer the purpose without any appreciable loss to the general revenues.'[64]

The new conciliatory approach had certainly made it more difficult for Europeans to engage in the 'dispersal' tactics of the nineteenth century but the cost to the Aboriginal people was increasing containment on designated land not necessarily their own. Protector Galbraith was only too aware that by 1904 the

Act which had been intended to improve the lot of the blacks, was working more for the benefit of the Europeans in the district. He noted that the cases of killing, cattle-stealing and so forth were rare and this gave white settlers more security. 'Country that a few years ago settlers would not take up, is now occupied with impunity.' Conversely Aboriginal hunting grounds were much more restricted.[65]

In spite of this situation, employers were far from happy with the way the Act was administered. In 1904 and 1905 there was considerable public debate—at meetings, in newspapers and in Parliament—concerning its operation. By 1905 the main target for employers' attacks was Chief Protector of Aboriginals Walter Roth, whom the editor of the *North Queensland Register* described as 'the best hated official in the Queensland Government service'.[66] In Roth's eyes, the general opposition to his administration was mainly due to his intervention into Aboriginal labour arrangements.

The Act required employers of Aboriginal labour, from 1 January 1898, to enter into a written agreement in the presence of a justice of the peace or a member of the police force. Contracts were to contain particulars of the names of the parties, nature of the service, periods of employment, wages or other remuneration and the type of accommodation to be provided. The aim of this legislation was to eliminate the serious abuses of Aboriginal labour, particularly in the maritime industry. It is clear that Police Commissioner Parry-Okeden wanted a deal of discretion exercised in implementing the provisions of the Act; he did not want the status quo disturbed. In reporting on the Act's operation in 1898 he noted that his 'instructions to Dr. Roth and to the various Protectors under [his] direction, have been to work the Act in a conciliatory and generous spirit, causing as little friction as possible'.[67] Roth however was intent on a much more rigorous application of the Act and set about ensuring that all employed, including those on cattle stations were properly signed on. Individual protectors also had considerable discretion in whether or not to enforce the signing of agreements, the portion of the pay which had to be banked and how the savings were spent.

Although the original intention of the Act may have been protection, within a short period its main thrust was the regulation of employment. By 1908 the stated aim of Chief Protector Howard was to obtain employment for 'each and every individual impressing upon them the desirableness of doing their best to satisfy their employer, and at the same time saving some of their earnings for a rainy day'.[68] In addition, Aborigines were subjected to ever increasing control because of the government's desire to close loopholes which employers might otherwise use.

With time, removal orders became the major mechanism for controlling Aboriginal lives and it would appear that they were used more rigorously in Queensland than in any other Australian state. The number of people removed to missions and settlements varied from year to year. In 1934 it was reported that 136 people were forcibly relocated including 45 for their own protection and 62 because they were destitute and unemployed. 'Half-caste' children, particularly girls, were early targets for removal to missions and reformatories. Roth argued that his chief aim was 'to ensure the future welfare and happiness of the children themselves'.[69] Aboriginal people remember it differently. Jerry Hudson of Mapoon recalled that, 'the government took our fathers and mothers away from our grandparents. Some were six and seven years old. Well, you can guess how our dear grandparents felt about our mothers and fathers who they will never see anymore . . . that's one thing we will never forget until we die.'[70]

While the 1901 amendment to the earlier Act made provision for the removal of people deemed to be 'incorrigibles', by the 1920s Protectors were continually using removal orders to modify behaviour. For instance Jimmy was removed from Gunnawarra Station in 1922 for being 'bad tempered and abusive' and Aggie from Gregory Downs for 'poor conduct'. The Cardwell Protector requested the removal of an Upper Murray man for causing discontent among Aborigines by advising them not to sign agreements. In another incident the Maytown Protector threatened to send nine Wrotham Park Aborigines to Barambah if they did not renew their agreements. The Charters Towers Protector recommended the removal of a man to Palm Island Reserve because

As late as 1924 Aboriginal people were sent to Palm Island for spearing cattle on Cape York Peninsula. *NORTH QUEENSLAND REGISTER*, 30 JUNE 1924

he caused 'discontent amongst those blacks who were under agreement'.[71] The threat of being removed to Palm Island caused a great deal of anxiety amongst the Aboriginal population and was just as pronounced in the more remote parts of the state. Jack Punch remembered that 'everybody was sort of frightened. They used to think they'd be sent to Palm Island . . . They didn't know what Palm Island was. They thought it was a sort of Jail.'[72]

It was so easy to defuse potential trouble by removing offenders to Palm Island. The fate of Albert Hippi in 1923 markedly illustrates this point. He was dissatisfied with the small amount of money he could withdraw from his bank account while on holidays in Richmond and organised a petition to the Minister for Justice. 'We do not ask that a big amount be paid to us in one sum but that we be permitted to draw at least £1 a day during our holidays,' he pleaded.[73] As with most complaints, the matter was investigated but no further action was taken. It was however, somewhat alarming to discover Hippi's name amongst those being removed to Palm Island the following year. The reason given was that 'he frightens women and tries to get liquor'.[74]

Once a removal order was obtained, Aborigines had no redress; the Chief Protector advised the Under Secretary in 1937 that there was no provision in 'the Aboriginal Protection Acts for an aboriginal to be brought before a Magistrate and given a hearing before being sent to a Settlement'.[75] In many instances Aboriginal people were unaware of the reason for their banishment and it was not uncommon for people who were the victims of a crime to be removed. A former protector explained that he had sent blacks from the Gregory Downs district because they were a 'nuisance'. 'They were being worked without pay and were being bedded down,' he said.[76]

Notwithstanding the numerous accounts of protectors readily invoking removal orders, there are instances of protectors objecting to this action. The Annual Report for 1938 notes that 48 Aborigines were removed from the Burketown camp to Doomadgee Mission because they were 'destitute and too old to maintain themselves in employment'.[77] Correspondence from the local Protector gives a totally different view. When the matter was raised with him in October 1937 he advised the Chief Protector that he did not favour the proposal as it was not in the 'best interests of the natives concerned'. He maintained that while some were aged and infirm, others were not.[78] One woman listed on the removal order was not even at the Burketown camp; she was living with her daughter and son-in-law in Camooweal. Clearly Aboriginal people who came under the jurisdiction of the Act had little choice in where they lived. Many opted to lived on missions.

The presence of missions helped to alleviate some of the state's welfare obligations. Roth noted in 1905 that 'the mission stations are year by year becoming of greater assistance to the State in dealing with the pauper aboriginal waifs and strays, adults and children, on the most economic lines'.[79] There were some people including Governor MacGregor who would have preferred to see Aboriginal welfare handed over completely to the churches. While he was governor he submitted a scathing report on the government's handling of reserves in Queensland.[80] Others such as neighbouring pastoralists resented the missionary presence in their area. Bowman of Rutland Plains Station drafted a letter complaining of the impact of the Mitchell River Mission. 'When it first started', he wrote, 'the blacks about here were well behaved and respected a white man; now they seem to think they have a right to do what they like and go unscathed. In my opinion and I have a life's experience amongst outside blacks—there will be bloodshed before long.'[81]

With missionaries' attention focussed mainly on Aboriginal children, there was a need for the construction of dormitories in which they would be housed. Dormitory life was highly regimented and spartan; it formed a 'crucial part of a systematic attempt to socialise Aboriginal children into new modes of thought and behaviour'.[82] Reflecting on the system, a former Aurukun missionary said that they believed they were acting wisely,

> and only a few Aborigines seem to have 'realised' that such a policy was undermining their social structure and dealing a heavy blow to their culture . . . [Missionaries] saw the unhappy side of Aboriginal life, the dirt and the consequent bodily ills, the crippling sores, the blindness, the high infant mortality rate, things that most anthropologists failed to see.[83]

By 1934 two-thirds of Aboriginal adults on the west coast of Cape York Peninsula, although still living in the bush, were under the influence of the missions. On the east coast the only camps were at Port Stewart and Cape Melville. The Chief Protector noted in his report that those at Cape Melville were in the process of being transferred to Lockhart River Mission and it was hoped to 'secure' those from Port Stewart in the near future.[84] There were some officials who could foresee the problems in having the majority of Aborigines living on missions where there was 'limited scope for employment'.[85]

The original Act had been open ended in regard to wages but this was rectified in 1901. Aborigines employed on boats were to receive ten shillings a month and those engaged elsewhere five shillings. Notwithstanding the introduction of this legislation many Aboriginal workers remained unpaid or underpaid for their services and this was a matter of some concern for the Northern Protector of Aborigines.[86] As there were insufficient police to adequately enforce the payment of Aboriginal wages it was decided to begin with the wages due to women. From 1904 money earned by them was to be paid to Protectors every three or six months. All money collected was to be banked to the credit of the employee in the Government Savings Bank with the Protector as trustee. With the successful introduction of this system for women, the practice of having men's wages paid through a protector was introduced in 1909.[87] It was argued that this not only ensured that Aborigines got the full benefit of their labour but that it would be easier to instil the notion of thrift. Protector Sweetman of Charters Towers claimed to have had considerable success in this regard as he had been

> trying to educate some of the boys up to a spirit of thrift and save their money by showing the Savings Bank Pass-Book of the gins wherein some have as much as £18: They express wonder and surprise at so much money being the property of one gin. I am opposed to aboriginals having much money to squander, except a few shillings as pocket money but the native should get the full benefit of his labour for a rainy day.[88]

From 1909 Aboriginal men's wages were to be paid to individual Protectors who had considerable discretion in determining what proportion was to be banked and what was to be retained by the employee as pocket money. In most instances deductions ranged from 20 to 50 per cent 'according to intelligence'. In 1915 it was ruled that two-thirds of the adult wage was to be banked if clothing was provided, one-third if not. For men and women with families to support, it was recommended that only one-fifth be paid to the bank.[89]

> Although the initial idea behind bank accounts was to ensure that Aborigines were properly paid, successive protectors viewed savings as a form of insurance to tide workers over periods of unemployment; this had the advantage of reducing the cost of Aboriginal welfare to the state. Because of this, most Aborigines found it a frustrating experience to withdraw money from their personal savings accounts. The humiliation of having to wait outside the police station all day was vividly etched in the

memory of Marnie Kennedy who said that she would sit there all day frightened to go away and get a feed for fear that you would miss out. Then at 5 o'clock the protector would come out and say, 'Nothing today. Come back tomorrow' . . . It was just like a big kick up the ribs when it was your own money anyway.[90]

This was one of the tactics used to disempower Aboriginal people and 'keep them in their place'. The Member for the western seat of Gregory told parliament in 1945 that he had:

> seen the treatment that policemen have given them, not because they desired to be cruel but because they wished to demonstrate to the native that they, the policemen, were their masters. If they had not done that, then the native would have assumed an air of equality or superiority.[91]

Protectors had no hesitation in vetoing purchases deemed by them to be inappropriate. The Cardwell Protector expressed 'shock' when a newly married Aboriginal women applied for £4 from her savings for personal items for herself and home. She was advised that 'You must be more prudent with your pocket money that Mrs. Henry pays you for should you get sick your money will be handy to you then. However as it is Christmas I will let you have £1/5/- out of your Banking account to buy lollies with.'[92]

Apart from compulsory savings taken out of Aboriginal wages, a second deduction was made for the Aboriginal Provident Fund. From 1919 all workers not living on reserves were to contribute a portion of their wages for the relief of 'indigent natives'.[93] There seemed to be some confusion about the purpose of this fund. Was it for needy Aborigines generally or for the benefit of those temporarily unemployed who had contributed to the scheme? The Chief Protector explained in his 1921 report that it entitled contributors 'to relief for themselves and dependants when in want, out of employment, sickness etc'.[94] This point was further clarified in a circular to all Protectors in 1922. 'Benefits are limited to contributors to the fund and those actually dependent upon them in distress, including widows.'[95] The Department had consistently maintained that this was the purpose of the individual savings accounts. It therefore seems likely, particularly in view of later developments, that the Chief Protector himself was confused about the purpose of the fund. By 1935 the State Government held £293,549/4/11 of Aboriginal money in trust. It is small wonder that the prevailing belief in the 1930s was that Queensland would never surrender the management of Aboriginal affairs to the Federal Government because of the loss of control over Aboriginal bank accounts.[96] Aboriginal people were given little opportunity to manage their finances, even those exempted from the Act.

The provisions of the 1897 Act were to apply to all Aboriginal people unless they were specifically exempted. To control their own affairs they had to basically deny their Aboriginality. For instance in 1912 representation was made on behalf of 22 Aborigines employed on cattle stations. Fifteen were 'full-bloods' and automatically disqualified from applying for exemption from the Act. Only one of the remaining seven did not 'unnecessarily associate with Aborigines' and was therefore deemed suitable to handle his own affairs.[97] Even when Aborigines were granted exemption, it did not mean that they had the same rights as non-Aboriginal people. One well-known North Queensland identity had a twelve months' restriction imposed on his banking account when he was exempted in 1932. Expecting this to be raised at the end of the year, he entered into negotiations to purchase a truck. However he found himself in an embarrassing situation when the application for the release of his money was refused on the recommendation of the local Protector. His non-Aboriginal father-in-law was forced to appeal to the local branch of the Country Women's Association for help: 'You all know Dick as a decent fellow sober and hardworking courteous in his dealings and meetings with all concerned. You all know him as a good horsebreaker and as a man who is very fond of his wife and children.'[98]

These were indeed the attributes desired in Aborigines and on the recommendation of the minister, the man was allowed £60 to service his debt. His account, however, continued to be subjected to departmental control.

Although the 1897 legislation was based on the assumption that the Aboriginal population would eventually disappear, by

'In town for Christmas': the trip into Charters Towers at Christmas time was a rare opportunity for Aboriginal workers to personally have access to their savings accounts. *NORTH QUEENSLAND REGISTER*, 5 DECEMBER 1921

1924 with the Aboriginal and Islander population stabilised at 17 000 there was a realisation that this was not going to happen. Of particular concern was the increasing number of part-Aboriginal people whose numbers rose steadily from 4052 in 1931 to 6451 in 1941.[99] As a result, an amendment to the legislation in 1934 brought 'half-castes who previously could not legally be regarded as aboriginals' under the provisions of the Act. There were many instances of people being placed under the Act for the first time in the late 1930s. The folly of such a decision was recognised by some including the Chief Protector who confided to his deputy that: 'I am satisfied that the type of crossbreed seen in my recent inspections, although now embraced by the new Amendment Act, should not have such Act rigidly applied to them in regard to their business affairs as though they had been returned to the aboriginal fold.'[100]

Nevertheless before the legislation was changed countless Aboriginal people experienced the 'heavy hand' of the Department. A letter from one such person outlining the circumstances of his removal to Palm Island and the conditions on the settlement was published in the *North Queensland Guardian* in 1937. A resident of New South Wales, Saunders was sent to Palm Island for being 'an absconder and addicted to drink'. He maintained that he was sent there because he would not 'work under the Aborigines Act and pay into the settlement'. He pointed out that he 'was transferred here to a penal settlement to remain here how long I don't know. I wish to get out of here as soon as possible. I did no wrong outside. The condition of living does not suit me at all. I don't get paid for the amount of work I do and have very bad food.'[101]

The acting superintendent advised the Chief Protector that Saunders was 'so little coloured and his bearing and intelligence is such that he cannot be thought of as anything but a white man'. He believed that Saunders 'would be better regarded as a white man and, if he offended against the law, dealt with in the ordinary way'.[102]

New Aboriginal legislation was introduced in 1939 addressing the 'half-caste' issue. The Director of Native Affairs[103] argued that the main feature of the legislation was 'the upliftment of the civilised half-castes by automatically conferring freedom and full citizen rights where their circumstances and associations qualified them for such privilege'.[104] For those people resident on settlements there was no improvement in the repressive conditions under which they lived.[105] Heather Wearne has pointed out that the tone of the debate in Parliament was significantly different in 1939 from 1897. She maintains that while the earlier legislation grew out of a sense of guilt, this had clearly dissipated in 1939, with the debate more concerned with making the institution of reserves a success and 'preventing the Aboriginal population from disrupting white community standards'.[106]

Long before the 1939 legislation was enacted an increasing number of Aboriginal people were incarcerated in these institutions. As late as 1962 almost 10 000 Aboriginal people lived on government settlements and missions with a further 17 652 living on country reserves and Torres Strait Islands.[107] As already suggested, Palm Island, established in 1918, quickly gained a reputation as a 'punishment place'.[108] People were transferred there from all parts of the state and were often unaware of the reasons for their removal. On government settlements, as with missions, children were normally separated from their parents. Fred Clay recalled that when his family was removed to Palm Island in the 1930s the members were separated; his mother and two sisters were sent to the female dormitory and the three sons to the boys' residence. 'We saw each other only when permission was granted. There was a white person there they called a matron, you know. We had to get permission from her to visit the dormitory and see our mother. Pretty stiff when you've got to get permission to see your own mother.'[109]

Years before they were formally recognised in the 1939 Act Aboriginal Police on settlements were used to maintain divisions within the black population. Residents were well aware of the injustice of such a system, Willie Thaiday arguing that 'the policemen on Palm Island should not be called policemen . . . They are only trackers from far away inland and they know nothing about law, not a scrap. They never been to school and all they do is what the superintendent tell them.'[110] The overwhelming majority of incidences on the settlement were dealt with by the Aboriginal Police and Courts where there was no right to a defence lawyer and no provisions for appeals against rulings made arbitrarily by the superintendent. On Palm Island even children were gaoled for insignificant misdemeanours. Marnie Kennedy recalled her experiences as a child in the late 1920s: 'I was singing this song "Who Said I was a Bum". I didn't know that the matron was coming through the dormitory. Next thing I found myself in jail for the night because I was singing that song and using the word "bum".'[111]

There seemed to be little logic in the way that punishment was dispensed. One inmate reported that 'a married man cleared out with a single girl for a couple of days'. They were sentenced to fourteen days gaol. After this the man was appointed to the police force and the girl was sent to Fantome Island.[112] In 1937 Tommy Ryan was charged with disobeying the orders of the superintendent and sentenced to seven days' imprisonment; Ted Bosun, sergeant of police was charged with trying to commit suicide and allowed to carry on as police sergeant; Constable Ross was found ill-treating his wife and when he reported the matter to the superintendent he was told to go home and that it was all right.[113]

A multitude of other practices compounded the sense of powerlessness experienced by those Aboriginal people unfortunate enough to be incarcerated on Queensland Aboriginal settlements. All inward and outward mail was censored in much the same way as occurred with soldiers in a theatre of war. From the 1930s, Aborigines living on settlements had to obtain permission from the superintendent before they could marry.[114] Even though most residents had committed no crime, they had to have the superintendent's permission before leaving the settlement. All residents could be ordered to work for 32 hours a week without pay. For those sections of the Aboriginal community subjected to increasing controls and regulations it must have been extremely difficult to maintain a sense of self-worth.

From 1904 Torres Strait Islanders were also subject to the provisions of the Act after it was discovered that white employers were exploiting them. Once again this was a situation where the victims paid the penalty for crimes committed against them. By the 1930s administrators looked favourably on Islanders who owned the largest pearling fleet in the north and marketed their products through the Native Trading Station and branch stores. As a result when new Aboriginal legislation was drawn up in 1939 it was decided that Torres Strait Islanders should be treated differently in a separate Bill, a large part of which dealt with local government. A departmental report noted that:

> This Bill has been introduced to give constitutional effect to a system of self-government which with sympathetic departmental assistance, has been evolved by these people, and to direct and assist them further towards perfecting such a system, at the same time fully preserving their racial entity and protecting their interests when such conflict with those of the European race.[115]

Like the *Aboriginal Act, 1939*, the notion of protection and preservation was still an integral part of the *Torres Strait Act*. In 1946 provision was made for elected councils on mainland

'King George of Saxby Downs and his consort': some Aboriginal workers were rewarded with King plates for their service. This did not prevent them ending up in a government settlement in their old age. QUEENSLAND PARLIAMENTARY PAPERS, 1910, VOL. 3

reserves and settlements in a bid to have more uniformity between the two Acts. However superintendents still controlled the proceedings of these councils when they were established. The superintendent could, for instance, declare a candidate ineligible 'for any reason whatsoever'.

By the 1950s it was becoming increasingly difficult to contain Aboriginal resentment of white bureaucracy on some settlements. When Roy Bartlam took over as Superintendent of Palm Island in 1954 he enforced the rules and regulations much more rigorously than his predecessor. Indignation at Bartlam's authoritarian style reached a peak in 1957; the catalyst was a disagreement between Len Croker, the white hygiene officer, and Albie Geia, an Aboriginal foreman. Eventually the whole island was drawn into the dispute leading to a general strike of all workers who were opposed to the administrative style of the superintendent. With the situation at flash point Bartlam called in twenty armed police officers from Townsville to arrest the six strike leaders. Without any charges being laid, these men were sent to three different settlements simply through the invocation of removal orders.[116]

Apart from the protest by residents on missions and settlements, those in towns who were less constrained by the Act were also becoming more politically active. Two of the most powerful identities to emerge from Cairns were Gladys O'Shane and Joe McGinness,[117] the latter subsequently becoming the Federal president of the Federal Council for Aboriginal and Torres Strait Islanders (FCAATSI). This organisation and others such as the Queensland State Council for the Advancement of Aborigines and Torres Strait Islanders which was formed in 1958 were important in putting Aboriginal issues on the political agenda and giving Aboriginal and Islander people the confidence to voice their grievances of the system. Evelyn Scott recalled that she

> never thought the day would come when I could tackle politicians, bureaucrats in government departments, and stand up in universities and address students. When growing up as a child in North Queensland I never thought I could achieve those things. Meeting people like [Faith Bandler] and Dulcie Flower, Joe McGinness and Kath Walker gave me confidence.[118]

In 1962 the State Government set up a review of Aboriginal affairs and the recommendations from this committee formed the basis of new legislation in which the general thrust was away from protection towards assimilation.[119] The concept of Protectors was abandoned in favour of the term District Officers who tended to be clerks of magistrate's courts rather than police officers. The Director of Native Affairs became the Director of Aboriginal and Islanders Affairs, superintendents were to be called managers and the terms 'settlement' and 'mission' were to be replaced with 'community'. Provision was made in Section 44 of the 1965 Act for Aboriginal Councils and Courts and under the Regulations of 1966, the structure of both institutions was to change. The Councils on each of the designated communities[120] were to consist of two assisted Aborigines to be appointed by the Director and two assisted Aborigines to be elected by residents. The Council was responsible to the manager for the conduct, discipline and well-being of assisted Aborigines residing within the reserve or community. Councils had the power to make by-laws, resolutions and orders for the well-being and progressive development of assisted residents. This appeared to be much more democratic than the previous situation but in reality little had changed as the Director could remove any of the members of an Aboriginal Council and all by-laws had to receive the approval of the Director before they were officially sanctioned.

In 1971 the Aboriginal and Torres Strait Islander populations once again came under the jurisdiction of separate Acts of Parliament. A major feature of these Acts was the abolition of the 'assisted Aborigine' category but the Department continued to manage the financial affairs for those who requested that this continue. Objectionable terms such as 'full-blood' and 'strain or preponderance of Aboriginal blood' were dropped in favour of a less complex definition of an Aborigine; 'a person who is a descendant of an indigenous inhabitant of the Commonwealth of Australia other than the Torres Strait Islands'. However after years of living under the cloud of the Act, these cosmetic changes may have made little difference to Aboriginal people. In 1982, when an Aboriginal man was asked if it would be possible to borrow his 50 year-old exemption certificate to copy, his response was 'No, no the government might ask for it.'

The 1971 Acts dealt almost exclusively with reserves specifying who could and could not enter them. An Aborigine who wanted to live on a reserve indefinitely or for a period of more than one month, had to apply to the Council chairman. A residence permit was then granted 'if and only if' the Council and the Director were satisfied that such residence was 'in the best interests of the applicant'. If a resident left a reserve, the permit was automatically terminated unless the departure was for a short term. Whereas under the 1965 Act it had been difficult for residents to leave reserves, under the new legislation it became difficult for them to return. Garth Nettheim was concerned that there was a 'danger that any past repression in this matter may be superseded by a sense of insecurity'. In his opinion neither condition was conducive to achieving 'the confidence of citizenship'.[121]

Mounting national pressure in the 1970s and 80s forced the Queensland Government to repeal its 1971 legislation and replace it with the *Community Services (Torres Strait) Act* and the *Community Services (Aborigines) Act* in 1984. The most important aspect of the new Acts was the granting of local government powers to community councils. While Minister Bob Katter claimed that the legislation reflected 'the government's desire to unfetter Aboriginal and Islander people in formulating decisions which affect the development of their communities', a number of restrictions were contained in the legislation. For instance, councils were required to submit an annual budget to the minister who had the power to reject it. Frank Brennan has observed that in general these councils 'were not viewed as responsible, elected councils expending their own funds but as public servants expending government funds and therefore accountable to the Queensland government through its officers'.[122] An amendment subsequently introduced by the Goss government has given the Aboriginal and Island Councils more autonomy in financial accountability but many other problems remain unresolved.

In the early decades of the twentieth century, Queensland was seen as the authority in the administration of Aboriginal affairs. With hindsight it was an accolade which clearly was misplaced. A large proportion of the state's Aboriginal and Islander population has experienced institutionalism either on a mission or a government settlement or community. Subjected to so many changes, these people have been left, in many cases, insecure and unsure of their identity. Moreover State paternalism has saturated every piece of legislation dealing with Queensland Aborigines and Torres Strait Islanders. The effect has been to slowly extract any power they had over their own lives. It is a situation to which four and five generations have been exposed, effectively crippling initiative and self-esteem. The traditional authority of elders has been replaced with the authority of the State. With the passage of time Aboriginal people have been subjected to less overt physical violence but there has been little improvement in the recognition of their human rights. The destructive impact of European colonisation is as evident in the twentieth century as it was in the nineteenth.

NOTES

1. See D.J.Mulvaney and J.Peter White (eds), *Australians to 1788*, Fairfax, Syme and Weldon, Sydney, 1987.
2. For a more detailed analysis of maritime, pastoral, rainforest and mining frontier experience see N.Loos, *Invasion and Resistance*, ANU Press, Canberra, 1982.
3. George Leslie to his parents, 10 Dec. 1839, 24 June 1841; Walter

to William Leslie, 14 April 1844; Patrick to his parents, 2 March 1843, K.G.T.Waller, 'The Letters of the Leslie Brothers in Australia 1834–54.' B.A. Hons. thesis, History Department, University of Qld, 1956 pp.85, 97, 102, 104. For a recent account see M.French, *Conflict on the Condamine: Aborigines and the European Invasion*, Darling Downs Institute Press, Toowoomba, 1989.

4 G.S.Lang, *The Aborigines of Australia*, Melbourne, 1865, p.77.

5 The early history of the Native Police is discussed in L.E.Skinner, *Police of the Pastoral Frontier*, University of Qld Press, St Lucia, 1971. For the later history consult N.Taylor, 'The Native Mounted Police of Queensland', B.A. Hons. thesis, James Cook University, 1970.

6 See the letters of Frederick Walker to Colonial Secretary, 18 Oct. 1849, 1 July 1854. Letters re Moreton Bay and Native Police, Mitchell Library mss. A2/19, A2/48; 1 March 1852, *NSW Legislative Council Votes & Proceedings (V & P)*, 1852, vol.1, p.789.

7 There is much debate currently about the original Aboriginal population. See for instance 'How Many People?' in J.P.White and D.J.Mulvaney (eds), pp.115–17.

8 See J.Camm and J.H.Quitton, eds, *Australians: An Historical Atlas*, Fairfax, Syme and Weldon, Sydney, 1987, p.65.

9 *Moreton Bay Courier*, 27 May 1862.

10 *North Australian*, 6 Dec. 1861.

11 ibid, 21 Sept. 1860.

12 For the question of the pastoral leases see H.Reynolds, *The Law of the Land*, Penguin, Ringwood, 1988, pp.137–46.

13 For material on the two attacks see G.Reid, *A Nest of Hornets: the Massacre of the Fraser Family at Hornet Bank 1857*, Oxford University Press, Melbourne, 1982. J.Wright, *The Cry for the Dead*, Oxford University Press, Melbourne, 1981.

14 Select Committee on Murders by the Aborigines on the Dawson River, *NSW Legislative Assembly*, *V & P*, 1858, p.849.

15 Ipswich correspondent, *Moreton Bay Courier*, 14 Nov. 1857.

16 *Queensland Guardian*, 6 Nov. 1861.

17 ibid.

18 Select Committee on Native Police Force, *Queensland V & P*, 1961, p.151.

19 Reported in *Queensland Guardian*, 27 July 1861.

20 *The Courier*, 25 July 1861.

21 H.Reynolds, 'The Unrecorded Battlefields of Queensland',

H.Reynolds (ed.), *Race Relations in North Queensland*, James Cook University, Townsville, 1978, pp.34–36.
22   19 April 1876.
23   M.Collison, 'The Recent Outrage on the Blacks', *Rockhampton Bulletin*, 25 June 1867.
24   A.Knaplund, 'Sir Arthur Gordon and the New Guinea Question', *Historical Studies of Australia and New Zealand*, 7, 1955–57, pp.330–31.
25   Diary of Caroline Creaghe, Mitchell Library, mss, 2982.
26   E.Thorn, 'A White Australia—The Other Side', *United Australia*, 25 Oct. 1901.
27   Anti-Slavery Papers, S22/697, Rhodes House, Oxford.
28   Report on the Board of Inquiry in the Aboriginal Reserve at Mackay, *Queensland V & P*, 1876, vol. 3, p.166.
29   For a discussion of racial ideas see H.Reynolds, 'Racial Thought in Early Colonial Australia', *Australian Journal of Politics and History*, 20, Apr. 1974, pp.45–53.
30   J.H.C., 'Civilization Based on Moralization', *Moreton Bay Courier*, 16 Aug. 1856.
31   *Moreton Bay Courier*, 19 Jan. 1856.
32   *Moreton Bay Free Press*, 29 Jan. 1852.
33   *Brisbane Courier*, 25 March 1865.
34   For a discussion of Social Darwinism see H.Reynolds, *Frontier*, Allen & Unwin, Sydney, 1987, pp.115–23; A.Markus, *From the Barrel of A Gun*, Victorian Historical Assoc., West Melbourne, 1974.
35   C.Lumholtz, *Among Cannibals*, London, 1889, p.348.
36   Letter from A.C.G., *Queenslander*, 5 June 1880.
37   Report by A.Meston on the Government Scientific Expedition to the Bellenden Ker Range, *Queensland V and P*, 1889, 5, p.1213. See also R.Evans, K.Saunders and K.Cronin, *Race Relations in Colonial Queensland*, University of Queensland Press, St Lucia, 1988.
38   A generalised picture of the Aboriginal response to Europeans is found in H.Reynolds, *The Other Side of the Frontier*, Penguin, Ringwood, 1982.
39   For an assessment of the impact of frontier see N.A.Loos, *Invasion and Resistance*. ANU Press, Canberra, 1982, N.A.Loos and H.Reynolds, 'Aboriginal Resistance in Queensland', *Australian Journal of Politics and History*, 22, Aug. 1976, pp.214–15.

40 'Report on the Aborigines of North Queensland', *Queensland V & P*, 1896, 4, p.3.
41 *Port Denison Times*, 12 June 1869.
42 *Queenslander*, 12 Jan. 1884.
43 ibid, 5 June 1880.
44 On the Aborigines West of the Warrego, June 1890, Queensland State Archives, COL/144.
45 *Brisbane Courier*, 29 Jan. 1863.
46 'Here and There in Queensland', *Illustrated Sydney News*, 24 Oct. 1885.
47 Report on the flogging by Constable Kind of an Aborigine, Queensland Colonial Secretary Files, CSP/A2894 of 1876.
48 N.A.Loos, p.433.
49 L.R.Smith, *The Aboriginal Population of Australia*, ANU Press, Canberra, 1980, pp.122–43.
50 A.Meston, 'Report on the Aboriginals of Queensland', *Queensland V&P*, 1896, pp.723–40.
51 Meston clearly subscribed to the notion of survival of the fittest. See above p.15.
52 *The Native Labourers' Protection Act* was passed in 1884 but this related specifically to those employed in the fishing and pearling industries.
53 H.Reynolds, *Aborigines and Settlers: the Australian Experience 1788–1939*, Cassell, Stanmore, 1972, p.162.
54 Meston had an ambivalent attitude to Aborigines. He felt that those who were foolish enough to trust blacks were likely to pay the penalty with their life. Yet in the same report he noted that 'Every white man murdered by blacks is represented by at least 50 blacks murdered by white men. The white man has, beyond all question been the most unscrupulous and deliberate murderer of the two.' A.Meston, 'Bellenden-Ker Range (Wooroonooran) North Queensland', *Queensland V & P*, 1889, 4, p.1213.
55 W.Thorpe, 'Archibald Meston and Aboriginal Legislation in Colonial Queensland', *Historical Studies*, vol.21, no.82, April 1984, p.62.
56 A.Meston, *Queensland Aboriginals: Proposed System for their Improvement and Preservation*, Brisbane, 1895, p.28.
57 *Queensland Parliamentary Debates*, 78, 1897, p.1541.
58 *Queensland Government Gazette*, 2 April 1904.
59 'Measures Recently Adopted for the Amelioration of the Aborigines', *Queensland V & P*, 1897, 2.

60 Annual Report Northern Protector of Aboriginals, *Queensland Parliamentary Papers (QPP)*, 1904, p.870.
61 McG.Watson to Police Commissioner, 10 Aug. 1898, POL/J16, Queensland State Archives.
62 Quain to Galbraith, 27 Dec. 1902, A/44679, Queensland State Archives.
63 Cited in Annual Report of Northern Protector of Aboriginals 1902, *QPP*, 1903, 2, p.471.
64 Annual Report Northern Protector of Aboriginals 1899, *Queensland V & P*, 1900, 5, p.590.
65 Annual Report Chief Protector of Aboriginals 1904, *QPP*, 1905, 1, pp.773–74.
66 *North Queensland Register*, 25 Sept. 1905, p.4.
67 'Condition of the Aborigines', *Queensland V & P*, 1898, 4, p.499.
68 Annual Report of Chief Protector of Aboriginals 1908, *QPP*, 1909, 2, p.975.
69 Annual Report of the Northern Protector of Aboriginals for 1900, *Queensland V & P*, 1901, 4, p.1335.
70 *Mapoon Story by the Mapoon People*, International Development Action, Fitzroy, 1975, p.7.
71 For more discussion of this see D.May, 'Aboriginal Labour in the North Queensland Cattle Industry 1897–1968', PhD thesis, History Dept, James Cook University, 1986.
72 Cited in B.Rosser, *Dreamtime Nightmares*, IAS, Canberra, 1985, p.85.
73 Petition from Albert Hippi, Charlie Anderson, Jimmy Keyes, Harry No.2, Sandy Woolgar, Willie Cooktown, Douglas and George Kane to Minister for Justice, 1 Jan. 1923, 25/593, HOM/J453, Queensland State Archives.
74 24/9082, Home Secretary's Register 1924, HOM/B64, Queensland State Archives.
75 Chief Protector to Under Secretary, Dept. of Health and Home Affairs, 17 Nov. 1937, TR1227/107, Queensland State Archives.
76 Bob Hegarty interviewed by Dawn May in Cooktown, 4 May 1984.
77 Annual Report of Aboriginal Dept. 1938, *QPP*, 1939, 2, p.1330.
78 Burketown Protector to Chief Protector, 5 Oct. 1937, TR1227/5, Queensland State Archives.
79 Annual Report of Chief Protector of Aboriginals 1904, *QPP*, 1905, 1, p.761.

80 Governor's Outward Dispatches, 1905–14, GOV/68, Queensland State Archives.
81 Soon after drafting the letter, Bowman was killed by blacks when he attempted to disperse them from his property. Bowman's letter was sent to the local member who read it out in Parliament during the debate on supply. (*Queensland Parliamentary Debates* 1910, 107, p.2186–87.)
82 D.Martin, 'Background Paper on Social and Family Factors for the Aurukun Case', Prepared for the Royal Commission into Aboriginal Deaths in Custody, 1988.
83 G.MacKenzie, *Aurukun Diary*, Aldersgate Press, Melbourne, 1981, p.199.
84 Chief Protector of Aboriginals, 16 Aug. 1933, TR1227/3, Queensland State Archives.
85 Protector of Aboriginals, Thursday Island to Chief Protector of Aboriginals, 11 June 1935, 35/2512, TR1227/4. Queensland State Archives.
86 Annual Report of the Northern Protector of Aboriginals for 1902, *QPP*, 1903, 2, p.452,
87 Annual Report of Chief Protector of Aboriginals 1908, *QPP*, 1909, 2, p.974.
88 Annual Report of Chief Protector of Aboriginals 1905, *QPP*, 1906, 2, p.914.
89 Circular from CPA to all Protectors, 17 Dec. 1914, Clerk of Petty Sessions, Cardwell, 1914–25, CPS 12J/W8. Queensland State Archives.
90 Interview with Marnie Kennedy by Dawn May in Townsville, 15 Feb. 1982.
91 *Queensland Parliamentary Debates*, 1945–46, 186.
92 Aboriginal Protector, Cardwell to Lucy, 16 Dec. 1917, Letterbook of Protector of Aborigines, Clerk of Petty Sessions, 1914–25, CPS 12J/G2, Queensland State Archives.
93 *Queensland Government Gazette*, 6 June 1919, Section 1 (1) para (4).
94 Annual Report of Chief Protector of Aboriginals 1921, *QPP*, 1922, 2, p.472.
95 Circular 22/7, CPA to All Protectors, June 1922, Papers and Circulars relating to Aborigines, 1914–25, Clerk of Petty Sessions, Cardwell, CPS 12J/W8, Queensland State Archives.
96 *Queensland Parliamentary Debates*, 1933, 163, p.920.
97 12/654 HOM/J83, Queensland State Archives.

98 Leandro Illin to Queensland Country Womens Assoc., Upper Stone branch, 4 Aug. 1933, 33/10018, A/3667, Queensland State Archives.
99 Smith, p.138.
100 Chief Protector of Aboriginals to Deputy Chief Protector of Aboriginals, 11 Jan. 1935, 35/2737, TR1227/4, Queensland State Archives.
101 *North Queensland Guardian*, 17 July 1937.
102 Julian to Chief Protector of Aboriginals, 30 June 1937, 33/480, TR1227/107, Queensland State Archives.
103 The office of Chief Protector of Aboriginals was retitled the Director of Native Affairs under the *Aboriginals Preservation and Protection Act of 1939*.
104 Report of Director of Native Affairs 1939, QPP, 1940, 1, p.1077.
105 *Aboriginal Preservation and Protection Act 1939*, Section 12.
106 H.Wearne, *A Clash of Cultures: Queensland Aboriginal Policy 1824–1980*, Uniting Church in Australia, Brisbane, 1980, p.14.
107 Annual Report, Director of Native Affairs 1962, p.2.
108 See D.May. 'A Punishment Place' in B.Gammage and P.Spearritt (eds), *Australians: 1938*, Fairfax Syme and Weldon, Sydney, 1987, pp.95–103.
109 Cited Rosser, p.129.
110 W.Thaiday, *Under the Act*, N.Q. Black Publishing, Townsville, 1981, p.27.
111 Marnie Kennedy interviewed by Dawn May in Townsville, 23 Nov. 1983.
112 *North Queensland Guardian*, 17 July 1937. A lock hospital was erected on Fantome Island in 1926 to deal with the numerous cases of venereal disease and by the early 1930s all people being transferred to Palm Island had to pass through Fantome Island first.
113 Report of R.Cilento, Director-General of Health and Medical Services on Palm Island Feb.–March 1937, TR1227/236, Queensland State Archives.
114 Under the provisions of the 1901 Amendment it had been only necessary to obtain permission in writing if an Aboriginal woman wanted to marry a non-Aboriginal.
115 History Leading to the Introduction of the Torres Strait Islanders Bill 1939, TR1227/150, Queensland State Archives.
116 W.Thaiday, *Under the Act* NQ Black Publishing, Townsville, 1981; A.Burger, *Neville Bonner: A Biography* Macmillan, South Mel-

bourne, 1979; Information received by the TLC TR1227/260; Report by Director of Native Affairs to Under Sec., Dept of Health and Home Affairs, 12 July 1957, 57/4883, TR1227/260, Queensland State Archives.
117 See J.McGinness, *Son of Aiyandabu*, University of Queensland Press, St Lucia, 1991.
118 Cited in F.Bandler, *Turning the Tide*, Aboriginal Studies Press, Canberra, 1989, p.150.
119 By 1951 all Australian governments claimed to have adopted a policy of assimilation but it was to be another decade before a common definition of the term was adopted.
120 Cherbourg, Hope Vale, Palm Island, Lockhart River, Yarrabah, Edward River, Woorabinda, Mitchell River, Weipa, Mornington Island, Cowal Creek, Doomadgee, Umagico (Bamaga), Aurukun, New Mapoon, Bloomfield River.
121 G.Nettheim, *Outlawed: Queensland's Aborigines and Islanders and the Rule of Law*, ANZ Book Co., Sydney 1973, p.34.
122 F.Brennan, *Land Rights Queensland Style*, University of Queensland Press, St Lucia, 1992, p.64.

5
South Australia

COLONISATION of the region now known as South Australia conformed to the pattern of dispossession and colonial settlement imposed on other parts of the Australian continent. From the European-Australian perspective, South Australia had some unique features. The colony was established by a private commercial company and land was distributed on a systematic basis to private, free citizens. There were no convicts. However, for indigenous people the process of alienation of land for urban, agricultural, pastoral and mining development was the same as in other regions.

Although Aborigines in South Australia were not subjected to the systematic brutality of early Tasmanian colonisation, and missed the harsh ironies of indirect rule using Native Police, they did not escape thefts of land, violent conflict or high mortality rates from introduced diseases. Government policies introduced to control and manage Aboriginal people strongly resembled those of other colonial and state parliaments, particularly Queensland and Western Australia, although their implementation was perhaps less doctrinaire than in those two states.

While the colonisation of South Australia was preceded by much debate in Britain over how rights to land in the 'occupation and enjoyment of the Natives' might be protected, in practice they were afforded no more protection than Aboriginal rights in any other colony. Ultimately the colonisation process and its impact on Aborigines was determined by the type of settler

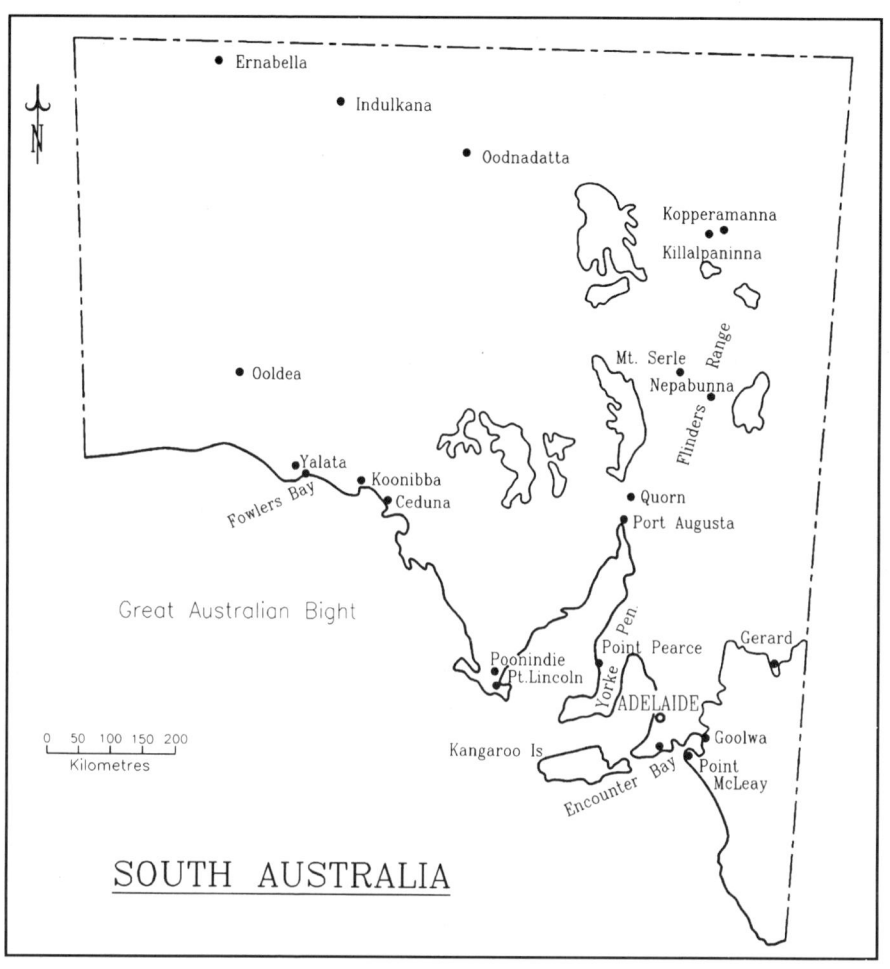

capitalist development (for example, mining, agriculture) and Aboriginal responses to it, rather than state policies.

Yet Aboriginal people did survive. Before tracing the familiar stories of dispossession, discriminatory legislation, institutionalisation, and harsh treatment by the courts and police, it is important to emphasise the capacity of suppressed peoples to triumph over adversity through many generations.

The history of the Wilton family of the north Flinders Ranges encapsulates the experiences of many Aboriginal people in South

Australia: initial dispossession, economic change, the threat of dispersal, periodic unemployment, Christian missions and government interference, and, most recently, a return to control of some of their lands and their own lives. Susie Noble, an Adnyamathanha woman, was born at Owieandana in the Flinders Ranges in South Australia in the latter part of the nineteenth century. Her generation grew up on land which they shared with non-Aboriginal pastoralists, working for rations, supplemented by food they gathered and hunted themselves. They learnt English, while maintaining their own languages, rites of passage and beliefs. For a long time they were relatively free from missionary influence or government interference. Yet only a decade or two earlier there had been a strong police presence in the district as the Adnyamathanha fought to retain control of their lands and established food sources. Susie Noble's uncle, Mount Serle Bob (also known as King Bob) told stories of violence and resistance when the first white men came to the Flinders Ranges. Those Adnyamathanha who survived the first years of contact adjusted their lives to new circumstances, until the 1890s brought economic depression and drought. A number of pastoral stations closed down, leaving Adnyamathanha people destitute and starving. The pastoral station, Mount Serle, initially acquired by the government as a camel depot and transport centre for the far north, became an Aboriginal ration depot, providing a tenuous life support system.

Susie Noble was first married to Ti-Tree Jack and then to Albert Wilton, but in 1909 she also had a son, Rufus, by George Edinton, the white caretaker at the Mount Serle camel depot. Rufus was brought up by his mother and his Aboriginal father, Albert Wilton. His biological father tried, but failed, to have Rufus taken from his Aboriginal family.[1] There were also attempts to remove Rufus under the *Aborigines Act, 1911*, which allowed children of mixed descent to be taken from their mothers and placed in institutions. Susie used to darken Rufus' skin with black ochre so he would not stand out from the other children. So, while the South Australian Government was quite remote from the Flinders Ranges, decisions taken in Adelaide did impinge on the Adnyamathanha.

In 1914 members of the South Australian Royal Commission on the Aborigines visited the Ranges and heard evidence from Susie Wilton. She explained that children at Mount Serle needed a school. Reading, writing and arithmetic would help protect them against unscrupulous employers. She said she was not interested in Christianity.[2] Rufus never got the schooling his mother asked for. But he did get full Adnyamathanha training culminating in the *wilyeru*, or second stage initiation ceremony. He taught himself to read and write while moving from one pastoral station to another with his parents. As a young adult he continued to follow stock work as it became available in the Ranges.

In the late 1920s another major crisis faced the Adnyamathanha—more drought, another Depression. Mount Serle ration depot closed and most Adnyamathanha were out of work. They established a settlement for themselves in the corner of a pastoral station called Ram Paddock Gate, where they sank wells and built cottages. Albert and Susie Wilton built their home alongside that of Rufus and his wife Ethel.[3] In 1929 the Adnyamathanha were introduced to Christianity by a missionary from the United Aborigines Mission (UAM), who also distributed rations, perhaps saving the people from starvation. The missionary negotiated land for a permanent settlement at Nepabunna which became the focal point of Adnyamathanha community life. Both Albert and Susie Wilton died at Nepabunna in the 1940s and Rufus lived there for sixteen years. He met and worked with the anthropologist, C. P. Mountford.

Rufus resented the missionaries' interference in Adnyamathanha ceremonial business and, when the elders discussed discontinuing the ceremonies, he strongly favoured maintaining them. Nevertheless the last initiations were held in 1947. By this time Rufus had left Nepabunna in search of work. While the missionaries realised they could not influence Rufus, they tried to retain his children. They used the power of the Aborigines Protection Board to force Rufus to return his children. His only means of escaping the control of the Protection Board was to apply for exemption from the Aborigines Act. Henceforth he was not legally defined as Aboriginal. He could no longer visit family and friends at Nepabunna nor seek any form of assistance from the Board.

Rufus worked at Leigh Creek coalfields from 1943–73, but as Aborigines (even exempted Aborigines) were barred from living in Leigh Creek township, his family lived at Beltana and he visited them on his bicycle at weekends. In 1973 the UAM withdrew from Nepabunna and an Aboriginal Council was elected to administer the settlement, but Rufus never returned to live there. The Adnyamathanha also gained control of the Nepabunna land and the Mount Serle pastoral lease in the 1980s.

In the 1970s and 1980s Rufus worked closely with the Aboriginal Heritage Branch recording Adnyamathanha sites of significance, history and language as a means of ensuring the continuity of this knowledge for posterity. He epitomised the Adnyamathanha ability to respond to changing circumstances, while maintaining strong links with the Adnyamathanha past.

Against the background of many similar stories of adaptation and survival, this chapter surveys two linked processes. First we follow the long process which Europeans called 'the spread of settlement' but which Aboriginal people experienced as dispossession and subjection to a new political and economic hegemony. Second we consider how that new hegemony was maintained through legislation, institutionalisation and the judicial system.

COLONIAL SETTLEMENT AND ABORIGINAL DISPOSSESSION

Although 1836 is the date generally given as the start of British colonisation in South Australia, direct and indirect contacts between Aborigines and non-Aborigines predate the establishment of Adelaide as the capital of the new British colony.

Whalers and sealers had lived on Kangaroo Island since about 1803 and are known to have come to the mainland and abducted women from the south-east coast and lower Eyre Peninsula. In 1829–30 Charles Sturt led an exploring party down the Murray River, encountering many Aboriginal people along the river as he went. He saw evidence that smallpox or some similar disease had infected people along the river sometime prior to his expe-

The Kuri Dance, George French Angas (detail from hand-coloured lithograph). ART GALLERY OF SOUTH AUSTRALIA 667G46

dition. George French Angas recorded that an epidemic, which originated in New South Wales, had killed many people on the lower Murray before any direct white contact, decimating whole communities.[4] It is possible that the disease spread further through South Australia, so that many Aboriginal people only encountered Europeans after indirect effects of colonisation had caused major disruption to their lives.

Permanent occupation of land in South Australia by the British began in 1836. Governor Hindmarsh landed at Holdfast Bay and established a town on the River Torrens which grew very rapidly. In 1844, eight years after the British landed, South Australia had a non-Aboriginal population of 17 366, which had increased to 85 821 by 1855.[5] Most of these people lived in Adelaide and its environs. Almost from the time they landed they vastly outnumbered the Kaurna people, who occupied the Adelaide Plains.[6] The intrusion of these outsiders onto the land of the Kaurna, the Aborigines on the coast south to Goolwa and Encounter Bay, and the people in the Mount Lofty Ranges, was devastating; many died and no doubt some tried to avoid the devastation by leaving the area.[7] Yet despite the disastrous effects of the arrival of the British on the Kaurna, Aboriginal people from the Murray River were attracted to Adelaide. They came out of curiosity, to collect rations and blankets (a substitute for their fur capes) and to take advantage of the disarray of the Kaurna to move over their lands. This pattern of devastation, revulsion and attraction continued to be an ingredient of Aboriginal/non-Aboriginal relations for the next century.

Although most Europeans came to South Australia by sea, in the early years of the colony much of the livestock came overland from New South Wales along the well watered route of the Murray River. The overlanders who accompanied the stock had no respect for the Aboriginal people over whose land they trespassed. Many made unprovoked attacks on Aborigines, 'marauding, shooting, molesting and abusing women as they went'.[8] The Aborigines along the Murray retaliated, attacking the overlanders and driving off stock. The colonists responded by sending a number of punitive expeditions up the river, some of which were repulsed by the Aborigines. In 1841 an expedition, led by the Protector of Aborigines, went to Rufus River in New South Wales where over thirty Aborigines were killed:

> The firing commenced before spears were thrown on account of inequality between the two parties; the natives at least were 150 strong whilst the Europeans had only thirty-six that could be spared apart from the sheep, cattle and drays. Some natives had two and three spears each, every spear being equal to a musket if sufficiently near an object to be thrown, and to have waited until the Natives were within that distance would have been to expose the Europeans to certain defeat.[9]

This massacre was officially condoned and therefore well documented, unlike many mass killings of Aborigines in South Australia. The incident also shows that Aboriginal people did not passively accept the process of dispossession and destruction but often made carefully planned attacks on the invaders of their lands.

From Adelaide Europeans moved out in search of land and wealth. They almost immediately moved south to Encounter Bay and Goolwa and by the early 1840s had extended eastwards. In 1846 there were 263 Europeans living south of Rivoli Bay.[10] This south-east movement was accompanied by violent conflict as

Aborigines continued to try to defend their rights over land until about 1848.[11]

At the same time colonists pushed north and west of Adelaide. Copper mining and pastoralism were established on Yorke Peninsula in the 1840s. Europeans had also established a toehold on Eyre Peninsula. In 1840 there were 190 Europeans in the Port Lincoln district and 48 houses in Port Lincoln.[12] Initial encounters between the Aborigines and the intruders were particularly violent in that region, a legacy of distrust engendered in the era of the whalers and exacerbated by the rough, lawless behaviour of some of the early settlers. The Nauo were determined to protect their territory and they almost succeeded in forcing the Europeans away from the lower Eyre Peninsula. But the Europeans persisted and gradually occupied the western and eastern coasts of the Peninsula. There was also movement into the interior of South Australia, extending in the 1850s through the mid-north and the Flinders Ranges to the salt lakes. Initial encounters in the Flinders Ranges and to the north were also characterised by violence. Inabuthina (also known as Pompey) was the most notorious of the Aborigines who resisted European incursion through direct attacks on Europeans, their stock and stores. In 1867 two missions in the salt lakes area were temporarily abandoned because of fears of attack by Aborigines.

By the 1880s, though, non-Aboriginal people were well entrenched over much of South Australia, excluding only the north-west and the western interior. They were continually demanding more land, leading to pastoral runs being subdivided into smaller blocks for agriculture in the late nineteenth century, which increased pressure on many Aborigines. While Aborigines could maintain many elements of their traditional life within the pastoral economy, agriculture prevented movement over land, forcing them on to missions or the outskirts of towns. Large numbers of Aborigines died or were displaced by the pastoral industry, especially in the north-east.

The distribution of Aboriginal people and land ownership-usage patterns of the period prior to 1836 in southern South Australia had been completely disrupted by the turn of the century. There were two large communities at Point Pearce on

People receiving weekly rations at Oodnadatta c 1908. SOUTH AUSTRALIAN ABORIGINAL HERITAGE PHOTOGRAPHIC COLLECTION, DEPARTMENT OF STATE ABORIGINAL AFFAIRS

Yorke Peninsula and Point McLeay on Lake Alexandrina in the south-east. There were also a few families scattered through the south-east and in the Riverland picking up seasonal work. Nevertheless, Aboriginal people's knowledge of their ancestors' origins was still extant.

On northern Eyre Peninsula, the west coast and in the Flinders Ranges and other pastoral areas, Aboriginal people worked on farms and stations or tried to live off the land. They supplemented their own efforts with rations for the aged and infirm distributed by the police at Koonibba and Killalpannina missions, Fowlers Bay, at the Mount Serle camel depot, and by some pastoralists.

The north-west was the only area where Aboriginal people had little or no direct contact with non-Aboriginal people. A few exploring parties passed through the region in the nineteenth century and the telegraph line to Darwin was built, but there were no permanent non-Aboriginal settlements. Nevertheless, there were shifts of population since the 1830s, indicating that non-Aboriginal intrusion had indirect as well as direct impacts on Aboriginal people. In the north-west, population movement had five phases: there was a movement south to Ooldea and the transcontinental railway line from 1917 to the 1940s; Ngaanyatjara speakers in the late 1920s moved from the Warburton Ranges and the Gibson Desert in Western Australia to Laverton, Mount Margaret, Kalgoorlie and Wiluna; by 1921 Antikirinya were moving east from Granite Downs to the Oodnadatta area, and Yankunytjatjara from the Everards were also moving east; and into the area they previously occupied came the Pitjantjatjara from the Mann and Tonkinson Ranges.[13]

In 1921 a reserve of 73 000 square kilometres was declared in the north-west to protect the Aboriginal people there from encroachment on their lands. They had no legal control over these lands, the declaration of the reserve was supposed to prevent pastoral or mining activity on the land.[14] Notwithstanding, the first pastoral lease was established on Pitjantjatjara and Yangkunjatjara lands in 1932 and other leases in the area followed.[15] These were originally used as dogging camps rather than pastoral runs, so the initial contacts of the north-west people were with doggers collecting dingo scalps. Scalps were collected from the Aborigines in exchange for flour, tea and sugar.[16] In 1937 Ernabella Mission was established to protect the Aborigines from this exploitative contact, yet its very establishment intensified contact between Aborigines and non-Aborigines. Earlier, people from this region had been attracted further south to the east-west railway line built in 1917. The ethnographer, Daisy Bates, fed and protected these 'remnants', as she referred to them, at Ooldea Siding from 1919 to 1934.

In 1933 the United Aborigines Mission established a mission for these people at Ooldea Soak (a few kilometres from the Siding) but by the early 1950s, this site had become uninhabitable, coinciding with the establishment of the Woomera Rocket Range. Soon after atomic tests at Maralinga and Emu began. These incursions forced Aboriginal people away from the area. Thus, by the 1950s the process of invasion and dispossession, which had begun in South Australia prior to 1836, had run its course.

Aboriginal people responded to the invasion of their lands in many ways. Some resorted to direct physical confrontation by attacking stock which monopolised water sources and replaced their own native game or by directly attacking the Europeans. As farmers and pastoralists became entrenched on the land and Aboriginal life was increasingly disrupted, many Aboriginal people tried other strategies to ensure their survival. Some made the decision to move onto missions, accepting their protection and acquiring skills which would facilitate their adaptation to the new economic conditions. Missions also enabled people to continue a communal life and retain a communal identity.

Others adapted their lives to the pastoral industry while maintaining their religious life and close relationship to the land. For over 90 years the Adnyamathanha of the Flinders Ranges kept in touch with their past, while becoming skilled stock and domestic workers.

More recently, Aboriginal people have confronted and infiltrated the Australian political and bureaucratic system, demanding that it respond to their unique position in this country. The disruption of their lifestyle and the dispossession of their lands sets Aboriginal people apart in Australian society, and, despite concerted attempts to undermine it, the continuity of Aboriginal culture and values provides a key source of strength.

The broad impact of colonisation on Aborigines in South Australia is similar to that experienced by Aboriginal people in other Australian states. South Australian Aborigines were dispossessed of their land and then marginalised economically and politically. But the process of settlement on Aboriginal lands in South Australia had some unique features. Urban development in Adelaide proceeded very quickly compared to other colonies. Movement out from the urban centre took place in a relatively orderly way. This reflected Edward Gibbon Wakefield's ideas of systematic colonisation, as well as South Australia's establishment as a separate colony, unlike Victoria and Queensland which began with 'illegal' settlement.

In South Australia, the rule of law generally kept pace with

Two girls carrying buckets on their heads, Ooldea. It appears they were gathering native plants.
SOUTH AUSTRALIAN ABORIGINAL HERITAGE PHOTOGRAPHIC COLLECTION, DEPARTMENT OF STATE ABORIGINAL AFFAIRS

expanding colonisation. Not that the rule of law was any guarantee of Aboriginal rights. The process of appropriation of Aboriginal lands was condoned by the state and was supported by para-military and police intervention.

The pattern of white settlement was dictated by the distribution of resources valued by Europeans and the accessibility of those resources to markets and transport. Noel Loos has suggested that there were three main resource frontiers in the colonisation of northern Queensland: pastoral, mining and pearl fishing, and that these had varying impacts on Aborigines.[17] Colonisation of Western Australia could also be said to be dominated by these three frontiers. South Australian expansion, in contrast, was directed from Adelaide, and in southern South Australia was dominated by urban, agricultural and pastoral development (with some mining in the 1840s). Northern and western South Australia attracted pastoralists (mining did not have major impacts on Aborigines until the mining boom of the 1960s).[18]

The greater the density and concentration of European settlement and resource use, the more immediate was the impact on indigenous peoples. Urban development on the Adelaide Plains with its density of population and intense use of the land resulted in rapid dispossession of Kaurna land but low levels of violence. Agricultural development also had an immediate effect of forcing Aboriginal people off their land. Pastoralism was more compatible with continued (although greatly disrupted) Aboriginal occupation of their lands. It depended on Aboriginal labour over an extended period and attracted a relatively sparse European population. Aborigines, therefore, outnumbered the intruders in pastoral areas. This asymmetry often resulted in high levels of violence exacerbated by European aggression and fear, in face of Aboriginal defence of their land and other resources. The result of these tensions was a more prolonged competition over resources than in regions of dense European settlement.

MAINTAINING THE NEW ORDER

The process of settlement and dispossession in South Australia took place over a century or more. At the same time authority structures were developed to maintain this new order. This development had four major phases. In the early years of the colony there was some notion that Aborigines would be quickly trained to assimilate and adopt the lifestyle of the colonisers. This soon was replaced by a view that Aborigines could not withstand the impact of a superior 'civilisation' and would die out, all that could be done for them was to feed and protect them until their inevitable demise. By the 1930s attitudes had changed. The number of Aborigines was increasing, not declining, especially people of mixed descent. The government worried that a group of people who looked increasingly like white people but lived and behaved like Aboriginal people was developing. To counter this trend some argued that people of mixed descent should be assimilated into the general population but it took another twenty years before these policies were embodied in legislation. This policy of assimilation was in turn modified in the 1960s to 'integration', predicated on the belief that Aboriginal people should be able to determine the rate at which they assimilated. More recently a policy of self-determination has developed, allied to multiculturalism.

In their broad application these changing policies parallel developments in Western Australia, Queensland and the Northern Territory but differ in fundamental ways from New South Wales and Victoria. When the colonies of South Australia, Port Phillip Bay and the Swan River Settlement were established in the 1830s, the Humanitarian movement was at its peak in Britain. Anti-slavery legislation had recently been enacted and there was optimism that future British colonisers would have to acknowledge the rights over land of indigenous peoples. But South Australia was colonised by a private company and, despite the concerns of the British Colonial Office, commercial considerations prevailed over the land rights of Aborigines. The *South Australian Constitution Act* was drafted by the South Australia Colonisation Commission and not by the government, and was rushed through the House of Commons with little debate.[19] The preamble of the Act declared South Australia to be 'waste and unoccupied lands which are supposed fit for the purposes of colonisation'.[20]

Although this Act was seen to be out of step with British Government policy, the Colonial Office accepted it under pressure. The Office tried to protect Aboriginal rights by insisting on the appointment of a Protector who would ensure that land occupied by Aborigines was only acquired if the Aborigines sold it voluntarily. If they did not want to sell it, he was to protect their right to occupy it.[21] A clause was also included in the Letters Patent which was designed to protect Aboriginal rights over land,

> Provided always, that nothing in these Letters Patent contained shall affect or be constrained to affect the rights of any Aboriginal natives of the said Province to the actual occupation or employment in their persons or in the persons of their descendants of any lands now actually occupied or enjoyed by such Natives.[22]

Neither of these measures could override an Act passed by Parliament and proved ineffective. Aborigines became citizens of the new colony and subject to British law. A Protector was appointed, who acted more often in defence of non-Aboriginal property than Aboriginal rights. At first, with the help of missionaries, Protectors attempted to educate and assimilate Aborigines in European ways but soon they were involved in 'pacifying' the Aborigines, first through brutal police and citizen action, then through distribution of rations.[23] The German missionary, Clamor Schürmann, who was appointed sub-protector of Aborigines in Port Lincoln in 1840, found that his duties as a Protector, which often involved assisting in the apprehension of Aborigines accused of attacking whites, conflicted with his own calling as a missionary. The high sounding intentions of the British Government and the Colonial Office in relation to Aboriginal rights to land were never implemented in South Australia.

In 1842 the *Waste Lands Act* was passed which enabled the Protector of Aborigines to establish reserves for Aborigines. These reserves, in line with the prevailing but short-lived policy which anticipated that Aborigines would be 'civilised' and trained to live like Europeans, were small. The intention was that Aborigines would settle down on them and 'cultivate the soil'.[24] When this did not occur, most of the reserve lands were leased to non-Aboriginal farmers. By 1860 of the 8000 acres allotted as Aboriginal reserves, most were leased out to non-Aboriginal farmers, generating £1000 income which went into general revenue.[25] Nevertheless, there are at least two recorded instances where Aboriginal reserve land was let to Aboriginal women who had married white men. The first was Kudnarto from the Crystal Brook area, who married Thomas Adams. But in each case when the Aboriginal woman died the land reverted to the State and did not pass to her children.[26]

By the late 1850s any remaining 'humanitarian' idealism about state obligations to Aborigines had been extinguished in South Australia due to a concern to cut governmental spending, and also because of the prevailing belief that 'primitive' Aboriginal culture could not withstand the onslaught of European 'civilisation' and was therefore doomed. This belief suited the governmental purse and for the next 50 years government confined its role to distributing food and blankets to aged and infirm Aborigines through the police, pastoralists and missionaries.

Rations were palliative but were also used to control Aboriginal movements and behaviour. Food was distributed to prevent raids on shepherds' huts or killing sheep for food, both common causes of violence. Ration distribution also enabled the police to get to know the Aborigines, so if trouble arose they could identify them. In addition rations were used to control their movements. After Eyre Peninsula settlers complained that a ration depot set up near their runs would encourage Aborigines to come into the area, the depot was moved beyond the area of settlement.[27] Later in the century rations were used to control the supply of Aboriginal labour. Some pastoralists requested rations to entice Aborigines to their runs so they would have a ready workforce. Others wanted police to distribute them so as to keep large numbers of Aborigines away from their properties. Distribution of rations in towns was also controversial. Some police advocated this distribution so an eye could be kept on Aborigines; others believed that distribution away from town centres would discourage Aborigines from entering towns.

The administrative vacuum left by the government's withdrawal from financial and administrative responsibility for Aboriginal affairs was partially filled by philanthropic and church groups. A number of missions were established in the second half of the nineteenth century, with the aim of segregating and protecting the Aborigines in their declining years. These included two missions in the salt lakes area in the north, Killalpannina and Kopperamanna (1866); and, in the south, Poonindie (1850),[28] Point McLeay (1859), Point Pearce (1868), and at the turn of the century Koonibba (1898).

Poonindie was planned as an ideal Christian village, isolated from both Aboriginal and European influence. Initially, recruits were taken from an Aboriginal school in Adelaide (many of whom came from the River Murray region) to continue their training as farm and domestic workers. Only volunteers were taken to Poonindie and most stayed there despite extremely high deathrates and low birthrates in the first ten years. Later, local Eyre Peninsula people were also admitted on a voluntary basis and children of mixed descent were sent there over the years. Poonindie people were, on the whole, dedicated to the institution, which was a self-sufficient farming community. It created a tight-knit community of people from all over southern South Australia. Therefore, these people were devastated when their home, for which they had worked over decades, was closed down by the government and subdivided into blocks for white farmers.

Poonindie stood both for Aboriginal people succeeding in the non-Aboriginal world and white people's determination to stop them. The history of this mission has parallels with Cumeroogunga in New South Wales, where Aboriginal people also lost their land after establishing a successful farming enterprise.

Other missions initially attracted local Aboriginal people, who moved onto the missions of their own volition. Some were attracted by the availability of food and the chance to learn new skills and a European education. For others there was nowhere else to go as their land was taken up by non-Aboriginal people for farming. Others used the mission as an occasional retreat from unemployment, drought or harassment. Many were encouraged by mission authorities to leave their children in mission dormitories, to be educated at the school and indoctrinated in Christianity. This also ensured that the parents were tied to the mission, either permanently or returning periodically to visit their children. Many left their children at the missions to prevent them being taken away to Homes in Adelaide. For Aboriginal people missions were often the best of the limited options available to them and ensured that they retained a communal Aboriginal identity, which the missionaries themselves had hoped to eradicate.

Aborigines who were not associated with one of the mission stations either lived independently from white people, obtained casual work on farms and stations, or subsisted on rations distributed by pastoralists and the police. In the latter part of the nineteenth century the police were generally the only government representatives in outlying areas. Their work in relation to Aborigines included, not only law enforcement but also ration distribution, census taking and implementation of government directives.

By the early twentieth century white attitudes towards Aborigines were changing. It was acknowledged that the assumption that the Aborigines would solve the problem of their administration by disappearing was wrong, and that the number of people of mixed descent was, in fact, increasing. A new era of racially based policies opened. The mixed descent population increased despite government and mission attempts to prevent miscegenation. Aboriginal women were often taken from their people without consent and forced to live with white men, or forced to work as domestic servants where they were vulnerable to exploitation by their male employers. Because there were very few marriages between white men and Aboriginal women, the children of these inter-racial liaisons were brought up by their Aboriginal mothers and Aboriginal stepfathers. Aboriginal people accepted children of mixed descent as Aboriginal. In Aboriginal society the factors determining a person's inheritance are complex and not solely dependent on the identity of the natural father. This adaptation was particularly easy in matrilineal societies such as in the Flinders Ranges and the north-east of the state where descent was determined through the mother but it did occur in all Aboriginal societies.

Non-Aboriginal people, on the other hand, measured descent in terms of 'blood'. The racial terminology of 'full-blood', 'half-caste', 'quadroon', 'octoroon' became common in South Australia as it did in other states. Aborigines were perceived, not only as being low on the evolutionary scale but as being disadvantaged on biological grounds.

In 1911 an Act was passed to provide 'for the better Protection and Control of the Aboriginal and Halfcaste Inhabitants of the State of South Australia'. Modelled on legislation passed by the Queensland (1897) and Western Australian (1905) governments, it stepped up government involvement in Aboriginal administration.

The Act established an Aborigines Department with a Chief Protector at its head. As with the legislation on which it was modelled, the *Aborigines Protection Act* broadly defined 'Aboriginal', bringing large numbers of people of 'Aboriginal' descent under direct government control. 'An aboriginal' was defined as 'an aboriginal native of Australia' or 'a half-caste' married to an 'aboriginal native' or habitually associating with them, or a 'half-

School children at Ooldea, 1940s.

caste' child under sixteen years. The Chief Protector was made the legal guardian of all Aboriginal children under 21 'notwithstanding that any such child has a parent or other relative living'. With such powers the Protector could take charge of all 'half-caste' children found 'wandering and camping with aborigines' and put them under the control of the State Children's Department.[29]

The Act also gave the Chief Protector enormous authority over adults. He could move them to a reserve or institution, (or from one reserve or institution to another), control their movements in and around towns, manage their property and finances. Although these clauses were described as 'protective', from our historical distance they appear to have been controlling. Every aspect of an Aboriginal person's life was open to control by the state from the time she or he was born. There were only a few protective clauses. It was, for instance, illegal to remove certain classes of Aborigine (especially women and children) from a district or reserve without authority. Many of these controls were enforced by the police, who had the often conflicting responsibilities of Protector and law enforcement officer. The only section of the Act which might have positively helped Aboriginal people establish themselves independently was Section 18, which allowed a block of Crown land 'not exceeding one hundred and sixty acres' to be allotted to Aborigines or suitable land to be purchased for them. Only a few people benefited, however. Those who obtained land to farm had no security of tenure and therefore had little incentive to improve it. An arbitrary decision of the Protector could end their tenure. The prevailing attitude of the time was that Aborigines should be kept on reserves administered by non-Aborigines because they were incapable of living independently.

The passing of the 1911 Act was followed by a Royal Commission on the Aborigines which issued a progress report in 1913 and a final report in 1916. The Royal Commission responded to general demands that there should be more direct government involvement in Aboriginal affairs. It recommended that four missions be taken over by the government as these privately run stations lacked the resources to train Aborigines past primary education.[30]

But the main concern of the Royal Commission was to distinguish between 'full-bloods' and 'half-castes'. It recommended that 'full-bloods' be separated from 'half-castes' and that each live in a separate community and that 'half-castes', 'quadroons' and 'octoroons' be compelled to go outside their communities and become self-sufficient.[31] There was no recognition that these different 'races' were often part of the same nuclear family.

Most of the Aboriginal witnesses before the Commission, especially those from Point Pearce and Point McLeay, were adamant that they wanted their own land to farm. Despite recommendations by the Royal Commission that a few Aboriginal men be given small farms as an experiment, Aboriginal people continued to be denied access to land.

While legislation and policy were largely segregationist and paternalist, there was occasional acknowledgement that these policies were preventing Aborigines from becoming independent and self-supporting. This ambivalence continued well into the twentieth century. It was not only government which displayed this ambivalent attitude; non-government bodies similarly imposed contradictory pressures on Aboriginal people. Koonibba Mission administered by the Evangelical Lutheran Church of Australia is one example. It wanted to maintain total control over its Aboriginal charges while financial constraints on the mission dictated that people had to move away in search of employment. The Aboriginal people were vulnerable to controls established by the 1911 Act and later acts of the 1930s. Only by staying at the mission where they were supervised and 'controlled' were they free of the threat of other interference.[32]

When people moved away in search of work they lived a camp life on reserves with no basic facilities or services. They were often harassed by police or local councils for living in unhygienic conditions. They could only find seasonal work. Their children were often not accepted in state schools. Many hospitals would not treat them when they were sick. In these conditions many could not sustain an independent existence and returned periodically or permanently to the mission. By the 1940s a few people had made a permanent break with the mission but only the most determined survived the harassment in the general community. Yari Miller, who made a committed attempt to establish his family in the town of Ceduna, wrote in frustration to the Secretary of the Protection Board in 1946. He complained that despite living independently of Board support, he and his family were continually harassed by police and other officials.[33] The Secretary to the Board responded with a threat: 'the Board has power to remove you to Koonibba if it deems such course to be necessary but I sincerely hope you will so order your life and those of the members of your family that you will become a useful citizen.'[34]

The purported aim of the 1911 Act, 'for the better Protection and Control' of Aborigines was not fulfilled. From the Aboriginal viewpoint the Act was all controlling with no protection. Yet its implementation was not as draconian as similar legislation in Queensland and Western Australia. While South Australian Aborigines did not enjoy the same freedom of movement as other

Aboriginal men on the Murray River c 1930. Judging by their appearance and paraphernalia, they had joined the Australia-wide march to rural areas in search of work. STATE LIBRARY OF SOUTH AUSTRALIA SSL: M B22421

citizens, they were not forcibly removed to isolated institutions as happened in Queensland (for example, Fraser and Palm Islands) and Western Australia (for example, Moore River Settlement). The Protectors of Aborigines in South Australia do not appear to have been driven by the same commitment to racial ideologies as Bleakley (Queensland), Cook (Northern Territory) or Neville (Western Australia).

By the 1930s the emphasis of government policy began shifting away from segregation and control towards assimilation of people of mixed descent into the general population. Assimilation was proposed on both racial grounds (through interbreeding Aboriginal 'blood' would disappear) and social grounds (Aborigines would be brought up to the 'standard of western civilisation').[35] It took two decades for administrators and legislators to fully implement such policies.

In the meantime, South Australia followed most of the other

states when it introduced amendments to the 1911 Act. In 1939 both South Australia and Western Australia broadened the legislative definition of Aboriginal, forcing more people under legal controls. The *Aborigines Act Amendment Act, 1939* brought all Aboriginal people under one definition,

    4.(1) Every person—

      (a) who is of the full blood descended from the original inhabitants of Australia; or

      (b) who being of less than full blood is descended from the original inhabitants of Australia (Section 5).

It then went on to make exceptions by establishing a mechanism through which some people could be exempted from the Act and 'cease to be an aborigine for the purposes of this Act'. An exemption could be unconditional and irrevocable, or conditional for up to three years. In Western Australia such exemptions (introduced in 1944) were always conditional, even though they conferred voting rights on Aborigines. In South Australia male Aborigines had gained the right to vote when the male population was enfranchised in the 1850s, and had maintained the right, although few exercised it.[36]

The exemption system, like earlier methods devised for separating people of full descent from people of mixed descent, ignored Aboriginal familial and social ties. It also ignored cultural, linguistic and historic differences between Aboriginal and non-Aboriginal people. It caused great social dislocation and trauma, splitting families and communities. Exempted people could drink alcohol legally but were prohibited from living on an Aboriginal institution or from 'consorting' with Aboriginal women other than a wife. They could receive Commonwealth social services but no assistance from the Aborigines Protection Board in the form of rations or blankets etc. Many exempted people found themselves caught between two societies and not legally a member of either. Two examples will illustrate this point. A girl who was exempted without her approval at the same time as her parents, later married an Aboriginal man. She was refused permission to live with his family on an Aboriginal mission while he was in the armed forces and was compelled to live with her young children in the local town. In another instance a woman was exempted so that she could receive a pension but when she became sick the local hospital would not treat her because she was Aboriginal and she could not return to live at the mission where she could receive medical care because she was exempted.[37] There are many other examples of the no-man's-land in which people were placed through the exemption system.

A clause in the 1939 Act which caused Aboriginal people much grief was the insertion of Section 34a which prevented 'exempted' men associating with Aboriginal women. There were also provisions under the *Police Offences Act* which made it illegal for Aborigines to associate with non-Aborigines.[38] These provisions ensured that if people attempted to follow the path of assimilation, they were cut off from family, friends and associates and had to carry a piece of paper proving their new racial identity.

By the 1950s the South Australian Government was actively assisting Aboriginal people to move into the general community by providing housing, education and other services which might enable Aboriginal people to raise their standard of living. In 1954 the first Housing Trust standard house was built for the Department of Aboriginal Affairs for an Aboriginal family and by June 1959, 60 houses had been built.[39] The Department also advanced money to Aboriginal people so they could furnish and equip their houses and not appear disadvantaged. In other areas too, Aboriginal welfare was catered for away from Aboriginal institutions. Increasing numbers of children were accepted into the state school system. These changing expectations of Aboriginal living standards put great pressure on the privately run Aboriginal institutions. Administered on minimal government support, these institutions did not have the financial resources to improve living conditions—housing was substandard, education often below Education Department standards and vocational training nonexistent. The inability of private organisations to improve living standards drove the government to take full responsibility for Aboriginal affairs. In the 1960s and 1970s, at a time when the Western Australian Government was relinquishing its tight control of Aboriginal institutions to the churches, the South Australian Government took over financial and administrative responsibility for all Aboriginal institutions. In this and a number of other ways South Australia began to take the initiative in reforming policies and practice towards Aborigines.

Another, perhaps, unforseen result of Assimilation Policies was a dramatic increase in Aboriginal arrest and incarceration rates after the 1950s. In the 1850s Aborigines made up 4 per cent of prisoners.[40] In the 1860s the imprisonment rate was around 7 per cent falling to an average of between 2 and 3 per cent for the rest of the century.[41] Figures for the years 1905 to 1930 on admissions of Aborigines to gaols and prisons in South Australia show that 2.4 per cent of admissions were 'black and coloured' people.[42] There was an average of 40 Aborigines admitted to prisons and gaols per year over the period. This represents less than 1 per cent of the estimated Aboriginal population of South Australia at the time.[43] In the era of assimilation these figures increased dramatically. By 1956 Aborigines accounted for about 13 per cent of admissions to prisons. This figure steadily increased over the period to approximately 25 per cent of admissions in 1968–69.[44] These percentages are much higher than for the first 30 years of the century and rise steadily over the period that the Assimilation Policy was finally implemented and Aboriginal people were encouraged to move away from segregated institutions into the general community.

Despite this evidence of institutionalised racism, there were major changes in the status of Aborigines in South Australia. Legislation passed in the 1960s set the agenda for the reform of Aboriginal administration throughout Australia. Aboriginal control over their own affairs increased, based on a policy of 'integration' rather than assimilation. An approach 'which recognises the right of a person to decide his own future and enables him to make the transitional stages at his own pace'.[45] The policy emphasised consultation with Aboriginal people and self-help and self-determination.

A landmark was the *Aboriginal Affairs Act, 1962* (amended 1966 and 1968). Its stated aim was to 'promote the welfare and advancement' of Aborigines. Most of the old 'protective' clauses were removed from the legislation (Aborigines could, for example, now buy and sell property freely). A section of the Act allowed the allocation of land to Aborigines and also made special assistance available to Aboriginal people to help them establish themselves in 'primary, mechanical or business pursuits'. In addition, by 1965 the Act had legalised the drinking of liquor by Aborigines throughout the state.[46]

The 1966 amendment to the *Aboriginal Affairs Act* allowed, ahead of the rest of Australia, Reserve Councils to be set up which empowered Aboriginal people to run their own institutions and control entry to them. For the first time since 1836 Aborigines in South Australia were legally able to run their own communities. In the same year the *Aboriginal Lands Trust Act* was passed, giving Aborigines some control over their own lands. The Trust, a completely Aboriginal body with a non-Aboriginal adviser, acquired all Aboriginal reserve lands but could only 'sell, lease, mortgage or otherwise deal with land vested in it' if the minister consented. This Act has been hailed as the first 'land rights' Act in Australia.

The legislative and policy changes which took effect in the 1960s reflected gradual changes in attitudes among the non-Aboriginal population but were also a response to Aboriginal political action. Increasing numbers of Aboriginal people were moving to Adelaide and other urban centres. There they had greater access to politicians and other influential non-Aboriginal people as well as the freedom to organise themselves. Aboriginal women were especially quick to take advantage of these changed circumstances. A number of them, including Gladys Elphick, Maude Tongerie, Faith Thomas, and Margaret Lawrie established the Council of Aboriginal Women of South Australia in the mid 1960s.[47] The Council acted both as a self-help group, establishing its own welfare and support services, as well as an effective political lobby group. Gladys Elphick, for instance, had direct access to Premier Don Dunstan and his photograph still hung proudly in her house in the 1980s.

By the late 1970s Aboriginal political action was effectively being pursued in the north-west of the State, culminating in the *Pitjantjatjara Land Rights Act, 1981*, followed by the *Maralinga Tjarutja Land Rights Act, 1984*. South Australia, however, does not have any general land rights legislation to cover the entire state. These Acts were introduced after the land rights legislation passed by the Federal Government for the Northern Territory. Along with the *Northern Territory Act*, these two Acts represent the strongest land rights legislation in Australia, giving freehold title over large tracts of land, and the power to negotiate over mining and other intrusions on that land.

Recognition of Aboriginal rights to land has taken two distinct forms in South Australia. First, there are rights for people living in remote, arid areas. These people, who lived on lands which were not regarded as productive by non-Aboriginal people were able to maintain strong traditions. They fought long and hard to re-establish control over their lands. Their strong assertions, refusal to give up, rapid appreciation of the Australian political process and ability to manipulate it resulted in the passing of the two land rights Acts. In contrast, Aboriginal people in the rest of the state suffer two disadvantages not experienced by the Pitjantjatjara and Maralinga people. Their traditional lands have many more non-Aboriginal people living on them and their lives have been more systematically disrupted over a longer period of time. The land available to them is Crown land, highly fragmented and based upon historically demarcated Aboriginal reserves administered through the Aboriginal Lands Trust, and land procured through Federal Government funding.[48] Aboriginal people making land claims in this region insist that their historical associations of the last century and a half are important to them and must be recognised. At the same time they are fighting to have their traditional rights to land recognised.

The 1960s brought dramatic changes to the legal status of Aborigines and governmental interest in Aboriginal affairs, both at the state and Federal level.[49] In this period of liberalisation many Aboriginal people moved away from segregated communities into towns and cities, where they could now obtain housing and schooling for their children.

They took immediate advantage of the changing political climate to establish a strong political presence in Australian society. Some became prominent in public life, although no Aboriginal person has as yet been elected to the South Australian Parliament. Sir Doug Nicholls in South Australia became the first

Aboriginal person appointed Governor of a state. Many more Aboriginal people have joined the public service or found they could act more effectively outside the formal political system. They have worked with their own communities to establish better living conditions, to improve standards of health and housing, to ensure a continuation of their own culture and cultural identity, to fight for land rights, to protect Aboriginal sites from destruction, and to create antidotes to the despair which can overwhelm people who fear that the future offers no more hope for them and their children than was offered in the past.

COLONIALISM IN SOUTH AUSTRALIA

South Australia has often been represented as progressive and innovative in its administration and treatment of its Aboriginal population. Certainly, in the early years of the colony there was much discussion of Aboriginal rights but little action. From the latter part of the nineteenth century until the 1960s, South Australia followed the policy lead of other states, particularly Queensland and Western Australia, although more moderate in its practice than these two states. Since the 1960s, however, the state has been in the forefront of reform in Aboriginal affairs. People in the remote north and west have benefited most from these reforms, mainly through land ownership and rights. Yet, South Australia has a large urban-based population in the south of the state which is still struggling for recognition of rights to land and a quality of life equal to that of other South Australians.

The story of the Wiltons with which this chapter began, highlights a range of Aboriginal experiences and responses to colonial relations in South Australia. Within the colonial situation in which Aborigines found themselves, many maintained a strong community base, which protected them from some of the impacts of colonisation—family cohesion was maintained, cultural information was transmitted and contact with country continued. Nevertheless this community base was always vulnerable to outside interference. Economically, the Adnyamathanha were, until the 1960s, dependent on employment in the pastoral industry. Although they were less affected than many other Aboriginal people, the threat of having children removed was often present. The remoteness of the community and the discriminatory practices of both government and non-government agencies made access to education, health, welfare, and housing facilities difficult.

The Adnyamathanha experience in the 1970s and 1980s stands between the Pitjantjatjara of the north-west who have gained control over much of their lands, and the people in the south with virtually no access to land. The Adnyamathanha have gained control of their own community organisations, won back partial control over small tracts of land, gained access to services not previously available to them and some obtained employment in government authorities and Aboriginal organisations. They now depend on government funding rather than the vagaries of the pastoral economy and individual pastoralists. Government funding carries with it a wide range of administrative and organisational obligations imposed by funding authorities. So the guise of colonial control has changed dramatically for the Adnyamathanha but it has not disappeared.

Nevertheless, the history of the Wilton family indicates that while colonialism continues to have an impact on the lives of Aboriginal people, it is not the only factor which has shaped their lives. While the history of Aboriginal/non-Aboriginal relations needs to be understood in the context of colonial relations, Aboriginal initiative and agency has never been overwhelmed and continues to assert itself.

NOTES

1 Unless otherwise indicated this biographical sketch is based on a number of interviews by the author with Rufus Wilton in 1985–86.
2 Royal Commission on the Aborigines, South Australia, South Australian Government Printer, Adelaide, 1916, p.16.
3 Heritage Unit, *Minerawuta, Ram Paddock Gate*, SA Department for the Environment, Adelaide, 1981, p.7.
4 Graham Jenkins, *Conquest of the Ngarrindjeri*, Rigby, Adelaide, 1979, p.29.
5 Fay Gale, *A Study of Assimilation: part Aborigines in South Australia*,

Libraries Board of South Australia, Adelaide, 1964, p.39, quoting *South Australian Parliamentary Papers*, 1857, no.47, p.1.
6 Philip Clarke in his article, 'Adelaide as an Aboriginal landscape' *Aboriginal History* vol.15, no.1, 1991, p.69 suggests that the label Kaurna has been loosely used in the past and includes many peoples from other districts.
7 Although there are some violent incidents recorded between the Kaurna and the British colonisers, the major factors contributing to the high death rate appear to be associated with the trauma of being dispossessed, losing their traditional food and water supplies, having their religious and cultural life undermined and being forced to wear clothes which became wet and dirty instead of traditional fur cloaks. These changes were all imposed within a few months of first contact without any time to adjust. Another major factor was exposure to diseases for which they had no immunity.

There are no accurate estimates of the number of Kaurna and other peoples in the region in 1836 but there is evidence that their numbers rapidly diminished after contact. See Report of the Select Committee of the Legislative Council upon the Aborigines, *South Australian Parliamentary Papers (SAPP)*, no.165, 1860, p.5.
8 Christobel Mattingly and Ken Hampton (eds), *Survival in our own land: 'Aboriginal' experiences in 'South Australia' since 1836*, Wakefield Press, Adelaide, 1988, p.38.
9 Matthew Moorhouse to Colonial Secretary, 13 Sept. 1841, quoted in Christobel Mattingly, ibid, p.40.
10 Robert Foster, 'The Bunganditj: European Invasion and the Economic Base of Social Collapse', unpublished MA thesis, University of Adelaide, 1983, p.3.
11 ibid, p.3.
12 A. Brauer, *Under the Southern Cross: A History of the Evangelical Lutheran Church of Australia*, Lutheran Publishing House, Adelaide, 1985, p.172.
13 Phillip Toyne and Daniel Vachon, *Growing up the country: the Pitjantjatjara struggle for their land*, McPhee/Penguin Books, Ringwood, Victoria, 1984, pp.25–26.
14 ibid, p.23.
15 Winifred Hilliard, *The People Inbetween: The Pitjanjatjara People of Ernabella*, Funk and Wangnalls, New York, 1968, p.80.
16 The doggers collected a government bounty on each scalp, an attempt to eradicate the pest from pastoral land.
17 Noel Loos, *Invasion and Resistance: Aboriginal–European relations on*

the North Queensland frontier 1861–1897, ANU Press, Canberra, 1982. Loos actually includes a fourth frontier, the rainforest frontier, but this refers not to resource development as do the other three, but to natural vegetation. While logging was undertaken in the forests, pastoralism and mining also seem to have had an early impact on the region.

18 A possible exception to this generalisation might be the Leigh Creek coalfields which began operating in the 1940s.
19 Henry Reynolds, *The Law of the Land*, Penguin, Ringwood, Victoria, 1987, p.103.
20 ibid, p.103.
21 ibid, p.107.
22 ibid, p.110.
23 For instance, the Protector accompanied a police expedition to the Rufus River area on the Murray River, where Aborigines had been reported to be attacking overlanders bringing stock into South Australia. He approved the police action which resulted in the deaths of large numbers of Aborigines.
24 *APP*, 1860, no.165, p.4.
25 ibid.
26 Peggy Brock and Doreen Kartinyeri, *Poonindie: The Rise and Destruction of an Aboriginal Agricultural Community*, SA Government Printer, Adelaide, 1989, p.25.
27 ibid, p.70.
28 Poonindie was the only mission to survive from the early period of Aboriginal administration. It was established by the Anglican Church, but with government financial support which was withdrawn in 1860.
29 Protector of Aborigines Report, South Australia, 30 June 1909, p.3.
30 Point Pearce and Point McLeay became government stations, Killalpannina closed and Koonibba remained a Lutheran mission until 1963.
31 Echoes of the policies implemented in New South Wales and Victoria.
32 Peggy Brock, *Outback Ghettoes: A history of Aboriginal institutionalisation and survival*, CUP, Sydney, 1993.
33 South Australian Public Record Office GRG/52/1/1946/9 reproduced as in the original.
34 ibid.

35 M.S. Brock, 'Africans and Aborigines: a comparative study of government policies in South Africa and Australia', 1969, p.44.
36 Pat Stretton and Christine Finnimore, 'Black fellow citizens: Aborigines and the Commonwealth franchise', *Australian Historical Studies*, vol.25, no.101, 1993.
37 South Australian Public Record Office GRG 52/1/1944/10; GRG 52/1/1948/28, 1948/58, 1951/33.
38 Mattingly and Hampton (eds), p.47.
39 South Australian Public Record Office, GRG 52/1/1959/147.
40 Report of the Select Committee of the Legislative Council of South Australia, 1860, p.87.
41 Statistical Register for South Australia, *SAPP*, 1860–1900. The majority were in gaols outside Adelaide.
42 These and the following figures are based on the Annual Reports on Gaols and Prisons, *SAPP* for the years 1905–30.
43 There are no figures available for the period 1930–56. However, in 1973 David Biles produced statistics for the period 1956–69. David Biles, 'Aborigines and Prisons: a South Australian Study', *Australian and NZ Journal of Criminology*, 1973, vol.6, no.4, pp.246–50.
44 ibid, pp.246–47.
45 ibid, p.30.
46 Fay Gale, 'The History of Contact in South Australia', University of Adelaide Publication, 19, p.13. SA Government Gazette, 25 July 1963, 16 April 1964, 1 April 1965.
47 Mattingly and Hampton (eds), p.153.
48 At the time of writing the Trust legislation was under review and is likely to be revised.
49 In 1967 a referendum gave the Federal Government power to legislate for and administer Aboriginal affairs and it subsequently took over primary responsibility for Aboriginal affairs from the states.

6

Western Australia

SUCCESSIVE colonial and state governments of Western Australia adopted similar approaches to Aboriginal matters, primarily facilitating settler land acquisition and the procurement of cheap labour. Legislation and 'settlers' laws' defined and controlled many Aboriginal lives. Extreme positions were sometimes tempered by humanitarian concerns but rarely were Aborigines consulted. This chapter has a special focus on the various government inquiries, including Royal Commissions, which were central to processes of administrative change.

Western Australia, as it became known, is the largest subdivision in the Australian continent. Geographically diverse, it contains fertile regions in the south, arid conditions in the centre and east and a tropical north. Such diversity provided excellent conditions for pastoral and agricultural development, and rich mineral deposits were also lucrative. Unimpeded mineral exploration is seen as central to the state's economy.

Varying periods and types of colonial contact, and the differing responses of various groups of Aboriginal and non-Aboriginal people, have engendered a complex history. However successful, much development has been non-intensive, and there are still vast areas of the state where Aboriginal people predominate or are a visible presence. A relatively large amount of land also remains Crown land.

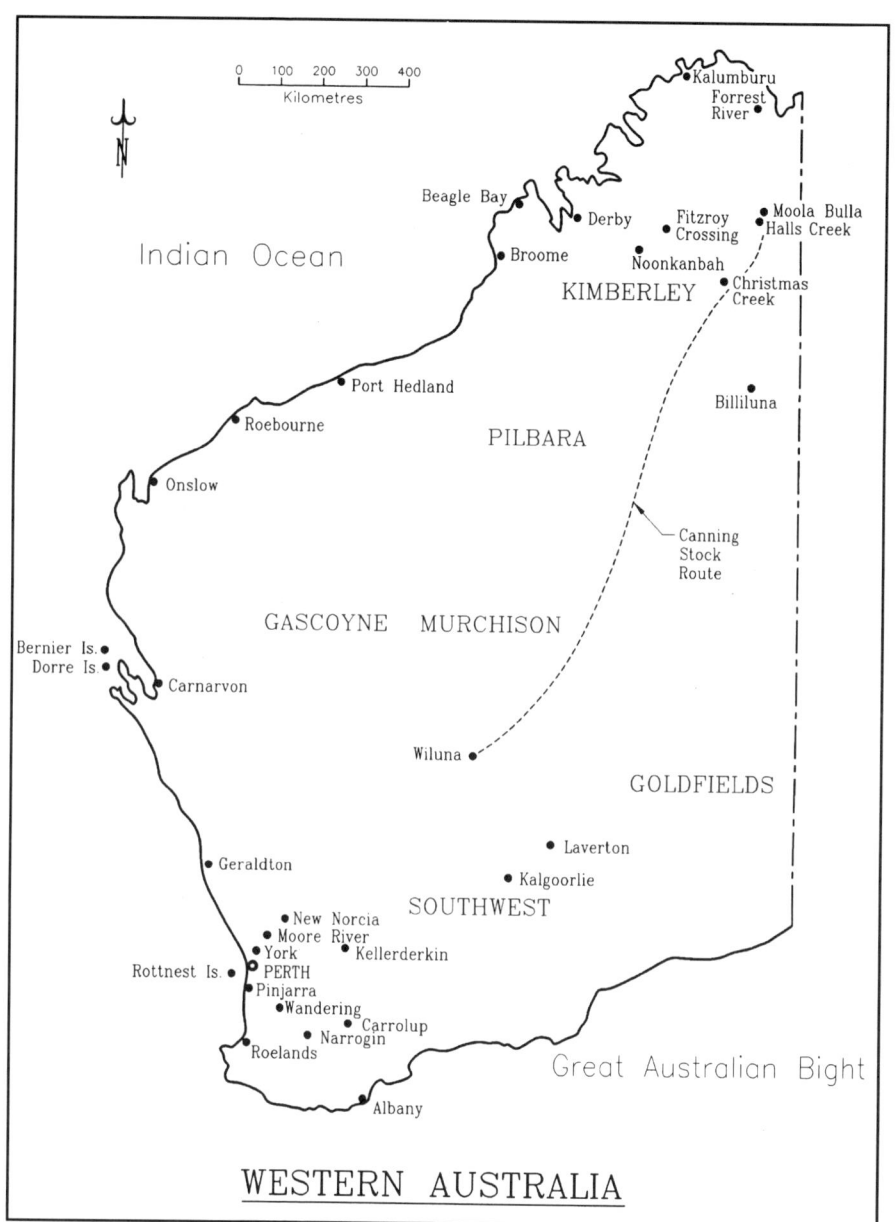

PRIOR TO BRITISH INVASION

Aboriginal people lived in and traversed the area now identified as Western Australia for at least 50 000 years prior to European invasion in 1829. As in other parts of the continent, their intelligent and responsible occupation and use of the environment revealed a remarkable resilience and approach to human ecology that has only recently been appreciated by many Europeans. In Western Australia, Aboriginal land was divided into approximately 98 territorial blocs, excluding the Western Desert (the last area to come under European influence), and the population has been conservatively estimated at around 60 000.[1]

Cycles of Aboriginal life and death found expression in Aboriginal Law, which derived from religious beliefs and practices generally known as the Dreaming. A hunter–gatherer mode of production led to small family groupings or bands. People travelled in a range of environments, including coastal, desert and riverine settings but mostly stayed in areas where they had sociocultural, religious and economic ties. They sometimes met with other larger groupings for ceremonial activity, dispute settling and marriage organisation, and traded along routes like *wunan*, which stretched across northern Western Australia and into the Northern Territory.[2]

Land was of great importance to life and cosmology, providing a connecting link between people, various plant and animal species, and the Dreaming. Knowledge about relations to land, kinship, religious rituals, political systems, hunting and gathering, material resources and artefacts was transmitted via oral traditions. Stories about the exploits of the mythic beings and spirit children were recounted in ceremonial settings and were often accompanied by dance, song cycles, visual and practical art.

Mythological accounts were also passed on in everyday contexts such as when families were hunting or fishing together. Children were socialised by kin and learnt through observation and verbal instruction. Some knowledge was restricted until children reached adult status or until puberty, when they commenced initiation and eventually married. The use of resources such as wildlife, roots, fruits, seeds, bush honey, wood, and water were managed efficiently, bringing about a viable hunting, foraging and fishing economy. The exploitation of these resources took place in accordance with seasonal or climatic changes where a highly organised and nomadic lifestyle allowed for their timely usage and regrowth.

An extract from the 1830 diary of an early European settler, Anne Whatley, revealed British perceptions about kangaroo hunting amongst south-west Aborigines. Her surgeon husband, she wrote, had enjoyed the honour 'of dining with a party of Natives who were assembled to eat a fine kangaroo they had speared'. Whatley recounted how her husband was asked to trade a brace of cockatoos he had recently shot.[3] This account reflects the early potential for reciprocal exchanges between the two groups but such attitudes proved to be all too rare among Europeans.[4]

THE BRITISH INVASION

The British colonisers initially invaded the south-west coast of Western Australia in 1826, 38 years after the landing at Sydney Cove in 1788; they settled permanently in 1829. The British were not the first outsiders to land on the western coast of Australia. Prior to 1826, the south-west was explored by the Dutch in 1658, the British in 1791 and the French in 1803.

The British assumed that the dispossessed indigenous peoples would 'benefit' from the extension of British justice to them. The first governor appointed to the Swan River Colony, Governor Stirling, proclaimed on its founding that:

> the Right of the Natives to the Protection of the British Laws was formally declared. On every possible Occasion their Equality, in this respect with all his Majesty's Subjects has been urged . . . [and explained] . . . to those Classes of the Community who might be most prone to act offensively toward them.[5]

Governor Stirling's proclamation was directed towards the European settlers and made no effort to inform Aboriginal people that their own beliefs, practices and Law had been usurped.

While *terra nullius* defined the indigenous people as being 'without property' and therefore unable to contest British imposition, some Europeans made their own observations. In 1836 the European settler Francis Armstrong observed the land management of south-western Aboriginal people. The land appeared to be 'apportioned to different families . . . [and was] . . . beyond doubt an inheritable property among them, and they boast of having received it from their father's fathers to an unknown period way back'. The predominantly patrilineal nature of land succession was also noted by Bishop Salvado, a Benedictine monk who established the first Roman Catholic Mission at New Norcia in 1848.[6] But more generally, and often brutally, the colonisers ignored Aboriginal interests in land.

Pastoralists, graziers and agriculturalists often baited or shot wildlife, causing rapid depletion. Lamenting their loss, John Watson, a member of the Nyikina language group, commented that 'lot of those things, such as kangaroos and emus were shot out for nothing. They [Europeans] cut the kangaroo right down because they said it was a pest.' He explained that the kangaroo was 'one of the real cultivators. Even though they were digging up the roots of the grass to eat, kangaroos were making holes which grass seeds would wash into. They actually helped to cultivate those grasses.'[7]

European 'settlers' were enticed to the Swan River Colony by decrees and advertisements that advised they would not have to pay for their lands. Land grants were conveyed to them in fee simple which would automatically be inherited by their descendants, though they still had to meet certain conditions. All land granted was to be cultivated or improved or could revert to the Crown. The colonisers believed their own endeavours to expand 'settlement' and 'develop' the land were justified. One Western Australian 'settler' in the north instructed his manager to shoot at Aboriginal people, arguing that once they conceded defeat, 'the less bloodshed there will be—the less expense and the greater security to property'.[8] Europeans resented continuing Aboriginal occupancy of land, especially their technique of 'firing' or 'burning' the bush. This practice ensured regrowth and flushed out small animals during hunting and foraging expeditions. (Ironically it had earlier created ideal conditions for pastoral and agricultural development.)[9]

Opposing views towards land ownership and use engendered an often violent history. By the mid 1830s several tragic incidents had already occurred around the most central point of colonial administration, the Swan River Colony (which now encompasses the Perth metropolitan area). In 1833 the south-west Aboriginal leader, Yagan, was shot and killed and his smoked head removed, to be placed on public exhibition in England. And in 1835 the Pinjarra massacre by the colonial police followed a punitive expedition led by Governor Stirling. Fatal clashes were also reported in the York district in 1835 and 1836.[10] Aborigines were punished by imprisonment in some cases; from 1841 many Aboriginal men were exiled to Rottnest Island, a penal institution. A government recommendation was made to close the prison in 1903 but Aboriginal prisoners were not actually allowed to leave until 1922. The cold weather and 'crowded and filthy conditions claimed many lives—nearly 400 Aboriginal men died there'.[11]

Colonial violence is the strongest recurring theme in the history of Aboriginal–European relations in Western Australia. While violent behaviour between different Aboriginal groupings occurred prior to colonisation, this took place in a traditional context of retaliation and small-scale warfare, sometimes discussed in Aboriginal narratives as the 'wild times'.[12] Aboriginal informants have provided evidence of massacres that were not only part of their forebears' history but which had also taken place in their own lifetimes. Such experiences are epitomised in the following account: 'We been hung out. Our people got shot, even the mustering men. If we ran away the station people went after us and put a bullet in us like dogs . . . we lost our country through bullets, rifles and chains.'[13]

When disappointed gold prospectors in the eastern goldfields region allegedly found their food pilfered by Aboriginal guides, they retaliated by turning on some young Aboriginal women. They captured and, 'kept them chained to trees for their pleasure. When the tribesmen retaliated with a night attack and a hail of spears, the white men arranged a counter attack and relentlessly massacred thirty warriors near a water hole.'[14]

European explorer A. W. Canning was accused of chaining Aboriginal people in order to force them to reveal well locations.

Blackwood natives returning from a kangaroo hunt, c 1870–1880. BERNDT MUSEUM OF ANTHROPOLOGY, UNIVERSITY OF WESTERN AUSTRALIA

In pioneering an 800-mile stock route from Wiluna to Halls Creek in 1906–1907, he arranged to liaise with local Aborigines, attributing much of his success to their knowledge. Later 'settlers' continued to rely on Aboriginal informers as they further explored and colonised the north of the state, largely via the Canning Stock Route.[15]

Despite such reliance, Aboriginal people were treated atrociously and some Europeans, like the Anglican Minister, Gribble, campaigned vigorously for the recognition of their rights. He was ostracised, however, for his views and eventually hounded out of the colony. His condemnation struck a humanitarian chord both locally and in Britain, giving rise to several future Royal Commissions and inquiries.[16]

As the colonisers' power increased, they took up more land and the dislocation of Aboriginal people intensified. Dispossession from homelands, violence undertaken with technologically superior instruments such as rifles, and the introduction of diseases to which Aborigines had no immunity, such as tuberculosis, smallpox, influenza, and venereal disease, all combined to create devastating effects. The indigenous people suffered alienation, widespread violence and often fatal illness. While indigenous population estimates have inherent problems, one estimate of the south-west Aboriginal population is that a people once numbering around 13 000 (in the southern region) were reduced to 1419, of whom 45 per cent were classed as 'half-castes' by 1901.[17]

Many Aboriginal people were coerced onto missions throughout the latter part of the nineteenth century and the early twentieth century. Belief in Social Darwinism and European supremacy led to various forms of 'de-Aboriginalisation' and 'evangelisation'. In the south-west, the New Norcia Mission opened in 1848, and in the north-west the Beagle Bay Mission opened in 1891. While these were Catholic, other denominations established missions throughout the colony during the proceeding hundred years, including Busselton, Carrolup, Mt Margaret, Gnowerangerup, Warburton, Moore River, Roelands, and Balgo Hills.[18] Some government settlements were not overtly identified as missions, although they zealously carried out certain missionary-style functions. Alfie Gerrard, who was removed from his family and placed at the Moola Bulla Native Settlement (opened 1910) commented:

> They [Native Welfare] picked up all the half-caste kids . . . They didn't care much for the full-blood, only for the halfbreed . . . And we had to be Christianised. All new boys that came in were flogged on the Saturday morning . . . I don't know why, don't ask me why it happened . . . but they had to Christian the boys by giving them a good flogging.[19]

Such institutions trained Aborigines for certain types of employment.

Many European pastoral stations, agricultural developments and pearl-shell fishing industries relied upon Aboriginal labour from the 1840s on. Notwithstanding the introduction of convict labour in 1850, Aboriginal people continued to be exploited as cheap labour in a variety of tasks such as pearling, shearing, stock work, fencing, gardening, domestic tasks, and general labouring. In the late nineteenth century, Malaysian and Japanese pearl fishers increasingly dominated that industry. Many developed intimate relationships with Aboriginal women or used them as prostitutes, leading to a prominent racial mix.

Some Aboriginal people established and ran their own farms through the provisions of the state's *Land Act, 1898*, where any 'aboriginal native or descendant' could be granted a lease of up to 200 acres. Haebich argues that specified conditions of occupancy created 'insurmountable' difficulties for potential Aboriginal applicants. Without security of title they could not borrow capital from lending authorities, and consequently were unable to develop and cultivate the land as did the Europeans.[20]

The Swan River Colony remained under formal colonial administration longer than other colonised states. According to Rowley, one result was that colonial patterns of indentured labour applied longer. In Western Australia during the first decade of the twentieth century, only 369 of 4000 pastoral workers were employed under 'agreement' and the others were not entitled to a cash wage. No legal responsibility existed to provide food or accommodation.[21] It was not until 1968 that such inequities were seriously addressed.

The fact that European women initially formed only a small proportion of the colonial population heightened the often brutal sexual exploitation of Aboriginal women by European men. It is erroneous to assume, however, that all relationships between European men and Aboriginal women were entirely coerced. Sometimes Aboriginal men were compliant with Europeans regarding the sexual services of women but relationships of affection and loyalty also occurred. Sexual unions between Aboriginal and European women and men led to an increasing number of mixed-descent children. Government concern about 'miscegenation' increased, and the institutionalisation of children of mixed parentage and isolation from their own families led to devastating long-term psychological effects. Nor was venereal disease delicately handled. In 1908, the Lock Hospital Scheme was established on Dorre and Bernier Islands off the Carnarvon coast. Aboriginal women and men, believed to be suffering venereal disease, were taken there to be isolated from infecting others, principally Europeans.[22] This scheme was to remain in place for ten years.

RESISTANCE, COERCION AND 'PROTECTION'

Striking expressions of Aboriginal resistance can be seen in the stories about Jandamarra, also known as 'Pigeon'; many Aboriginal narratives continue to recount his exploits. A member of the Bunaba language group in the central Kimberley, Pigeon challenged the authority of the colonisers in a number of ways. He carried out raids on sheep and cattle stock in the late 1800s and evaded capture numerous times. In 1894, in what was known as the Windjana Gorge Rebellion, Jandamarra was caught, along with several others, chained by the neck and taken to Derby. Eventually, he was released on the grounds that he assist the police by working as a 'police tracker' and that he care for the horses. The police became reliant on Jandamarra's skills and knowledge of the local country and he helped them track down Aboriginal cattle killers. In the 1880s Jandamarra escaped from his Derby police post and was killed by Mingo Mick, a 'police tracker' from Roebourne. Jandamarra had witnessed many dramatic changes to Bunaba country but died before a large pastoral station was finally established there.[23]

Through the *Aborigines Protection Act, 1886*, the government sought to implement greater control and under the Protection Board, appointed men as Protectors. Mainly drawn from police ranks or local settlers, they were ostensibly there to 'protect' Aboriginal well-being. One of the major problems with the Protector System was the dual role of being both a Protector and a police officer.[24] John Watson explained:

> The police used to ride right down into the desert to capture Aboriginal people and bring them back to work on stations. If any of the station owners or managers told the police that they were short of workers, the police would bring some of their captives back to the station. In those days, the police were also the official protectors. They used to give the station managers a permit to hold them on the station, and to work them as they saw fit.[25]

Station owners and managers were also given the status of Protector. In many instances, as revealed by a Walmajarri man, Eric Lawford, 'the station manager could do pretty much as he liked. That included the stealing of women.' While some stations brought in their own rule of not employing single European managers, 'the rule only applied to the managers; there was no attempt to stop the *kartiya* [white] stockmen and station hands

Schoolgirls at Mt Margaret Mission, 1950. BERNDT MUSEUM OF ANTHROPOLOGY, UNIVERSITY OF WESTERN AUSTRALIA

from taking Aboriginal women'.[26] Sexual relations between Aboriginal women and European men were influential in shaping race relations generally, including straining relations between Aboriginal and European women.[27]

Government concern about the increasing numbers of 'half-caste' children, as they were described, resulted in greater regulation and control of the Aboriginal population. John Watson never had the chance to meet his two eldest brothers because they were taken away before he was born. He goes on to stress that:

> My sisters and another brother were sent away to the Catholic Mission School at Beagle Bay [on the western coast of the Kimberley region in northern Western Australia]. My parents had

no say in that, it was government policy . . . The police could take away any Aboriginal child with bits of colour in them, any kid with a bit of white blood in them . . . When it looked like the younger brother and I were going to be taken away as well, our parents got talking and decided they weren't going to part with us. So, whenever a police party came out to Mt. Anderson [pastoral station in the West Kimberley] they sent us off to the bush.[28]

John Watson further explained that his parents 'sent us down to our father's and grandmother's country with some old people . . . that's why I'm able to speak my own people's language and several other languages'.

As in other parts of Australia, some people recall their faces being smudged and blackened with burnt cork so that they would be identified as 'full-bloods' and thus not removed from families. And Haebich states that parents who lost children this way were 'broken hearted'. She observed: 'They frequently rebelled against this and in 1911 an elderly woman in the Bremer Bay district took to the bush with her grandchildren to avoid losing custody of them.'[29]

Targeting children was the most significant ideological and practical means by which the colonial government attempted to consolidate colonisation.[30]

ATTAINING SELF-GOVERNMENT FROM THE BRITISH

Although Western Australia eventually attained self-government in 1890, the British Government continued to retain control over Aboriginal affairs until 1898. Introduced into the Western Australian Constitution in 1889, Section 70 allowed for the sum of 5000 pounds sterling for 'the welfare of the Aboriginal Natives'. If and when the gross revenue of the colony exceeded 5000 pounds in any financial year, an amount equal to 1 per cent of that revenue was to be substituted. In 1890, however, the then Premier of Western Australia, John Forrest, challenged the authority of Section 70, whereby the British Government retained control over Aboriginal affairs. Whether or not his challenge was successful remains a significant and not entirely forgotten point of contention.[31]

Meanwhile the south-west was becoming an increasingly attractive proposition for agricultural 'settlers'. By 1903 the government had commenced an extensive and soon successful programme of agricultural development, especially wheat, which produced a profitable export.[32] Contemporary Aboriginal policies and laws combined strategies of restriction and humanitarian relief. Anxiety and controversy about the worsening conditions of Aboriginal people were felt within the colony and also in Britain where allegations of European brutality persisted. This concern led to Government Inquiries and Royal Commissions.

COMMISSIONS AND INQUIRIES, POLICIES AND LAWS

In 1883 the first inquiry was established to consider what was described as 'the Aboriginal problem'. Generally referred to as the 'Forrest Commission' after the first premier, it inquired into the treatment of Aboriginal prisoners on Rottnest Island, and the various relief measures provided to the 'poor and sick natives'. Although revealing concern about social conditions, the Commission confirmed prevailing European beliefs that Aboriginal people were 'dying out'. In this and other commissions and inquiries, non-interventionist approaches to 'the Aboriginal problem' were underpinned by the view that there was nothing further the Europeans could do but 'smooth the dying pillow'.[33] Pastoralists, however, were anxious about the impact of depopulation upon their cheap labour force.

Commencing late in 1904, the Royal Commission into the Condition of Aborigines was held, headed by Dr W. E. Roth, an ethnographer and the Chief Protector of Aborigines in Queensland, considered a national expert on Aborigines. Roth spent several months travelling the state observing conditions and taking submissions, mainly from pastoralists. Of the 42 witnesses from whom he took evidence, only two were Aboriginal people.[34] Roth's Report to the government contained some compassionate findings and progressive recommendations. He criticised unlawful police practices, especially with respect to arresting and chaining Aboriginal witnesses, and the system of indentured Aboriginal labour.[35] Yet Roth's Report also reflected his ethnocentrism, and overall, he recommended greater control of Aboriginal people.

Nonetheless, police and local newspapers were highly critical of the Report. Eventually, a Select Parliamentary response to Roth's Report resulted in the *Aborigines Protection Act, 1905*. All Aboriginal adults and children, including those labelled 'half-castes', were included but provisions were made for certain forms of exemption for those who were thought to have attained a suitable degree of 'civilisation'. Few people, however, were granted exemption from the provisions of the Act, and this could be revoked at any time.[36]

The Chief Protector of Aborigines had the authority to compulsorily remove 'part-Aboriginal' children from their natural parents, and to establish more government settlements, reserves and missions where Aboriginal people could be contained and controlled. The role of Protectors was reinforced and the police were given power to arrest Aborigines without warrant for offences against the Act. Many of the severe conditions imposed by the 1905 Act were not completely repealed until 1963. If not in lawful employment, Aborigines were barred from towns and cohabitation between European men and Aboriginal women was prohibited.[37]

Due to complaints by Europeans, the Minister for Education authorised the wholesale expulsion of Aboriginal students from most schools in the south-west during the early decades of the twentieth century. Such action directly affected Nyungars, one of the largest Aboriginal groups in that region, as John Kickett explained in 1916 to the Minister of Education:

> Sir, I wish you would let me Know if there would be any Objection my Children attending the State School at Quairading. Some time-agoe there were a few of them going Native Children and Some were not Clean so the Schools Board put a stop to them . . . I was thinking to Write first to you see what you got to Say am living on My Block My children wants to learn something I have been to School . . . this is my own handwriting . . . Probbley this is the only letter you ever got

from an Half-Cast . . . I want to Bring My Children up the Best away . . . Sir do what you can for me.[38]

The Director of Education refused permission for Kickett's children to attend the local school at Quairading and recommended that they could be sent to the 'Carrolup Native Settlement for the sum of 4s per week', where they would be 'properly fed, clothed and educated . . . moreover it is a native school'.[39]

Allegations of maltreatment of Aborigines by an exploration party along the Canning Stock Route led to the third Royal Commission into Aboriginal matters. Its findings acknowledged incidents of chaining Aborigines, feeding them with salt beef and not providing water, and 'running down prospective informants with horses' but it failed to lay any criminal charges and all members of the Canning exploration party were exonerated.[40] A. O. Neville, Chief Protector of Aborigines in Western Australia from 1915, was a strict administrator of Aboriginal affairs; Aboriginal people today still often recall 'the time of Mr Neville', with disdain.[41]

The fourth Royal Commission was required to look into the 'facts' relating to the alleged killing and burning of Aborigines in 1926 in the Forrest River District of the Kimberley region. Established in 1927, it was headed by George Wood, Magistrate of the Local Court in Perth. It found that there had been at least 'eleven natives' burned as retaliation against the alleged murder of 'settler' William Hay by a 'native called Lumbia'. Yet only cursory acknowledgement of the incidents was made and no one was prosecuted.[42]

Each successive inquiry led to amendments which further enhanced the power of the *Aborigines Protection Act, 1905*. In 1934 H. D. Moseley was appointed to lead another Royal Commission.[43] Moseley's recommendations led to the *Native Administration Act, 1936*, which gave the Chief Protector of Aborigines almost complete control over Aboriginal people's lives. For example, any wages earned were not to be paid directly to them. Some aspects, however, were more innovative; native courts were introduced to consider offences against Aborigines and 'tribal law' could be taken into account in mitigation of the sentence, though there was no right of appeal. Native Courts were disbanded in 1954, partly due to difficulties in ascertaining 'tribal law'. The case of Lumbia, charged with 'unlawful killing' of his wife, provides an example of the ineffectiveness of the 'Native Court' system. Despite official requirements, there was no representative from Lumbia's 'tribe' present during the court proceedings and instead of the Commissioner of Native Affairs, the local publican represented the government. Lumbia was represented by the Officer in Charge of the local hospital, who had no experience as an advocate. No witnesses were called in his defence, and Lumbia was eventually found guilty of murder, although he had been charged for a lesser offence. Lumbia was finally pardoned because of an error at law.[44]

The Moseley Commission had discouraged any form of recognition of Aboriginal rights, responsibilities and aspirations. It urged that Aboriginal camping grounds be entirely abolished and replaced by settlements with separate schools. Moseley recommended greater 'protection' of Aboriginal women but regulations mainly limited women's mobility; they were prohibited from being within two miles of the mouth of a river or inlet between sunset and sunrise. The *Native Administration Act, 1936*, following his report, was based on the underlying principle that 'the destiny of the native of aboriginal origin lay in their ultimate absorption by the people of the Commonwealth'. As in the Northern Territory, the increasing number of mixed-descent people was thus a special concern.

Missions and settlements with 'native' schools continued to be generated to enable 'absorption'. Moore River Settlement, also known as Mogumber, was established in 1937; Roelands Mission in 1938, and in 1940 Carrolup Settlement, which provided a setting for the production of an innovative school of art generally referred to as 'the Carrolup artists'[45], and in 1944 the Wandering Mission. Settlement and mission life provided much of the foundation for the contemporary relationship between Aborigines and Europeans. Children were placed there for their own 'good' or 'benefit', according to government rhetoric, under the 'guardianship' of the Chief Protector of Aborigines. While the number of children removed in Western Australia has not been calculated, thousands of families were certainly affected. Aboriginal poet, Jack Davis, wrote:

> They have buried my past
> those pink legislators
> and stolen my name
> They knew my mother was black
> so they took me away
> And pinned on a label
> one that's a lie[46]

During the Second World War, Aboriginal people were perceived as a security threat. Under National Security Regulations from 1942, Aboriginal employees over the age of fourteen years were required to be issued with a 'military permit' in either red or black; red indicated the bearer was believed to be 'subversive' and black that the bearer was deemed to be 'trustworthy'.

In 1944 policies were designed to provide 'citizenship rights' for Aboriginal people. A Bill was lobbied for by various Members of Parliament and others involved in Aboriginal affairs to give 'those aborigines prepared to adopt a higher standard of living an opportunity to uplift themselves'. This Bill eventually became the *Native (Citizenship Rights) Act, 1944* and it provided for the granting of citizenship rights to Aboriginal people who could prove, among other things, that they had adopted the manner and habits of civilised life, could speak and understand English, were not suffering from leprosy, syphilis or yaws, and were reasonably capable of handling his/her own affairs.[47] The granting of citizenship rights could be suspended or cancelled if any of these stipulations were not met and recipients had to carry a certificate showing their exemption at all times. As in New South Wales and the Northern Territory, many Aboriginal people referred to this certificate as their 'dog tag'. This trial citizenship did not extend automatically from parent to child. As persons from each new generation reached adulthood, they too had to apply for citizenship and be subjected to the same official scrutiny. People were left with very little choice; you could be a citizen or an Aboriginal but not both.[48]

Superficially, the movement toward greater citizenship rights could be considered as a small step toward recognising Aboriginal humanity. While many Aboriginal men and some women fought for Australia in the Second World War, as they had also done in the First World War, they were still not entitled to vote or receive pensions until the 1960s.

After the late 1940s it became increasingly evident that Aboriginal people were not 'dying out'. They were able to resist and/or accommodate some forms of European intrusion. They maintained oral traditions, kin obligations, knowledge about the custodianship of land, performed ceremonial ritual, and harvested natural resources. The adaptation and persistence of certain Aboriginal beliefs and practices could occur because Aboriginal people were segregated from Europeans in mission settings, on settlements, on declared 'Aboriginal reserves' and seasonally on pastoral stations. An insight into this process can be gleaned through the comments of Lochy Green, a Mangala man from the north-west:

> That law business used to be held during the wet season . . . The managers used to let the Aboriginal people alone during that time . . . We used to set up our camp quite close to the stations . . . We'd collect our rations for the week . . . Then the law men used to call people from all the other stations to come down for a big meeting.[49]

This is not to imply that the force of dominant European ideologies and practices could be ignored.

Assimilationist ideas started to influence inquiries and policies from the 1940s on. Referring to the Moola Bulla Native Settlement, a Native Welfare official thus argued that:

> educational aspects will never be completely successful at this station until it is possible to transfer the camp children to special institutional accommodation and thus remove them from the camp influence of the adult full-bloods, parents and otherwise . . . Nomadic habits and tendencies must be eliminated if the child is to be given a sense of responsibility sufficient to take its place in the community both economically and in all other respects.[50]

In 1948, an ex-Commissioner of Native Affairs in Papua New Guinea, S. G. Middleton, reorganised the Western Australian

Rations day at Kalumburu, 1963. BERNDT MUSEUM OF ANTHROPOLOGY, UNIVERSITY OF WESTERN AUSTRALIA

Department of Native Affairs, decentralising and expanding it. He tried to loosen restrictions on Aboriginal people but mixed-descent children continued to be removed from their families, and he worked in with the missionaries to teach European Christian values via a process of institutionalisation and evangelisation.[51] Further changes were touted in 1953, when a state Labor government passed the *Native Welfare Act, 1954*. While it removed some of the more onerous measures of the prior legislation—for instance, employment permits, prohibition on Aboriginal people entering towns—it still legally sanctioned child-removal and denied pensions and maternity allowances to any person who was a non-exempted person more than 'one-half Aboriginal'. For an Aboriginal person to leave her or his employment of their own accord, remained an offence, as did marriage without the permission of the Commissioner of Native Affairs and Welfare. After 1963, restrictions eased and the State Housing Commission was called in to develop a programme of improvements in housing facilities in town and country areas.

The conditions of Aboriginal people generally lay outside the interest and knowledge of most Europeans throughout the 1960s. Those who were deemed to be 'Australian citizens' because they conformed with the criteria of the 1944 Act and thus gained exemption from the requirements of the 1905 Act, were entitled to vote in 1961. Unlike non-Aboriginal people, however, Aborigines were not legally required to do so until 1985. Drinking rights were granted to Aboriginal people of the south-west of the state in 1964 and to the north-west population in July 1971.

Despite the fact that Aboriginal men and women were making a vital contribution to the Australian economy, as a non-unionised and industrially weak labour force they continued to be denied standard industrial conditions. They had primarily received a form of remuneration through rations such as flour, tea, tobacco, and clothing. Referring to the 1940s, 1950s and early 1960s, Eric Lawford states that their pay as stockmen was 'perhaps two shirts and two pairs of trousers a year, working boots, hat, canvas swag [bedding that could be rolled up], and a couple of blankets . . . no money!'[52] While a strike by Aboriginal pastoral workers in the Pilbara region in 1946 raised the issue of social and economic inequities, it was not until 1969 with the Federal Pastoral Industry Award that many Aboriginal workers were theoretically ensured 'equal wages for equal work'. The contribution of women is often underestimated. Maggie Milangga, from the Western Desert region of the state, explained, 'I used to cook, used to ride horses too—out on the muster. Night time we used to take turns watching cattle: man and woman took turns. Talk about tired, don't say! [53]

As in the Northern Territory, the change in the Award structure meant that it was uneconomical for station owners to maintain the same number of Aboriginal employees on full Award Rates together with their dependants. This coincided with greater mechanisation and fencing, and the introduction of helicopter mustering. Many Aboriginal people were subsequently evicted from stations while others, following kin, simply walked off. Many were forced to set up camps outside rural town centres. A hospital administrator at Fitzroy Crossing, one of the areas most affected by the changes recounted:

> The Award created a multitude of problems affecting the natives

... as the stock work declined, more people drifted in ... and by the end of December there were some 500 people in Fitzroy Crossing ... Local names for this were and are the 'ghetto' or 'refugee camp'.[54]

Some workers, like Jack Britten, a Kija man from the Kimberley, lamented the loss of patronage: 'that [European] manager he ... never trying to belt em or he never trying to shoot em, nothing. He was a good kartiya [white man]. That's the way all blackfellas bin like em, living la [near or alongside] him.'[55]

Relocation of Aboriginal people and labour utilisation most profoundly affected the pastoral north-west, and the south-west agricultural and farming properties.[56]

AFTER THE 1967 REFERENDUM

Following the sweeping results of the 1967 National Referendum, which enabled the Commonwealth to legislate on behalf of Aborigines, and later the coming of the Whitlam Labor government in 1972, Aboriginal policies changed. The Federal Government began providing State assistance to support programmes to 'upgrade' Aboriginal education and living standards. Yet such 'assistance' remained subject to European ideologies and practice. The words of a Nyungar woman, living on a reserve in the south-west, epitomises an Aboriginal perception about this form of supposed 'upgrade':

> One day some men from Native Welfare came along to our camp and told us we were moving. We hardly had time to put our things together. They put us into a house in town away from our relatives. It was hard because it was different from the house and living on the reserve. We had built a lot of that house ourselves and though it was rough it was our home. We went back later to have a look. But they had bulldozed it all down. Some people say we were moved because the Shire wanted the gravel there. We didn't like the house in town. So we left it to move to Perth to stay with some relatives. My husband thought he might get some work up there ... [57]

In 1972 the Western Australian Parliament introduced the Aboriginal Affairs Planning Authority (AAPA), cementing co-operation between the Department for Community Welfare and the State Housing Commission. The AAPA co-ordinated Aboriginal policies throughout the state, acted in an advisory and mediating role, and administered the Aboriginal Lands Trust (ALT). The *Aboriginal Heritage Act*, introduced in 1972, ostensibly gave the Western Australian Museum, through the Department of Aboriginal Sites, the responsibility to protect areas of religious and cultural significance to Aboriginal people. The weakness of the Act was clearly demonstrated during what is now well-known as the Noonkanbah drama of 1980. The State Government amended crucial sections of the Act in 1980, further weakening the legislation so that mining exploration, through Amax, a multinational subsidiary company, could proceed despite the protests of the Yungnora people at Noonkanbah and their supporters. Dickie Skinner, a Walmajarri man and spokesperson for the Yungnora people at that time, comments on the 'secrecy' which took place with respect to mining and government operations. He states:

> Mining people came secretly and did not talk to the Aborigines. Later people were going around mustering and they found samples and told the old people. When Aboriginal people found out about the holes [drilled for exploration purposes], they wondered why the mining people didn't come and talk to them. After one year all the kangaroos disappeared and the people knew they had gone back to the spirit hole because of the mining.[58]

The Federal Labor Government's policy of 'self-determination', while somewhat ambiguous, recognised in principle the 'equal right of Aboriginal people along with other Australians to determine their own future within the Australian community'. In 1975, when the Liberal–Country Party Coalition replaced Labor, the policy of 'self-management' was adopted. In Western Australia in 1974, yet another Royal Commission was established to consider all concerns 'affecting the wellbeing of persons of Aboriginal descent in Western Australia'. L. C. Furnell, a Queen's Counsel and former judge of the District Court, drew heavily on documentary material, consulting little with Aboriginal people.[59] In 1976 another Royal Commission, known as the Laverton or the Skull Creek Commission, inquired into a police incident against

Aboriginal people and, despite criticism of police evidence, it was concluded that 'no-one involved acted improperly'. The prior historical legacy, however, could not be ignored.

> While nothing can excuse what was done at Skull Creek . . . It is obvious that many of the problems develop out of the historical development of the relationships between Europeans and the Aboriginal people whose way of life and culture have been affected. The problems lie at the door of the whole society and not just at the door of the police force or any other section of society.[60]

Greater Aboriginal independence resulted with the Aboriginal Medical Service (established in Perth in 1973), and the Aboriginal Legal Service (established in Perth in 1975). Regional resource agencies, land councils, Aboriginal language centres and programmes, community schools, and outstations also emerged throughout the latter part of the 1970s and continued to proliferate throughout the 1980s. Some of these developments were government funded, others received financial assistance from various church bodies and aid agencies, while other developments were supported by independent Aboriginal communities and organisations.

The *Aboriginal Communities Act*, for example, was instituted in 1979 with the aim of enabling certain Aboriginal communities to institute and monitor their own by-laws. Also in 1979, the Aboriginal Child Care Agency (ACCA) was established with a brief to liaise between Aboriginal families and the Department for Community Welfare (formerly the Department of Native Welfare). Though not without their problems, government recognition of the need for community by-laws, and an organisation such as ACCA, indicated a minor shift in the relationship between Aboriginal people and the state.

In the Aboriginal Land Inquiry (ALI) of 1983, Mr Paul Seaman QC was asked to consider the most appropriate form of title over land for the use and benefit of Aboriginal people, what kinds of land should be protected, issues of conservation and land management; the question of compensation and royalties, the operation of the *Aboriginal Heritage Act* (1972–80), the relationship of granted areas to resource development.[61] The ALI carried out extensive consultation throughout Western Australia with Aboriginal people and other residents. But sectors of the mining industry, who feared a decline in resource development, waged a rabid anti-land rights campaign, and the Liberal Party Opposition objected to any form of security of title for Aboriginal people.[62] A Final Report was released in 1984 which, among other things, recognised the extensive nature of Aboriginal relationships to land and recommended the right of Aboriginal people to negotiate about, and ultimately have the ability to say 'no' to mining on their land. The ALI also recommended land rights legislation claims to be heard by a tribunal. Ten days after public release of the ALI's report, the State Government rejected its findings, replacing the report with its own set of principles. A drafting committee was established which put together its own Aboriginal Land Tenure Bill, but this was not supported by the majority of Aboriginal people in Western Australia. Nonetheless, a Bill was tabled in 1985, to be defeated in the Upper House. Meanwhile the Federal Government proposed national land rights legislation but backed down due to mining interests and an alleged lack of popular support.[63] Western Australia, then under a Liberal government, was one of the few states which refused to endorse the Mabo-inspired *Native Title Act, 1993*.

CONCLUSIONS

In Western Australia, despite some humanitarian concern, 'settlers laws' have always taken precedence over Aboriginal sociocultural interests or economic and political justice. This has generated a race relations history that will not easily fade from the state's social and political memory. The Royal Commission into Aboriginal Deaths in Custody recorded 32 deaths in Western Australia, the highest number of deaths investigated by the Commission for the period 1980–89. The deaths were especially disturbing considering that Aboriginal people currently constitute only 2.7 per cent of the state's total population at around 40 000 people.[64] In 1993 the Western Australian Premier was the most vocal opponent of federal land rights, and mounted an unsuccessful High

Court challenge to the validity of the *Native Title Act* in relation to Western Australia.

A frontier development ethos amongst non-Aborigines continues to inform contemporary race relations. Over-representation in the prison system, public and police over-reactions against Aboriginal crime, racial stereotyping and anxieties about the threat of Aboriginal land rights continue to endure. Western Australia, however, is a state where the Aboriginal population is a visible presence and even predominates in many areas. Its large tracts of Crown land and areas of non-intensive development have often meant Aboriginal people could maintain relatively close contact with their traditional lands. Western Australian Aborigines have been politically active in protecting sacred sites and persisting in land rights campaigns. Western Australia has also produced Aboriginal people who have made outstanding cultural contributions, bringing the experience of Aboriginal Australians to a wide audience. These include writer Jack Davis, writer and artist, Sally Morgan, and Jimmy Chi, creator of the powerful and optimistic musical, 'Bran Nue Dae'.[65]

NOTES

1 R.M. Berndt, 'Traditional Aboriginal life in Western Australia as it was and is', in R.M. and C.H. Berndt (eds), *Aborigines of the West: Their Past and Their Present,* University of WA Press, Nedlands, 1980, p.7.

2 P. M. Kaberry, *Aboriginal Woman Sacred and Profane,* Routledge and Sons, London, 1939, p.132.

3 Typescript of Anne Whatley's diary held in Battye State Library, Perth. See also B.T. Haynes et al, *W.A. Aborigines 1622–1972,* History Association of Western Australia, 1972, pp.4–5.

4 See A. McGrath, 'Europeans and Aborigines' in N. Meaney (ed.), *Under New Heavens,* Melbourne, 1989.

5 Report of Governor Stirling, 1835. Despatches to Colonial Office, Letter No. 53, Battye State Library, Perth. See also Haynes et al, 1972, pp.10–12.

6 N. Green, *Nyungar: the people,* Creative Research, Perth, 1979, pp.194–195; E.J. Stormon, (translator and editor), *The Salvado Memoirs: Historical Memoirs of Australia and Particularly of the Bene-*

dictine Mission of New Norcia and of the Customs of the Australian Natives by Dom Salvado, University of WA Press, Nedlands, 1977, pp.267–75.
7 John Watson quoted in P. Marshall (ed.), *Raparapa*, Magabala Books, Broome, 1988, pp.248–49.
8 C.D. Rowley, *The Destruction of Aboriginal Society*, Penguin, Middlesex, 1970, p.71.
9 S. Hallam, *Fire and Hearth: A Study of Aboriginal Usurpation in the south-west of Australia*, AIAS, Canberra, 1975, p.76.
10 N. Green, 1979, P. Hasluck, *Black Australians, 1829–1897*, MUP, Melbourne, 1942, and L. Tilbrook, *Nyungar Traditions*, University of WA Press, Nedlands, 1983.
11 P.L. Dodson, 1991, p.18; see also Haynes et al 1972, pp.28–29.
12 Jack Britten cited in H. Ross and E. Bray, *Impact stories of the East Kimberley*, ANU, Canberra, 1987, p.20.
13 P. Seaman, *The Aboriginal Land Inquiry Final Report*, Government Printers, Perth, 1984, p.89.
14 W.J.K. Christensen, 'The Wangkayi Way: Tradition and Change in a Reserve Setting', unpublished PhD thesis, Anthropology, University of WA, 1981, p.97.
15 Haynes et al, 1972, p.48; see also A.W. Canning, 'Mr Canning's Expeditions in Western Australia, 1906–1907 and 1908–1910', *Geographical Journal*, vol.38, 1911, pp.26–29.
16 J.B. Gribble, *Dark Deeds in a Sunny Land*, University of WA Press, Nedlands, [1886] 1987; see also S. Hawke and M. Gallagher, *Noonkanbah*, Fremantle Arts Centre Press, Fremantle, 1989, p.57.
17 Neville cited in R.M. Berndt, 'Aborigines of southwestern Australia', in D. Merrilees et al, 'Aboriginal man in southwestern Australia', *Journal of the Royal Society of Western Australia*, vol.56, 1973, p.53; see also A. Haebich, *For their own good: Aborigines and Government in the Southwest of Western Australia 1900–1940*, University of WA Press, Nedlands, 1988, p.1.
18 P.L. Dodson, *Final Report of the Royal Commission into underlying issues into Aboriginal Deaths in Custody in Western Australia*, AGPS, 1991, pp.853–62 provides a historical chronology which contains reference to the establishment of various missions in Western Australia.
19 Gerrard, cited in B. Gammage and P. Spearritt (eds), *Australians 1938*, Fairfax, Syme and Weldon, 1987, pp.55–56; see also Rumley and Toussaint, 1990, for discussion of Moola Bulla Native Settlement.

20 Haebich, 1988, pp.30–31.
21 C. D. Rowley, *The Remote Aborigines*, Penguin, Middlesex, 1976, p.243.
22 M. A. Jebb, 'The Dorre and Lock hospitals', in Reece and Stannage (eds), 1984, pp.68–87.
23 H. Pederson, 'Pigeon: An Australian Rebel', in R. Reece and C.T. Stannage (eds), *European–Aboriginal relations in WA history*, 1984, pp.7–14, *Studies in Western Australian History*, History Department, University of Western Australia.
24 E. Eggleston, *Fear, Favour or Affection*, ANU Press, Canberra, 1976, makes available relevant material concerning the 'dual role' played by Protectors in Western Australia.
25 John Watson quoted in Marshall, 1988, p.331.
26 Eric Lawford quoted in Marshall, 1988, p.15.
27 A. McGrath, *Born in the Cattle*, Allen & Unwin, Sydney, 1987, pp.68–94, and M. Tonkinson, 'Sisterhood or Aboriginal servitude? Black women and white women on the Australian frontier', *Aboriginal History*, vol.12, no.1, 1988, pp.27–40. See also P. Grimshaw, M. Lake, A. McGrath, M. Quartly, *Creating a Nation*, Penguin, Ringwood, 1994.
28 John Watson quoted in Marshall, 1988, p.220.
29 Haebich, 1988, p.113.
30 It is revealing to note that between 17 and 21 of the 32 Aboriginal people whose life and death were investigated by the Royal Commission into Aboriginal Deaths in Custody in Western Australia had been removed from their families and placed in missions and government institutions as a result of such polices; Dodson, 1991, and E. Johnston, *Royal Commission into Aborginal Deaths in Custody. National Report*, vol.1, AGPS, Canberra, 1991, p.44 provide details. See also D. McCotter, *Children in Limbo*, Dept of Community Welfare, Perth, 1981 for discussion of the removal and placement of Aboriginal children under the auspices of the state's Community Welfare Department (previously known as the Department of Native Welfare).
31 *Statutes of Western Australia*, vol.11, 1883–1892, pp.384–85; see also Seaman, P., 1984, pp.245–47.
32 Haebich, 1988, p.11.
33 S.T. Woenne, 'The true state of affairs', Commissions of inquiry concerning Western Australian Aborigines in R.M. Berndt, *Aborigines of the West: Their Past and Their Present*, University of WA Press, Nedlands, 1980, pp.324–56.

34 ibid, pp.324–56.
35 P. Biskup, *Not Slaves, Not Citizens: the Aboriginal Problem in Western Australia 1898–1954*, University of Queensland Press, St Lucia, 1973, pp.59–65; Haebich, 1988; Woenne, 1980.
36 Haebich, 1988, p.89.
37 C.D. Rowley, 1976, pp.242–43.
38 John Kickett quoted in Haynes et al, 1972, p.53.
39 ibid, p.54.
40 Haynes et al, 1972; see also Canning's Report dated 1911.
41 P. Jacobs, *Mr Neville*, University of WA Press, Nedlands, 1990.
42 Wood Commission, 1927, 'Royal Commission of Inquiry into Alleged killing and burning of bodies of Aborigines in the East Kimberley', *WA Parliamentary Votes and Proceedings (WAPV&P)*, vol.1, no.3.
43 H.D. Moseley, 'Report of the Royal Commission in Relation to the Condition and treatment of Aborigines', *WAPV&P* vol.1, no.2, Perth, 1935.
44 Dodson, 1991, p.28.
45 Carrolup became the setting for a school of young Aboriginal artists; see J. Stanton, *Nyungar Landscapes*, Occasional Paper No. 3, published by the Berndt Museum of Anthropology, 1992.
46 Jack Davis, *Black Life: Poems*, University of Queensland Press, St Lucia, 1992, p.59.
47 Biskup, 1973, p.207.
48 See A. McGrath, 'Beneath the Skin: Australian Citizenship, Rights and Aboriginal Women' in R. Howe (ed.), *Women and the State*, La Trobe University, Bundoora, 1993.
49 Lochy Green quoted in Marshall, 1988, p.191.
50 Department of Native Welfare, Annual Report, 1950, Battye State Library, Perth.
51 T. Long, 'The Development of Government Aboriginal Policy' in R.M. and C.H. Berndt, 1980, and Biskup, 1973, provide extensive discussion on the Bateman and Middleton years.
52 Lawford quoted in Marshall, 1988, p.15.
53 Milangga quoted in M. Tonkinson, 1985, p.171. See also A. Lawrie and A. McGrath, 'I was a drover once myself: Amy Lawrie of Kununurra', in I. White et al, (eds), *Fighters and Singers*, Allen & Unwin, Sydney, 1985, pp.76–89 for discussion of Aboriginal women working in the pastoral industry.
54 Australian Inland Mission, Hospital Administrator's report 1969.

Typescript held at Department of Community Services, Fitzroy Crossing.
55 Britten quoted in Ross and Bray, 1987, p.20.
56 S. Hodson, 'Nyungars and work: Aboriginal labour in the great southern region, WA, 1936–1972', unpublished MA thesis, Anthropology, University of Western Australia, 1989, and Haebich, 1988, pp.28–35.
57 Quoted in S. Toussaint, 'Nyungars in the city: a study of policy, power and identity', unpublished MA thesis, Anthropology, University of WA, 1987, p.115.
58 Dickie Skinner quoted in Hawke and Gallagher, 1989, p.226.
59 L.C. Furnell, *Report of the Royal Commission into Aboriginal Affairs in Western Australia*, Perth, Government Printers, 1974; see also Woenne, 1980.
60 Report of the Laverton Royal Commission, 1976.
61 P. Seaman, 1984, p.iv.
62 Dodson, 1991, p.333.
63 Dodson, 1991, pp.334–35.
64 Dodson, 1991, p.2.
65 Jimmy Chi, *Bran nue dae*, Currency, Paddington, 1991.

7

Northern Territory

The White people named this place Lake Nash but its real name, its Aboriginal name, is Ilperrelhelame. Aboriginal people own this waterhole. We look after this place as those before us have always done. White people have got no right to push us out . . .
    They don't own the country—we are the true owners. They only brought in the cattle and horses and drilled bores on our land . . .
    I was born here at Lake Nash. I've always lived and worked here. Even when I was a small boy, I worked with horses in the stock camp. We Aboriginal people ran the stock camps on our own. Lots of us were working then . . .
    You should hear the real story—our story, not the company's. They can't tell you the true story because they don't own the country. We are the real owners of this country—they only manage it.[1]

THIS statement is by Harry Campbell, an Alyawarra man from Lake Nash station north-east of Alice Springs. His community fought for many years for a living area on the station, and was at last successful. 'They can't tell you the true story because they don't own the country.' Campbell's words indicate how strongly the traditional life flourishes in the Northern Territory.
    Several other features set the Northern Territory apart from other areas of Australia. The proportion of White people[2] to

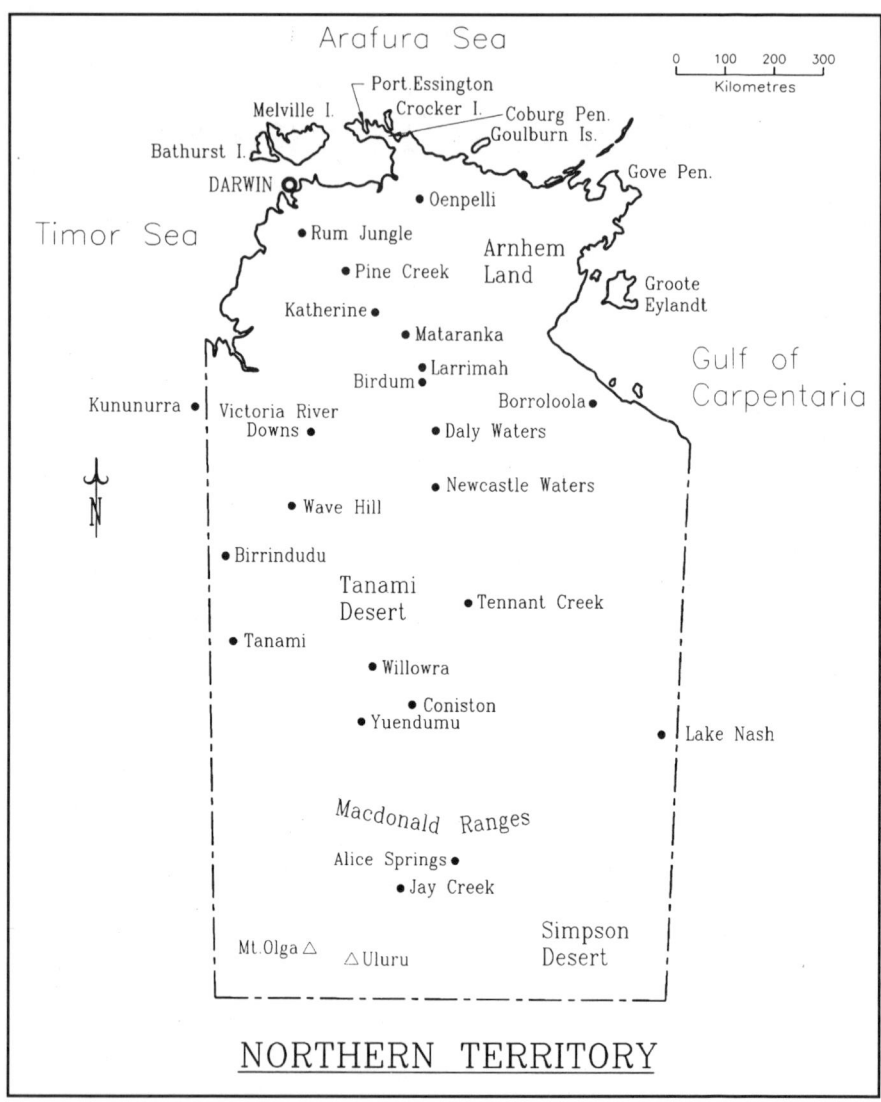

Aborigines and other races such as Chinese, Japanese and Malays has been very different to that in the southern states. The nature of the soils and climate made many areas useless for primary production, so that much of the Northern Territory is even now unoccupied by Whites. The Territory was developed intermittently. Large areas proved to be uneconomic and were abandoned. Such differences continue to affect the history of the Northern Territory. Partly because more uncontested land was available for claim than elsewhere, more land was granted. The long periods of very low White populations offered comparatively little threat to traditional lifeways.

A long period of Commonwealth Government control (1911–78) attracted numerous critical observers, left an unusually large quantity of records, and from time to time enabled progressive legislation to be enacted which Federal governments hoped might become a model elsewhere. The White population was so small and, in some areas, so stable that many pastoralists, police and missionaries are still remembered by Aborigines: in the 1970s older Aborigines of the Victoria River district were still able to name two policemen present in the area in 1896 and 1909.[3] 'Punitive expeditions', in which police and settlers rode upon a camp at dawn and shot all the men, a practice which ceased in southern states more than a century ago, are still recalled by living people.[4]

The White presence in the Northern Territory has been comparatively recent, and much smaller than elsewhere. Peter Horsetailer, of Tara Community, could remember how his father acted as a guide to Charles Chewings in 1909, in the same way as Aborigines helped the Whites in the Sydney region a hundred years before that.

> Yeah, well two men bin comin' with camel from Alice Spring. They come here and find'em old feller mine, my father, longa Barrow Creek. Longa old Telegraph Station. They bin pick'em up that old fella. They ask'em him, 'You want like to show us country to go longa desert? We tryin to look that gold.'
>
> 'All right then,' my father said, 'All right. I'll take you. But you know'em all that country to go through with the camel because I don't think we can get water now, I-I can show'em where we can get water.'[5]

Even areas generally thought of as 'occupied' were in fact often inhabited by Whites for a short period only. Many commercial ventures like sheep, sugar, rice, peanuts, tobacco and tropical fruit were tried, but failed. The memory of these failures is now preserved only in the minds of the descendants of the original inhabitants whose lands were, sometimes only temporarily, wrested from them. Throughout the twentieth century most Aborigines, like Harry Campbell, believed that the pastoralists merely squatted on land that was rightfully theirs. Even the findings of Mr Justice Blackburn in the famous 'Yirrkala' case in 1971, has not changed their minds that the land is rightfully theirs and has always been so.[6]

Unlike the Whites, Aborigines have lived in Northern Australia for a very long time indeed. Some Aborigines maintain that they have lived in their land from the beginning of time, others believe that, long ago, their distant ancestors came from over the sea. The oldest ground-edge axes in the world, dating from some 20 000 years ago, have been found in Arnhem Land. In the mid 1980s an upper limit of occupation was thought to be about 40 000 years, which happened also to be the limit of the radiocarbon dating method. Scientists testing old occupation sites by thermoluminescence, a newer method of dating which does not rely on the decay of organic material, have suggested a presence of up to 50 000 years. There is no theoretical reason, according to western-trained scientists, why Aborigines should not have occupied Northern Australia for a much longer period than that. The upper limit, on the basis of scientific knowledge, indicates an Aboriginal occupation of not more than 100 000 years. Elsewhere in the world modern humans have first been identified distinct from other near-human forms at about this time, and no scientific evidence indicates that Aborigines evolved separately from all other modern humans.[7]

TRADERS AND EXPLORERS

The Aborigines of Arnhem Land encountered and worked with Macassan trepang-gatherers from at least 1700 to the early years of the twentieth century.[8] Relations seem to have been generally harmonious, probably because the Macassans only came for a period of each year, occupied areas not much further than the beach, and traded with, rather than merely exploited, the Aborigines. The Europeans intended to stay. If the first European explorers like Leichhardt and Stuart, and a few sea-borne venturers like those at Port Essington (1838), maintained non-hostile relations with the indigenous people for most of the time, the second wave of the European invasion was often marked with violence. The excursions into the Territory from South Australia in the 1870s degenerated into destruction of traditional living areas, and many massacres. The Overland Telegraph Line, constructed in the 1870s, provided a route for gold miners as well as pastoralists, and the gold rushes at Pine Creek (1872) and Arltunga (1897) gave traditional owners little choice but to co-operate with the miners after the local water, food and firewood resources were destroyed.[9]

The second land route to the Territory was eastwards from Queensland but European and Aboriginal evidence suggests that here the initial friendly contact was often not even attempted. In Queensland, where the 'Black Police' were brought to their most deadly pinnacle of organisation and bushcraft, the pastoralists had more or less determined their own relations with Aborigines. Entering the Northern Territory via the 'Barkly route' from the 1870s they probably thought of the new grasslands as an extension of Queensland where they could simply continue the same methods of invasion and control.[10] Nevertheless the domination of the Whites was completed neither easily nor quickly. Many areas officially known as 'pastoral stations' were not completely controlled until half a century after the first incursions by Whites.

THE CATTLE INDUSTRY

The pastoral industry, which gave to the Northern Territory its particular flavour of ringers (stockmen), enormous droving trails and cattle stations the size of small European nations, also gave a particular characteristic to race relations. Unlike many other areas of Australia, Aboriginal men and women were not only useful but vital in maintaining an economy which would have been impossible without them. A typical large station might employ half a dozen White people, (including the manager, head stockman and book-keeper) one or two Aborigines of mixed descent who took superior roles such as stock-camp boss, and twenty or more Aboriginal 'ringers'. Though men did much of the most dangerous work of culling and marking beasts, the historian Ann McGrath notes that frequently women performed hard manual labour such as road mending as well as working at 'the big house' (the station homestead) or cattle mustering; old people swept the yard, chopped wood, and looked after the garden; children learned to ride at six or seven years of age.[11] The economy was seasonal. The 'wet season' in the north, and the summer shut-down in Central Australia was the signal for Aborigines in station camps to 'go walkabout', and live off 'bush tucker' for several months before being encouraged (or allowed) to enter the station precincts in February–March.

The pastoral industry, however, could at no time compete successfully with southern markets. Poor pastures, cattle diseases, lack of water and meatworks, and enormous distances made survival almost impossible without government co-operation or direct aid.[12] Several stations in Arnhem Land in the early years of the twentieth century failed completely, while many others survived only through their reliance on unpaid Aboriginal labour.[13]

The most remarkable feature of the pastoral industry was the very large number of Aborigines associated with it. In the first years after the establishment of a new station, Aborigines already working would sometimes visit the bush people to explain that the choice was either to co-operate with the pastoralists or be shot at; those who chose to remain 'myalls' (bush people) were forced into a life of guerilla warfare, or relied on their younger working kinfolk to supply them with food at night.[14] Nor were the station Aborigines always friendly. The historian Debbie Rose wrote of the bush people in the 1880s:

> Increasingly the 'enemy' was not only the whitefellows but also station blackfellows. Some of the station 'boys' and police trackers were from far away; others were local. Some had relations still living in the bush carrying on warfare and other acts of subversion; many had had ceremonial-ritual and marriage ties across this boundary of allegiances. Some were brutal; others tried to minimise the violence.[15]

People living on large government reserves frequently spent periods in employment on adjacent stations. Aborigines of mixed descent living in or near towns found regular employment as fencers or well-sinkers. Outside Arnhem Land, it is probably true that every Aboriginal person in the Territory born before 1950 in contact with Whites and not removed from his or her family, was involved in the pastoral industry in some way.

THE MISSION STATIONS

The earliest missionaries at Hermannsburg in the south (established in 1877) and Roper River in the north (established in 1908) acted in part as Aboriginal protectors against the attacks of pastoralists on the bush Aborigines. During the rule of the South Australian Government over the Northern Territory (1863–1911), missionaries were no more than tolerated but the Commonwealth Special Investigator J.W. Bleakley argued in 1929 that the missions were 'working on the right lines' towards a responsibility which was in reality the State's, and ought to be financially supported.[16] By this time the Lutherans (Hermannsburg), Catholics (Daly River, Bathurst and Melville Islands), Methodists (Milingimbi, Goulburn Island, Elcho Island, Yirrkala), and the Anglicans (Roper River, Groote Eylandt, Oenpelli) were established in mutually respected 'patches'. Unlike many southern mission stations of the previous century, individual missionaries stayed for long periods; the missions remained and in the 1970s formed bases of new and independent communities even after Christian influence had declined. Like the pastoralists, missionaries brought mixed blessings. Almost all children raised on mission stations before 1970 were likely to be separated to some degree from their older close relatives. In this way they were deprived both of traditional teachings but also of role models of parenting and family life. Hagar Roberts recalled her days at the Roper River Mission in the 1920s: 'Missionary didn't let us go, you see. She bin learn us to speak, like, White man way. Know about a White God story, teaching us to know what to do longa White man way, that story. They didn't let us go to mother and father.'[17]

COMMONWEALTH CONTROL, 1911

The Commonwealth Government, anxious to take seriously its new responsibility of governing the Northern Territory in 1911, commissioned the newly-appointed Chief Protector of Aborigines, Baldwin Spencer, to report on the Aborigines. Spencer, who had wide experience as an anthropologist in the Northern Territory, recommended that some 11 000 hectares be set aside as Aboriginal reserves, a necessary procedure, he thought, 'if any serious effort' was to 'be made for their betterment'. His proposals were generally accepted. Many of today's large Northern Territory reserves were created at this time.[18]

Spencer gave much thought to what extent customary (that is, Aboriginal) law should continue to operate. He thought it 'manifestly advisable' not to interfere in matters which concerned Aboriginal law or custom only. Spencer approved the Chief Protector's power to remove offending Aborigines to a place other than prison. He understood that a sentence to Fanny Bay gaol might be regarded as a mark of distinction and that some prisoners emerged worse than they had entered.[19]

In the regulation of the lives of Aboriginal town dwellers, however, Spencer's recommendations illustrated a long-standing tension between laws to protect Aborigines from Whites and laws to protect Whites from Aborigines. While his recommendations for overseeing living conditions on remote stations were fairly conscientious and sympathetic (though unenforced) Spencer believed that in Darwin and Alice Springs it was the rights of the Whites which must be protected. Under regulations of the *Aboriginal Ordinance* of 1911, Aborigines in those towns had to reside with their employer or in 'the [Kahlin] compound'. Spencer recommended that no Aborigine be allowed to wander between sunset and sunrise on penalty of being locked up for the night. No Aborigine should leave Darwin nor be allowed to enter without permission. Spencer thought it probable, however, that 'in view of the scarcity of labour for domestic purposes, that the numbers of servants would have to be replenished periodically'.[20] Spencer's concern for the welfare of traditional Aborigines in remote areas, but for the welfare of Whites in the towns, set a precedent which arguably still remains entrenched in Northern Territory legislation.

Seventeen years passed before the next major investigation of Aboriginal living and working conditions. In 1928 the Queensland Protector of Aborigines, J.W. Bleakley, was asked by the Commonwealth Government to report on the status and conditions of Northern Territory Aborigines. Though he observed that a small wage was occasionally paid to Aboriginal workers, very little attempt was made to provide adequate shelter for station workers as required by the regulations. Bleakley found it remarkable that the pastoralists, though recognising their absolute dependence upon the Aborigines, made no attempt to 'elevate or educate them, though this should enhance their value as machinery'.[21]

So the tension between controlling Aborigines and protecting them was as apparent in Bleakley's 1929 Report as it was in Spencer's of 1911. Like Spencer, Bleakley approved imprisonment for Darwin Aborigines found wandering after dark, and disapproved of films, such as American westerns, likely to lower respect for Whites. Yet further from the European settlements Bleakley was rather more humane: he recommended that missions be established in suitable areas, not to draw Aborigines unnecessarily from tribal life but to 'win their trust by kindly ministrations'. In 1929, though the most serious alarms were still caused by bush people, (the 'Coniston Massacre' took place as Bleakley was conducting his field work) the most restrictive legislation again applied most of all to the people gathered around the towns.[22]

Merely identifying bad living conditions by investigators did not guarantee that they would improve, and though Bleakley recognised that regulations were virtually ignored in remote regions he recommended no prosecutions or cancellations of licences to employ Aborigines. It was scarcely surprising that conditions probably deteriorated during the following decade. The government was quite prepared, for instance, to give over the Haasts Bluff Reserve to the pastoralists, and was only dissuaded from doing so after the well-known Christian medico, Dr Charles Duguid, threatened to publicise the plan in England.[23] In 1945, the Australian Investment Agency (Vesteys) asked the anthropologists R. and C. Berndt to investigate why the Aboriginal populations on its stations were declining. It was not hard to find out, for Vesteys, like most other company stations, had a much worse record of labour relations than family-owned stations. The Berndts found apathy, hopelessness and acute malnutrition in the station camps. There was a question constantly implied and sometimes asked by the Aborigines: 'Why should we breed more children for *Kadia* [Europeans] to use the way they use us?' At Limbunya Station, only 10 out of 21 children survived the first year of life. At Wave Hill, where the mortality rate was calculated at 31.6 per 100, the Berndts reported that three births took place during their period of study at the station. The first, unknown to the White station community, was stillborn. The second was normal but in the third case, mother and child died within a few hours of each other. In each case the mothers had subsisted on the standard ration of damper, beef and tea. At Birrindudu Station, the Aborigines lived on dry bread three times a day and usually a piece of goat meat. Twelve to sixteen people shared a three-litre billy of tea.[24]

Why did conditions remain so bad? Part of the answer lies in the continuing phenomenon of official and unofficial support for the pastoral industry at the expense of Aboriginal welfare, to the extent of belittling or ridiculing critics of the pastoral regime. The pastoralists often defended themselves by economic arguments; the Western Australian, M.P. Durack stated that Aboriginal stockmen returned to employment each year because they valued food, clothing, tobacco and were willing to work for them.[25]

Like government settlements in the south, a particular station gave a person a local identification, so that a man called 'Willowra Freddie Jampijinpa' might be known by the station he grew up on (Willowra) as well as by his Christian and subsection or 'skin' name (Jampijinpa). In the absence of other areas where Aborigines were allowed to gather, the stations became focal points of population and community life. On most stations religious and secular ceremonies were allowed at times which did not interfere with the pastoral routine. Traditional teachings, languages and stories often continued whatever the pastoralist's wishes. Today there are over one hundred smaller stations, or excisions, now designated as Aboriginal land, which have been carved off from the older pastoral properties. These are occupied by Aborigines, some of whom once worked on them under a White manager.

FRINGE-DWELLERS AND PEOPLE OF MIXED DESCENT

In 1929 Bleakley repeated Spencer's unexamined assertions about the 'degradation of the blacks' camp' from which 'half-castes' should be removed, and recommended that 'No half-caste child should be allowed to remain in any native camp'; the 'best and kindest thing' was 'to place them on reserves along with the natives, train them in the same schools and encourage them to marry among themselves'.[26] The justification for such a policy was that as the Northern Territory became more populated, those people with an Aboriginal and White parent, colloquially known as 'half-castes', would decline in proportion to the rest of the community. In 1927 Patrol Officer Strehlow (the later owner of the famous Strehlow Collection of Aboriginal artefacts) reported that the Alice Springs ration depot was attracting 'scores of natives' from all parts of Central Australia. In his judgement, 'Ngalia, Ilpara and Pitjentara' peoples were 'useless, drifting wreckage', and likely soon to degenerate into 'unemployable hooligans, beggars and wasters'.[27] Ten years later Strehlow reported that the same ration depot was now attracting people from the desert in 'whole clans'. 'It is a disgrace,' he wrote, 'that all these dirty camps are allowed not only to exist but to increase at a place rich in press-reporters and frequented by crowds of tourists.'[28] Strehlow urgently recommended the establishment of new reserves at Jay Creek and Haasts Bluff. During the 1920s and 1930s, removals to the White institutions increased.

The anxiety of the Alice Springs and Darwin Whites at these developments was indicated in the new *Aboriginals Ordinance* of 1933, which gave the Administrator powers of control even greater than those which he already possessed. He could now declare any place to be prohibited to an Aboriginal person, remove him or her to any place in or beyond the Northern Territory and nominate any mission station as a children's institution. The Chief Protector could order local removals, control real and personal property, forbid marriage to non-Aborigines and prohibit the possession of firearms.[29]

At the same time the problem of 'half-castes' continued to concern Alice Springs residents even more than the increasing town camps. Despite Bleakley's advice to remove 'mixed-blood' children to the large *Aboriginal* reserves, it was removals to *White* institutions which were increasing during the late 1920s. The original 'Bungalow', a tin shack occupied by a single family in Alice Springs in 1913, had become by 1930 a large institution housed at the old Telegraph Station two miles from the town. Bleakley reported 64 children at the Bungalow; seven years later, in 1935, this had risen to 106. The writer Ernestine Hill probably did not exaggerate her claim made in 1933 that Aboriginal children of mixed descent were being gathered in by police from 'Port Keats to the Petermann Ranges'. In the institutions, she wrote approvingly, the children were given every opportunity to 'outgrow their heredity'. The intention was that the children would be 'encouraged to live white, think white and to marry, if possible, into the white race, or failing that, with each other'. She estimated that twenty years would pass before the end of the story would be written.[30] Twenty years later Bleakley's total of 140 children held in official institutions had risen to 337.[31]

Like other inmates of the Bungalow, the young Charles Perkins absorbed the place of the 'half-caste' in the Northern Territory of the 1930s. Sometimes he would climb over the fence to the camp of his elderly full-descent relatives, to hear a few words of his banned Arrernte language and to poke a stick into a billy full of porridge before returning to the Bungalow for a second breakfast. At other times he'd climb the ridge between the camp and the town to peer down at the Whites who seemed so strange, so powerful: 'They were the bosses. The top people. Never argue with them, always say yes, always be frightened. If they come towards you, take off.'[32]

The more the 'mixed-blood' Aboriginal population increased the more anxious the Whites became. The very wide definition of Aboriginality of the 1918–33 *Aboriginals Ordinance* ensured that the Administrator or Chief Protector could bring a person of any degree of Aboriginal descent under legal control.[33] In 1931 the Chief Protector reported that it was a matter of social and economic urgency to improve the living standard of 'half-castes', since they were already one-third of the European population and increasing rapidly. Accordingly, under a new directive, illegitimate children of not less than 50 per cent European descent would continue to be removed from the camps and placed in Homes, ultimately to marry 'higher-grade half-caste males and whites'.[34] The Northern Territory Chief Protector, Cecil Cook, argued that if the Commonwealth followed a policy of laissez-faire, probably all Aborigines would be extinct in 50 years. That was impossible; therefore the policy of the Commonwealth was to 'do everything possible to convert the half-caste into a white citizen . . . We have to absorb the Aborigines, as well as protect them, or a little later the white population of the Northern Territory would be absorbed by the black.'[35] Non-Aborigines at this time probably made up no more than a quarter of the population of the Northern Territory, and the frontier—the violence, the living conditions of Whites as well as Blacks, the rudimentary services—were at a stage which the southern states had passed a generation before.

The Federal Government, which oversaw the Chief Protector's actions, followed rather more slowly. The 1939 'McEwen Statement' of Commonwealth policy was nominally based on Aboriginal, not White, concerns. McEwen announced that a Native Affairs Branch would be established. Under the revised policy, all Aborigines, over many generations, would become citizens but in the meantime only children with one White parent would be removed.[36] But back in the Northern Territory, the Administration proceeded along its already well-trodden course of taking into institutions Aboriginal children of any 'caste' who came under notice.

ABORIGINES AND THE SECOND WORLD WAR

The most significant effect of the Second World War probably was to further integrate Aborigines of both full and part descent into European mainstream. Some integration was compulsory:

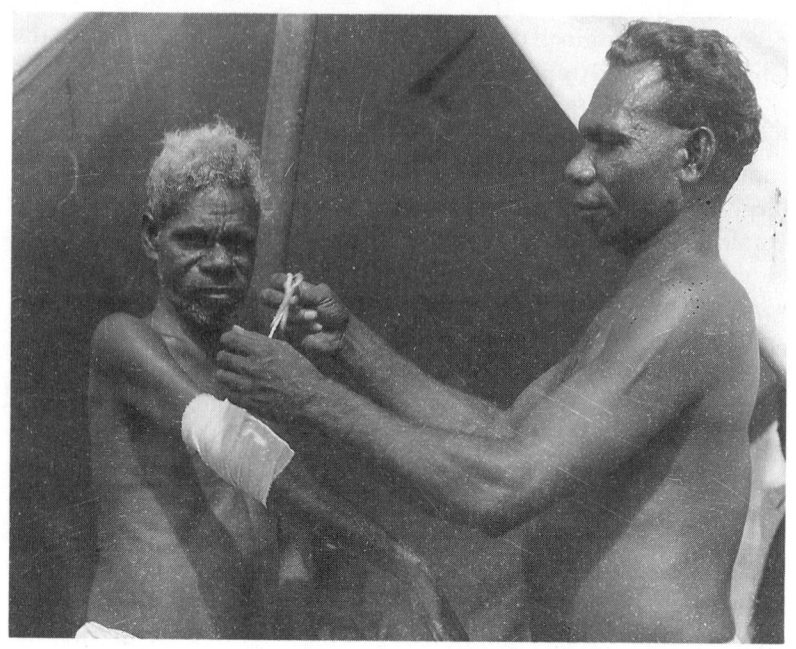

An Aboriginal orderly at 121 Australian General Hospital assists in the treatment of Aboriginal sick and wounded in 1942. During the war Aborigines were often treated with greater respect and accorded good living conditions and pay. AUSTRALIAN WAR MEMORIAL 27835

---

scores of children were sent south from the Centre and the islands, and some did not return. Kwementjaye Jampijinpa of Willowra Station recalled bringing in the bush people to Army camps by the promise of rations if they came and shooting if they did not.[37] Nevertheless many Aborigines in the postwar period retained very fond memories of the war as an exciting experience, the time they were treated equally with Whites with regular hours of work, regular rations (including rice, potatoes, onions and soap) and a regular wage (five shillings a week).[38] Tim Japangardi recalled:

> Treated pretty well, Army time, no cheeky [ie nobody harmed Aborigines]. Nobody get cheeky. You know, they got provost police, and soldier policeman, somebody get cheeky. You know,

they never treat 'em wrong way. Some people never, never treat an Aboriginal wrong way. That's really kind. Never. And the good fun always.[39]

Unlike mandated New Guinea, Australia at no stage possessed a truly colonial Aboriginal administration, with special courts and measures to expose exploitation. Perhaps because such an administration might imply that potentially Aborigines possessed rights other than those of ordinary Australian citizens. Nowhere was this deficiency more clearly exposed than when an alternative was presented, briefly, by the Army's Inspector of Native Personnel in 1945. In a summary of the Army's work, the Officer quoted Article 22 of the League of Nations Covenant which declared the well-being and development of 'certain' peoples to form a sacred trust of civilisation. He noted that Aboriginal service personnel had become concrete workers, drivers, mechanics, quartermasters, and hygiene supervisors. He claimed that bushcraft was encouraged, as was the practice of traditional rituals—'The natives have certainly not been detribalised'. Aborigines could arrive and leave at will except where health or security restrictions applied. The Report concluded with the pertinent observation that civilian authorities had now to 'seriously consider' bringing Aboriginal living standards to the level of the Whites.[40]

The Report was noteworthy for the implied internationalist view that Aborigines might be as good as *but did not need to be the same as,* White Australians. But when the Army withdrew from all settlements and camps in 1946, it left its one thousand Aboriginal employees with an uncertain future. The Administrator, evidently unimpressed by this Report, noted an 'acute restlessness among certain individuals' who would not remain in long-term employment.[41] The bureaucracy concluded that a firm control should be reasserted. Yuendumu Settlement (1946) was one administrative answer to the population shifts and 'acute restlessness' caused by the war.

POSTWAR ENQUIRIES AND CONFERENCES

The administration was conscious of criticism of its lack of progress towards better living conditions or in 'training for citizenship'. In October 1945 the Native Affairs Branch, sent V.C. Carrington to investigate Aboriginal living and working conditions on the northern pastoral stations. Carrington reported the working men 'reasonably well treated', though accommodation, sanitation and ablution facilities for 'non-workers' was practically non-existent. The majority of pastoral lessees paid no wages, instead, as entitled under the *Aboriginal Ordinance,* they merely supported the workers' dependants and relations.[42] In fact, he argued, many people categorised as 'dependants' were actually workers and ought to be reimbursed. Carrington recommended that men over 21 be awarded the non-cash sum of two pounds five shillings (70 per cent of the pastoral Award for non-Aboriginal males), and women ten shillings per week. Carrington thought Aboriginal drovers were particularly exploited, since they were highly skilled, were seldom off duty and travelled very far from their homelands. He concluded his Report with the assertion that were it not for the fact that Aborigines could leave at will and were protected from ill-treatment, their position would be little less than slavery.[43] In reality both Carrington's provisos were frequently violated.[44]

A serious consequence of the lack of payment was that Aborigines, directed by McEwen eventually to become part of one Australian community, were being given no practice in that aspect of European society which distinguished it most sharply from Aboriginal. But it was probably an increasing concern at the denial of human rights to Aboriginal people at the United Nations which caused the government to call a conference between the Native Welfare Branch and the pastoral lessees in June 1947, where it sought to extract an agreement from the pastoralists to raise wages and improve conditions. Here the Chair confessed that the government had failed to enforce the policy which it had ratified at the League of Nations (the UN's predecessor). There was no legal sanction, for instance, for the practice of penalising Aborigines for refusing to work or for going on strike. The pastoralists opposed most suggestions for improvements to ablutions, accommodation and housing. The new wage structure was provisionally fixed at two pounds thirteen shillings for a male worker over 21, and for an unmarried female at one pound twelve shillings and eight pence.⁴⁵ In truth the Commonwealth was arguing from a position of some weakness, having generally ignored its own protective regulations for many years. Like Bleakley, Carrington had discovered gross breaches of the health, housing and ration regulations, but had not found it necessary to recommend the revocation of the employment licences of any of the stations which he visited. Nor was government supervision of the mission stations very much more conscientious: in 1951 Winifred Wilson, a Commonwealth health official, found that, in addition to the sixteen of the seventeen pastoral stations she visited which provided rations rated nutritionally as 'D' or 'E', the inmates of six out of ten missions also received rations below internationally acceptable levels.⁴⁶ A political scientist, Colin Tatz, found that many missionaries still used banishment as a punishment for 'troublemakers', although in apparent contravention of Section 71 of the Ordinance which forbade the deprivation of food, clothing or shelter.⁴⁷ Nor, finally, was the administration of the government's own settlements in some respects any better: Wilson found ten out of eleven settlements also distributed 'D' or 'E' levels of food, with 'E' being the worst grade possible in the scale.

THE 1953 WELFARE ORDINANCE

The early 1950s were looked upon as the beginning of a new era in Aboriginal administration. In 1951 Paul Hasluck, the innovative and idealistic historian and politician, became the Minister for Territories. He believed that 'for good or ill, the future of Aborigines . . . lies in close association with the white community',⁴⁸ and the planning of new legislation to govern Northern Territory Aborigines was immediately begun. Proclaimed as a significant advance, the legislation embodied in the *Welfare Ordinance, 1953* was later criticised by the social scientist Charles Rowley as 'one of the last big efforts to use authoritarian legislation to control the processes of social change'.⁴⁹ The Administrator could now declare any Aboriginal person a 'Ward' who, in his opinion, was in need of special care.⁵⁰ Soon it was apparent that an important purpose of the Ordinance was to

Children under supervision of a teacher, Northern Territory, c 1950. Note the symbols of Imperialism: the noticeboard contains posters of the Queen's Canadian visit, the young royal family and Sandhurst Royal Military Academy. AUSTRALIAN INFORMATION SERVICE

legally separate people of full-descent from those of mixed-descent. On the passing of the new Ordinance, some 2000 mixed-descent people suddenly became non-Aborigines but some 15 700 Aborigines of the full-descent became Wards. Their names were entered in the much-resented Register of Wards (known colloquially as the 'Stud Book'). They were now also subject to a multitude of restrictions relating to the consumption of liquor, the owning of property, movement, marriage and sexual relationships.[51] Families were split under quite arbitrary categorisations, as Jack McGinness, a well-known member of the Darwin 'Half-Caste Association' angrily told a public meeting:

> I am a married man with seven daughters and two sons. Four of my daughters were born before my wife and myself were exempted [ie declared to be legally non-Wards]. They are classed as non-exempted half-castes but the other children are classed as

exempted. What a farce. Brothers and sisters having different classifications. My second daughter married a white man and had two children before the authorities discovered she was an unexempted person. Under the *Aboriginal Ordinance* her husband is liable to arrest and prosecution for consorting with a female half-caste Aboriginal . . . You can see, gentlemen, that we are worse than foreigners in our own country.[52]

Nor was it only the government to blame for the break-up of mixed marriages. Men returning to town were often shamed by other Whites into ending a relationship. Bob Randall, who grew up at the Bungalow and later at Croker Island, put the tragedy of sudden break-ups into song:

On the mustering camps out bush you always kept me
By your side without no shame and no care
It seems to me like horses I am treated

Just used for the season and then let out to graze.

Black velvet, my darling, you used to say
I'll love you always please don't go away
You taught me kisses that I never knew
Though my heart is breaking, it will never show[53]

Compulsory separations of unapproved couples, and even compulsory marriages, were most likely to occur on the large reserves like Beswick (Barunga) and Warrabri (Ali Curung). These settlements were designated not just as living areas but key instruments in the shift from Black to White. Employees of the Welfare Branch, as the new administrative section was known from 1953, were instructed that the 'only possible future' for Aborigines was assimilation, which involved the 'discarding of tribal ideas, values, traditions, loyalties and an acceptance of standards of conduct, social conventions and general purposes of the Australian community into which the native will eventually move'.[54] Nowhere was the Australia-wide push towards compulsory assimilation in the 1950s stronger than in the Northern Territory.

By the 1960s progress towards both the amelioration of living standards and towards citizenship remained, to the Whites, disappointingly slow. The Aboriginal infant mortality rate stood at 208 per 1000 in Central Australia, which was one of the highest in the world.⁵⁵ On the settlements, selected families were allowed to live in a 'Kingstrand', a verandah built around a small aluminium hut on a concrete base. Those who managed their Kingstrand satisfactorily might in time expect to exchange their 'half-way' house for a real house in Darwin, while those who failed might be deemed to be unassimilable. The test was unfair, however, since many people found Kingstrands disagreeable to live in. A survey found one to be 9 degrees C hotter than a spinifex-grass humpy at mid-morning.

In the 1950s the pastoralists and administration relied on a similar 'half-way' principle to justify substandard wages and conditions on pastoral properties. Abuses were common. The Director of Welfare conceded in 1965 that only 20 of 200 pastoral stations had made a genuine attempt to meet the legal requirements of employment: he did not state how many had actually achieved them. Rowley in 1970 could not find a single instance of revocation of an employment licence.⁵⁶ Tatz discovered only one attempted prosecution of an employer for damages on behalf of a ward.⁵⁷ The historian Frank Stevens found the pastoral-worker wage payable under the *Wards Employment Ordinance* was only approximately one-fifth of the rate payable to Whites. One week's sick leave was granted to Aborigines instead of two to Whites; eighteen food items rather than the 50 which Whites received were provided in the ration schedule.⁵⁸ A multitude of offences both against natural justice and against the Ordinance and Regulations continued despite the 'new era'.

Obviously there were local difficulties of inspection: six patrol officers could not make much of an impression on 230 properties spread over more than half a million square kilometres. Yet there were much deeper issues than administration. Probably, as Rowley argued, a few cancellations of employment authorities would have ensured some improvements, but an insistence would have involved enforcing and/or subsidising changes at the expense of the national development agenda.⁵⁹ Neither the local administration, nor the Federal Government, was prepared to do that. The doctrine of *terra nullius* had set a particular perception, or lack of perception, of the indigenous people. Aborigines, as it were, did not exist before the invasion and those who survived were owed no rights except those of legal children who would ultimately inherit no more than the rights of other Australians. The view of the Aborigines as *potential* citizens, coupled neatly with the theory of partially competent workers, was used perpetually to delay hard decisions about awarding or enforcing equal pay and conditions. Apparently by an ad hoc national consensus, Aborigines were seen to be fundamentally unlike indigenous peoples elsewhere.[60] The 'child-race' theory (seldom rationally explored as to its responsibilities rather than its exploitative potential) allowed Aborigines no room for expansion as a people *independent* of White Australia.

We have seen how, in the bureaucracy, White Australian ideology and its economic motivations took precedence over Aboriginal community or individual rights. In the postwar era that same relationship was affirmed in sentences awarded to Aboriginal law-breakers. Naturally there were humane pastoralists, concerned Protectors and dedicated missionaries; but in the many conflicts between an issue of law and order and the infringement upon the rights of an individual, the judgement of the Courts was almost certainly in favour of the Whites. In 1927 two Methodist missionaries were attacked at Milingimbi for having tried to prevent promised marriages, and for whipping those men who resisted the missionaries. At the trial of the assailants the Judge ruled that there had been 'no provocation which would amount to a defence in law . . . Aborigines in the wild condition have to be controlled . . . The mission cannot allow its work to be destroyed if not prevented by the actions of a few recalcitrant natives.'[61] Thirty-four years later a Papunya Aborigine, Johnny Wheeler, resisting arrest, kicked and broke the settlement superintendent's rib. The Magistrate, in sentencing Wheeler to six months hard labour, found that, although Wheeler had been unlawfully taken into custody, it was nevertheless 'necessary to maintain the authority of a superintendent of a Welfare settlement'.[62]

In many cases, however, Aborigines were able to exercise freedom of choice in this period, even when they were under the direct rule of superintendents or pastoralists. From the late 1950s, for instance Pintubi and Pitjantjatjara peoples began making

A typical 'shanty camp' in the Northern Territory. Many of the outstations started up like this. AUSTRALIAN INFORMATION SERVICE L35417

their way from the Western Desert to settlements such as Papunya. Although the migration has sometimes been regarded as an example of forced assimilation, the anthropologist/patrol officer Jeremy Long, who witnessed these events, insisted that the exodus from the desert was voluntary:

> The decisions to leave traditional country which the Pintubi and their neighbours to the south in the Petermann Ranges took were consistent with a tradition of opportunist exploitation of resources when and where they appeared. It was not a helpless 'drift' but a series of highly motivated and purposeful moves . . . If their migrations meant that they abandoned, for a time at least, the care and use of the land they knew best, they also allowed them to re-establish links with their relatives and establish new ties to many more people and this maintenance and extension of personal and ritual links was also a strong tradition.[63]

THE ADMINISTRATION UNDER SIEGE

Southern and northern Aborigines like Doug Nicholls and Davis Daniels began to combine as trenchant critics of the status quo. The Northern Territory, alone of the big Aboriginal administrative areas, remained under Commonwealth control, and the administration was seldom far from critical analysis. The Council for Aboriginal Rights was established in 1951 partly to investigate allegations of human rights abuses in the Territory and Charles Duguid brought his expert knowledge of Central Australian affairs to his role of Chair of the Federal Council for the Advancement of Aborigines (later FCAATSI) after 1956.[64] The southern organisations backed and publicised the Aboriginal initiatives, the most celebrated of which was the walk-off by 200 Gurindji from Wave Hill Station in 1966.[65] Though sometimes portrayed as a triumph of workers' solidarity, the walk-off is better seen in the context of resistance to racially inspired poor pastoral conditions. The historian Ewan Morris, investigating postwar race relations in the Victoria River Downs Station—Wave Hill area, found six instances of defiance, small strikes or fights between Aborigines and Whites between 1946 and 1956, in nearly all of which a racial element was specifically invoked. For example, in 1947, several Aboriginal stockmen claimed they were just like Whites and could leave their job whenever they liked. Stockmen at a nearby camp followed suit by demanding extra supplies, and one Aborigine told the head stockman, 'We are just as good as you . . . whites' before striking him.[66] Morris also identified various disturbances at Lake Nash and Berrimah, which taken in consideration with the better-known incidents in the Pilbara in 1946, makes it clear that the mass walk-outs from Newcastle Waters and Wave Hill in 1966, were not only the result of actions by certain brave individuals but also evidence of a general growing self-confidence as well as dissatisfaction with existing conditions. The Wave Hill walk-off, therefore, may be described as the most spectacular confrontation of this phase of postwar Aboriginal resistance, less overtly aggressive than the spearings but no less effective at striking the pastoralists at what was then their weakest point, their labour supply.

The walk-off followed the judgement of the Commonwealth Conciliation and Arbitration Commission the previous year that Aboriginal stockmen, with some exceptions, must be paid the same wage as non-Aborigines engaged in similar work by the end of 1968.[67]

Co-operation between southern and northern critics in these and other issues, in each of which Aborigines were prominent, increased to some degree a 'siege mentality' on the part of the Aboriginal administration. Suspicion grew following the establishment of the Council for Aboriginal Affairs by Prime Minister Holt in 1967. The Council, chaired by H.C. Coombs, was anxious to make changes both in Aboriginal living conditions and race relations but found itself frustrated by the local administration, which generally regarded advice from 'Canberra' as interference. The Federal Government was itself split: the Department of Interior arranged the transfer of additional mining leases to the bauxite producer Nabalco on the Gove Peninsula, and carried out negotiations with the Australian Investment Agency, the owners of the Wave Hill pastoral lease and the Gurindji, as if the Council for Aboriginal Affairs did not exist.[68] The tensions were powerfully illustrated in Central Australia in 1969 when a Welfare Branch officer complained of Aborigines wanting to buy the Haasts Bluff Reserve, becoming 'more independent' and 'losing all respect for authority'. It was 'becoming dangerous', he wrote, 'to reproach Aboriginals in a firm manner'. The Council replied that such views were more appropriate to 1869 than 1969. Coombs responded that the Aborigines were 'not children or prisoners but Australian citizens whom it is the Commonwealth's policy to help to full and equal participation in our society'.[69]

It was a timely reminder that the sign of a successful policy of assimilation might be expected to produce exactly such a reaction to arbitrary authority rather than passive acquiescence in the conservative spectrum of the European mainstream. The disturbances demonstrated that Aborigines in the postwar decades were indeed gaining the confidence necessary to take part in the world of the Whites. Nevertheless the bureaucratic war between the old administration on the one hand, and the Council for Aboriginal Affairs, the Federal Council for the Advancement of

Aboriginal and Torres Strait Islanders and bodies such as the North Australian Workers Union and the Northern Territory Council for Aboriginal Rights on the other, continued until the Department of Interior was abolished by Whitlam soon after coming to power in 1972.⁷⁰

THE 1970s

For at least the following decade after Whitlam's election the view of both the Labor and Coalition governments favoured the recognition of Aboriginal demands as the partly legitimate rights of an indigenous people rather than those of an intractable welfare problem. One of the government's first actions was to approve the purchase, on behalf of the traditional landowners, of Willowra cattle station.

Most significant of 1970s developments was the *Aboriginal Land Rights (NT) Act,* introduced by Prime Minister Fraser in 1976 but based on principles laid down by the Whitlam government. The Act established the Northern and Central Aboriginal Land Councils, and the mechanism of Aboriginal claim on reserve and vacant Crown land to which traditional attachment could be demonstrated. Though there were certain major exceptions, including the Ranger Uranium Project Area near Oenpelli, the Act in its recognition of indigenous rights was far in advance of legislation in any of the states except South Australia. Mining royalties were now available to Aboriginal traditional landowners, though it was clear that both the Federal Government and the semi-autonomous Northern Territory legislature (established by Fraser in 1978) would block the transfer of land held to be especially valuable. By 1981 Aborigines held over 30 per cent of the Northern Territory total area under the Land Rights Act.⁷¹

Another Aboriginal initiative which accelerated in the 1970s was a return to homeland centres. In Central Australia people began to return to traditional lands outside the cattle areas, in some instances almost as soon as they had arrived at the large settlements of Papunya and Yuendumu.⁷² In the north, early outstation communities were established at Oenpelli, Goulburn Island, Milingimbi and Yirrkala, and by 1987, though numbers

This sign displays the strong anti-alcohol position adopted by numerous Aboriginal councils. Many communities have declared their residential areas 'dry' and anyone carrying alcohol into such a township or 'outstation' can be fined. AIATSIS N194.10

fluctuated through seasonal and other factors, there were at least 5500 Aborigines living in 328 Homeland Centres in the Northern Territory.[73] The number of Homeland Centres in other states was very much smaller, indicating again that in this period the Commonwealth Government, unhindered by State Government objections, was prepared to set new benchmarks in the conception as well as the mechanics of Northern Territory Aboriginal programmes. Yet the areas where Whites and Aborigines mixed together in the greatest numbers—the towns and settlements of the Stuart Highway—continued to resist the efforts of Canberra legislators. At Alice Springs in 1975, nearly 500 people lived in 18 separate fringe camps almost entirely without water, sewage or nutrition. Untreated trachoma, ear and skin infections affected many of the population.[74]

It was the local Aborigines who began in the 1970s to grapple with the continuing phenomenon of desert communities who had wandered from, or had been forced to leave, their homelands and had sought sanctuary in the town. With government assistance, Alice Springs Aborigines formed the Central Australian Aboriginal Congress in June 1973 partly to attack what they described as the 'national disgrace' of the fringe camps. Unlike Strehlow in the 1930s, and the Northern Territory administration in 1946, the Aborigines did not seek forced repatriation to distant centres nor the further creation of large settlements. Instead, their starting point was that most of the fringe campers were there to stay. Remedies were in part practical: Congress organised 200 tents as temporary accommodation and a daily pick-up service along the Todd River for people needing medical treatment. They were also psychological: Alice Springs Aboriginal leaders had recognised what the White bureaucracies were much slower to grasp, that the supply of endless welfare benefits alone would not give Aborigines a pride in themselves or their heritage. By 1975, for the first time Aborigines of full descent owned buildings in town, sought their own federal funds and managed their own organisations.[75]

Not all the urban Whites of the Northern Territory were content with the prospect of Aborigines living in towns. The 1970–80s, the period of substantial improvements in law and federal funding, also saw a deterioration in race relations as Aboriginal political and economic power increased. A particularly offensive example of this more explicit racism was in 1978 scribbled on a wall of the bar at the Daly Waters Hotel: 'For Sale, Gas Ovens (German made) will accomidate at least 30 coons.'[76]

The graffiti was probably also a reaction to the long familiar phenomenon of increasing town-fringe Aboriginal populations. The rapid depopulations from many of the stations after the 1966 Award put an end to any further walk-offs which might have followed the Gurindji strike. Though some communities, such as the Mangarayi people near Mataranka, found new living areas when ejected from the head-station, the more common result of the equal pay legislation was massive evictions of the old station populations which in turn created these bigger camps on the fringes of all the towns of the Stuart Highway, and in some new areas like Kununurra, Western Australia. Older people, unless successful in a land claim, could not return to their birthplace or traditional country. Young people did not necessarily want to return permanently. Just as the Western Desert people's arrivals caused punitive legislation at Alice Springs in the 1930s, the growth of the fringe camps in the 1970s–80s caused similar reactions. White townsfolk petitioned authorities to open new settlements, asked for greater police protection, and tried to remove the fringe dwellers by methods of doubtful legality. It is alleged that in 1977 a police officer at Mataranka, describing a town camp as unpleasant for tourists, warned the inhabitants to leave, then set fire to the humpies and drove a truck over anything that remained. Such town-camp dwellers often had been forcibly evicted from stations, in this case the famous Elsey Station.[77] The anthropologist Diane Bell described how unalienated Crown land near Tennant Creek, claimed by Warramungu people under the *Land Rights (NT) Act,* was abruptly withdrawn from claim by the Northern Territory Government while the hearing was in progress.[78] The 'two-kilometre rule', by which no person may drink in a public place nearer than that distance from a liquor outlet, seems to have been enacted solely to keep Aborigines off the streets.[79]

THE NORTHERN TERRITORY IN CONTEXT

We began this chapter by outlining the ways in which the Northern Territory was historically different from the rest of Australia. Today the Northern Territory still remains substantially different. More than 25 per cent of the population is of Aboriginal descent. More than half of the still existing 50–100 Aboriginal languages are spoken in the Territory.[80] The Homelands movement is probably more firmly established in the Northern Territory than elsewhere, as is traditional bushcraft, ceremonial life and cosmology. Because more Aborigines remained apart from the Whites for longer, more people than in the southern states retained a freedom to choose their futures. A greater distance from mainstream Australia allowed men and women the psychological space to meditate upon and present powerful alternative interpretations of their recent history. Hobbles Danayirri of the

Victoria River District, for instance, chose Captain Cook as the key representative of English institutions. He reasoned that Cook, under direct order from England to exploit and abuse the Aborigines, carried a book of instructions to Darwin for distribution to the settlers. Why else did the Whites behave so appallingly towards the owners of the country:

> [Cook] brought a book out from big England; brought a lot of book from England to Sydney Harbour. And made a new building. Put all the book and all the government too, from England right there now . . .
> [The book said] Right. If anybody get sick, anybody get blind; anybody get blind, anybody get broken leg, [they] shot him. And just work. That's his law. because he took the land from the people, Aboriginal people. Some of them alive yet, running away. Lot of whitefellows come up from Darwin, Sydney Harbour, look round, and they didn't ask [Aborigines] for their country. What for this mob wasn't telling we [why didn't they explain], asking we, huh? And my people started to work around, old people, and really frightened for the White people coming from big England. They didn't ask. And they were really really sad, poor buggers.[81]

Both the unattractive and attractive features of its past history of race relations remain in the present Northern Territory where Aborigines continue to be arrested in very high numbers.[82] On the positive side, Aborigines own an increasing proportion of the Northern Territory through the operation of the Land Rights Act, though much of this land had been unused by the Whites. It is the old Aboriginal stockmen and women who are now showing Heritage Commission investigations where the early *White* pioneers had their homes. The Land Councils wield considerable national political and economic power. The Aboriginal Areas Protection Authority makes negotiations between developers and traditional Aboriginal owners obligatory, leading to the preservation of innumerable sacred places. Dozens of organisations, such as the Central Australian Aboriginal Media Association, Yipirinya School, and the Tangentyere Town Council have shown a lead to other Aborigines. The Northern Territory has produced many famous figures such as Albert

Charles Perkins (*centre*) at the Aboriginal demonstration at the opening of Parliament by Queen Elizabeth in 1974. As the reigning monarch, Aborigines recognised the Queen as having ultimate authority over the delivery of justice for Aborigines. Despite the British takeover of Australia, she has not made any strong statements about Aboriginal dispossession. COURIER MAIL

Namatjira, Rosalie Kunoth-Monks, Charles Perkins, Galurrwuy Yunupingu, and Pat Dodson, Chair of the Federal Government's Reconciliation Committee. Mick Dodson held the key role of Social Justice Commissioner and has been an outspoken conciliator in Mabo-related negotiations. Yothu Yindi is an internationally known band blending traditional and rock music, whose lead singer, Mandawuy Yunupingu, was Australian of the Year in 1993. Darwin is a very cosmopolitan city in which Aborigines and non-Aborigines marry more frequently and with less adverse comment than elsewhere. The police have initiated a number of remarkable changes including the appointment of Aboriginal police. Perhaps most importantly, many Aboriginal leaders like Pat Dodson, Gallarwuy Yunupingu and Charles Perkins believe it is both desirable and possible for Aborigines and Whites to live together, without the domination of one by the other. Like Peter Horsetailer who was prepared to help Charles Chewings find gold in 1909, Northern Territory Aborigines are taking the lead in offering to share their civilisation. They believe that if the offer is again rejected, it is the non-Aboriginal Australians, not the indigenous people, who will again be the losers. As Perkins stated:

> My expectation of a good Australia is when White people would be proud to speak an Aboriginal language, when they realise that Aboriginal culture and all that goes with it, philosophy, art, language, morality, kinship, is all part of their heritage. And that's the most unbelievable thing, that it's all there waiting for us all. White people can inherit 40 000 or 60 000 years of culture, and all they have to do is reach out and ask for it.[83]

NOTES

1. Harry Campbell, in P. Lyon and M. Parsons, *We Are Staying*, IAD Press, Alice Springs, 1989, pp.1–2.
2. Editor's note: This chapter refers to non-Aborigines as White people. This terminology has not been adopted throughout the book but it is included here to demonstrate the problems of naming colonial actors and the diverse solutions chosen. Peter Read has a point: 'White people' is just as valid a categorisation as 'Aboriginal people'.
3. Personal communication, Little Mick Yanuwinma and Daly Pulkara to P. Read, Aug. 1977
4. For example, see 'A Homeland Deserted', (accounts of the Coniston Massacre, 1928), in P. and J. Read (eds), *Long Time Olden Time: Aboriginal Accounts of Northern Territory History*, IAD Press, Alice Springs, 1992.
5. G. Koch, compiler and ed., H. Koch, trans., *Kaytetye Country: an Aboriginal History of the Barrow Creek Area*, IAD Press, Alice Springs, 1993.
6. *Milirrpum vs. Nabalco Pty Ltd (1971)*. The Court held that the Aboriginal clan and land did not amount to proprietorship as understood in White Australian law, and that no doctrine of common law required recognition of land rights under Aboriginal

law which might have existed before 1788; for an analysis of the judgement see C.H. Coombs, *Kulinma,* Australian National University Press, Canberra, 1978, p.168 ff.

7 For a discussion of the use of the thermoluminescence technique in the Northern Territory see R.G. Roberts, Rhys Jones and M.A. Smith, 'Thermoluminescence dating of a 50,000-year-old human occupation site in Northern Australia', *Nature,* vol.345, no.6271, May 1990, pp.153–56. I am grateful to Dr Colin Pardoe for information supplied in this section.

8 For details of the probable duration of Macassan visits to Australia, see C.C. Macknight, *The Voyage to Marege,* MUP, Carlton, 1976, ch.1.

9 For a description of the effects in Central Australia see B. Spencer, *Wanderings in Wild Australia,* Macmillan, London, 1928, (I), pp.382–86, 'Even in 1909 the condition of the Arunta [Arrente] tribe was very different from what it was six years earlier, and the "rush" to the Arltunga goldfield, in 1902, practically completed its demoralisation.'

10 For an account of killing by Queenslanders of eastern Northern Territory Aborigines, see Isaac Joshua, transcribed by Jeffrey Heath, 'Massacre at Hodgson Downs', in L. Hercus and P. Sutton (eds), *This Is What Happened: Historical Narratives by Aborigines,* Australian Institute of Aboriginal Studies, Canberra, pp.177–81

11 A. McGrath, *Born in the Cattle,* Allen & Unwin, Sydney, 1987, chapter 3.

12 For example, failure to prosecute pastoral lessees who defaulted on rent payments.

13 Among the several official reports to note the fact was J.W. Bleakley, who observed (1929, pp.7, 12) that neither the pastoral industry nor Darwin family life would be able to continue without Aboriginal labour. For a discussion of Aboriginal award wages, see below.

14 For an example of persuasion and the reliance of bush people on station food see evidence of Powder (Brunette Downs), in Read and Read, 1992, pp.76–78.

15 Deborah Bird Rose, *Hidden Histories,* Aboriginal Studies Press, Canberra, 1991, p.90.

16 For an unsympathetic official South Australian view of the work of the missions, see 'Report of a visit of a Deputation to the South Australian Minister of Education', *Adelaide Advertiser,* Feb. 1889; J.W. Bleakley, 'The Aboriginals and Half-Castes of Central

Australia and North Australia', *Commonwealth Parliamentary Papers*, No.21, 1929, pp.25–26.

17 Hagar Roberts in Read and Read, 1992, p.101; see also C.H. and R.M. Berndt, 'An Oenpelli Monologue', *Oceania*, vol.XXII, no.1, Sept. 1951, pp.28–30.

18 W. Baldwin Spencer, 'Preliminary Report on the Aboriginals of the Northern Territory', Melbourne, 1913, p.24; further large reserves were set aside following Bleakley's 1929 recommendation.

19 Spencer, 1913, p.20.

20 Spencer, 1913, pp.23–24; see also Northern Territory of Australia, *Regulations Under the Aboriginal Ordinance,* 1918–33, No.40 of 1933, Nos. 29–31; ibid, 1918–37, No. 57 of 1938, Nos.1, 2.

21 Bleakley, p.6. Typical accommodation, where provided at all, was a small galvanized iron hut without light or ventilation.

22 Bleakley, pp.6, 7, 9, 33.

23 A. Markus, *Governing Savages,* Allen & Unwin, Sydney, 1990, p.67.

24 R.M. and C.H. Berndt, *End of an Era: Aboriginal Labour in the Northern Territory,* Aboriginal Studies Press, Canberra, 1987, pp.76, 90–103.

25 M.P. Durack, quoted by Patsy Durack, *Kings in Grass Castles,* pp.331–32.

26 Bleakley, p.21.

27 Strehlow to Chief Protector, 18 March 1927, Australian Archives NT, CA 1070, Administrator NT, CRS: F 126, item 37, p.1.

28 Strehlow to Chief Protector, 11 Nov. 1937, p.1; Australian Archives, ibid.

29 Northern Territory of Australia, *The Aboriginals Ordinance 1918–33,* (No. 9 of 1918, as Amended) ss.11, 13, 15, 17, 45, parts V, VI.

30 Bleakley, pp.14,17; 1935 figure, Head Teacher to Deputy Administrator, 27 Feb. 1935, Commonwealth Archives 1070 F1 37/30; E. Hill, *Sydney Sun,* Commonwealth Archives F1, 214/33.

31 Acting Director of Native Affairs to Administrator, 3 Feb. 1954, p.1, Australian Archives, CA 1070, F 1, 52/250.

32 P. Read, *Charles Perkins: A Biography,* Viking, Ringwood, 1990, p.16.

33 *The Aboriginals Ordinance* 1918–33, s3: an Aborigine was defined as 'an aboriginal native of Australia or any of the islands adjacent or belonging thereto'; other 'Aborigines' included 'half-castes' who lived with an Aboriginal de facto spouse, associated with

Aborigines, was a child under 21 years, a female living unmarried to a person substantially of European descent, or a person over 21 years apparently incapable of managing his own affairs. Like the definitions employed in some of the southern states, the authorities had decided that the most useful were those which could be manipulated for administrative convenience.

34 Extract from *Annual Report of the Chief Protector,* quoted by Director of Native Affairs to Secretary, Department of Territories, 28 Feb. 1952, 'Removal of partly coloured children from Aboriginal camps', p.1.
35 C. Cook, in *Aboriginal Welfare: Initial Conference of Commonwealth and State Aboriginal Authorities,* Canberra, 21-23 April 1937, AGP, 1937, p.13ff.
36 Hon. J. McEwen, 'Commonwealth Government's policy with respect to Aboriginals (Northern Territory of Australia)', Feb. 1939, Government Printer, Canberra, p.5.
37 Kwementyaye Jampijinpa, in Read and Read, 1992, pp.123–25.
38 For instance, recollections of Tim Japangardi, Tommy Tracker, Read and Read, 1992, pp.125, 128.
39 Tim Japangardi, in Read and Read, 1992, p.133.
40 Inspector of Native Personnel, Administration of Native Affairs Section, 'Care and Guidance of Native Race by Army', HQ NT Force, 23 April 1945.
41 'Report on Native Affairs, 1945–6', in *Report on the Administration of the Northern Territory of Australia for Year 1945–46.*
42 *Regulations under the Aboriginals Ordinance* 1918–33, No. 14a.
43 V.C. Carrington to Administrator, 10 Oct. 1945, Report contained in Bovril Australian Estates, 1941–55, ANU Archives of Business and Labour, 42/14/1.
44 For example of allegations concerning north-western Western Australia, see *The World,* 14 Jan., 7 July 1932; in the Northern Territory, see letter by Mathew Thomas to *Northern Standard,* 20 Aug. 1937.
45 'Conference held in Alice Springs, 8, 9 June 1947, transcript; Bovril Australian Estates papers, ibid.
46 W. Wilson, 'Dietary survey of Aborigines in the Northern Territory' [1951], Commonwealth of Australia, Department of Health, p.101; 'E' was the worst grade possible, while 'A' represented a nutritionally adequate diet. The deficiencies were in Vitamins A and C, and calcium.

47 C.M. Tatz, 'Aboriginal Administration in the Northern Territory of Australia', PhD thesis, ANU, 1964, p.251.
48 Tatz, p.12.
49 *An Ordinance to provide for the Care and Assistance of Certain Persons,* No. 16 of 1953; C.D. Rowley, *The Remote Aborigines,* Penguin, Ringwood, 1970, p.296.
50 *An Ordinance to Provide for the Care and Assistance of Certain Persons,* No. 16 of 1953, III (1) (14); ss. 25, 26, part V.
51 For example, ss 25,16, part V, ibid; for discussion see Tatz, 20ff.
52 J. McGinness, *Son of Alyandubu,* University of Queensland Press, Brisbane, 1991, p.63.
53 B. Randall, 'Black Velvet', Cassette produced by Central Australian Media Association, Alice Springs, nd.
54 'Handbook of Instruction for the Guidance of Settlement Supervisors and Staff under the Control', Dept of Territories, nd, c 1953; quoted by Tatz, p.12.
55 F. Lancaster Jones, *A Demographic Survey of the Aboriginal Population of the Northern Territory, with Special Reference to Bathurst Island Mission,* Australian Institute for Aboriginal Studies, Canberra, 1963, p.96.
56 *Conciliation and Arbitration Act 1904–1961,* Case No. 830, transcript, p.1448, quoted by Rowley, p.306.
57 Tatz, p.258.
58 F. Stevens, *Aborigines in the Northern Territory Cattle Industry,* 1974, pp.23–25. Stevens drew evidence from the *Wards Employment Ordinance,* 1953 and 1959, and the Wards Employment Regulation, No.4 of 1959.
59 Rowley, p.307.
60 For example, while many Australian patrol officers in Papua and New Guinea attended the Australian School of Pacific Administration in Sydney, no Aborigine, and very few Northern Territory Welfare officers, are believed to have done so.
61 Incident reported in *Northern Territory Times,* 3 March 1927.
62 Tatz, p.244.
63 J. Long 'Leaving the Desert: Actors and Sufferers in the Aboriginal Exodus from the Western Desert', *Aboriginal History,* 13, 1989, pp.40–41.
64 Aboriginal founding members of FCAA included Doug Nicholls and Bert Groves.
65 Two organisers of the walk-off were Lupgna Giari (Captain Major) and Dexter Daniels.

66 Ewan Morris, 'Like the bends in an old tree', BA Honours thesis, Department of History, ANU, 1990, quoting Director of Native Affairs Branch to Administrator, NT, 10 Sept. 1947, Australian Archives (Canberra), A 431 46/450; other Whites and Aborigines carrying spears joined the argument but the incident was defused.
67 Commonwealth Conciliation and Arbitration Commission, No.830 of 1965; for summary of the arguments see Stevens, chapter 10.
68 Council for Aboriginal Affairs, memo for Minister in Charge of Aboriginal Affairs, 'Relationship with Interior', 12 Jan. 1970; H.C. Coombs to W.C. Wentworth, 26 July 1968, Dexter Papers.
69 Correspondence and Memoranda, Chairman, Council for Aboriginal Affairs to Secretary, Department of Interior, 11 Aug. 1970, Dexter Papers.
70 The NTCAR (1961) led by Jacob Roberts and Davis Daniels, based its campaigns for justice for all Aborigines on the Universal Declaration of Human Rights.
71 For further discussion see R. Broome, *Aboriginal Australians*, Sydney, Allen & Unwin, 1982, pp.189–93.
72 'Return to Country: the Aboriginal Homelands Movement in Australia', Report of the House of Representatives Standing Committee on Aboriginal Affairs, March 1987, p.13.
73 ibid, p.28; the DAA estimate was rather higher than this.
74 DAA Report, 'Appreciation of Alice Springs situation', 30 Sept. 1974, Dexter papers; *Centralian Advocate*, 22 May, 5 June, 24 July, 28 Aug. 1975.
75 Neville Perkins, Trevor Cutter, interviewed by P. Read, 1988, 1989.
76 Charles Perkins, personal communication; for other examples from the same 'noticeboard' see S. Harris, *Its Coming Yet, Aboriginal Treaty Committee*, Canberra, 1979, p.75.
77 The Mangarayi community at Elsey Station was prevented from returning to the station after the whole community attended the Mataranka races in the early 1970s: see Jessie Roberts Garalnganjag, 'Talking History' in *Land Rights News*, 2/12 (Jan. 1989), pp.30–31.
78 Mataranka: personal communication to author, 1990; Tennant Creek: D. Bell, 'A fight for land', *Aboriginal Law Bulletin*, 6, Dec. 1982.
79 *Summary Offences Act, 1983*, s45D; for discussion of the operation

of the 'two-kilometre' rule in Tennant Creek see Brady, p.13 pass.
80 Personal communication, Dr Ian Green.
81 Hobbles Danayirri in Rose, 1991, p.138.
82 According to figures provided in M. Clifford, *Aboriginal Criminological Research: Report of a Workshop Held 3–4 March 1981,* p.29, the Aboriginal arrest rate was 446.5 per 100 000 and for non-Aborigines, 113 per 100 000. The proportion between the rates was less than in other states because the arrest rate of non-Aborigines is greater in the Northern Territory than elsewhere; see also J. Walker, 'Prison cells with Revolving Doors: a Judicial or Structural Problem', in K. Hazlehurst, *Ivory Scales,* UNSW Press/Australian Institute of Criminology, Kensington, pp.106–107.
83 Charles Perkins, in Read, 1990, p.315.

8
Tasmania: 1

TODAY there are approximately 8000 Tasmanian Aborigines, many of whom are politically active and who challenge the assumptions of the white nation. Outspoken leaders such as Michael Mansell have argued for a separate Aboriginal nation and recognition of Aboriginal sovereignty. Although Mansell continues a long family tradition of struggle for Aboriginal rights, anxious whites attempt to discredit him by asserting that his blue eyes and fair skin prove he is 'not a real Aborigine'. Others say he is not a 'real Aborigine' because of his education and militancy, a stereotype which he wittily rebukes.

As it is so widely believed that Tasmanian Aborigines disappeared from history, the survivors are under a greater historical burden than the mainlanders. Their struggle is to be recognised at all.[1] Recent Liberal governments continue to deny land rights to Tasmanian Aborigines and in a recent parliamentary speech, Premier Groom denied that Aborigines were subjected to genocide or that they were 'deliberately' exterminated. Writer Robert Hughes reinforced a racially-based cliche when he described Tasmania's history as the 'only true genocide in English colonial history'.[2] Yet historian Lyndall Ryan reminded us that in terms of the United Nations Convention on Human Rights, a form of genocide indeed took place. Part of the problem with the term 'genocide' is whether people are using it in reference to a final destruction, or an *intention* to destroy, and whether 'extermination' means *total* destruction. It is worth noting that in the

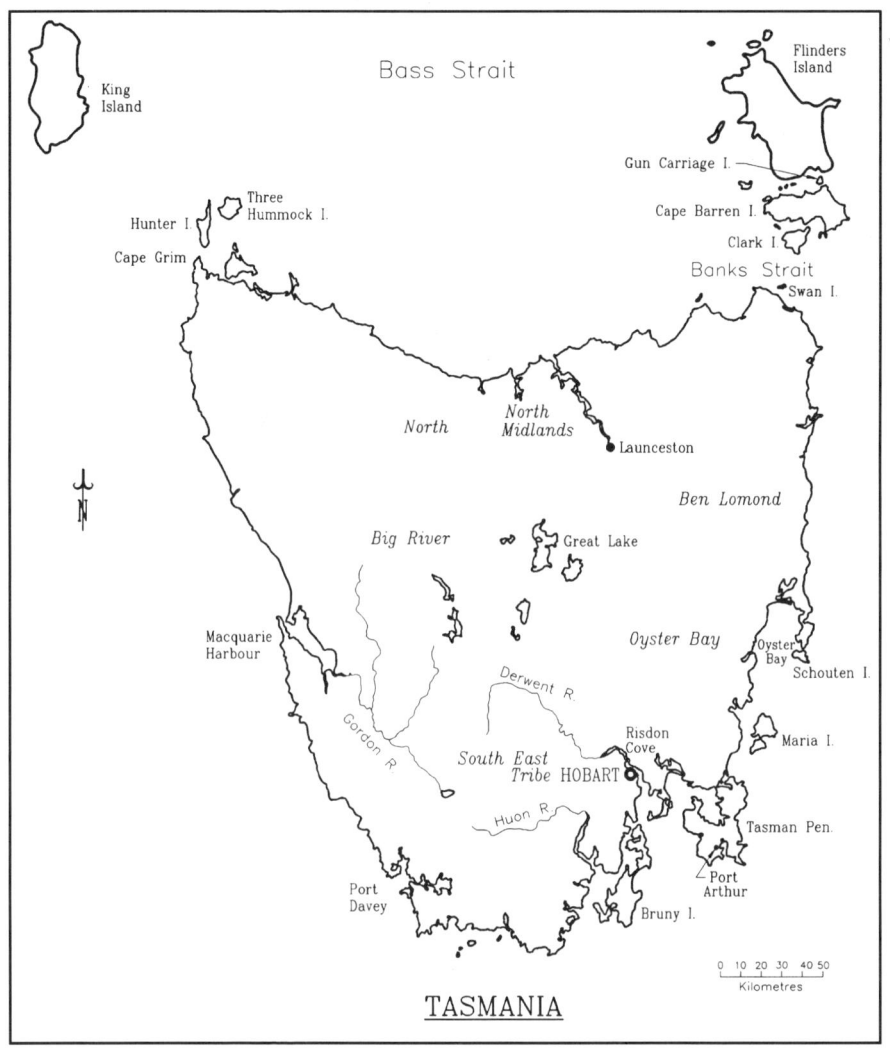

early 1830s, the Colonial Secretary, Sir George Murray, observed settler support for a genocidal policy, warning against its implementation by the colonial government: 'the adoption of any line of conduct, having for its avowed or secret object the extinction of the native race, could not fail to leave an indelible stain upon the British government.'[3]

Truganini/'Truggernana', c 1833–40. Showing her necklace and ceremonial markings on her forehead and arm, this portrait also suggests the striking beauty and presence which so enamoured British male writers. DIXSON LIBRARY, STATE LIBRARY OF NEW SOUTH WALES

By 1837 the Select Committee on Aborigines reported that his dire prediction had come true, as the 'race' had almost died out.

The physical appearance of today's Tasmanian Aborigines are a material manifestation of their continuing history, as in another way, are their current political struggles. Their story is written into their skin-colours, into their political campaigns, and their poetry. Tasmanian Aborigines have a strong sense of having been shaped by a particularly oppressive and destructive history, where they were viewed as inferior and socially excluded. They are aware of cultural difference and allegiance to distinctive communities. There are many family sagas, and most Tasmanian Aboriginal families know of each other's existence. Constantly told they are an extinct race, knowledge of their past has been crucial to their regaining an even stronger sense of cultural pride.

The story of Tasmanian Aborigines has indeed been one of virtual destruction and attempted genocide but not of successful extermination. Strangely, a total 'disappearance' was a tidier, more comfortable history to serve the ambitions of white Australia, for then colonial takeover was seen as complete. Western scientists thought Tasmanian Aborigines the most primitive form of humankind. It followed that they must die out in the struggle for 'survival of the fittest'. Their story could be seen as foretelling the eventual doom of Aborigines on the mainland and confirming the inevitable demise of all 'native' peoples. Like tracts about the American Indians such as *The Last of the Mohicans* (and the more recent film *Dances with Wolves*), Charles Bonwick's *The Last of the Tasmanians*, published in 1870, dramatised the sadness of their 'passing'.[4]

In the first half of the twentieth century, most westerners thought that only ghosts of a 'lost people' remained. A 1940s children's book told of an encounter between the spirit of Truganini and the small white boy 'Digit Dick' when lost in the Tasmanian bush. Fortunately the melancholy though kindly spirit led him to safety. Strangely, the white boy is heroic for keeping the lonely spirit company.[5] After all, who could be lonelier than the last of one's people? Perhaps ghosts were easier to portray and control than living humans. The myth of a Tasmania empty of Aborigines was reinforced by such films as Rhys Jones' *The Last Tasmanians* and more recently the rock band Midnight Oil's song 'Trucanini'. Midnight Oil, who have distinguished themselves as politically aware and even activists for Aboriginal causes, apologised in early 1993 to the Tasmanian Aborigines, stating that they had thought Truganini was indeed 'the last Tasmanian'.

By contrast, the 1992 film *Black Man's Houses* tells us a great deal about the recent struggle of Tasmanian Aborigines to reclaim their history by identifying the graves of their ancestors. The white people's power was corrosive; when they whispered 'Aboriginal blood', it meant something to be ashamed of, someone to reject. Such discrimination encouraged Tasmanians of Aboriginal descent to stick together.

Before the British invasion of Tasmania, the Tasmanians probably numbered between three and four thousand, although the number could have been higher. There were at least 50 bands, organised into nine regional 'tribes' or wider political units. These people regularly met, shared adjacent areas of land, exchanged rituals and intermarried. Their movements and diverse hunting and gathering activities varied regionally. The largest tribe was the Oyster Bay people, which comprised ten bands, and totalled over 700 people. Their territory spanned 7800 square kilometres, covering 515 kilometres of coastline. They ate shellfish from estuarine beds, birds, possum, wallaby and kangaroo from open forests and plains, and a wealth of vegetables. Various groups travelled to exchange ochre, shells and necklaces and to obtain the potentially intoxicating Eucalyptus gunii of the Big River country.[6] Amongst the North Oyster Bay people, seasonal movements took place in spring and autumn. They spent winter on the coast and summer inland. The North Midlands country was often visited, though usually they would return to the coast at the end of January for sealing and muttonbirding. Another tribe, the North East people, travelled to muttonbirding and sealing areas in April and May. They also hunted emus, swans, ducks and seals, and used the eggs of swans and ducks for food. Echidnas, wombats, and ferns, roots and fungi were included in the diet. From July to September, bands congregated around lagoons and estuaries to collect freshly laid swan and duck eggs.

Cut off from the mainland for 10 000 years after the last ice age, Tasmanian Aborigines adapted their culture to the environment. About 4000 years ago they ceased to eat scale fish and stopped making bone tools. Stone tools were refined, however, and along areas of the west coast, many people lived in village-like settlements, where they could almost continuously exploit shellfish, seals, muttonbirds and kangaroos.[7] They also had a distinctive appearance; they greased, ochred and twisted their hair and applied reddish ochre to their skin.

Isolation made Tasmanians a culturally distinct people from mainland Aborigines. Their languages showed links to the mainland groups but also unique characteristics. The men carried fire, and often wore ornaments consisting of the bones of dead kin. Like mainland Aborigines, the women usually procured the staple foodstuffs; they transported babies on their shoulders, and carried water containers and baskets, digging sticks and stone tools. Tasmanian Aborigines believed in 'star gods', a good spirit who governed the day and a bad spirit who dominated the night. They believed that a guardian spirit or 'soul' occupied their left breast and went elsewhere after death.

Waves of white visitors were to have a dramatic effect on their lives. While Abel Tasman's expedition of 1642 made no contact with Aborigines, that of the Frenchman, Captain Marion du Fresne in 1772, ended in conflict and misunderstanding, with at least one Aboriginal person killed. Early visitors to Van Diemen's Land such as the French naturalist Labillardiere described Aborigines in 1792 as peaceable, though in a state of shock at sighting white men. They eventually approached, accepting handkerchiefs and binding them round their heads. But when shown a sword, they became terrified.[8]

M. Peron left fascinating accounts of the earliest encounters between Aborigines and Frenchmen of the Baudin expedition of 1802. At Port Cygnet on the D'Entrecasteaux Channel, two Aboriginal men joined the French. They were astonished by the whiteness of the newcomers' skin, and opened their waistcoats and shirts, reacting with 'loud cries of surprise' and 'extremely quick stamping of the feet'. They then gazed at the ship, its timbers, construction, masts and sails. When one man was offered a bottle of 'grog', he was shocked by the brightness of the glass, threw it into the sea, then ignored it. A family group who joined the members of the expedition attracted interest, especially a woman in her twenties, who was:

> of pretty robust constitution . . . entirely naked, with the exception of a kangaroo skin, in which she carried a little girl, who she still suckled. Her breasts, a little withered already, appeared otherwise pretty well formed, and sufficiently furnished with milk . . . The girl's eyes had expression, and something of the *spirituel* which surprised us . . . She appeared, also, to cherish her child much; and her care for her had that affectionate and gentle character which is exhibited among all races as the particular attribute of maternal tenderness.[9]

Like the British observers at Port Jackson, Peron was fascinated by the women's appearance, referring to the charcoal which the charming girl Oura Oura smeared on her cheeks as 'the rouge of these regions'. After its application, she appeared more confident, leading Peron to remark that the taste for ornament and 'the sentiment of coquetry' were 'innate in the heart of woman'. As a gallant gesture, before bowing to her beauty, Peron drew off his glove; she was horrified, thinking that he had peeled off his skin. When an old Aboriginal man invited the French arrivals to a meal of cockels and mussels, Peron joined them, singing the

'Marsellaise' and other 'more tender airs' which the party approved with excited gestures.[10] These first encounters were times where each party gazed with intense interest if not amazement at the other. In retrospect these were moments to be cherished: moments of promising warmth and openness, of recognition of a common humanity. They were rare times of mutual trust between the indigenes and the foreigners and certainly the last time the visitors, the strangers, would all return permanently to their homelands.

The earliest regular visitors to Tasmania were less cultivated, although equally interested in the Aboriginal women. The sealers, who first arrived in 1800, were a rough fraternity of entrepreneurs. Initially ships were sent from the United States, Britain and Sydney to take as many fur seals as possible; later this was rationalised so that groups of ten to fifteen men would catch the seals from November to May, then return next season. They needed the peaceful co-operation of the Aborigines and keenly sought female company. Only a few hundred men arrived each year but it was an intensive industry, with over 100 000 seals slaughtered for skins between 1800 to 1806.[11] From 1804, whalers also visited the D'Entrecasteaux Channel and in 1822 a temporary whaling station was opened at Port Davey and others followed.

Local Aborigines customarily visited the islands for the muttonbird season around May. At first wary of the newcomers, they eventually began a trade in kangaroo and seal skins in exchange for tobacco, flour and tea. Later, in an attempt to integrate the white men into their society, women's sexual services were offered in exchange for hunting dogs, flour and other gifts. Such payments had parallels in customary marriage negotiations, and these new-style marriages had the potential to be mutually advantageous. Since the sealers did not require large areas of land or permanent settlements, there was more scope for co-operative arrangements than in later phases of white occupation. Local bands incorporated the sealers into their own economy; they met them upon arrival, held a dance then a conference where women partners were allocated for the men. For such purposes, Aboriginal men abducted women from neighbouring bands, to be exchanged with sealers for sought-after commodities. Where possible, the local economy and inter-band relations were thus adapted to take advantage of the sealers' presence.

Often Aborigines had no choice. When the sealers failed to obtain women voluntarily, they murdered Aboriginal men and subjected women to abduction and rape. Gun-wielding raiders made women submit by chaining, whipping or starving them. It was not uncommon for girls of eight or nine to be forced to cohabit with white men, as in the case of Jumbo, employed by James Munroe. Another young woman named Moretermorrerlunener, alias Poll, loyally cared for the invalid Charley Peterson.[12] Sealers and whalers often enjoyed the services of several wives.

Aboriginal men like Mannalargenna also undertook voyages with the sealers, although the women were preferred. They performed all tasks associated with sealing, becoming indispensable to the industry. One woman, Fanny Hardwick, could navigate a schooner and 'could hand reef and steer'.[13] Women also supplied the men's diet, including shellfish, native vegetables, kangaroo, and other necessities. Unwilling workers were brutally coerced: one man called Harrington, had ten to fifteen women working for him, each placed on different islands. If they procured insufficient kangaroo skins, he tied them to trees for up to 36 hours and flogged them intermittently. When women defiantly resisted, sealers murdered them in cold blood.[14]

Sometimes the women preferred to be with the sealers rather than face tribal punishments. They also avoided being removed again by government agents. At Bruny Island, young women frequented the whalers' camps to obtain food and they were sometimes in a strong bargaining position.[15] Aboriginal men often disapproved, complaining to white officials. George Augustus Robinson, a builder and evangelist who led numerous expeditions to liaise with Aborigines on behalf of the government, noted that the men were fond of their wives and children. Women who became captives of sealers or whalers could only communicate with their men via smoke signals. As a result of the trade in women, Aboriginal men faced severe difficulties finding partners, upon whom they had previously relied for many things, including an adequate diet. Pondering the importance of women's tasks, Aborigines asked Robinson of his wife Maria's activities in England; did she swim in salt water and get crawfish and muttonfish?[16]

Aboriginal men's desperation to find women also led to serious tensions between the clans and tribes. Dejection and loneliness often set in, exacerbating sickness. Venereal and other diseases were spreading rapidly and the death toll was high.[17] Resulting infertility posed devastating consequences for the future, with many women never producing any children, and of those born, many died young. Of the nine women at Oyster Cove in 1869, only two ever had children; one had a single child and the other had two but all soon died. When asked why there were so few children, one woman laughed abrasively; another asked, 'What por? blackfellow, him all die.'[18]

Convicts were transported to what was known as Van Diemen's Land from 1803. These included the toughest recalcitrants, exiled anew. Until 1809, severe food shortages meant they were encouraged to forage in the bush, leading to unrecorded conflicts and brutality against Aborigines. Bushranging became widespread, and Aboriginal women were frequently abducted as partners.[19] The first large-scale massacre was inflicted by soldiers at the official settlement of Risdon, near Hobart, on 3 May 1804. A party of 300 Aboriginal men, women and children were approaching the settlement, singing and carrying boughs as a symbol of peace, when the military panicked and opened fire. The assembly may have been about to conduct a ceremony, as they were reported to be carrying numerous kangaroo carcasses. Reports conflicted: one stated that the soldier who first fired was suffering an overdose of rations' rum; another alleged that a white woman had been 'ill-used'. British officers explained that they feared the size of the Aboriginal party and had sighted spears; another witness said they had waddies, not spears. Whatever took place, the previously friendly Aborigines thereafter avoided the settlement and were increasingly violent.[20]

Between 1807 and 1820, free agricultural 'settlers' arrived in Van Diemen's Land, and after 1822, a contingent of pastoralists occupied the remaining land for sheep-farming. The free settlers used convict labour extensively. From a non-Aboriginal population of 2000 in 1817, numbers rose dramatically to 13 000 by 1824, and 23 500 by 1830. The second wave of immigration saw large grants of land given to pastoralists; by 1830 a million sheep occupied Aboriginal lands, more than in New South Wales. The speed and intensity of the pastoral invasion had devastating consequences on Aboriginal life.

Many Aboriginal children were captured by whites and brought up by white families. This was often justified as 'saving' them from barbarism or starvation. George Van Diemen was one boy supposedly 'found' in the bush. Baptised and taught 'letters and prayers', he was 'weaned from his wandering habits'. He was taken to England, partly as an 'experiment' to see if he could be civilised. His mentors were pleased with their results but he died prematurely in 1828. By 1817, at least 50 Aboriginal children were being used as cheap labour in settlers' homes. If the children survived to puberty, they then rebelled, seeking their own people or taking to the streets.[21] Girls who drank, stole or prostituted themselves were classed as 'bad', relieving onlookers of any concern for their physical or mental well-being.

Settler attitudes hardened: they bragged of the number of 'black crows' they destroyed, and of killing Aborigines for dog food. Stock-keepers wantonly fired at and killed Aborigines, leaving the remains around their properties. Other terrible slaughters took place as 'inoffensive' camps of Aborigines slept. Chilling stories abound. A white man called Carrots murdered an Aboriginal man in order to acquire his Aboriginal wife; he then forced her to wear her husband's head tied around her neck. Bonwick told of two white men out shooting birds who sighted an Aboriginal woman hiding in a tree. Her advanced pregnancy had prevented her from fleeing with her kin. One of the men planned to shoot but the other objected. Undeterred, he dropped behind and fired at her. After a shocking scream, a new-born infant fell from the tree.[22]

Aborigines resisted but at a cost of further violence, either against them or their community. One Aboriginal woman who was caught and chained to a log managed to slip the bullock-chain from her leg and escape. Her captor was later found in a state of near-starvation, as he was used to relying on the food she supplied. Another cruel abductor gave his traumatised captive a flogging each morning with a bullock whip to 'subdue her sulks', then tied her to a tree until his evening return. This man was later found speared to death.[23]

Indeed, the Tasmanian frontier saw bitter struggles. The height of the conflict was between 1824 and 1834, when increasing areas of land were being exploited by sheep farmers. In the early period, disease did not take as many Aboriginal lives as in New South Wales, perhaps because they continued to obtain a good high-protein diet with a good intake of vitamins. Frontier conflict, however, was intense. It was much worse and within closer range of townships than experienced on the Hawkesbury in the 1790s but it was perhaps comparable to the Bathurst and Hunter Valley regions in the 1820s. Specific revenge killing progressed to general attacks on the British as a whole.[24] One white observer recorded that chiefs of bush clans had told him that they acted violently against whites because 'they and their forefathers had been cruelly abused, that their country had been taken away from them, their wives and daughters had been violated and taken away and that they had experienced a multitude of wrongs . . . '[25] One of the great rebel heroes was Mosquito, who had been exiled to Van Diemen's Land after being held on Norfolk Island; he was allegedly responsible for serious Aboriginal resistance in New South Wales. His Tasmanian raids upon James Hobbs' property at Eastern Marshes in 1823 infuriated the white residents. With a keen sense of British offensive strategies, he waited until the muskets had discharged, then attacked the British. Governor Arthur offered a reward for his capture but he was not caught until an Aboriginal man, Tegg, tracked him. Although unarmed and alone, Mosquito was shot in the groin before being brought to trial for murder. He had desperately wanted to return to Sydney but past promises for his return had not been kept. His farcical trial offered him no translators and relied upon convict witnesses. He was hanged on 24 February 1825.

According to Robinson, Tasmanian Aborigines exhibited a 'Determined Spirit of Hostility', with 'acts of outrage' committed on the lives and property of non-Aborigines in every 'settled' district. Massacres had led to their 'bloodthirsty temper'; they wanted to atone for aggression by murdering their enemies.[26] Such Aboriginal men often eluded their pursuers, their tracking and bush skills putting them at an advantage. Governor Arthur thus wrote: 'They suddenly appear, commit some act of outrage and then as suddenly vanish; if pursued it seems impossible to surround and capture them.' Rugged mountain and thick forest areas provided excellent opportunities for Aboriginal escape from British. The relatively small number of horses on the island and British inexperience at rough mountain riding worked to their advantage.[27] They also exploited the inefficiency of pre-1850s European weaponry.

By the 1830s, Tasmanian Aborigines had a generation of experience of the British and their weapons, and many spoke English proficiently. Aborigines took a variety of items from the invaders' camps or huts, including guns, shot and powder. They abused the invaders, shouting such things as, 'Get out you white buggers, what are you doing here?'[28] A six-foot tall woman called Walyer or Mary-Ann, was described as an 'amazon'; the tribal leader, she stood on a hill giving orders for the men to spear the whites. Walyer swore at the white men, taunting them to come out and be speared.[29] She was considered very dangerous; she had killed whites and was feared by her own people. Walyer attempted to murder the sealers who were exiling her to Penguin Island. She also plotted the murder of Turnbull, the man who transported her to George Augustus Robinson at Swan Island, because she wanted to steal his boat and return to the mainland. Robinson separated her from his other captives, for he saw her as able to incite a mutiny. He also prevented her from rejoining her clan, whom she would rally for aggression.[30]

Successive governors had been in a bind. Their first interest was the settlement's success but the influence of the anti-slavery movement meant they must appear to have humane sentiments towards indigenes. Governor Collins thus condemned the 'abominable cruelty and murders' suffered by Aborigines. Governor Davey wrote in 1813 that he 'could not have believed that British subjects would have so ignominiously stained the honour of their country and themselves, as to have acted in the manner

they did towards Aborigines'.³¹ Occasionally someone was punished: one white man for exposing the severed ears of an Aboriginal child who had been mutilated, one man flogged for cutting off the finger of an Aboriginal person. No white man was ever brought to trial, however, for murdering an Aborigine. With a background of humanitarian concern regarding the treatment of slaves in British Honduras, Governor George Arthur's arrival in 1824 looked auspicious. Yet he underestimated Aborigines. He blamed murders of whites upon the corrupted 'civilised' Aborigines and attempted to establish native institutions. Aborigines refused to stay there, for they did not want to move permanently off their country, or be separated from their children. Following the colonial policy in Canada and the Cape Colony of southern Africa, Arthur imagined a large reserve on the north-east coast. Fearful of Aboriginal attacks, the British tried to justify their plan by resort to Christian teachings about 'husbanding' the land.

In April 1828, Arthur's Proclamation of Demarcation had ordered a 'temporary separation of the Coloured from the British population of this Territory' but it was the Aborigines who were forced to depart. A line of military posts demarcated the settled districts. With the aid of the soldiers and well-armed constables, all magistrates and others were to effect 'the retirement or expulsion of the Aborigines from the Settled Districts of this Territory'. If persuasion did not work, Aborigines were to be captured. Thenceforth they became 'prisoners', treated, so the proclamation read, 'with the utmost humanity and compassion'. Force was to be used with 'the greatest caution and forbearance' but it *was* to be used. Aborigines were to be captured, with whatever consequences. In order to travel in their own country,

---

Opposite: Governor Davey's Proclamation to the Aborigines, 1816. Many slightly different versions of this illustrated order were hand-copied or hand-coloured. It is dated as c 1828–30? The text, suggestive of black American creole and pidgin English, reads: '"Why Massa Gubernor" said Black Jack "You Proclamation all gammon . . . How blackfellow read him eh? He no learn him read book." "Read that then" said the Governor, pointing to a picture.' MITCHELL LIBRARY, STATE LIBRARY OF NEW SOUTH WALES

Aboriginal leaders had to possess 'a *General Passport* signed and sealed by Governor Arthur'.[32] Although clothed in acceptable humanitarian rhetoric, the actual intentions of the proclamation could not be disguised. Aborigines were to be considered enemy aliens in their own country, and if they survived capture, were to be interned—first by imprisonment and later by convincing them to adopt a European lifestyle in a confined area.

When hostilities continued, Arthur declared martial law against Aborigines in the 'settled districts' in November 1828. This declaration of war authorised the military to shoot any Aboriginal person upon sight. Martial law was to stay in force for three years.[33] Arthur set up six roving parties to hunt down or capture the 200 Aborigines residing near settled districts. Some were caught and gaoled, or conscripted to work in the parties.

Arthur justified his actions to the Colonial Office:

> All the Aboriginal Tribes of this island with which we are acquainted, except the tribe who visit Brune Island, are actuated with one common purpose of murdering the white inhabitants whenever met with . . . their attacks had been unhappily attended with a degree of success . . . well calculated to produce the great state of alarm which appeared to be felt generally by the interior settlers and servants in husbandry.[34]

Attacks against white women and children caused the most extreme responses. Aborigines were blamed for their own fate; writing to the *Hobart Town Press*, Gilbert Robertson criticised Aboriginal men for their role in prostitution and Aboriginal women for their willingness. Associated murders were blamed 'as much to the depraved taste of the aboriginal as to the moral turpitude of the Whites'.[35]

Military operations now extended to remote districts. In 1830 a bounty was introduced with five pounds for every adult Aborigine captured, and two pounds for each child. Warfare by the Oyster Bay and Big River Aborigines against the settlers led to a full-scale military expedition. In October 1830, the notorious 'Black Line' was established. Every able-bodied male colonist, convict or free, was to form a human chain which would move across the settled districts, forming a pincer shape which would be cordoned off by military forces. The aim was to drive Aborigines off their lands to the Tasman Peninsula. On 7 October, 2000 free men, 500 troops and 700 convicts were assembled. For three weeks this intimidating force beat through bushes, built defensive huts and battled pouring rain. But they captured only two Aborigines and shot two. Various groups may have been driven away and a dozen more captured afterwards. Obviously Aborigines had been vigilantly watching whites and had prior intelligence of the event.[36] Once again, it seemed that the Aborigines had temporarily beaten their foe.

Humanitarians, newspaper commentators and even those most involved in conquering the Aborigines, had uneasy consciences. By 1832 Governor Arthur regretted the horrific violence of settlement, blaming the lack of an initial treaty. Stating that this was 'a great oversight', he urged that in any future colonies, an understanding should be reached before settlement commenced and that land be purchased from indigenous people.[37] After describing a 'diabolical outrage' against men and women, George Augustus Robinson wrote in one of his journals:

> Thus it is that their wrongs are handed down from generation to generation. The children have witnessed the massacre of their parents and their relations carried away into captivity by these merciless invaders, their country has been taken from them and the kangaroo, their chief subsistence, have been slaughtered wholesale . . . Can we wonder then at the hatred they bear to the white inhabitants? This enmity is not the effect of the moment. Like a fire burning underground, it has burst forth. We should make some atonement for the misery we have entailed upon the original proprietors of this land.[38]

An 1836 article in the *Hobart Town Times* stated:

> They have been murdered in cold blood. They have been shot in the woods, and hunted down as beasts of prey. Their women have been contaminated, and then had their throats cut, or been shot, by the British residents, who would fain call themselves civilized people. The Government, too, by the common hangman, sacrificed the lives of such of the Aborigines . . . to its shame be it recorded, in no one instance, on no single occasion, ever punished, or threatened to punish, the acknowledged murderers of the aboriginal inhabitants.[39]

Yet British invaders were deeply threatened by their courageous, strategically ingenious adversary. Between 1824 and 1831, at least 60 British were killed by Aboriginal people in the Big River district alone. They speared sheep and cattle, burnt homes and wheatstacks, raided huts and stole firearms. On the other hand, the Big River people suffered dreadfully, with some 240 of them killed. Of the 300 alive in 1823, only 60 remained by 1831. Women had been abducted, and many others shot. About 700 Tasmanian Aborigines were killed by violence, and about 176 British were killed by Aborigines. While the indigenous people came off far worse, they mounted an effective resistance, killing more of the British than elsewhere—a ratio of one British to four Aboriginal people as compared with one to ten elsewhere in Australia.[40] Umarrah, a North Midlands leader, explained that the murders of whites were intended to stop them driving kangaroos off their hunting grounds. Aborigines continued to wage war in the areas of British settlement, even when their numbers were depleted.

Desperate to improve the colony's image to prospective settlers, Governor Arthur had wanted to contain Aboriginal aggression by forcing them to relinquish their traditional lifestyle, which demanded extensive land-use. Capture was his chosen technique. In July 1829, three women were thus caught, treated 'kindly' then told to distribute presents to their tribe. Released from their detention, they were delegated to 'assure them of the friendly feeling of the government towards them, and invite them to be conciliated'. The female 'embassy', as he saw it, brought in the chief and nine men for clothing and food but the mission was declared a failure, as the group soon plundered their providers and deserted.[41] Arthur later decided to obtain a missionary who would gain the sympathy of Aborigines and convince them to move to a reserve from which they could not escape. The rhetoric of 'protecting' their welfare sounded better than 'confinement' or exclusion from their own lands. The project to curb Aboriginal assaults was thus referred to as a 'friendly mission'. In 1829, George Augustus Robinson was employed on 100 pounds a year to help the friendly Aborigines on Bruny Island and to make arrangements for those captured from settled districts.

Robinson's diaries provide important insights into the tragedies endured by the Tasmanian Aborigines. His records also reveal the extent of depopulation. At Bruny Island, he found only nineteen Aborigines from tribes which six years previously had numbered 160. Even those who had agreed to co-operate with whites had been ill-treated. Nelson, the leader of the island, suffered attempted rapes by the soldiers and her husband was shot dead when attempting to escape. Robinson set up a mission station along South Pacific lines, distributed clothing and convict rations. None of these arrangements were conducive to good health; the death toll was shocking. Where possible, Aborigines left when illness struck, some moving to a nearby whaling station. Bruny Island Mission failed and in 1831 the survivors were moved to Gun Carriage Island but they died of sickness, depression, confinement. Flinders Island Settlement was then established in 1835 with 123 residents but by 1838, 59 people had died. Despite illness, they were expected to work hard; the women collected heavy loads of thatching grass and the men built roads. Robinson claimed they were superior to white men at this work.[42] Arguing that they were suffering 'mental irritation', Robinson lobbied for the Tasmanians to accompany him to his new job in Port Phillip,[43] so fifteen more Aboriginal people were taken from Tasmania.

Writer Viviene Rae Ellis saw Robinson as a mesmeriser of Aborigines, who tricked them into capitulation, especially agreement to surrender their country. Henry Reynolds disagrees, arguing that they were not passive dupes; the process was one of active Aboriginal negotiation. They agreed to move to an island only on the firm condition that their needs would be fully met, including their requirement to make regular return journeys to the mainland. They were not to know that this verbal contract would be broken. Robinson knew Aborigines were insulted by interference so he gained their trust by taking an interest in their language, customs and welfare without overtly trying to change them. Robinson was to 'work on their feelings' then resort to whatever was required to ensure 'their voluntary submission to the British yoke'.[44] Whether this truly comprised 'conciliation' is highly debatable, as the outcome was already decided.

By 1829, Robinson estimated that only two or three hundred

'Woureddy' of Brune Island c 1833. Truganini's husband appears a forceful, strong and dignified man. DIXON LIBRARY, STATE LIBRARY OF NEW SOUTH WALES

Aborigines had survived, far fewer than fearful white 'settlers' imagined. Robinson gained important intelligence regarding which Aborigines had committed recent murders, and their strategies of warfare. He formed especially close relations with Truganini, whom he first met as a seventeen-year old, and for whom he did not disguise his sexual attraction. She was reported by many observers as good-humoured, with a beautiful face and body. Her father, Mangana, was chief of the Bruny Island tribe. Truganini's life was indeed tragic; as a small child, her mother was stabbed to death by British men, then her two sisters were kidnapped, and one of them, Moorinna, was later shot dead by a sealer. At the age of sixteen, when her promised husband tried to save her from abduction, she watched as he was mutilated and drowned.[45] Between 1830 and 1834, Robinson travelled with a party of about thirteen Aborigines, including Truganini, Wooraddy, who later became her husband, his sons Peter and Davy, Truganini's companions, Pagerly and Dray, and a British escort party including fourteen convicts. They journeyed around the coastline and interior of Tasmania attempting to locate and negotiate with the remaining Aborigines.[46] By 1831, several Aborigines from New South Wales were brought in to act as trackers and intermediaries in the roving parties. Others were released from gaol on condition that they work in the expeditions.[47]

During their west coast journey, Robinson began a sexual relationship with Truganini, whom he called 'my Lydgugee'. Her devotion and their intimacy became a subject of discreet comment. Robinson secretly mentioned 'pargener' or kissing in his own journal of 1837, perhaps to keep the affair from his wife Maria,[48] but probably more so from his own employers. Truganini knew that she would have better survival chances if she stayed with Robinson, who she understood to be a powerful man in the new social order. She became Robinson's mistress to achieve a political alliance and protection, and when Robinson failed to fulfil them, Wooraddy tried to kill him.[49] Truganini refused to mediate with certain Aboriginal people; when travelling in the Big River region, a woman from that group mediated with the locals. Truganini criticised Robinson's strategies and later flouted his authority. On an 1839 journey with Robinson to Port Phillip, she absconded, raided and looted shepherd's huts, and successfully tracked down and shot one of the whalers who had abducted her sister eleven years earlier.[50]

When Truganini died in 1876, it became legend that she was the last 'real' or 'full-blood' Tasmanian Aborigine. This was not true, however, as another woman living with a sealing community on Kangaroo Island, Suke, lived until 1888. Fanny Cochrane-Smith also survived her, living until 1905, but on the basis of contemporary genetic theories, scientists believed that Fanny could not be a 'real Aborigine'. Count Strzelecki's theory propounded that an Aboriginal woman could not give birth to a black child if she had produced a white man's child, like Fanny's mother. In 1884, Fanny successfully gained title to 300 acres of land and a government annuity, which she saw as compensation for the loss of Aboriginal land.[51]

The surviving Aboriginal communities mainly inhabited certain islands off Tasmania. Most, like the Cape Barren Island community, were descendents of the Aboriginal women who lived with whalers and sealers.[52] In 1871, the colonial government offered those living on Cape Barren Island blocks of land, and gave Aborigines exclusive rights to the muttonbird rookeries on

The Conciliation by Duterrau. A dramatic sketch of Robinson befriending and negotiating with different Aboriginal peoples, 1835. Truganini stands in the background. According to Benjamin Brau, his etching was part of a 'National Picture'. MITCHELL LIBRARY, STATE LIBRARY OF NEW SOUTH WALES

Chappell and Big Dog islands. Muttonbirding was an integral part of the economy and lifestyle of many Aborigines. They continued traditional movement patterns, valued singing, and pursued crafts such as making shell necklaces. In 1881, land was reserved for their occupation but they had no security of tenure, leading some to depart to Flinders Island.[53]

Nor did the geographic isolation of island life guarantee freedom from interference, for the Anglican bishop, Charles Bromby, objected to their lifestyle, demanding they become a 'settled community' that tilled the soil. Missionaries imposed their notions of 'civilisation' and godliness upon an often unwilling community. When Edward Stephens, a missionary school teacher, arrived on Cape Barren Island in 1890, the community of 110 people soon objected to his attempt to control their lives. Extreme tensions and mistrust arose, with islanders withdrawing their children from the school, accusing Stephens of adultery, being intoxicated in front of the school children, and even of attempted murder. Hilarious rumours spread about the night-shirt clad Stephens singing 'God save the Queen' on the roof of the toilet, then engaging in drunken revelry with the Bishop. Stephens was indeed having a horrific battle with his alcoholism, and contemplated suicide. After he suffered a nervous collapse, his son Charles replaced him, only to face a resurgence of islander resistance. The residents had rejoiced in driving his father away and formed an Islander association, rather pointedly stating that they did not want to become 'like white people'. They knew how to goad young Stephens by testing him on his own terms; one strategy was for parents to wait outside the school checking his punctuality against the school clock. By 1899, Stephens despaired, telling the Bishop that the Aborigines would give 'more trouble than the Boers are giving Great Britain'.[54]

Unlike all the other colonies and later states, the Tasmanian Government had no specific legislation concerning Aboriginal people. It was the Islanders' agitation which led to some relevant enactments. Insecurity of tenure continued to trouble them, for they were often criticised for their land-use styles, and knew that white graziers and other settlers were eager to take over their island lands. The Aborigines actively campaigned for independence and less restrictive allocation and conditions regarding blocks of land. In 1911, they sent a petition to Parliament; having a strong sense of community identity, they objected to young women being entitled to blocks because they did not want outsiders marrying into their community in order to acquire land.[55] In the 1930s they lobbied against further missionaries, stating, 'we decidedly object to people coming here to save us . . . '. Instead, they wanted work.[56] Although not well off, the people supported each other, and enjoyed sharing sports days, dances and hunting excursions. Nonetheless, they were closely policed by the school teacher, who enforced regulations regarding visitors and behaviour on the island.

The *Cape Barren Island Reserve Act, 1912* represented an achievement in its acknowledgement of Aboriginal existence and occupation. While it officially entrenched the belief that Islanders were the only Aboriginal people or descendents of such in Tasmania, their hold on the land remained insecure, and from 1945 the leases of many families were cancelled. The *Reserve Act, 1945* was intended to phase out the reserve by 1951, ensuring its residents would become part of the wider community. As part of the assimilation policy, the Islanders were thus encouraged to leave—sometimes by the offer of a house, or the withholding of social service benefits. On the one hand, the State Government claimed there were no Aborigines, yet they accepted federal grants to rehouse them. Unemployment, withdrawal of government spending on the island, concern for their children's future, and several poor muttonbird seasons all contributed further pressure towards mainland migration. Aborigines were relocated to small run-down houses in suburbs such as Invermay and Mayfield Creek, and allocated unskilled jobs. They often suffered overcrowding, poverty and discrimination by employers, police and in public places such as hotels.[57]

Many Aborigines refused to leave Cape Barren Island, taking out leases or merely 'sitting' on the land, arguing they had already paid for it after the 1912 Act and would not pay again. They also believed they deserved compensation because their country was taken over by the whites.[58] By the 1960s, the Social Welfare Department was offering them jobs and homes in Launceston and many accepted.[59] Government policy continued to encourage them to relocate, whilst the Islanders argued for redevelopment of the island. Rifts developed between those who had refused to leave the islands and those who left for jobs. Discrimination against Aborigines also led many to deny their ancestry. As Albert Deverall recalled, 'If people could get away with passing as white, they did. It saved a lot of heartbreak.'[60] For many other Aborigines, the experience of discrimination led to a stronger sense of self-identity. Their island bases or origins gave Aborigines a strong sense of shared community and they returned regularly.

Official Aboriginal population figures reflected changing state policies towards Aborigines. Before 1967, Aborigines were not counted in the National Census, and any other enumeration excluded Aborigines according to 'caste', with anyone below 'octoroon' omitted. In 1971, 675 Aborigines were enumerated, by 1976, 2943 and by 1986, this had jumped to 6712.[61]

Tasmanian Aborigines, especially those based on the Tasmanian mainland, strengthened their political activities, establishing the Tasmanian Aboriginal Centre in 1973 and the Aboriginal Legal Service as bases for political action, struggles for education and justice. They also agitated for Aboriginal studies in schools and at tertiary level. Land rights and recognition of sacred sites became a central part of their struggle. Sites of former reserves such as Oyster Cove, Cape Barren Island, Wybalena, Cape Grim and other islands had associations with massacres and the 'decline of our tribal ancestors'. So far the claims have had only marginal success. Aborigines object to having to pay for hunting or fishing licences, as they see these as traditional land-use rights.[62] A 1976 land rights claim was presented to State and Federal Governments, and in the following year, at Wrest Point Casino, Michael Mansell presented a petition to the Queen. In 1978 an 'Aboriginal Parliament' was set up in the parliamentary reserve. The State Government established an Aboriginal Affairs Study Group to consider certain requests but consultation with Aboriginal people was inadequate.[63] After 1978, some land was acquired: this included Trefoil Island, 20 hectares of Cape Barren Island and some blocks in Launceston, purchased through the federally funded Aboriginal Land Fund Commission. These properties became important bases for community and political development.

Traditions such as muttonbirding continue.[64] Aboriginal families return to the islands for the season, often in their own sailing boats, where the birds are plucked, cleaned, cooked and preserved. Wild berries and vegetables such as grass-tree centre, pig-face and she-oak nuts sometimes accompany the feasts. Muttonbirding is a family activity and a direct link with the past. Ida West remembers the dances held after birding. 'You had to shampoo your hair, wash it two or three times before you could go to the dance. You never could get rid of the smell of the birds or the feathers.'[65] Older Aborigines still teach children about native foods and bush medicines. They remember their childhoods, and reminisce about catching wallabies, possums and echidna and collecting choke apples, wild potatoes, fern roots, and shellfish.

Ida West's family—the Everett-Armstrongs—liked fishing, though the 'old folk' now advised they should only eat fish 'with scales on'. Ida West has her own brand of spirituality which combines Christianity with belief in premonitions, ghosts, and the spirits associated with graves and land.[66] For her, such spiritual feelings authenticate the past in the contemporary landscape.

Aboriginal heritage was recognised by the High Court in the Franklin Dam case in 1983, where ancient archaeological sites played an important role in the argument against the dam's construction. Justice Murphy argued that their preservation could strengthen Aboriginal identity and promote tolerance of Aborigines amongst the general community. 'Because of the attempted genocide of the Aboriginal race in Tasmania, which extended to their customs, tribal structures and culture, a law aimed at the preservation, or the uncovering, of evidence about their history is a special law with respect to the people of that race.'

Counsel for the Tasmanian Government argued that the Tasmanian Aborigines were extinct but the majority judgement stated the significance of sacred sites and land to Aboriginal people.[67] Despite active Aboriginal campaigns, including marches and protests, and the support of the 1989 Labor government, the Legislative Council rejected the Aboriginal Lands Bill 1991 and the Liberal government, elected in 1992, closed down the Aboriginal Affairs Policy Unit and refused to support land rights, even withholding its federal funding from the Tasmanian Aboriginal Land Council.[68]

Another important Tasmanian-led struggle has been 'bone-rights'; that is, the return of the bones and preserved anatomical parts of Aborigines acquired by Australian and overseas museums during the nineteenth century in the name of science. Tasmanian Aborigines see this as a continuing insult and a desecration of their ancestors' remains.

Despite her dying pleas that her body not be mutilated or displayed,[69] Truganini's body was exhumed two years after her death and eventually put on show at the Tasmanian Museum and Art Gallery between 1904 and 1947. In the 1970s, a campaign by

Aboriginal activists succeeded in having her remains returned. A hundred years after she died, Truganini's wishes were finally enacted; in May 1976 she was cremated and her ashes later scattered over the D'Entrecasteaux Channel near her birthplace.[70] In 1984 the introduction of bone rights legislation meant the return of skulls and other skeletal material, to be disposed of by members of the Aboriginal community.[71] Overseas campaigns have been more protracted, and while some remains have been returned, hundreds of items are still held by British museums alone.

In 1980, a research report commissioned by the Tasmanian Aboriginal Centre found the community suffered problems of unemployment, alcoholism and ill-health. In many walks of life, Aborigines considered they were treated unfairly because of their 'race'.[72] In recent decades, Aborigines have been over-represented in courts and gaols. Although the Aboriginal Legal Service led to some improvement, relations between police and Aborigines were often tense.[73] Aboriginal women complained of being verbally abused as sluts and whores by arresting officers, reflecting historically-shaped stereotypes. For generations, police and white overseers had enforced white law in Aboriginal communities. The deaths by hanging of the young men Glenn Clark and Mark Revell whilst in police custody reveal deeply troubled lives. A 1988 survey showed that Aborigines were over-represented in police custody at five times the rate of non-Aboriginal people. Hal Wootten, the relevant Commissioner for the Royal Commission into Aboriginal Deaths in Custody, found that Tasmanian authorities lagged behind other states in acting to improve the situation.[74]

There can be no understanding of the contemporary situation of Tasmanian Aborigines without an attempt to comprehend their past. For these people bear a strong sense of pride about Aboriginal history and a sense of pride in Aboriginality today which permeates their current sense of community. As Jimmy Everett wrote in his poem, *Yes, I know what you mean*:

> Am I Tasmanian Aboriginal,
> my bloody oath I am
> What! Not Black enough,
> well that don't mean a damn.
> Only part Abo is what they say,

you really are a charm.
Is it my leg, my head, my foot, or is it my right arm.
Oh! I see, I'm not full blood,
well that's a funny thing.
Always thought I was full of blood,
a pumpin' like a spring
. . .
Why is it that if I get drunk,
and stagger down the road.
I'm called a drunken blackfeller,
that boozing is my code.
But! If I conform and show my wit,
and still claim I'm a Koorie.
Whites deny my right as one,
and deny me my identity.
Oh! You say I'm not one of those,
and I know what you mean.
Then how come you distinguish those!
YES, I KNOW WHAT YOU MEAN[75]

Tasmanian Aborigines have produced substantial educational materials about their culture, including school kits, oral history interviews, and the publication of Ida West's *Pride Against Prejudice*. All have strengthened their common sense of identity. Forums for Aboriginal prose and poetry included the Tasmanian Aboriginal Centre's Pugganna and Black Action.

Despite a horrifying history, Tasmanian Aboriginal people did not in fact suffer as many massacres, poisonings, or ambushes as those elsewhere in Australia. But whereas the murder of whole tribes or groups of Aborigines on the mainland could go unnoticed, the finite nature of the island of Van Diemen's Land made their rapid decline more obvious. Nineteenth century scientists, with their keen interest in racial hierarchy, encouraged interest in the 'genocide' story, and their speculation raised the value of Tasmanian skulls. This is not to deny the sufferings of Tasmanian Aborigines, which were great. Nowhere else in Australia was such a frightening concept as the 'Black Line' tried, nor such a wide-ranging mission of 'conciliation' intended to force them to quit their lands.

It is paradoxical that in the island state of Australia, the

This painting by John Glover recorded the Hobart Aboriginal people who were sent to Great Island, 1832. DIXON GALLERIES, STATE LIBRARY OF NEW SOUTH WALES

Aborigines only survived on islands away from the main island. From the early nineteenth century, islands were used to exile the toughest recalcitrants or to isolate sufferers of contagious disease. Islands were also seen as appropriate places to isolate Aborigines to ensure they were not just fringedwellers but totally exiled from colonial society. Today many Tasmanian Aborigines again live on the mainland but identification with smaller islands, especially those in the Furneaux group, remains significant. Indeed, island links are crucial identifiers; anyone claiming origins from mainland Tasmania is viewed suspiciously by their fellows, who believe only islanders survived.

Greater insights into Tasmania's history from Aboriginal perspectives might enable more Australians to know what Jimmy Everett means. Aboriginal studies courses and historical research by Tasmanians such as Errol West and Vicky Matson-Green will greatly assist that process. For while Aboriginal 'blood' is biological nonsense, the metaphor is meaningful. Blood was lost and blood remains. There is still bad blood between whites and blacks in Tasmania.

During the campaigns of the 1970s, the majority of Tasmanians were found to support land rights and to strongly back the return of bones from local museums. But atonement is controversial, and, as indicated by the grudging attitude of Mr Horman, a former Commissioner of Police, in response to the Underlying Issues Paper of the Royal Commission into Aboriginal Deaths in Custody, white denials have not lost their momentum. This Commissioner argued that white families who lost their land suffered similarly; he also rejected that the pain of Aboriginal dispossession could be passed down through so many generations.

Tasmanian Aborigines had to live with the contradiction that while their existence was denied, they suffered the same discrimination as Aborigines elsewhere.[76] They have not yet had their entitlements recognised. Despite the denigration by past writers about their 'primitive culture', and past classifications as 'half-caste'/outcast, they are still very proud.[77] While the tragic ghosts of the past may never be laid to rest, today's Tasmanians are 'real' Aborigines, testimony of a long struggle for survival. It is good to know them; they are people of blood, bone, intellect and a lot of guts.

NOTES

1. L. Ryan, *The Aboriginal Tasmanians*, University of Queensland Press, St Lucia, 1982, p.1.
2. *The Age*, 18 June 1993; *The Australian*, 18 June 1993.
3. Report from Select Committee on Aborigines, 1837, *British Parliamentary Papers (BBP)*, Anthropology, Aborigines, vol.2, pp.13–14.
4. J. Fenimore Cooper, *The Last of the Mohicans*, [1826] Dent, London, 1906; J. Bonwick, *The Last of the Tasmanians*, London, 1870 [hereafter facsimile 1969 is used].
5. L. Rees, *Digit Dick and the Tasmanian Devil*, Sydney, c 1950. For a discussion of the Jindyworobaks and other aspects of cultural transmission and exchange, see A. McGrath, 'Europeans and Aborigines', in N. Meaney (ed.), *Under New Heavens*, Heinemann, Melbourne, 1989.
6. Ryan, p.17, 20.

7 Ryan, p.10; See N.J.B. Plomley, 'The Tasmanian Aborigines: A Research Report' in *Bulletin of the Centre for Tasmanian Historical Studies*, vol.1, no.3, 1987.
8 From M. Labillardiere, *Voyage in search of La Perouse* (translation), London, 1800, p.134, cited in M. Yarwood and M. Knowling, *Race Relations in Australia: A History*, Methuen, North Ryde, 1982, p.73.
9 Bonwick, pp.18–19. The French observers, like the early English visitors, were influenced by romanticism, enlightenment principles and the notion of the noble savage. For comparisons, see A. McGrath, 'The White Man's Looking Glass: Aboriginal Colonial Gender Relations at Port Jackson', *Australian Historical Studies*, April 1991.
10 Bonwick, pp.20–21.
11 Ryan, p.66.
12 Robinson in N.J.B. Plomley (ed.), *Friendly Mission: The Tasmanian Journals and Papers of George Augustus Robinson*, Tasmanian Historical Association, Hobart, 1966, pp.271–72.
13 Robinson in Plomley, p.82.
14 Robinson in Plomley, p.39, 418.
15 Ryan, pp.66–69.
16 Robinson in Plomley, p.80, 625.
17 V. Ellis, *Black Robinson*, Melbourne University Press, Carlton, 1988, p.30.
18 Bonwick, p.386. Of nine women at Oyster Cove, only two ever had a child. Truganini had no children.
19 Arthur to Murray, 19 Mar. 1830, *BPP*, vol.4, p.60.
20 Yarwood and Knowling, p.74. See also M. Nicholls (ed.), *The Diary of the Reverend Robert Knopwood, 1803–1838*, T.H.R.A., 1977, p.51, and J. Bonwick, pp.32–36.
21 H. Reynolds, *With the White People*, Penguin, Ringwood, 1990, pp.184–86.
22 Select Committee on Aborigines, 1837. See Bonwick, pp.58–59.
23 Bonwick, pp.65–66, 60 [facsimile, 1969].
24 H. Reynolds, 'The Black War: A New Look at an Old Story', Hobart, 1984, pp.1–2.
25 Reynolds, *The Black War*, p.2.
26 Robinson in Plomley, p.87.
27 Reynolds, *The Black War*, pp.3–4.
28 Reynolds, *The Black War*, pp.2–3.
29 Robinson in Plomley, pp.472–74.

30 Robinson in Plomley, p.296.
31 Bonwick, p.59.
32 Bonwick, pp.78–83. *BPP*, 1831, vol.19, no.259, Correspondence between Lieut. Governor Arthur and His Majesty's Secretary of State for Colonies; see also Ryan, pp.4–7, 24, 97.
33 Bonwick, p.84.
34 Copies of all correspondence between Lieutenant Governor Arthur and His Majesty's Secretary of State for the Colonies, *BPP*, 1831, vol.19, no.259, p.10, cited in Ryan, p.99.
35 Cited Bonwick, p.64.
36 Ryan, chapter 6, map of military operations, p.111. Bonwick, ch.5.
37 Select Committee on Aborigines, 1837, p.17.
38 Robinson, Mission to Port Davey, 20 Aug. 1830, in Plomley, p.202.
39 Cited Bonwick, p.70.
40 Ryan, pp.122, 174. Reynolds, p.3.
41 *BPP*, vol.6, Nov. 1830.
42 Robinson, *BPP*, vol.5, pp.10–11.
43 Select Committee, 1837, *BPP*, pp.123–24.
44 Ellis, p.28; H. Reynolds, 'Did George Augustus Robinson Negotiate a Treaty with Tasmanian Aborigines?', AHA History 90 Conference, 1990.
45 Ellis, p.32.
46 See map, Ellis, p.40.
47 Robinson, pp.472–74.
48 Ellis, pp.48–49.
49 Lyndall Ryan to author, 21 July 1993, letter in author's possession.
50 Ryan, p.218.
51 See Bonwick, pp.386–87; D. Reeman, 'Adaptation and Survival: The Culture and Identity of Tasmanian Aboriginal People in the twentieth century', unpublished BA (Hons) thesis, 1992, UNSW, pp.26–28.
52 See B. Plomley and K. A. Henley, *The Sealers of Bass Strait and the Cape Barren Island Community*, Blubber Head Press, Hobart, 1990, p.29.
53 Ryan, chapter 16.
54 Ryan, pp.235–37; Montgomery Papers, cited in Ryan, p.236.
55 D. Reeman, Adaption and survival: Tasmanian Aboriginal people in the twentieth century, unpub. honours thesis, UNSW, 1992, p.45.
56 *Examiner*, 19 Sept. 1936 and B. Mollison and C. Everitt, *A*

Chronology of Events Affecting Tasmanian Aboriginal People, Hobart, 1976, p.212, cited in Reeman.
57 M. Mansell, 'A Short history' in *Racism in Tasmania*, p.4.
58 Reeman, p.50; A.W. Burbury, *Report on the condition of half-castes at cape Barren Island Reservation*, 16 Sept. 1929, TSA, CSD 22/336/104/37. See also H. Reynolds, *The Law of the Land*, Penguin, Ringwood, 1987, pp.139–41.
59 Ryan, p.249.
60 Cited Reeman, p.16.
61 Reeman, p.105. See Graeme Hugo, *Atlas of the Australian people: Tasmania*, 1986 census, Canberra, 1989, p.23. See also J.H. Wootten, *RCIADIC: The Report of Inquiry in NSW, Victoria and Tasmania*, AGPS, Canberra, 1991.
62 Tasmanian Aboriginal Centre, *Land Rights in Tasmania*, March 1982, p.2.
63 I. West, *Pride against Prejudice*, AIAS Canberra, 1984, p.86; Reeman, p.57.
64 Many Aborigines agreed to work for pitiful wages as Europeans took over the muttonbird industry; they also wrought serious ecological damage.
65 West, p.62.
66 West, p.62, passim.
67 See *Commonwealth vs Tasmania*;(1983) *Australian Law Reports*, 46, pp.629, 677–78, 737–38.
68 Reeman, p.62.
69 B. Smith, *The Spectre of Truganini*, ABC Sydney, 1980, p.10.
70 West.
71 Reeman, p.96.
72 H. Sculthorpe, 'Tasmanian Aborigines: A Perspective for the 1980s', Tasmanian Aboriginal Centre Research Study, 1980, p.103–104.
73 Clyde Mansell in *Racism in Tasmania*, University of Melbourne Students Union, Carlton, 1978.
74 Wootten, pp.280, 310.
75 J. Everett and K. Brown, *The Spirit of Kuti Kina*, Eumarrah, Hobart, 1988, p.17. See also *Tasmanian Aborigines in Their Own Write*, Tasmanian Aboriginal Centre, Hobart, 1989.
76 Wootten, pp.310, 312.
77 West, p.87.

9
Tasmania 2: 'You cannot deny me and mine any longer'

A MESSAGE:

> Pallawah[1] identity cannot be denied any longer. Such attempts will not be tolerated. The Pallawah community has taken control of that right. No longer will questioning of Pallawah identity be permitted. For it is not up to non-Aborigines, be they parliamentary ministers, bureaucrats, public servants, media personnel, teachers or the average person in the street, to determine the terms under which me and mine exist and grow. You cannot take our identity from us whiteman because you didn't give it. Our mothers and fathers of 2000 generations gave us this, and we will carry it with pride and determination, regardless of the persecution and prejudice heaped upon us because we dare to identify as we choose rather than how you dictate. We have a responsibility to our mothers and fathers of the past as well as to our generations of the future to continue the struggle for our freedom and we will. You cannot change who we are by mere rhetoric for our heritage is stronger and older than your words, written or spoken.

Since invasion Tasmania has sought to rid itself of the 'Aboriginal problem'. The first and most obvious means were via the atrocities of rape, massacre, dispossession and persecution. This was the first attempt at genocide against the Pallawah. These events have previously been well documented by historians and will not be dealt with in detail here. Then there was the establishment and perpetuation of the belief that the Pallawah had passively submitted their lands to the invaders. There was also the myth that when Truganini died, a race had been entirely exterminated. The instigation of the policy of assimilation was the second attempt at committing genocide.

The most prolonged attempt at ridding Tasmania of the Pallawah has been to challenge our very existence through a denial of identity. This is the latest attempt at genocide. Many non-Aborigines hope it will prove to be the final solution. But be warned, the Pallawah community will no longer tolerate the continued injustice of past government policies and historical inaccuracies. Pallawahs now demand that our cultural and racial history be recognised as being an unbroken, continual survival. The Pallawah community from now on will set the agenda for our future and rewrite history from an Aboriginal perspective.

The ancestors of today's Pallawahs fought with tenacity and guile in an attempt to keep their lands. The perception that the Pallawah meekly submitted to the British invaders is based upon historical writings, which were in the majority authored by the invaders themselves. Such writings gave birth to racism that became embedded in language and is perpetuated through the spoken word. It eventually became institutionalised.

The writings of early colonial Tasmanian history were biased and racist, with good reason. The written message was an instrument used to sustain racial propaganda, in order to ensure the continued perception of British superiority and the rightness of the illegal invasion. But more than that, it developed a negative view of Pallawahs which was (and still is) maintained through language use. Such propaganda motivated people to go forth to new colonies and 'settle' them.

Men perpetuating atrocities and taking illegal possession of land, by definition do not say or write positives about the people towards whom they are inflicting torture and death with the intention of committing genocide.[2] Such an action asserts that the victim is scarcely more deserving of better treatment, and perpetuates the notion that they bring about this action themselves by their savagery, brutality and lack of intellectual capacity. Ethnocentrism and justification of actions, through religion and science, provide the basis for the development of stereotypical perceptions.

Thus ideas, such as the Pallawah meekly submitting to the British invaders, are perceived and then continually perpetuated through language.

In this way Aboriginal defence of land, women and children was/is viewed as treachery and bloodthirsty ferocity.[3] Concepts such as this take away the nobility and justification for the struggle. Instead they allow the struggle to be viewed as an action with no direction or consequence except to kill for the sake of killing and to accommodate cannibalism, as was mistakenly reported to be the case with the Pallawah.[4] Broome supports the concept that British perceptions of black being evil, primitive and savage were rife during this violent period of Australian history.[5] Such notions were instilled and continually reiterated by colonial authorities to invoke the desire to colonise, possess and dominate.

The notion of meek submission by the Pallawah persists today despite the current writings of such notable historians as Reynolds, Pybus, Ryan and Broome, and the efforts of contemporary Pallawah society to dispel such fallacious ideas. The reason for this is that racism is embedded in the sociology of Australian society and is continually perpetuated through the spoken and written word. Racism has become an integral part of Australian identity through the good old Aussie joke, the education system which until recently continued to teach the lie of *terra nullius*, the White Australia Policy, the nepotism which became entrenched in the white male societal system, the media, and the government, specifically within the bureaucracy. It is interesting to note that within all of those systems the white male dominated and held the power, as they did in the period of colonisation.

The most damaging word in relation to this issue is 'settlement'. Settlement brings forth connotations of peace and negotiation, taking away the brutality of invasion and the bravery of the Pallawah resistance. Pallawah resistance to invasion and oppression was diverse and adapted over time according to circumstances. Initially the invaders were welcomed and attempts were made to accommodate them into the Pallawah kinship structure. This was done with the expectation of the reciprocation of rights and fulfilment of obligations on the part of the British invaders. These were expected in exchange for the concessions made by the Pallawah, such as allowing the British access to land.

An example of the attempt to accommodate the invaders, and consequently tie them into the traditional laws of the Pallawah pertaining to kinship and reciprocal obligations, was the giving of women. Broome states that the Aborigines quickly recognised the need for women by the invaders and offered them, with the expectation of 'establishing kinship and reciprocal ties in a traditional way'.[6]

Tying the British into traditional reciprocal obligations and kinship concepts was an attempt by the Pallawah to accommodate the invaders in Pallawah territory and consequently to ensure that the land, so sacred, would still be available to them. This action would also protect the women and children because they would still be within Pallawah society and have all the protection which that implied. If this plan had worked it would have given the Pallawah control over the lives of the invaders in such a way that they would, by necessity, be required to obey the tribal, social and spiritual laws of the group. If they chose not to obey, the Europeans would have been subjected to the same rigorous laws as the Pallawah themselves.

Accommodation, as a means of defence and offence, was attempted in many different forms, however the British did not see that it was necessary to reciprocate, especially in terms of land-use and the taking of the women and children. To the British, their right to land was divine. It had after all, been theologically and scientifically determined and justified.[7]

Pallawah resistance began in 1804 in response to the atrocities committed against them. Robinson and York suggest that the Pallawah were extremely talented, skilful and tactical fighters, provoking fear in the psyche of the invaders.[8] The Pallawah developed techniques to undermine the superior fire power of the British and quickly adapted to European weaponry by obtaining guns.

The ability to adapt to extremely diverse and threatening conditions is a measure of the bravery and intelligence of the Pallawah. Adaptation of fighting techniques was common. Through careful observation the invaders were seen by the

Pallawah to be at their most vulnerable after having emptied their guns of ammunition. It was at this stage that the Pallawah chose to attack, often wreaking havoc amongst the enemy.[9] The European need for women was also used as a means of setting up an ambush. The women acted as decoys to lead the European men into situations where the advantage was with the Pallawah. Other tactics were spearing of sheep and cattle, and the feigning of attacks at significant places to draw the enemy away from the real target.[10] These examples show the Pallawah's ability to gain an advantage against a more powerful force. The indication is that they quickly adapted to the lifestyles, needs and technology of the invaders in order to use that knowledge to the best advantage in the defence of land and kin.

Racist language, both written and spoken has, throughout history, been used in an endeavour to suppress knowledge of the bravery of the Pallawah resistance. This effectively denied recognition of the Pallawah ability to adapt to the prevailing circumstances and turn negatives into advantages. Reynolds demonstrates this when he quotes a 'settler' who wrote that, 'their whole art of war . . . consist[ed] of a concealed silent and treacherous attack'.[11] *The Cooktown Independent*, a widely read newspaper of the day, takes the same attitude, 'there was not a particle of manhood or even brute bravery about the aboriginal, his weapons being treachery patently nursed'.[12] Words such as these undermine the tenacity and strength of the Pallawah warriors and their style of warfare, much of which required quick and effective adaptation to previously unknown situations.

As earlier stated, the perception of meek submission was developed and sustained through the use of the English language. It was used in the rationalisation of the invasion, attempted genocide, destruction of cultural and ceremonial practices, and the dispossession of land. Language set the scene to portray the British invaders as the active agents of history and the Pallawah as the passive victims. The concept of settlement provided the vehicle with which to achieve the goal, whilst this strange interpretation of history loudly voiced the opinion that the Pallawah way of fighting was cowardly and treacherous. Language was used to embed racial attitudes in the mind of society and for white society to continually renew and justify its actions. The finality of such terms as extermination and genocide negate the adaptiveness, versatility and resourcefulness of the Pallawah.

The other forum used to attack Pallawah identity was the political structure which has initiated propaganda in order to develop racist social attitudes. Government policy has persistently, throughout Australian history, socialised the majority of the population to question Pallawah identity. As a consequence, the Pallawah community has become entwined in a battle for their own identity, and, indeed their very existence.

The current Federal Government's definition of Aboriginal identity has very strict and clearly stated criteria, which was developed and based on the values and ideals of the dominant society. Under that definition a person who identifies as an Aborigine must:

- be a descendant of the original Australians;
- identify as an Aborigine; and
- be accepted as such by the community in which s/he lives.[13]

This requirement of identifying gives the power to determine who is and who isn't an Aborigine to the dominant class, the descendants of the invaders of this country. But this European value-laden attitude also places the responsibility of daring to identify squarely on the shoulders of the Aboriginal communities. The Aboriginal people must deal with the social and political implications of a situation which renders them economically powerless, unless they comply with the rules of the dominant society. Aboriginal organisations are constantly held to ransom through the threat or the actuality of withdrawing government funds unless they take this ideology on board. In the past and now Aborigines have been dependent on the whims of the powerful white society in regard to their identity and place in Australian society.

Errol West, a well-known Pallawah, says that this definition was specifically developed in order to retain the essence of the segregation and assimilation policies. He states that, 'Each of these policies has an ideal, and as an active intention, the elimination of the Aboriginal people as a distinct group. The constant debate on the legitimacy of an individual's claim to Aboriginality, and subsequent power to accept or deny such a claim by white bureaucrats, confirms that view.'[14]

Aborigines have had their identity shaped by European power brokers since invasion. Power is a process of control. As a direct result of this control, the invaders not only determined but dictated Aboriginal identity. Attwood says that, 'the basis of the coloniser's power lay . . . in the possession . . . and . . . expropriation of land as an economic and cultural resource'.[15] This proved to be an ideal means of protecting the interests of the invaders at the expense of the indigenous people. The continued denial of the existence of the Pallawah, as a distinct race, was intended to prevent any claims for sovereignty, land, compensation, and economic independence. Pallawah society was totally dispossessed of its country.

During the invasion and up to the mid–late 1800s Aboriginality was defined by the dominant powers as being culturally based. It was at that time politically expedient to extinguish the racial identity, which they did by a mere flourish of a pen in legislation.[16] This appears to have been a deliberate political strategy employed to cut ties to land by making Aborigines British subjects. Overnight the indigenes were expected to forget all that tied them to their past—all that made them whole, spiritually and physically. In their attempt to sever Pallawah religious and spiritual ties to their country and sacred places the Europeans effectively denied Pallawah sovereignty. A further consequence of that was the severance of economic links to the land. Once these ties were destroyed the way was made clear for the British, and subsequent descendants or migrants, to claim the land without conscience. For, if there was proved to be no distinct race who could lay claim to the land, it became a matter of course that the British Crown owned Tasmania.

The process of dispossession, along with the implementation of segregation, made the Pallawah dependent on European society. The total disempowerment of today's Pallawah is the result. The traditional economy became almost non-existent and the Pallawah were forced to approach the British invaders for permission to use any land. This eventually meant a life of forced settlement on Cape Barren Island for the majority of the Pallawah population—in isolation on a reserve. It was a matter of out of sight, out of mind. For the remainder it meant living on Flinders Island, where racism was rife, or living in suburban Tasmania, and in many cases denying their identity in order to survive.

Adaptation to European economic values became necessary. The Pallawah communities on Flinders and Cape Barren islands did adapt economically and survived. However, the concept of racial identity continued to be submerged by representatives of the government. The stereotypes of 'half-caste', 'quarter-caste' and 'part-Aboriginal' began to be internalised by the communities. The government of the day had apparently rid European society of the 'Aboriginal problem', at least racially. This is demonstrated by a Pallawah from Cape Barren Island who, when interviewed for the film *The Last Tasmanian*, said that there were 'no full-bloods' left in Tasmania, in fact there probably weren't even any 'half-castes'. On the other hand, the Pallawah communities were, whether deliberately or not, employing strategies which would ensure that their uniqueness would be retained. They were developing a very strong cultural identity, and began calling themselves Islanders. The Pallawah people were being socialised into accepting the dominant society's definition of Aboriginality.

The Pallawah Islanders became intent on focusing on the 'white blood' which ran in their veins. They clung to their unique traditional cultural practices while integrating European values and practices. They were told that white was good and black was bad and internalised that idea.[17] Attwood says that the Aborigines demonstrated a 'willingness to adopt some of the mores of colonial bourgeois society and in doing so apparently began to gain a different sense of identity'.[18] An argument against that, however, is that the Pallawah were forced to accept European values in order to ensure the survival of their race. Thus they were involved in a process of strengthening their existing identity. What other options were available when they were incarcerated and policed to the extent that they were? This does not demonstrate a society weakened but one strong enough to recognise that in some matters you adjust and use what you can to your advantage.

There is no doubt that during this time the Pallawah were influenced by European social and racial doctrines. Darwin's theories in *On the Origin of Species* were influencing not only the way Europeans saw Aborigines but also the way Aborigines saw themselves.[19] During this period it became socially important to be able to say that you had more white blood than the next person. Auntie Ida West relates a story in the film *Black Man's Houses* of how the community used powder on their skins in order to look whiter.[20] White says that Darwin's theories gave the British justification for the oppression practiced.[21] Perhaps the British viewed Darwin's theories as being totally acceptable, probably as justification for their attempted genocide of the Pallawah peoples.

The negative racial identity of the Aboriginal people, espoused during this period was acceptable to European society. As long as people were not identified, or identifying, racially as Pallawah there could be no claim to the land stolen during the period of dispossession. It was essential politically, socially and economically to maintain the policies which would determine the identity of the Islanders who had descended from the original Pallawah. The Europeans defined an identity for the Aborigines which was 'heavily contingent upon their own approval'.[22]

This policy of segregation was developed to control a group of people on the basis of their racial origin or heritage. Discussions became focussed on the racial bloodlines of the group. Many Pallawah today see that the aim of this policy was to divide the larger groups into smaller ones, each with their own identity based on the amount of 'white blood' they had—the white blood component being the positive force whilst the Pallawah blood was to be viewed as negative and considered little more than 'animal'. (That was dependent upon the notion that such a difference is measurable.) In this way the very 'humanness' of the individual was questioned and determined. Errol West views this, in what he terms blood quantum ascription, as the 'basis of the labelling of Aborigines as "half-castes" or "quarter-castes" etc'.[23] While the authorities thought or hoped that this attitude would divide and conquer, it actually gave the message to the Pallawah that no matter how much 'Aboriginal blood' individuals had, everyone was equally Aboriginal.

The policy of segregation in Tasmania was developed to separate people of Pallawah descent from members of European society and to give legal status to the removal of Pallawah children from families. The intention was that once the children became adults, they would integrate into European society by taking on the white Australian work ethic and marrying whites, preferably from the lower classes, and so eventually breed out the Aboriginal race.[24] West voiced the opinion that the stealing of the children for 'enculturation into the white civilised worlds of the British and the Christians was a major aim' of the Segregation Policy.[25]

This policy was achieved in Tasmania by making Cape Barren Island a reserve in order to isolate the Pallawah from European society. Pallawah incarcerated on the reserve were controlled by European laws and values. Those Pallawah not resident in the Cape Barren Island Reserve were also controlled but in a less regimented and authoritarian manner. They were, nevertheless, required to gain permission to visit family on the reserve and had to be off the reserve by sundown. These restrictions had devastating effects on the families of the reserves inmates. Morton Green was one such person who was directly affected by the controls put into place to keep inmates of the reserve separate from the Pallawah on the outside. Morton Green, who is my father, was required to gain permission to visit my mother, who was a reserve inmate, in order to court her. Dad had to leave the reserve by sundown and return to Flinders Island.[26]

Some of the Pallawah residents of the reserve eventually internalised the concept of who they were that had been imposed on them by the dominant European culture. But at the same time, a political awareness was beginning to develop; the struggle was intensified to have Cape Barren Island declared as Pallawah land and to claim the muttonbird islands as a cultural and economic base. This struggle was seen by some Pallawah Islanders as central to their racial and cultural identity, and economic independence.

During the period between the late 1800s and the early 1900s it became even more important to retain a strong, distinctly

My maternal grandparents, Arthur and Alma West, taken soon after their marriage during the segregation period. VICKI MATSON-GREEN

Pallawah cultural heritage. This chapter of Pallawah history witnessed the development of a real sense of pride in themselves. This is evident in old photographs of the period where people were 'nicely attired'. The oral traditions often told of the cleanliness of the people with the words, 'She was so clean you could eat off her floor'. Ties to the land were being reinstated, as was a recognition of their own uniqueness as a distinct race. Unfortunately, this period also witnessed the development of conflict within the community. Some of the community still clung to the concept that having more 'white blood' made them better socially, while another group began to take pride in their Pallawah history, and racial and cultural identity.[27]

At all times since the invasion the Pallawah Islanders kept intact many cultural aspects of their ancestral heritage, despite strong opposition by white authorities. Kinship was central to their society and with that came obligations to others. Despite conflict which may have been lying under the surface, the Islanders kept in place those cultural practices which helped develop and maintain their unique identity.

My father, Morton Clare Green, and Bernard Maynard on Cape Barren Island in the late 1920s.
VICKI MATSON-GREEN

During the 1950s the Assimilation Policy was developed and put into place. This policy was an attempt to fragment the Aboriginal community. According to Errol West, 'the major thrust was to whiten completely the habits and philosophies, (such as the "pagan" beliefs of Aborigines) and to Christianise them, only not "save" them but destroy Aboriginal culture at the same time'.[28] The policy of removing children, which will be discussed in more detail later, was maintained.

In the opinion of contemporary Pallawah society, the political agenda in the 1950s was to weaken and obliterate the Pallawah community into non-existence. The Pallawah Islander community was growing stronger. They became politically aware and began to demand rights based on their racial heritage and their total dispossession which took place on invasion. The fightback had begun. They began to recognise the need to become economically independent in order to dictate and control their futures. Murray-Smith says that the Aboriginal Islander community sent,

> petitions and letters . . . [to] the Land Department . . . protesting at the distruction of mutton bird rookeries, appealing against eviction orders, asking for the reservation of rookeries for half-caste use, drawing attention to illicit robbing of graves and

even petitioning the governor to reserve Flinders Island for the Islanders.[29]

The government's agenda of assimilation was to break down this new-found strength. Before and during this period the Cape Barren Islanders were economically isolated.[30] As Aborigines they were not entitled to any Social Security benefits, and the government refused to spend any money on the Island to create employment. This was based on the convenient myth that there were no Tasmanian Aborigines.

The government's belief in this myth is intriguing given that Cape Barren Island was an Aboriginal reserve, established and maintained in that context by an Act of law, and simultaneously, the Tasmanian Government was applying for and receiving grants for Aboriginal programmes for having established an Aboriginal reserve. (This information has been told by the Elders many times within the Pallawah community however I do not know what grants were being referred to, with the exception of the Remedial Reading Programme. Under this programme funding was available for Aboriginal children at the school on Flinders Island, however when our community became aware of it we found out that the funds had been used instead to provide non-Aboriginal children with remedial assistance.)[31]

The government used the following strategy to justify taking our children. They would enter a house, look through the cupboards, find no food and take the children. The point to consider is, with no employment, no benefits and social isolation because Cape Barren Island was still a reserve, what were people supposed to do? They survived very well on their traditional tucker but this was not acceptable to the authorities.

The population on Cape Barren Island had put in place initiatives to create some economic base for their community. The men had become proficient boat builders, seamen and fishermen.[32] They also began tin mining on the island. Their produce was often taken by ship to Launceston for sale. But despite these highly commendable initiatives the authorities refused to recognise the Islanders' right to keep their children. In one family alone (that is in European terms aunt's and uncle's children) fifteen children were removed and placed with white foster parents. The authorities did not consider any member of the Aboriginal community to be an appropriate foster carer, for which our kinship structures are clearly designed to cope. Often these children ended up being little more than slaves but the official explanation was that the children deserved a better chance at life.

The repercussions of such government actions are still being felt by our community today. In the past four years, eight of those children, now adults, have found some of their brothers and sisters, three in the last year. They are currently suffering a terrible trauma: trying to find out who they are, and when they do, trying to fit into a family on terms which will suit all parties concerned. Other children are being told that they are Aboriginal and were fostered out but cannot make contact with their families for whatever reason.

The other intention of the Assimilation Policy was to forcibly remove families from Cape Barren Island to integrate them into urban white society. Many families, including my own, were promised employment and housing in Launceston and Hobart if they left the islands.[33] The *Cape Barren Island Reserve Act* was revoked in 1951 in order to encourage people to move to the major European areas of settlement.[34] The aim was to break up the community; through fragmentation the resolve to fight would be weakened. With integration the government hoped that a gradual breeding out of the Pallawah race would occur. But the bureaucrats responsible for policy development again underestimated the Pallawah strength and determination to maintain their identity.

Despite being uprooted in a major way yet again during the 1950s and early 1960s, the people removed from the islands in order to assimilate, congregated in areas such as Ravenswood and Invermay and maintained the kinship structures as well as the unique cultural activities. Thus a new Pallawah community emerged. Families travelled en masse to the islands each muttonbird season to continue important cultural traditions and to secure a meagre economic subsistence. This also allowed oral histories to be passed on, kinship obligations to be fulfilled and ties to place reinstated. The Assimilation Policy didn't work. The

Granny Mary Maynard and Uncle Vern Maynard holding his daughter (identity of third person not known) at 1 Bedford Street, Invermay in Launceston, Tasmania. Many of the ex-Reserve inmates gathered in Invermay during the assimilation period. Granny Mary was my paternal great grandmother. VICKI MATSON-GREEN

Pallawah community didn't want to assimilate and the majority of the white population didn't want to include these people in their community. And so the Pallawah community became established on the island of Tasmania once again.

According to J. Everett,[35] it was the period of assimilation which highlighted the conflict regarding Aboriginal identity within the Pallawah community. Recognition, by the Pallawah community, of the conflict did not occur until the 1970s after the Assimilation Policy had dispersed most of the Pallawah Cape Barren and Flinders Islanders, and during the growth of the Aboriginal struggle for identity, social justice and land rights.

Assimilation, for the first time, brought the Islander families into contact with other Pallawah families who did not have a historical association with the Furneaux Group of islands. The blending of different Pallawah groups led to internal conflict. As far as can be ascertained the question of who is or isn't Pallawah in the contemporary Pallawah community began when the old established Islander families were confronted by the descendants

Waiting for the boat to go mutton birding on Babel Island. Standing at the rear of the group is my father, Morton Green, and standing on the right hand side is my sister Ruby. In the background are the tin shacks the Aboriginal people lived in on the foreshore at Lady Barron on Flinders Island. VICKI MATSON-GREEN

of Fanny Cochrane-Smith in Hobart and Dolly Dalrymple's descendants on the north-west coast. In the words of June Sculthorpe, a descendant of Fanny Cochrane-Smith, at a community discussion on identity (at the Tasmanian Aboriginal Centre on 6 June 1993), 'It wasn't more than five years ago when anyone living south of Launceston wasn't considered Aboriginal by the Bass Strait Aboriginal community.'

This exemplifies the seriousness of the situation. Another case involves an Elder who, when questioned about her identity, and asked to provide evidence to a government department, said that she felt like a vacuum inside. She commented 'I now know how our old people felt when they were taken to Wybalenna and stripped of their identity, last century.' In the words of Errol

West, 'The more things seems to change, the more they stay the same.'[36]

Since the death of Truganini, the Islanders had considered themselves the only Tasmanian Aboriginal descendants, and generations were constantly told in their oral histories that they were unique and the last of a proud race of people. To be suddenly confronted by two other large community groups who also considered themselves Aboriginal, created an air of tension which started their questions regarding proof of Aboriginality.

Two historical events added to the burden for those who wanted to establish their identity through their family trees but couldn't because of a lack of available records. The first was the publishing of what has commonly come to be known in the Pallawah communities as the 'Stud Books', Bill Mollison and Coral Everitt's *Tasmanian Aboriginal Genealogies* compiled in 1978. It has created much anger and hurt within the Pallawah community. First, many untruths were printed, causing conflict, pain and harm to many individuals. People who are genuine descendants of Pallawah are questioned about their rights to claim their identity. Government departments and members of the general community use this work to deny the identity of some of those who claim Aboriginality. The worst aspect of Mollison and Everitt's work is that it is assumed to be a comprehensive and detailed documentation of all the descendants of the ancient Pallawah, through to the time that it was written. This is not correct.

Governments have almost required the general populace to question Aboriginality but more insidious than that, Aborigines have also been socialised to question the identity of his or her contemporary. In Tasmania in particular, the focus is directed towards this question because of the myth that Truganini was the last Tasmanian Aborigine and the race was extinct.

The second event which has created conflict is a paper recently found in the government archival records indicating that there were far more Pallawah in the state, than was always thought since the time of Truganini's death. Felton mentions Mary Patches, an Aboriginal woman who lived in Launceston in the early 1890s:

> During the last part of the nineteenth century there were many Aboriginal people living in places such as Launceston, Hobart, Tasman Peninsula and the North-West Coast. However, it is very difficult to find out much about these people. Often there were no written records . . . Many of these people were not accepted by the white people, were discriminated against when they tried to get jobs and so were usually very poor.[37]

It must be remembered that this was happening at the time that the government was acknowledging Aboriginal Islanders as the only 'part-Aboriginal' people in Tasmania. At no stage was this other group acknowledged. It appears that now some of the descendants of these people are beginning to surface and demand the right to identify as Pallawah. Other members of the Pallawah community are not accepting them, partly because they believe the information they have been fed, and because they are unable to prove their Aboriginality through a family tree. This is obviously because no records were kept of their ancestors, therefore how can they prove their connection.

The political and social renaissance of Aborigines during the 1960s, gave Aboriginal people some social restitution. Suddenly, various government grants and programmes became available to people because of their Aboriginal heritage. For many Pallawah families this meant at least food on the table. In Tasmania it also meant that for the first time our community was recognised as Aboriginal by law under the Federal Government policy regarding Aboriginal identity. Many people became fiercely protective of their identity and the programmes which offered some financial assistance.

The media must take some responsibility for the false perception which emerged—that Aborigines could get money for almost anything as long as they were identified as Aborigines and were accepted as such by the Aboriginal community. The other fallacious point is that Aborigines were perceived by the media as being privileged and receiving more social welfare dollars than other disadvantaged groups. These fabrications created conflict within and outside the Aboriginal community. Many Pallawah today, if asked why it is important to them that people supply a family tree to prove Aboriginality, will respond with 'To stop whites from getting Aboriginal money'. This was a response from a 19-year-old student attending the Bridging Course at Riawunna, the Centre for Aboriginal Education at the University of Tasmania, when asked that very question recently in class. The fact is that programmes funded for Aborigines are also funded for non-Aborigines but under a different name. Aborigines, as individuals, do not receive benefits, in some form or other, which other Australians are not eligible for. However, there are several instances where whites have been eligible for benefits, including land, which Aborigines were not considered appropriate to receive, even in recent times. An example of this was in the 1960s when the Tasmanian Government began the Soldier Settlement Development Programme on Flinders Island where returned soldiers were given large parcels of land to develop. The grants which enabled this to happen were based on a very low interest rate. Uncle Ken Everett, a Pallawah Elder, applied for one of the farms as he was a returned soldier. He was refused on the grounds that he was Aboriginal and not fit to own land.[38] Instead, the Tasmanian Government imported returned soldiers from New South Wales.

It is time that the Aboriginal community in Tasmania, and the rest of Australia, took their destiny into their own hands and demanded the right to determine their own identity.

Unfortunately many Tasmanians cling to the myth that Truganini was the last Tasmanian Aborigine in order to deny the indigenous people of Tasmania the right to identify as such. The saddest aspect of this process is that the various governments have manipulated the thinking of the Pallawah in relation to identity. Pallawah people have been taught to question their own contemporaries. The interesting point here is that Aboriginal identity, as dictated by government policy, is based on economics and has been since invasion. That will not change until Aborigines all over Australia, and particularly in Tasmania, gain land rights, sovereignty, and become economically independent. It is only then that Aborigines will be free to determine their own identity and say, without fear, **I am an Aborigine and I'm proud of it**, without the expectation of retribution or question from non-Aborigines.

NOTES

1. Pallawah is the spiritual name adopted by some Aborigines in Tasmania. Pallawah was the name of the first black man in the Spiritual Creations. The word 'Aboriginal' is an English term used to describe all 'indigenous peoples' throughout the world, taking away the unique identity of the people whose ancestors originated in this land known as Tasmania. The author of this chapter is a Pallawah and as such this term will be used to replace the words Tasmanian Aborigine/Aboriginal.
2. R. Evans, ' "A King of Brutes": Stereotyping the Vanquished', in R. Evans, K. Saunders, and K. Cronin, *Exclusion, Exploitation and Extermination: Race Relations in Colonial Queensland*, 1975, pp.67–84 in SACAE Aboriginal Culture and History.
3. H. Reynolds, *Frontier*, Allen & Unwin, Sydney, 1987, p.42.
4. ibid, p.109.
5. R. Broome, *Aboriginal Australians*, Allen & Unwin, Sydney, 1982, p.25.
6. ibid, p.55.
7. B. Smith, *The Spectre of Truganini: ABC Boyer Lecture, 1980*, in Hollingsworth, SACAE Aboriginal Culture and History Readings, part 2, 1980, pp.23–4.
8. F. Robinson and B. York, *The Black Resistance*, Widescope, Victoria, 1977, pp.23–24.
9. ibid, p.24.
10. ibid, p.24.
11. H.Reynolds, *Frontier*, p.43.
12. ibid, p.43.
13. D. William and B. Chambers, *An Evaluation of the Aboriginal Study Grants Scheme*, Canberra, AGPS, 1986, p.31.
14. Errol West, Aboriginal identity: the question or the answer, Masters thesis, Faculty of Education and the Arts, University of Tasmania, Launceston, 1989, p.1.
15. B. Attwood, *The Making of the Aborigines*, Allen & Unwin, Sydney, 1989, p.x.
16. ibid, pp.84–86.
17. Auntie Ida West, Pallawah Elder, Flinders Island, Tasmania, 1992.
18. B. Attwood, p.32.
19. R. White, *Inventing Australia*, Allen & Unwin, Sydney, 1981, p.69.
20. Auntie Ida West in S. Thomas, (Director) *Black Man's Houses*, Open Channel, Victoria, 1992.
21. White, p.69.

22 Attwood, p.57.
23 West, p.1.
24 B. Cummings, *Take this Child: From Kahlin Compound to the Retta Dixon Children's Home*, Aboriginal Studies Press, Canberra, 1990, p.11.
25 E. West, p.1.
26 M. Green (dec), Flinders Island, Family oral histories. All oral histories or personal remarks from individuals are as related to the author unless otherwise stated.
27 S. Murray-Smith, 'Beyond The Pale: The Aboriginal Community of Bass Strait in the Nineteenth Century', in *Papers and Proceedings*, vol.20, no.1, Tasmanian Historical Research Association, Dec. 1973.
28 West, p.1.
29 Murray-Smith, p.184.
30 ibid, pp.169–92.
31 P. Cameron, Family Oral histories, Launceston, Tasmania, 1993.
32 Murray-Smith, pp.169–92.
33 M. Green (dec), Family oral histories, Flinders Island.
34 L. Ryan, *The Aboriginal Tasmanians*, University of Queensland Press, St Lucia, 1981, pp.247–59.
35 J. Everett, *Observance of information*, University of Tasmania, April 23, 1992.
36 West, p.47.
37 H. Felton, *Living with the Land: Aborigines in Tasmania, Community and Change*, Book 6, Department of Education and the Arts, Tasmania, 1991, p.21.
38 Ken Everett, Pallawah oral histories, Flinders Island.

10

Contested ground: what is 'Aboriginal history'?

WHEN the then Prime Minister Bob Hawke launched the *Penguin Bicentennial History of Australia* on the grassy banks of Sydney Harbour in January 1988, a delegation of Aboriginal protesters ensured that it made quite a splash. An Aboriginal man hurled the book into the waters below and the television cameras rolled. The soggy copy was retrieved by a participant in the book launch and duly autographed. The Aboriginal spokespersons complained that this officially endorsed book did not tell their side of the story. Indeed, anticipating possible criticism, its non-Aboriginal author had stated that he did not attempt to present 'Aboriginal history' because he could not write on their behalf.[1]

On Australia Day, 26 January 1988, Aborigines from around the country, including the remotest parts of Australia, converged on Sydney's Hyde Park to celebrate their physical and cultural survival. Speakers Gary Foley and Galarrwuy Yunupingu ridiculed the relatively puny achievement of 200 years, pointing out that, having occupied the country for at least 40 000 years, Aborigines could be celebrating not their first but their 200th Bicentennary. It was an optimistic message, for Aborigines today suffer high rates of poverty, unemployment, alcoholism, imprisonment, disease, infant mortality, and premature death. That same January evening Aboriginal people gathered at La Perouse, named after the French expedition of 1788 and now home of a major urban Aboriginal community, to share sacred 'Dreaming stories', to

Aboriginal Protest on Australia Day, 1988. This protest was centred around Sydney Harbour, near where a re-enactment of the arrival of the First Fleet was to arrive and where Aborigines staged their own version of the landing. JOHN FAIRFAX PHOTO LIBRARY

Galarrwuy Yunupingu, Chairman of the Northern Land Council. NATIONAL LIBRARY OF AUSTRALIA

dance, sing and make music shaped by generations of people who lived in distant Australian landscapes.

These events highlight not only the vexed question of the place of Aborigines in Australian history generally but also the problem of modes of transmission and authorial voice. Questions of power relations, of colonialism, nationalism and the political functions of such historiography are also central to the debate. Indeed, the very term 'Aboriginal history' is problematic. Amongst academic historians, and now the general public, it has come to signify historical writing where the predominant subject matter concerns Aboriginal people. Aborigines, however, argue that the only true 'Aboriginal history' must be written by Aborigines. Some non-Aboriginal historians concur, defining themselves as historians of Aboriginal–white relations, claiming they have never attempted to write 'Aboriginal history'.[2] Others have decided to write only of textual representations—of the way non-Aborigines perceived or constructed the notion of Aborigines—and without actually writing about them as people.

The term also implies further questions: who are 'Aborigines?' A general category for indigenous people, 'Aborigine' was applied by Europeans to describe the indigenous people of Australia. The term 'Aborigine' is a historical construct, a product of time and of changing consciousness.[3] Prior to the arrival of Europeans, there was no unified indigenous consciousness nor use for a general term. Australian indigenous people now apply the term 'Aborigines' themselves, though, as shown in earlier chapters, those of the south-east prefer 'Kooris' or 'Murris', designations for their own people, as an Australia-wide category of identification. In pre-contact societies and in more traditional societies today, black Australians identify according to clan or band associations, sometimes dubbed 'tribal'. Regional diversity is indicated by the more than 500 languages spoken throughout the continent in 1788, and clan affiliation was flexible according to marriage, changing population and ecology.

Nonetheless, the term 'Aboriginal history' prevails in its wider usage as denoting history about Aborigines and by Aborigines—in print, art, voice and song. Its ambit is shifting and open to debate. In my opinion, the term usefully identifies a genre of writing, although it is a pluralistic one, without clear boundaries or prescribed authors. But then I am writing as a white female historian, trained in the academy in the liberal humanistic traditions of thought and knowledge. This chapter reflects this by the pre-eminence given to traditional academic 'historiography' over popular and Aboriginal traditions. I first look at the texts, the 'history books', which have been written almost exclusively by non-Aboriginal, mostly male, authors. Then I turn to Aboriginal history-making, and finally explore historiographical and political issues and debates about the discourse.

No consideration of the term 'Aboriginal history' could be complete without also questioning the meaning of the term 'history'. In the western cultural context, it is used for both academic and popular forms of historical representation, particularly written. As Lenore Coltheart argued, 'the moment of Aboriginal history' differs from the European version, for

> history is our familiar blend of the European ideas of time and knowledge and a 'natural' product of our system of thought. History is our second nature, the context of experience for our praxis, as for our contemplation; the source of explanation for us as political agents in public and in private.[4]

Men have made themselves the stars of the drama. Although subject to increasing challenge, 'history' encapsulated a linear notion of time, and the concept of unvarnished truth, or 'the triumph of logos over mythos'. 'Aboriginal history', originating in an oral tradition, thus forces us to reflect upon the cultural specificity of 'history' as understood by westerners.

But before focussing further on such problematic issues, a survey of the place of Aborigines in the earlier historiography will be provided. In the journals kept by the British men who arrived on the 'First Fleet' in 1788, (published in the 1780s and 90s) their meetings with Aborigines were described in fascinating ethnographic detail. Whilst these works were travellers' narratives rather than professional histories, they displayed a strong interest in the unique and exotic nature of the indigenous people of Australia, an interest shared by their reading public. Their physical appearance, rituals, adornments, economy, gender behaviour, morality, and interactions with the white men, were discussed alongside philosophical questions regarding the contemporary notion of the 'noble savage'. The journals of Lieutenant David Collins and Surgeon Watkin Tench were especially readable, and provided an important source for future writers, including historians.[5]

While Australian historiography in a formal sense was still in its infancy by the early nineteenth century, these efforts did not ignore Aborigines. J. Bonwick's *First Twenty Years in Australia* told the story of individual Aborigines such as Bennelong, who proved capable of 'civilisation'; 'failed' attempts at 'uplift' were also described. Bonwick wrote:

> The settlement of Australia was formed without any consideration of the claims of the natives, or scarcely a recognition of their existence. *They were too weak to present opposition, and too degraded to excite sympathy.* [my italics] The assumption of absolute jurisdiction over the new territory followed the occupation, just as if it had no previous inhabitants.[6]

G.W. Rusden's *History of Australia*, published 1883, discussed Aboriginal–white relations as part of its introductory chapter 'Natural Phenomena and the Australian tribes'. Rusden acknowledged the violence and rapid population decline, especially focussing on Tasmania. An apparent trend towards extinction in Tasmania confirmed the emergent ideology of Social Darwinism, proving the 'inevitable' consequences of colonisations. Rusden's was one of the last general histories to address frontier brutality and the moral issues of dispossession of the indigenous people. He tackled the issue of national guilt, arguing that 'by nearly half a century of contempt for justice', public opinion has been so debauched 'that Aboriginal rights were denied'. Rusden held the whole community responsible for the slaughter which continued in frontier regions as he wrote. More commonly, however, Australians were told they should not trouble themselves about the 'disappearance' of Aborigines. H. G. Turner's *History of the Colony of Victoria* concluded that its treatment of Aborigines should result in 'no serious stain' on the colony's reputation.[7] The earlier histories therefore used Aborigines to underline the strangeness or otherness of the new land and as a 'backdrop' for the coming of 'civilisation'. The hostility of indigenous peoples was emphasised to show the difficulties of conquest; frontier conflict was thus inescapably part of life as were ethical questions concerning land ownership.

By the turn of the nineteenth century, Aborigines were being increasingly expunged from published histories, and historians turned their attention to explaining away the 'convict stain' of white Australia's foundations. The trend was typified by Arthur Jose's bestselling *History of Australia from the earliest times to the present day* (1899), which opened with an image of Australia as waiting to be 'discovered' and 'colonised', then followed by a chapter entitled 'Filling in the Map', as though the land was a series of blank spaces waiting to be pencilled in by Europeans. In referring to Captain Cook's journey to Australia, Jose blames the 'blackfellows' for being unco-operative with the 'friendly' expedition. While Jose's section on New Zealand is a story of indigenous and coloniser clashing in warfare, his reference to Aborigines is to dismiss them as 'so small and scattered that their claims were rarely considered'.[8] Indeed, S.H. Robert's influential *History of Australian Land Settlement* (1924) started with British, not Aboriginal occupation. Reference to their presence, while minimal, sweeps them further into irrelevancy: 'Their grievances . . . were usually the result of their own ungovernable dispositions and their failure to see any sense in the white man's laws of property.' A. de Brune's *Fifty Years of Progress in Australia 1878–1929* (1929) proceeds as though the continent was empty. Overlooking the bloodshed of conquest on Australian soil, the story's climax comes with the Great War of 1914–18, from whose 'blood-stained battle-fields' a new nation supposedly emerged. Such studies of Australian history thus presented European men as actors—discovering, exploring, settling, fighting.

With the Federation of the Australian colonies as a nation in 1901, historians had a new agenda. Not surprisingly, they wanted to reflect contemporary goals and aspirations and bolster positive self-images. Twentieth century historians, including the labour 'radicals', were inevitably engaged in nation building and the construction of the unifying mythologies necessary to buttress it.

National immigration policies such as the 'White Australia Policy', designed to keep out Asian migrants, also served an ideological function in reinforcing the concept of an all-white nation. Despite its unusual acknowledgement of 'the Invasion of Australia', W.K. Hancock's *Australia* (1930) denied the Aboriginal presence by repeatedly referring to 'empty' and 'uninhabited' lands and 'virgin plains'. Whilst his assessment of the inevitability of Aboriginal destruction is tempered by criticism of those British who did their 'wrecker's work with the unnecessary brutality of stupid children', he simultaneously blamed humanitarians for being unable to agree on policy for the 'black man's preservation'. While rather naive to assume that any one policy was a cure for the havoc wrought by colonialism, Hancock more convincingly argued that Australians were unwilling to commit the necessary 'hard thought and hard cash. Australian democracy is genuinely benevolent but is preoccupied with its own affairs. From time to time it remembers the primitive people whom it has dispossessed, and sheds over their predestined passing an economical tear.'[9]

Until the 1970s, most general histories of Australia forgot to shed even the token tear. Despite its comprehensive mission, Gordon Greenwood's influential *Australia: A Social and Political History* (1955) only mentioned Aborigines in passing. Manning Clark's *Short History of Australia* (1964) stressed the offerings of British civilisation, and after chapter one Aborigines faded from the story. Building on an evolving mythology, Douglas Pike's *Australia: the Quiet Continent* (1966) depicted Australia as 'a lonely land', 'the remote continent', and contended that nothing dramatic or bloody ever occurred on Australian soil. A.G.L. Shaw's *The Story of Australia* (1967) spoke in negatives; Aborigines could offer 'no serious resistance' due to their 'primitive culture'; they 'knew nothing of agriculture', had 'no permanent settlements', had 'no domestic animal but the dog'. Humphrey McQueen's *A New Britannia* (1970)[10] represented a critical turning point, for although he did not provide a detailed discussion on Aborigines on the grounds that too little had been written about them, he recognised racism as central to Australian history.

In 1968, it was the anthropologist W.E.H. Stanner who, in the prestigious Boyer Lectures, challenged 'The Great Australian

Silence'—on the story of Aborigines. His survey of historical writing revealed a terrible neglect of the topic, leading him to argue that:

> inattention on such a scale cannot possibly be explained by absent-mindedness. It is a structural matter, a view from a window which has been carefully placed to exclude a whole quadrant of the landscape. What may well have begun as a simple forgetting of other possible views turned under habit and over time into something like a cult of forgetfulness practised on a national scale.[11]

Australian history as a separate study evolved alongside burgeoning nationalism, unashamedly written as the story of colonialism victorious, with varying degrees of deference to the British Imperial founders. The easiest way to tell such a tale without sounding callous was to forget the vanquished altogether, and certainly not to allow the uncomfortable possibility that the nation was founded upon dubious sovereignty. Equally influential was the author's subjectivity; as white male authors, they undoubtedly imagined a similar audience. Aboriginal people's meagre educational opportunities ensured that few would read these texts, let alone write them. Deaf to the few public voices of Aboriginal protest, the historians wrote within the comfortable western mind-sets of the dominant society.

The disciplinary boundaries of history and anthropology were also to blame. With the rise of anthropology in Australia during the early twentieth century, an artificial demarcation arose between those who studied the 'primitive' blacks, and those who studied the 'progressive' white past. The domination of the British structural-functionalist school of anthropology in Australia led to an emphasis on reconstructing past cultures, with its static cultural model deflecting attention altogether from processes of change. In the quest for 'traditional' society, fieldwork and analysis ignored both past and present economic and social environments. Although exhibiting some humanitarian concern, anthropologists such as A.P. Elkin attempted to nurture cosy research relationships with government policy makers and the pastoralists upon whose land many Aborigines resided. To these men, such charged issues as colonialism and indigenous exploitation were anathema.[12]

When female ethnographers such as Olive Pink[13] tried to combine scholarship with strong activism, her work was judged a threat to the status quo and the power-brokers refused its publication. The female protectors that Pink proposed to prevent Aboriginal women from sexual exploitation, threatened the attractiveness of outback employment for white males. Thus the anthropological establishment reinforced the notion that Aborigines, whilst having a static 'past' to uncover and preserve, did not have a history.

The establishment in Canberra of the Australian Institute of Aboriginal Studies in 1963–64 as a research centre did little to alter this, for its purpose was not to study change but essentially to retrieve what might otherwise be 'lost'. Anthropologists, linguists, and experts in material culture dominated the establishment; only 'prehistory', or history prior to white contact had its own special advisory committee and a mere sprinkling of historians were members of the Institute. When historians' interest in 'Aboriginal history' strengthened, they were viewed as untrained and unsuitable for research on Aborigines. Although there is now a History Committee, Fellowships at the Institute have rarely been held by historians, and in past years, historical researchers have sometimes met difficulty in gaining support due to lack of anthropological training.[14] Aboriginal writers in various fields complain that they, too, have trouble being taken seriously.

Specialist historical analysis of Aboriginal–white relations first appeared in the 1970s, in the tracks of important Aboriginal rights campaigns in the late 1960s, including the Gurindji's strike for equal wages and land rights. Effective lobbying by Aboriginal spokespeople like Oodgeroo Noonuccal (previously Kath Walker) in the lead-up to the 1967 Referendum further raised the consciousness of white Australians. They were also influenced by developments in the United States and decolonisation movements in Africa. Influenced by Althusser, Marcuse and the New Left, academics questioned progress models and committed themselves to activist scholarship. Recognition of the absence of Aborigines in Australian historiography thus led to a wealth of enthusiastic research.

In 1970, the political scientist C.D. Rowley published a pathbreaking historical trilogy, entitled *The Destruction of Aboriginal*

Society, Outcasts in White Australia and *The Remote Aborigines*. Rowley humanely appraised state administration of Aboriginal affairs, especially via government policies and the law. He keenly understood the political ramifications of breaking the silence:

> No adequate assessment of the Aboriginal predicament can be made so long as the historical dimension is lacking; it is the absence of information . . . which has made it easy for intelligent persons in each successive generation to accept the stereotype of Aborigines as an incompetent group.[15]

Frank Stevens, author and barrister, analysed the history of racism in Australia and issues of wage equality, especially in the northern pastoral industry. Peter Biskup's *Not Slaves Not Citizens* (1973) was another excellent study of state policy regarding Aborigines. Raymond Evans' work on Queensland Aborigines in *Exclusion, Exploitation and Extermination* (1975) applied sociological models to an analysis of racist ideology and practice.[16]

The belief of such authors, however, in the universality of humanistic and Marxist paradigms, left their cultural bias as author unchallenged, and led them to portray Aboriginal people as passive victims. Rowley and Biskup's near exclusive reliance on official sources meant that Aboriginal people's perspectives were ignored.

In *The Black Resistance* (1977)[17] Maoist authors Robinson and York similarly took no account of the different world-view of Aboriginal peoples, despite their efforts to present Aborigines as fighters rather than victims. They modelled Aborigines as a guerilla-style resistance, even turning a woman into a man to suit their cliched warrior paradigm. Nonetheless, a book which portrayed Aborigines as actors rather than helpless victims made a timely impact.

Some important work was published in the prestigious mainstream journal, *Australian Historical Studies*, now brought together in a volume edited by S. Janson and S. Macintyre entitled *Through White Eyes* (1990)[18] This selection shows that the first relevant articles—Mulvaney's excellent descriptions of changing attitudes towards Aborigines from 1606–1929—did not appear until 1958. A long pause followed until 1973, the year after the Aboriginal Tent Embassy was erected outside Canberra's Parliament House, then several important articles appeared in the 1980s. None were by Aboriginal authors.

Most importantly, however, a specialist journal *Aboriginal History* has been devoted to the subject since 1978. The product of the tireless efforts of its first editor, the late Dr Diane Barwick, from its outset the journal was characterised by a pluralistic definition of 'Aboriginal history' and the encouragement of contributions from Aboriginal authors and co-authors. A survey of editions reveal only a small proportion of Aboriginal-authored articles but a more substantial number collaborated with Aborigines who shared their life stories or perspectives. The journal also fostered an interdisciplinary approach, with contributions from anthropologists, linguists, archaeologists, prehistorians, cave art experts, musicologists, geographers, educationalists, archivists, and librarians.

Enriched by the insights offered by several disciplines, Henry Reynolds' *The Other Side of the Frontier* (1981)[19] was an extremely important monograph, for it attempted to portray the story of the frontier from Aboriginal vantage points, to get into the minds of Aboriginal people, and to acknowledge 'difference'. Aboriginal reactions to sighting the first white men, and their responses to frontier violence, were driven by their cultural imperatives, including Aboriginal belief and law. This book was indeed an attempt to present the perspective from 'the other side', the one which historians had thought could not be told due to inadequate evidence. While Aborigines had little control over the manufacture of historical records, Reynolds scoured the documents to find snatches of their voices recorded in newspapers, parliamentary papers, police and court records. Collecting then threading together evidence from throughout Australia, he created a patchwork picture of wider patterns of colonialism. Critics pointed out the need for closer regional studies, while others had doubts about Reynolds' resistance model and frontier paradigm. Reynolds' frontier implied rather firm boundaries, with Aborigines placed on 'the other side' as noble, and any who co-operated with the colonisers presented as collaborators. Reynolds made great progress in challenging the western mind-set, yet perhaps he gave some the impression that a white man could fully articulate

Aboriginal perspectives. He stated that he was not a dispassionate scholar but instead motivated by a desire to change an ignorant, racist society. The following year Richard Broome's compassionately written *Aboriginal Australians* appeared. It provided an excellent general synthesis of existing historical work and made sensitive use of Aboriginal perspectives.

Lyndall Ryan's *The Aboriginal Tasmanians*[20] was a detailed study located mainly in the late eighteenth and early nineteenth century materials. She sensitively took into account the feelings of the Aboriginal communities with whom she worked and intelligently portrayed the experiences of female Aborigines. My *'Born in the Cattle': Aborigines in the Cattle Industry* (1987)[21] departed from preceding interpretations, being described as using a dynamic cultural model and containing a more complex notion of power relations.[22] Here Aborigines were shown to inhabit *both* sides of the frontier. They agreed to work for the white men and women and indeed Aborigines excelled at stockwork, a highly prestigious activity, and domestic tasks, including caring for and virtually bringing up the manager's children. Working for the coloniser did not mean that they were traitors to their own people; they did not suddenly think 'white' but rather incorporated the cattle world into their own cultural frameworks; it was 'no shame job' and they worked for rather different reasons than Europeans might envisage. Unfamiliar with cash, they wanted a regular supply of food for their kin, and to continue to live upon, have access to and 'look after' their traditional lands. *Born in the Cattle* also made gender a central category of historical analysis[23], focussing upon the division of labour and the sexual relationships between coloniser and colonised. The inter-dependence created by such intimate relationships was shown to be central to frontier dynamics, further breaking down any stereotype of a fixed frontier boundary. Given the predominance of white–black unions in frontier regions, it was indeed problematic to ascertain who was on which side of the frontier during sexual intercourse!

Born in the Cattle was substantially shaped by the collection and incorporation of oral history interviews with Aboriginal and non-Aboriginal cattle-station workers. This enabled the piecing together of richer detail on the everyday labour routine of

Aborigines, and a greater understanding of Aboriginal cultural explanations for their work experience. In many ways, the research process enabled Aborigines to teach their history themselves. Their perspectives played an important role in shaping the questions asked of other evidence. Blurring occurred, however, between the voices articulated; was the author acting as a vehicle for the perspectives of Aboriginal interviewees, or was it her own voice as historian the reader heard? Those engaged in oral history collection often find it difficult to contradict their informants' accounts due to the nature of the relationships formed, and expectations of trust which arise. Tim Rowse argued that I had not paid enough attention to the influence of nostalgia in the accounts of older surviving station workers.[24] Attwood was especially suspicious of the value of oral history.[25] Rowse and later Attwood argued that my involvement in land rights work led to an effort to stress continuing traditional land associations. Also controversial was my contention that cattle station Aborigines were 'never truly colonised'[26], an assertion which demanded more careful definition of terminology and theory.

Marie Fels' study of the Port Phillip Native Police *Good Men and True* (1988) applied cultural history models and close ethnographically-informed textual readings. She tended to attribute a great deal of autonomy to the Native Police, pointing out how they mediated between cultures. The next significant study was Bain Attwood's *The Making of the Aborigines* (1989).[27] Drawing upon his research into Aboriginal missions in Victoria, he argued that Aborigines were more 'made' than making, more 'determined' than determining. Attwood argued that nineteenth century Aborigines were being 'constructed' as people by a dominant culture. Jan Kociumbas also dissents from the 'agency' model, arguing that, 'Like other oppressed people, they had no power to determine the choices available to them.'[28] Her work is heavily structured according to Marxist paradigms which tend to encapsulate all oppressed groups as victims.[29] Ann Curthoys has also argued for balance in this regard.[30] Like Reynolds, McGrath and Fels, Attwood was influenced by insights from a variety of disciplines, and drew upon intensive doctoral research, though with more overt reference to his historiographical influences. Distinguishing himself from other scholars on the grounds of being an 'outsider', a New Zealander rather than Australian born, and not being politically active, he claimed a greater monopoly on 'objectivity'.

Recently Reynolds also published some influential works on the question of land tenure and frontier violence, especially *The Law of the Land* (1989), and *Frontier* (1987), which questioned the *terra nullius* doctrine.[31] Drawing upon a wealth of recent scholarship, Reynolds' more recent *With the White People* (1990) is a study of Aborigines in a wide range of employment relationships with the colonisers. It allows for a more flexible frontier paradigm and slightly more recognition of the importance of gender relations.

General histories have not yet managed to integrate the story of Aborigines into their analysis. Those published in the 1970s and 1980s made only token mention of Aborigines, including the widely-used *New History of Australia* edited by F.K. Crowley. *A People's History of Australia since 1788*, edited by J. Lee and V. Burgmann, employed Left-wing and labour historian's perspectives, and included a number of articles on Aboriginal issues. The largest team project, the *Australians* series, invited Aboriginal discussion and participation, hoping to provide a history for everyone and about everyone. Authors of several volumes included Aboriginal content but Aboriginal people were reluctant contributors.[32] Its 1938 'slice' volume included the much-praised article on Aboriginal activism 'Day of Mourning' by Langton and Horner and a collection of Aboriginal oral histories.[33] The *Oxford History of Australia* devoted a special volume to pre-1788 history, which has not yet appeared, and authors of other volumes attempted to interweave 'Aboriginal history' into the texts but it is only a key theme in the 1770–1860 volume by Jan Kociumbas.[34] In the 'view from the window' of the general histories, Aborigines are only just starting to be seen, though the collaborative feminist history, *Creating a Nation*, represents a departure.[35]

ABORIGINES MAKING HISTORY

For many Aboriginal people, the only 'Aboriginal history' they recognise is that compiled by their own people. There are as yet no general histories of Australia written by Aborigines, and very few publications which claim to be all-encompassing regional histories.[36] Biographies and autobiographies are the most common form of Aboriginal historical writing. They contain a hitherto untold story, which readers are happy to absorb without the mediation of further historical interpretation. But within this medium, there are many possibilities. Biographies of 'outstanding Aborigines' first appeared in the 1970s and 80s: the story of well-known civil rights activists such as Kath Walker, *Stradbroke Dreamtime*, Margaret Tucker, *If Everyone Cared* and Charles Perkins, *A Bastard Like Me,* artist Dick Roughsey, and of 'ordinary people' such as Jimmie Barker (told by Janet Mathews), Marnie Kennedy, Ella Simon, Elsie Roughsey, Phillip Pepper, Ida West, Alice Nannup, G. Ward, and Ruby Langford.[37]

Sally Morgan's best-selling *My Place* (1988), while not a 'work of history' in the academic sense, was a compelling autobiographical narrative, a journey of discovery and a detective story whose main theme was family history. It included large slabs of oral history told in the words of Morgan's older and more traditional Aboriginal relations. This work received many accolades and won virtually every available literary prize. Since then, the market for Aboriginal autobiography has expanded, and new books are regularly coming out which narrate the story of Aboriginal women, men and families. Some of these have been compiled with the assistance of non-Aboriginal editors, in the style of *Two Worlds of Jimmie Barker*.[38] For academic historians, these works also present new historical data—a wide range of examples from which common threads and diversity of historical experiences emerge. The Aboriginal critic Mudrooroo criticised Morgan for borrowing European narrative styles[39], presumably because this perpetuated cultural hegemony.

But Aboriginal publications have distinctive qualities; kinship and loss of family are especially prominent. Tucker's *If Everyone Cared* fits this category, and more recently Ruby Langford's *Don't Take Your Love to Town*. Edwards and Read's *The Lost Children* contains stories of thirteen New South Wales people and their struggles to find their Aboriginal parents or kin. *Take This Child* also contains stories of child-removal in the Northern Territory.

More culturally-traditional northern Aborigines such as Ngabidj and Paddy Roe have recorded life stories via white intermediaries, and these also tend to emphasise stories of people's relationships to land and landscape. Cohen and Sommerville's *Ingelba and the Five Black Matriarchs*, the story of generations around the New England district of New South Wales, is another example of the land-based narrative, with a biographical format.[40]

It is worth pondering why Aborigines choose the biographical form for expressing their stories. Partly it may reflect a reluctance to speak about what has not been personally witnessed or what lies outside one's own clan area. Biography might have been chosen for its ability to touch a nerve, to get a message across. Dominance of the biographical medium can also be explained by the relatively few Aboriginal graduates. While limited educational opportunities have meant that most Aboriginal people had little choice, other Aborigines reject university training as a bastion of colonialism, determined to achieve their ends without being subject to such western hegemonic institutions.

Aboriginal students are more likely to choose law, anthropology, or medicine. Some recent graduates, including those with interdisciplinary backgrounds such as Marcia Langton, Gordon Briscoe, Noel Pearson and Jackie Huggins have continued their historical writing. But such talents often find they are called upon to fulfil senior executive positions in policy making, or decide to spend their energies working with their own communities rather than becoming career-path academics.[41] Universities thus suffer a 'brain-drain' of Aborigines with historical expertise.

Aborigines make history mainly outside the academies. Unlike the disciplines of anthropology or linguistics, history is considered a non-exclusive discipline, because its language or theory is not specialist, and because wider social perceptions of history stress its accessibility to the general public. (For example, newspaper articles constantly refer to 'history in the making', 'historic moments'; people enjoy historical television series and films.) History can be shared by storytelling, songs and art, so does not require high literacy or educational standards, and can be taught to people of varying ages.

Aboriginal student Anita Heiss receives her honours degree in history at the Faculty of Arts and Social Sciences, University of New South Wales, 1992. UNSW PUBLICATIONS

This probably explains why, of all the conferences held by Australian Institute of Aboriginal and Torres Strait Islander Studies (AIATSIS), 'Aborigines Making History' (1988) was one of the best attended by Aboriginal participants. They came from diverse backgrounds: educators at pre-school, primary, secondary and tertiary levels, genealogists, family historians, bureaucrats, and activists. Many were in some way involved in the practice of history; a group of Collingwood women had set up an Aboriginal History Group and had already published historical pamphlets. Others practised history by researching, writing or teaching, and saw such knowledge as intrinsic to their identity as Aborigines. They viewed history as something which belonged to them all, in which they could participate through sharing their personal experiences or acquired knowledge, through researching family history, by recording the reminiscences of older people. Some participants had studied at university level, often in general Aboriginal studies courses, or education, linguistics, literary criticism or anthropology. Most participants had picked up their historical skills through community involvement or actually practising history. Had they not been Aboriginal, they might be dubbed 'amateur historians' but given the special value and purpose of history by Aborigines, this label is not only elitist but quite inappropriate.

Many writers, including numerous older women, were most interested in writing the specific histories of their families and clans, emphasising genealogy rather than social history. While these less ambitious histories do not generally discuss the wider impact of power relations, they certainly raise consciousness, strengthening a sense of distinctive identity, boosting self-esteem and preserving cultural knowledge for their descendants. Many family histories have been published, especially by the government-backed Aboriginal Studies Press, alternative presses and increasingly by commercial publishers.

The historical novel is another form chosen by black authors. Monica Clare related the exploitation of a young Aboriginal girl in *Karobran*. Colin Johnson's *Dr Wooreddy's Prescription for Enduring the End of the World*, based his story of frontier brutality in Tasmania, and Eric Willmot's *Pemulwuy* dramatised the story of an Aboriginal warrior who led battles against the British in their early New South Wales settlements.[42] Philip McLaren's *Sweet Water, Sweet Land* told of brutal massacres and cultural exchanges.

Where historical circumstances have led to greater dislocation from their land and traditional culture, Aborigines are more likely to see 'Aboriginal history' as a means of retrieving that lost past, of piecing together an often romanticised 'lost culture'. The personal and political are fused. History is used as a means of explaining the personal pain suffered by their parents or near kin and for their current underdog status. Like the white history which excluded them, 'Aboriginal history' can serve pan-Aboriginal, nationalistic ends, for it enhances the anti-colonial struggles for recognition as an indigenous nation and for land rights generally. This might be termed 'oppression history' but Aboriginal stories such as that of the drover Amy Laurie and matriarch Ida West's *Pride Against Prejudice* often stress survival themes.[43]

'Aboriginal history' is thus used as a means of political consciousness-raising, affirming a shared sense of oppression, and a way of resolving identity problems caused by state interventions which broke up families and communities. Aboriginal ancestry

WHAT IS ABORIGINAL HISTORY?

need no longer be denied; the deepest hurts of bureaucratic cruelties can be aired. Children can learn why their parents refused to talk about certain issues; to open the locked doors is both saddening and empowering. As movingly rendered in books such as Morgan's *My Place* and C. Edwards and P. Read's *The Lost Children*[44], to discover the truth of the past, the pain of the past can heal. Improving self-knowledge and self-esteem can mean greater individual and community well-being.

The preceding discussion of history by Aboriginal people has been chiefly concerned with an end-product which is written down or published. Aboriginal people are a very diverse group, and approach their history from varying vantage points and in differing cultural styles. As Aborigines were a pre-literate people prior to the British arrival, they had no place for the 'written history' or even the recorded events which westerners usually assume to be 'real history'. The thousands of Aboriginal people in more remote regions still maintain a qualitatively different relationship with their own history. With more continuous relationships with land, language and culture, they see 'Aboriginal history' as a living tradition, of which written or published versions are a recent development. Nonetheless, Aboriginal elders are deeply concerned about their younger generation's loss of interest in traditional law, and consider the continuing life of 'the Dreaming' and education about land and history as essential to their survival as a people.

Another way of looking at 'Aboriginal history' is thus as something quite ancient, a complex and diverse tradition which has ensued for at least 50 000 years. This is the history which has been transmitted through the generations, not just 'orally' through spoken stories but through dance, music and song. Song cycles linked country, stories and people throughout the land. The Aboriginal philosophical and religious tradition or 'Dreaming' included creation stories relating animals, plants and humans together within the same landscape. Aborigines in northern and central Australia now swap Dreaming stories on cassette tapes or at large gatherings to which they travel by car, 4-wheel drive vehicles and bus. Dreaming stories are also told via traditional paintings and engravings on stone, patterns on sand, 'story sticks',

Northern Territory Land Commissioner Kearney with Pharlap Dixon during Murranji Land Claim Hearing, 1983. Aboriginal men and women have shared many traditional stories as part of the land claims process in the Northern Territory. R. BLOWES

and modern forms of painting on bark, canvas and paper. Traditional children's stories have also been translated into English and illustrated by Aboriginal artists. Some communities have also embraced film, video and multi-media CD-Rom. 'Traditional' forms of Aboriginal history are far from static, reflecting and explaining ever-changing contemporary circumstances.

Northern Aborigines such as the Mudbura and Gurindji tell stories of the coming of the first white men to their regions, sagas of exploration, settlement and Aboriginal negotiation with the newcomers. They explain how the arrival of white men dramatically altered their prior relations with their land, sustenance and women. Such contact sagas are referred to by Aborigines as 'history stories', or merely *'before'*. Some can be verified as accurate accounts, enhanced by unique Aboriginal understandings of events. Others, such as the Captain Cook myths, have attained a more mythologised form, where the white intruders become symbols of chaos and law-breaking. Other sagas formulate distinctive Aboriginal paradigms of colonialism—explanations for their current place in the world.[45] Although quite distinctive, they have partly evolved out of a dialogue with white Australian historiography, often conveyed via the classroom. For example, school children are told that 'Captain Cook' was the first white man to come to Australia. It is therefore extrapolated that whenever a first white intruder appears in the landscape, he will be called 'Captain Cook'.[46] Names become symbolic, characters archetypal. 'Dreaming stories' about sites in the landscape have also merged with some Christian traditions, such as the story of Noah's Ark.[47] Narrative style and the principles behind them deserve much further analysis but to do even a little justice to these forms of history requires much further study. That historians in Australian universities have not engaged in an analysis of traditional Aboriginal historical practice is a serious omission.[48] Such explorations could provide stimulating challenges to the discipline.

POLITICS OF BLACK AND WHITE

Several Aboriginal spokespeople have contended there must be no further appropriation of their history. Only Aborigines should write 'Aboriginal history'. All others should stay out. White historians have based their careers, got Doctorates, made money out of books by ripping off Aborigines of their life stories, of their evidence, of their history. Only Aborigines should gain. Only Aborigines know the 'correct' interpretation of their past. Only Aborigines can understand Aboriginal minds, and Aboriginal reactions.[49]

White historians sometimes reacted defensively to such attacks, partly because it threatened them with redundant specialisations. Others have been troubled because they hoped to prevent the damaging effects of black exclusion from Australian national history; to them 'Aboriginal history' is part of the story of humanity. They value the potential power of the white historians' voices: the impact of Geoffrey Blainey's *Triumph of the Nomads*[50] in heightening public awareness of Aboriginal cultural achievements, Rowley's exposure of their dispossession and oppression and Reynolds' calculation of the death rates on the frontier, the creative responses of Aborigines and the dubious justice of *terra nullius*. Historians should perhaps be more self-conscious of the culturally-specific nature of their liberal missionary zeal[51]. On the other hand, it is unfortunate that many talented historians, including highly-motivated students, shy away from the field because they fear offending Aborigines or being accused of not minding their own business.

The great diversity in Aboriginal culture and historical experience and their relatively few historians could mean that blacks-only 'Aboriginal history' might reflect the experience of a regional or political minority. This could be exacerbated by the dominant myth of 'the authentic Aboriginal voice', for like 'the feminist view', one Aboriginal author is often taken by outsiders to be representative of all, leaving no room for divergent political positions. While a generalist account of Aboriginal history by an Aboriginal author will undoubtedly be published before too long, Aboriginal scholars like Michael Williams and Noel Pearson are committed to following traditional protocol and avoid setting themselves up to represent knowledges to which they cannot claim.[52]

There are still many areas of potential conflict between Aborigines and non-Aboriginal researchers. One of these is access to records, for on the grounds of privacy, Aborigines are demanding full control over who inspects archival records concerning their people. This is an understandable position as it follows decades of the State exerting control over their private lives. Many things have also been insensitively published by anthropologists and other academics, including photographs or names of the recently deceased or sacred materials. Aborigines have every right to mistrust white promises. Yet to 'lock up' this information from non-family members threatens to keep the lid on an already censored past. It threatens to deny access to vital knowledge relevant to understanding colonial power relations.

Of more concern to 'traditional' communities is the propriety of knowledge-sharing according to the principles of Aboriginal law. The European concept of knowledge as universally accessible, fundamental in institutions such as universities and libraries, did not apply in pre-contact Aboriginal society. Information about Dreaming stories, land and ceremony were available according to gender, kinship classification, land ownership, and age. Important cultural information was for those worthy, ready or appropriate to receive it. In a special sense, knowledge was power but it must not get into the wrong hands. Knowledge bore importantly on custodianship of land, power over production and reproduction. To share secret knowledge could empower the receivers but endanger its articulators.

Like all peoples, Aborigines thus have many different histories. Some are more militant in interpretation than others. Some are extremely conciliatory, leading white radicals to say their political consciousness has not yet developed. Some Aborigines want to co-operate with non-Aboriginal researchers; some don't. Some people have very clear political agendas, others see education and culture as something separate from politics. Some believe that only elders can tell history stories; others believe anyone who knows them can do so. Revisionism and critique is also emerging in the ranks of Aboriginal writers, for example the work of Jackie Huggins, Mudrooroo, Paul Behrendt and Michael McDaniel.

Aboriginal spokespeople want their children to be taught about their own past in the school system. Some demand that it only be written about and spoken by Aborigines. This poses a serious dilemma for non-Aboriginal teachers who believe they must incorporate the story of Aborigines. Collaborative teaching approaches with increasing Aboriginal control are becoming more common, especially at tertiary level. Koori-controlled courses at Monash, New South Wales and Macquarie Universities have used texts written by Aboriginal and non-Aboriginal authors, and called in a variety of Aboriginal speakers. White historians are increasingly inviting Aboriginal guest lecturers to contribute to any relevant courses. White historians willing to teach or co-ordinate courses on Koori history have often interpreted their role as that of caretaker, awaiting a suitable Aboriginal applicant at a later date. This has often worked well, though students have sometimes had to suffer a constantly changing front-person. Aboriginal lecturers, although highly valued and sought after, have been offered little job security and had to work in locations distant from their home community. They have then confronted difficulties in fulfilling the multiple demands of students, of their local communities, and of the academic community. The Aboriginal Resource Centre of the University of New South Wales, directed by Paul Behrendt, presents an excellent model. Achieving some continuity, it independently runs its own courses, makes input into campus-wide subjects and runs a busy centre which makes knowledge of Aboriginal matters highly accessible.

Positive discrimination towards Aborigines has enabled many outstanding individuals to supply invaluable perspectives within universities but it also raises difficulties for others. Should Aboriginal historians be admitted to postgraduate degrees or promoted to lectureships within the history discipline without receiving any basic formal training? Is it justifiable because it offers the opportunity to sink or swim, or does it put them at a disadvantage, setting some people up to suffer from feelings of inadequacy or inevitably fail? Is the role-model function of such appointments more important than their historical skills? Or do Aboriginal people offer a *qualitatively different* history and sophisticated and unique skills which cannot be judged by the same standards?

While many Aboriginal scholars prefer the disciplinary autonomy of 'Aboriginal Studies' rather than having to conform to the parameters of a single discipline, Aboriginal voices are increasingly finding places to be heard within 'mainstream' historical accounts. For example, Aboriginal author Jackie Huggins has participated in *A People's History of Australia*, *Through White Eyes* and *Gender Relations in Australia*.[53] More importantly, Aboriginal groups are assuming greater control over the dissemination of knowledge about them. Tranby College circulates a list of books approved by black educators. Aboriginal education or other special officers have been appointed to the Australian Museum, the Powerhouse Museum, the National Museum of Victoria, and Aboriginal communities have set up their own cultural museums or 'keeping places' in Adelaide and various rural locations.

In attempting a new sensitivity, non-Aboriginal historians face the danger of overcompensating, being so over-concerned about offending Aborigines that they refuse to disagree with any person of Aboriginal descent. As Marcia Langton has pointed out, to not engage in debate with Aboriginal scholars is both condescending[54] and cowardly. Yet some white scholars are justifiably fearful of presenting ideas which might not conform with the political campaigns of the most high-profile Aboriginal spokespersons; indeed they fear informal 'blacklisting', receiving scathing reviews, being branded racists or banned from the black-approved books lists. With Aboriginal representatives now increasingly consulted by University appointment panels, career opportunities can be tangibly damaged. Sometimes such advice rightly penalises insensitivity towards Aboriginal issues but it can also reflect misunderstandings or misinterpretations which can stem from different orientations to knowledge and different educational levels. Applying a set of rules to such appointments is problematic. Fear of going against current political adages may inhibit exchange of ideas, and sometimes those who do not fear offending others have some very useful ideas. No one has a monopoly on 'truth', and often the only way to advance knowledge is to suggest interpretations beyond the currently perceived 'truths' or wisdoms. So while acknowledging the need for historians to be politically sensitive, this should not mean censorship.

While history is inevitably political and historians of Aboriginal history have been forced to face this from the outset, it is no easy task to recognise one's own place as part of an ongoing colonial process. White historians are inevitably part of the group oppressing Aborigines. To be challenged on this can be an educational experience, enhancing awareness of one's own society, the process of history and history-making.

Many white historians have worked alongside Aboriginal people on projects of vital current concern to their communities. Indeed, historians in the 'Aboriginal history' field have a high participation rate in public or applied history. Often they have been employed by Aboriginal bodies or government organisations with Aboriginal staff, been expected to work with cultural sensitivity and to deliver the required product. This represents a shift in power relations, for Aboriginal organisations are in the role of employer and historian as service provider. At the same time, the historians' expertise is respected and they are awarded some authority and independence.

Heather Goodall acted as Historical Advisor during the Royal Commission into British Nuclear Testing at Maralinga in Central Australia and has worked for numerous Aboriginal organisations, including Tranby Aboriginal Co-operative College, the Western Aboriginal Legal Service in New South Wales and the Pitjantjatjara Council in Western Australia. Henry Reynolds has advised various Land Councils, including the Cape York Land Council, and has taken an active role in land rights reform. Peggy Brock worked on an Aboriginal Sites Register for the Aboriginal Heritage Branch of the Department of Environment and Planning in South Australia.[55] The editor of *Aboriginal History* since 1990, Peter Read, began researching 'Aboriginal history' as part of his teaching job with Aboriginal children in the Northern Territory. He collected oral histories there and later in Cowra, New South Wales, and published a book on the Wiradjuri people. In between, he worked for Link-up, an Aboriginal organisation set up to trace parents or children separated mainly by state policies, which until the 1960s, had advocated separating children from their families to 'train' them as cheap domestic labour and in the benefits of 'white civilisation'. In 1990 Read was called upon to give evidence in the Californian murder trial of the Australian Aborigine, James Savage, who was taken from his young mother at birth, adopted and later deserted by white missionary parents. From 1979, the author advised and acted as expert witness for the Northern Land Council for several Aboriginal land claims. Lenore Coltheart, Ray Evans and Kay Saunders also advised Aboriginal Land Councils. Rae Frances and Bruce Scates collaborated with the La Grange Aboriginal community to erect a monument in Fremantle which would take issue with a nearby explorers' memorial; it would commemorate 'All Aboriginal people who died during the invasion of their country'.[56] Historians of Aboriginal history became the first to play a major advisory role for an Australian Royal Commission when from 1990–91 they contributed research papers and advised the Royal Commission into Aboriginal Deaths in Custody. Its National History Project, co-ordinated by the author, engaged consultant historians Peter Read, Richard Broome, Peggy Brock, Errol West, Henry Reynolds, Heather Goodall and Dawn May. In

1994, historian Tom Stannage (who earlier worked on the Seaman Inquiry in Western Australia) and Bob Reece conducted research relating to the *Native Title Act, 1993*.

Historians' involvement in Aboriginal politics has led to their being branded 'bleeding hearts', liberals or missionaries but experience with 'real life' has led to a growing sensitivity and awareness of cultural complexities: it has allowed historians to hear what Aborigines actually want rather than what others assume they want. Although some historians, such as Marie Fels and Bain Attwood, have eschewed involvement in Aboriginal politics, the practice of history has already involved them. Attwood, for example, tutored in an Aboriginal studies course at Monash University run by Aboriginal linguist Eve Fesl, and Aboriginal critics have responded sharply to his ideas.[57] Whether white historians work alongside Aborigines or not, in taking part in any historical dialogue on this topic, they are inevitably caught in the web of ongoing power relations, cultural clashes and conflicting nationalisms.

Such entanglement can mean positive attempts to shift the balance of power between whites and blacks, as has also taken place within the academies, in teaching. Despite its career problems, Aboriginal history as practised within the traditional history discipline has a special vitality and originality. The reasons for this are linked with the way it has borrowed insights from other disciplines, especially ethnography, linguistics and archaeology. It also leads the way in venturing towards 'cultural history', the successor of social history. Such recognition implies that Aboriginal history has not been marginalised as an obscure specialisation but is recognised as leading the discipline in new directions. The quality of recent works has been recognised by the award of numerous prizes, including human rights, literary and historians' awards.[58]

Historiographical questions become especially pertinent in an atmosphere of political engagement. These include whether a separate, an alternative field of study is warranted and whether it is methodologically possible to write 'Aboriginal history' in segregation. In my view it is impossible to analyse post-contact history in an isolated manner, for it is essentially relational. Just as feminist historians are recognising the need to understand masculinity and wider social power structures, historians interested in 'Aboriginal history' must explore the interface between the cultures, between coloniser and colonised. But the question of position, and of perspective, allows for many different vantage points. Some, like Evans and Saunders, have categorised it as part of the history of 'race relations'.[59] Many would quibble with using the term 'race' at all; others have referred to 'culture contact'. In the Australian context, the historical importance of Aboriginal–white relations requires that 'Aboriginal history' be integrated into the story of mainstream Australian history. A shift of paradigm is required, an incorporation of 'Aboriginal history' into an Australian history which is truly one of colonialism: one which analyses the economic, social and cultural conflict between indigenous peoples, the colonised, and the colonisers, as central to national settlement, development and nationalism.

DISCOURSE AND DIALOGUE

'Aboriginal history' is constantly under challenge. One dilemma is whether white authors cease to *collect* Aboriginal life stories. Aborigines have argued that this violates their privacy. Others point out that the story is inevitably 'channelled' via the white interviewer, with cultural bias shaping the questioning and responses. A second dilemma is whether white authors should cease to *analyse* 'Aboriginal history', on the grounds that this is a continuing appropriation of Aboriginal intellectual property. Perhaps they should only write about what whites *did* to Aborigines, not how they responded.

White authors have put their names to books where they have edited Aboriginal stories. Should they be authors or ghostwriters or co-authors? What is and should be their status? Are they facilitators or creators? Aboriginal oral histories have often been mediated through white authors, and this has become a subject of much literary criticism. In the late 1970s, early 1980s, Bruce Shaw collected and edited the stories of Ngabidj, Banggaiyerri and various other men of the Kimberley region in Western Australia. Ngabidj's story, *My Country of the Pelican Dreaming* is an invaluable source, allowing insights into the traditional world of an elder in the context of a volatile and changing frontier region. Ngabidj, who died before the book was published, told his story in English, which Shaw transcribed and rephrased into more 'readable' English for the imagined 'general reader'. Mainstream literary critics claimed the Aboriginal-colloquial style of Shaw and Ngabidj's narrative was too obscure for the general reader, whilst Aboriginal critic Mudrooroo accused Shaw of too much interference with the text, attacking such writing as 'captured discourse, captured lives'. Mudrooroo argued that an Aboriginal audience was left out of Shaw's category 'general reader', though this is somewhat dubious given the range of English spoken amongst Aboriginal groups throughout the country. *Reading the Country* used a contrasting strategy, presenting the words of Paddy Roe like poetry; the pauses are signified by new lines not punctuation, and little obvious editorial intervention. Mudrooroo argued, however, that the words are still trapped and subordinate to the artworks of Krim Benterrak and the philosophical discussions by Muecke, who studied in Paris and cites the ideas of G. Deleuze and F. Guattari on nomadology and the influence of French theorists such as Foucault, Barthes and Derrida.[60] Muecke's presentation of Roe's words (in Aboriginal English, a type of creole) are an attempt to avoid intervening with his words, yet his control over the form of the book, with instructions on how to read it, introductions and conclusions, inevitably privilege the voice of the white, highly educated male author, who unlike Paddy Roe, spoke cultured English as his first language.

The collection of oral history by white or black historians necessitates an intensely personal confrontation with the past, or more accurately, the individuals' different pasts. The power relations between interviewer and interviewee are constantly under examination. Aboriginal interviewers are now collecting valuable oral histories, which effectively places more control in Aboriginal hands but issues of power relations are still relevant.[61] The Aboriginal author, Bill Rosser, interviewed ex-drovers and pastoral workers in his *Dreamtime Nightmares*.[62] His angle of questioning showed marked differences of perspective to his Aboriginal interviewees, at least one of whom classed him as a 'white man'. His behaviour and skin colour had led to this perception, underlining the varying definitions of 'Aboriginality'.

Power relations are even more problematic when the interviewer is non-Aboriginal and part of the colonising class. Heather Goodall argued that the best way to prevent the exploitative mining of Aboriginal evidence by historians, was for interviewer and interviewee to collaborate in the historical analysis, with the historian sharing, maybe training the interviewee in her special skills. Though commendable, Goodall's position might only be applicable where there is shared ground regarding cultural outlook, education and age. It does not resolve the problem of whose voice will be used for the final presentation. Further, her argument could imply that the trained historian holds the more 'sophisticated' interpretation, one which tends to deny cultural difference and assume the same interpretation should be reached.

Anthropologist Diane Bell whipped up great controversy when she co-published with an Aboriginal collaborator Topsy Napurrula Nelson in *Women's Studies International Forum*. The topic itself was highly sensitive, about rape within Aboriginal communities. Aboriginal women, including Marcia Langton and Jackie Huggins, were outraged by the article, and various detractors spoke on *The Coming Out Show* on ABC National Radio, on 18 May 1990. The debate hotted up further when the editor of *WSIF* refused to publish a protest letter by twelve Aboriginal women. In her critique of the affair, Jan Larbalestier argued that despite Bell's assertions of cross-cultural collaboration, Bell as the privileged white academic was the one who located Nelson's voice in the text. Her voice was the authoritative white voice, the active voice, which she also placed in opposition to other 'hostile' Aboriginal women who she accused of not speaking out. By setting up the 'traditional' credentials of Nelson and positioning her as the 'authentic Aboriginal' voice, she thus invited the anger of black women. In emphasising women's shared oppression, Bell paid inadequate attention to difference, the need to consider the power relations of such collaboration, the forum for and mode of expressing its results and especially the need for Aboriginal women to formulate a distinctive voice.[63] Bell responded by arguing that her Aboriginal critics, like her collaborator, had powerful voices, and feared that Larbalestier's assertions would only mean a reversion to silence.[64]

To what extent will white authors really collaborate on an equal footing with Aboriginal historians? Nervousness on the part of some white authors about 'Aboriginal' topics could draw them to acquire Aboriginal co-authors. The practice might become merely a method of enhancing the white author's political credentials. The power relations implicit in such interactions, and the nature of the collaboration, must be more clearly articulated. Different types of contributions may be made without assuming either party is more important than the other but the readers are entitled to know to whose voice they are listening. It is important that collaborations do not cease but also that they be real, so that the dangers of tokenism do not arise.

Other scholars have attempted to create a safe haven by avoiding any discussion of Aboriginal experiences of history. Instead, they focus purely on critical studies of European representations of Aborigines, sometimes assuming that this topic relieves them of any obligation to include or co-operate with Aboriginal authors. Some indigenous people criticise such highly theorised studies as attempts to 'rise above' their concerns and render their writings 'inferior'. Typifying such studies is *Power, Knowledge and Aborigines*, edited by John Arnold and Bain Attwood.[65] Although many of its authors earnestly discuss the importance of indigenous voices and the politics of co-operation, there is no editorial reference to Aboriginal authors being invited to contribute to its analysis.[66] *Power, Knowledge and Aborigines* only admits Aboriginal representations in the cover art, thus perpetuating the type of primitivist trope it set out to critique. That is, Aboriginal people belong to the world of the visual, of colour and sensation rather than that of the intellect, words and theory. Despite good intentions, a retreat to studying 'our representations of them' can exaggerate the boundaries between 'us' and 'them', thus leading to a form of intellectual apartheid.

In debates about form, content must not be forgotten. There are still many important themes which demand further exploration. The evolution and meaning of Aboriginal identity is attracting increasing attention from scholars such as Beckett and

Attwood, and the results will be interesting. The gender dimension of colonialism has been largely ignored, and much more needs to be done on the ways in which Aboriginal men and women and relations between them were portrayed by white authors at different historical junctures. Trans-cultural relationships between the sexes also require further research: the relationships between white females and black, the relationships between white men and black, and the relationships between the genders of different societies. Where sexual unions occurred, what happened to the children and what sort of family cultures emerged?[67] As stated in the introduction, comparative studies are important, not only between different colonies and states but between regions, between mission and cattle station people, reserve residents and labourers living outside state controls (and often outside archival records). Furthermore, with the approaching centennial of Federation, we need to explore Aborigines' exclusion and conditional inclusion into the nation. We cannot understand the history of the Australian nation until we understand this.

'Aboriginal history' can be heard or read in many different ways—as a form of further colonialistic appropriation and exploitation, or as a means of decolonisation, of constructing Aboriginal nationalism, as a history for human rights, as a way of gaining control over the past and present, as a way of holding onto the land. Some might still see it as 'objective', politically disinterested[68] scholarship. Yet it can be a means of gaining a balance, with cultural exchange and a sharing of power as intrinsic to the making of history. In many ways, therefore, the process is as important as the product. The history of Aborigines in Australia is an interactive one, and it is also part of the story of the wider cosmos. Colonialism could not be confined to either an 'Aboriginal world' or a 'white world', for cultural change means cosmological vantage points were ever changing. A multiplicity of perspectives is therefore required.

As we have seen, 'Aboriginal history' challenges the very parameters of history as a discipline; it highlights its cultural embeddedness, and it throws up many questions regarding the nature and universality of knowledge: the importance of the interpreter and participant's perspectives, its ownership, manufacture and dissemination. The controversial nature of 'Aboriginal history' for both Aboriginal and non-Aboriginal practitioners has led to a special liveliness—a healthy introspection balanced by outward application of their expertise to the public sphere, which have necessitated interactions with contemporary Aboriginal communities.

Like the term 'Aborigine', 'Aboriginal history' is a site of conflict; it can be a site of exploitation, of privilege, hegemony, a meeting point, a site of separation, of coming together, of continuous tradition, of cultural resurgence. Like all historiography, it may be dated, burdened by outmoded paradigms and culturally bound. Equally it can be a site of cultural exchange and learning, on the edge of evolving, of understanding, of speaking, dancing or dramatising, something beyond itself. Colonialism, as typified by conflict over land, bodies and minds, created 'Aboriginal history' as pluralistically understood today. Traditionally a history rooted in the soil, 'Aboriginal history', like the very land of Australia, has become, and will continue to be, contested ground. The contest shapes the differing perceptions of what history is, of what the historical questions are. But this contest can involve collaborations which attempt to challenge wider power relations. The common ground of 'Aboriginal history' must remain a speaking place, one of co-existence and dialogue between all kinds of Australians. Hopefully the great Australian silence will not again shade the island continent, or its island state. On the land's edges, I hope there will still be places where history books fly like fish into the water below. Beyond will be further sites where histories, glittering and horrifying, will be salvaged. Released from their drowned muteness, they will ask questions of the dead and the living.

NOTES

1 J. Maloney, *The Penguin Bicentennial History of Australia*, Penguin, Ringwood, 1988. For a discussion of historians and the Bicentennary, see S. Janson and S. Macintyre (eds), *Making the Bicentennary*, Australian Historical Studies, Melbourne, 1988. Articles of special

interest are P. Spearritt's 'Celebration of a nation: The Triumph of Spectacle' and C. Bulbeck's, 'Aborigines, memorials and the history of the frontier'.
2. Henry Reynolds, paper at Australian history symposium, Maleny Folk Festival, 1988.
3. B. Attwood, *The Making of the Aborigines*, Allen & Unwin, Sydney, 1989, p.150. See also B. Reece, 'Inventing Aborigines' *Aboriginal History*, 11, 1987.
4. L. Coltheart, 'The moment of Aboriginal history' in J. Beckett (ed.) *Past and Present*, Aboriginal Studies Press, Canberra, 1988, pp.179–80.
5. W. Tench, *Sydney's First Four Years*, Augus & Robertson, Sydney, 1961, facsimile edition; D. Collins, *An Account of the English Colony in New South Wales*, Sydney, [1798] facsimile, 1975. For further analysis of these themes, see A. McGrath 'Europeans and Aborigines' in N. Meaney (ed.), *Under New Heavens*, Heinemann, Melbourne, 1989.
6. J. Bonwick, *First Twenty Years in Australia*, Low, Marston, London, 1882, p.178.
7. See A. Markus and A. McGrath, 'Sources on Europeans and Aborigines', in D. Borchardt (ed.), *Australians: Sources*, Fairfax, Syme and Weldon, Sydney, 1987.
8. A. Jose, *History of Australia from the earliest times to the present day*, London, 1899; S. H. Roberts, *History of Australian Land Settlement*, Macmillan, Melbourne, 1924; A. de Brune, *Fifty Years of Progress in Australia 1878–1928*, Halstead, Waterloo, 1929.
9. W.K. Hancock, *Australia*, Ernest Benn, London, 1930.
10. G. Greenwood (ed.), *Australia. A Social and Political History*, Angus and Robertson, Sydney, 1955; Manning Clark, *A Short History of Australia*, Heinemann, London, 1964, pp.34–35, 65; D. Pike, *Australia. The Quiet Continent*, Cambridge, London, 1966; A.G.L. Shaw, *The Story of Australia*, Faber, London, 1967, pp.17, 21; H. McQueen, *A New Britannia*, Penguin, Ringwood, 1970.
11. W.E.H. Stanner, *After the Dreaming: Black and White Australians—An Anthropologist's View*, Boyer Lectures, ABC, Crows Nest, 1968, p.25.
12. See R.M. and C.H. Berndt, *End of an Era*, Aboriginal Studies Press, Canberra, 1987. It is evident from this analysis that loyalty to Elkin stopped the Berndt's public expose of the fatal consequences of exploitation of Aboriginal workers by the Vesteys company.

13 C. Cheater in *Olive Pink Bulletin*, 1990.
14 See Annual Report of Australian Institute of Aboriginal Studies, 1965, its newsletters and journals.
15 C.D. Rowley, *The Destruction of Aboriginal Society*, ANU, Canberra, 1970, p.69.
16 F. Stevens, *Racism: the Australian Experience*, ANZ, Sydney, 1971-2; F. Stevens, *Aborigines in the Northern Territory Cattle Industry*, ANU, Canberra, 1974; F. Stevens, *Black Australia*, Sydney, 1981; P. Biskup, *Not Slaves, Not Citizens*, University of Queensland Press, St Lucia, 1973; R. Evans, K. Cronin, K. Saunders, *Exclusion, Exploitation and Extermination*, ANZ, Sydney, 1975 [republished 1988].
17 F. Robinson and B. York, *The Black Resistance*, Widescope, Melbourne, 1977.
18 S. Janson and S. Macintyre (eds), *Through White Eyes*, Allen & Unwin, Sydney, 1990.
19 H. Reynolds, *The Other Side of the Frontier*, James Cook, Townsville, 1981 [reprinted Penguin 1982]. Some of the critique below contains ideas from Ann Curthoys.
20 L. Ryan, *The Aboriginal Tasmanians*, UQP, St Lucia, 1981.
21 A. McGrath, *'Born in the Cattle': Aborigines in Cattle Country*, Allen & Unwin, Sydney, 1987. The amount of space given to the editor's own work is disproportionate, but it was requested to provide readers with an idea of my historiographical approach, which happened to highlight several relevant debates.
22 T. Rowse, 'Tolerance, Fortitude and Patience: Frontier Pasts to Live With?', *Meanjin*, vol.47, no.1, 1988; T. Rowse 'Paternalism's Changing Reputation', *Mankind*, vol.18, no.2; Bain Attwood, 'Understandings of the Aboriginal Past: History or Myth', *The Australian Journal of Politics and History*, vol.34, no.2, 1988; Bain Attwood, 'Aborigines and Academic Historians: Some Recent Encounters', *Australian Historical Studies*, 24, April 1990.
23 Attwood, *The Making of the Aborigines*, p.138.
24 Rowse, 'Tolerance, Fortitude and Patience'.
25 See Rowse, 'Tolerance, Fortitude and Patience'.
26 See Rowse, 'Paternalism's Changing Reputation'. See also R. Frances, B. Scates, A. McGrath, 'Broken silences? Labour history and Aboriginal workers', in T. Irving (ed.), *Challenges to Labour History*, UNSW Press, Kensington, 1994. D. S. Trigger, *Whitefella Comin'*, Cambridge University Press, Cambridge, 1992, also used Aboriginal oral history perspectives as evidence.

27 M. Fels, *Good Men and True: the Aboriginal Police of the Port Phillip District 1837–1853*, MUP, Melbourne, 1988; Attwood, *The Making of the Aborigines*.
28 J. Kociumbas, *The Oxford History of Australia: Possessions*, vol.2, Oxford, Melbourne, pp.101–102.
29 See review by M. Anderson in *Labour History*, 66, May 1994.
30 A. Curthoys, 'Agents or Victims', paper delivered to AHA Conference 1988.
31 H. Reynolds, *The Law of the Land*, Penguin, Ringwood, 1987; *Frontier*, Allen & Unwin, Sydney, 1987; *With the White People*, Penguin, Ringwood, 1990.
32 'The Working Party of Aboriginal Historians for the Bicentennial History, 1788–1988', 'Preparing Black History', *Identity*, 4, 5, Oct. 1981.
33 See S. Janson and S. Macintyre (eds), *Making the Bicentenary*, MUP, Melbourne, 1988; M. Langton and J. Horner, 'Day of Mourning', in B. Gammage and P. Spearritt (eds), *Australians, 1938*, Fairfax, Syme and Weldon, Sydney, 1987.
34 J. Kociumbas, *Possessions*, Oxford University Press, Melbourne, 1992. Kociumbas has stridently objected to the emphasis on agency in recent texts, implying on one occasion that such authors are apologists for colonialism. See pp.101–102.
35 P. Grimshaw, M. Lake, A. McGrath, M. Quartly, *Creating a Nation*, McPhee Gribble/Penguin, Ringwood, 1994.
36 J. Miller, *Koori: A Will to Win*, Angus and Robertson, Sydney, 1985.
37 K. Walker, *Stradbroke Dreamtime*, Angus and Robertson, 1972; M. Tucker, *If Everyone Cared*, Ure Smith, Sydney, 1983; C. Perkins, *A Bastard Like Me*, Ure Smith, Sydney, 1975; E. Simon, *Through My Eyes*, Collins Dove, Melbourne, 1987; J. Matthews, *The Two Worlds of Jimmie Barker*, AIAS, Canberra, 1977; M. Kennedy, *Born a Half-caste*, AIAS, Canberra, 1985; R. Langford, *Don't Take Your Love to Town*, Penguin, Ringwood, 1988; P. Pepper, *You are what you make yourself to be*, Hyland House, Melbourne, 1980; L. E.Roughsey, *An Aboriginal Mother tells of the Old and the New*, McPhee Gribble/Penguin, Ringwood, 1984; I. West, *Pride Against Prejudice*, AIAS, Canberra, 1984; G. Ward, *Wandering Girl*, Magabala Books, Broome, 1987; A. Nannup, *When the Pelican Laughed*, Fremantle Arts Centre Press, Fremantle, 1992. For an overview of Aboriginal literature, see A. Shoemaker, *Black Words, White Page*, University of Queensland Press, St Lucia, 1989.

38 Matthews.
39 Mudrooroo, *Writing from the Fringe*, Hyland House, South Yarra, 1990.
40 Tucker, Langford; B. Cummings, *Take this Child: From Kahlin Compound to the Retta Dixon Children's Home*, ASP, Canberra, 1990; P. Cohen and M. Sommerville, *Ingelba and the Five Black Matriarchs*, Allen & Unwin, Sydney, 1990.
41 Marcia Langton, currently at the Cape York Land Council, has held numerous influential positions: Director of the Australian Institute of Aboriginal Studies; Central Land Council; the Royal Commission into Aboriginal Deaths in Custody; the Queensland Ministry for Aboriginal Affairs; and the Anthropology Department, Macquarie University. Gordon Briscoe completed a postgraduate degree on the Royal Commission into Nuclear Testing at Maralinga and is currently working for the Commonwealth Government. Noel Pearson completed a BA Honours in history at the University of Sydney, studied law and is Director of the Cape York Land Council, which has been protesting against a proposed space station being built there. Jackie Huggins studied history and women's studies at the University of Queensland; she wrote *Auntie Rita*, Aboriginal Studies Press, Canberra, 1994, and her publications include 'Response' in S. Janson and S. Macintyre (eds), *Through White Eyes*, Allen & Unwin, Sydney, 1990, and (with Thom Blake) 'Protection or Persecution? Gender Relations in the era of Racial Segregation' and (with Heather Goodall) 'Aboriginal Women are everywhere: Contemporary Struggles' in K.Saunders and R.Evans (eds), *Gender Relations in Australia*, Harcourt Brace Jovanovitch, Marrickville, 1992.
42 M. Clare, *Karobran*, Alternative, Chippendale, 1978; Mudrooroo Nyoongah, (previously Colin Johnson) *Doctor Wooreddy's Prescription for Enduring the End of the World*, Hyland House, Melbourne, 1983; E. Willmot, *Pemulwuy, the Rainbow Warrior*, Weldons, McMahons Pt, 1987.
43 See A. Laurie and A. McGrath, 'I Once was a drover myself' in D. Barwick, B. Meehan and I. White (eds), *Fighters and Singers*, Allen & Unwin, Sydney, 1985; I. West, *Pride Against Prejudice*, 1984. D. Headon analyses the survival theme in 'Beyond the Years of the Locust: Aboriginal Writing in the 1980s, part 2', *Meridian*, vol.7, no.2, Oct. 1988.
44 C. Edwards and P. Read (eds), *The Lost Children*.
45 For fuller discussion of these themes, see introduction, chapter 1

and afterword of A. McGrath, *Born in the Cattle*, Allen & Unwin, Sydney, 1987.
46 D. Bird Rose, 'The Saga of Captain Cook: Morality and European law, *Australian Aboriginal Studies*, 2, 1984, pp.34–35; H. and F. Morphy, 'The "Myths" of Ngalakan History: Ideology and Images of the Past in Northern Australia', *Man*, 19, 1985, pp.459–78.
47 E. Kolig, 'Dialectics of Aboriginal Life-space' in M. Howard (ed.), *Whitefeller Business*, Institute for the Study of Human Issues, Philadelphia, 1978.
48 One book heading in that direction is by anthropologist D. Bird Rose. Her *Hidden Histories*, Aboriginal Studies Press, Canberra, 1991, presents and interprets oral accounts from the Victoria River region. A more recent large-scale work is Stuart Rintoul's *The Wailing: A National Black Oral History*, William Heinemann, Melbourne, 1994.
49 This is a summary of the proceedings of a special seminar on Aborigines and History at the Australian Historians Association Conference, 1984. One of the key speakers was Phyllis Daylight, then heading an enquiry into Aboriginal Women. See also J. Huggins and K. Saunders, 'Defying the Ethnographic Ventriloquists', *Lilith*, no.8, 1993.
50 G. Blainey, *Triumph of the Nomads*, Macmillan, Melbourne, 1975.
51 L. Coltheart, p.180.
52 Michael Williams' Doctoral research concerns his home community, and Noel Pearson was reluctant to write a general history of Aborigines in Queensland for the Royal Commission into Aboriginal Deaths in Custody partly due to this factor.
53 See J. Lee and V. Burgmann, the three-volume *People's History of Australia*, McPhee/Gribble, Ringwood, 1988; K. Saunders and R. Evans (eds), *Gender Relations in Australia*, specifically co-authored articles by J. Huggins.
54 Marcia Langton during RCIADIC discussions, May 1990.
55 P. Brock, *Women, Rites and Sites*, Allen & Unwin, Sydney, 1989.
56 R. Frances and B. Scates, 'Honouring the Aboriginal Dead', *Arena*, 86, 1989. See also C. Bulbeck, 'Aborigines, memorials and the history of the frontier', in S. Janson and S. Macintyre (eds), *Making the Bicentenary*.
57 Attwood, pp.142–43. See B. Attwood 'Portrait of an Aboriginal as an artist', *Australian Historical Studies,* 99, Oct. 1992 and 100, April 1993; T. Birch 'Half Caste' and J. Huggins 'Always was Always will be', *Australian Historical Studies*, 100, April 1993.

58 Henry Reynolds' *Law of the Land* won a peace prize in 1988, and Reynold's *Frontier* and McGrath's *Born in the Cattle* were nominated for A. A. Phillips Prize for Australian Studies in the Victorian Premier's Literary Awards for 1988 and 1990. *Born in the Cattle* won the Hancock Award for Young Historians, 1988 and *The Making of the Aborigines* was co-winner of this Award for 1990. Co-winners of the John Barrett Prize in Australian Studies, 1992–93 were Heather Goodall, ' "The Whole Truth and Nothing But": Some Interactions of Western Law, Aboriginal History and Community Memory', in B. Attwood and J. Arnold (eds), *Power, Knowledge and Aborigines*, LaTrobe University, Bundoora, 1992, and A. McGrath, 'Beneath the Skin', in R. Howe (ed.), *Women and the State*, LaTrobe University, Bundoora, 1993. Out of the wide interdisciplinary field known as 'Australian studies' it is interesting to observe that both related to Aboriginal history.
59 See K. Saunders and R. Evans (eds), *Gender Relations in Australia*, Harcourt Brace Jovanovich, Sydney, 1992, pp.vii–xiv.
60 Mudrooroo, *Writing from the Fringe*; K. Benterrak, S. Muecke, P. Roe, *Reading the Country: Introduction to Nomadology*, Fremantle Arts Centre Press, Fremantle, 1984.
61 The Australian Institute of Aboriginal Studies has trained numerous women in oral history techniques, as have various government projects. Others have gained expertise through experience.
62 B. Rosser, *Dreamtime Nightmares*, Aboriginal Studies Press, Canberra, 1985.
63 D. Bell, 'Speaking about rape is everyone's business', in *Women's Studies International Forum*, 12, 4, pp.403–16; J. Larbalestier, 'The Politics of Representation: Australian Aboriginal Women and Feminism', in *Anthropological Forum*, vol.6, no.2, 1990, pp.143–57.
64 D. Bell, 'A Reply from Diane Bell', *Anthropological Forum*, vol.6, no.2, 1990, pp.158–65.
65 J. Arnold and G. Attwood (eds), *Power, Knowledge and Aborigines*, La Trobe University, Bundoora, 1992.
66 B. Attwood, 'Introduction' to ibid, pp i–xvi.
67 The author has received a substantial grant from the Australian Research Council for a project, Gender and Colonialism, to explore state attitudes and Aboriginal responses to black/white sexual and family relations and childrearing.
68 For further discussion of this theme, see A. McGrath, ' "Stories for Country": Oral History and Aboriginal Land Claims', *Journal of the Oral History Association of Australia*, 1988.

Select bibliography

ROYAL COMMISSION PAPERS

Dodson, P. L., *Royal Commission into Aboriginal Deaths in Custody. Regional Report into Underlying Issues in Western Australia*, AGPS, Canberra, 1991.

The First Step: a Report on the Initial Community Consultations on the Royal Commission into Aboriginal Deaths in Custody, AGPS, Canberra, vols 1-3, 1992.

Johnston, E., *Royal Commission into Aboriginal Deaths in Custody. National Report into Underlying Issues*, AGPS, Canberra, vols 1–5, 1991.

Wootten, J.H., *Report of the Inquiry in NSW, Victoria and Tasmania*, AGPS, Canberra, 1991.

The individual case reports should also be consulted, though they are too voluminous to list here.

BOOKS

Arnold, J. and Attwood, B. (eds), *Power, Knowledge and Aborigines*, La Trobe University, Bundoora, 1992.

Atkinson, A. and Aveling, M. (eds), *Australians, 1838*, Fairfax, Syme & Weldon, Sydney, 1987.

Attwood, B., *The Making of the Aborigines*, Allen & Unwin, Sydney, 1989.

Bandler, F., *Turning the Tide*, Aboriginal Studies Press, Canberra, 1989.

Bandler, F. and Fox, L., *The Time Was Ripe*, Alternative Publishing Co-operative, Chippendale, 1983.

SELECT BIBLIOGRAPHY

Biskup, P., *Not Slaves, Not Citizens: The Aboriginal Problem in Western Australia 1898–1954*, University of Queensland Press, St Lucia, 1973.

Brock, P., *Outback Ghettos: A history of Aboriginal institutionalisation and survival*, Cambridge University Press, Melbourne, 1993.

—— *Yura and Udnyu: A history of the Adnjamathanha of the North Flinders Ranges*, Wakefield Press, Adelaide, 1985.

Brook, L. and Kohen, J.L., *The Parramatta Native Institution and the Black Town: A History*, NSW University Press, Kensington, 1991.

Broome, R., *Aboriginal Australians*, Allen & Unwin, Sydney, 1982.

Butlin, Noel, *Our Original Aggression*, Allen & Unwin, Sydney, 1983.

Cowlishaw, G., *Black, White or Brindle*, Cambridge University Press, Cambridge, 1988.

Daylight, P. and Johnstone, M., *Women's Business*, AGPS, Canberra, 1986.

Edwards, C. and Read, P., (eds), *The Lost Children*, Doubleday, Sydney, 1989.

Eggleston, E., *Fear, Favour or Affection*, Australian National University Press, Canberra, 1976.

Evans, R., Saunders, K. and Cronin, K., *Race Relations in Colonial Queensland*, University of Queensland Press, St Lucia, 1988.

Fels, M., *Good Men and True: The Aboriginal Police of the Port Phillip District*, Melbourne University Press, Melbourne, 1988.

Finnane, M. (ed.), *Policing in Australia: Historical Perspectives*, UNSW Press, Sydney, 1987.

Grimshaw, P., Lake, M., McGrath, A. and Quartly, M., *Creating a Nation*, McPhee Gribble/Penguin, Ringwood, 1994.

Haebich, A., *For Their Own Good: Aborigines and Government in the Southwest of Western Australia*, 1900–1940, UWA Press, Perth, 1988.

Horner, J., *Vote Ferguson for Aboriginal Freedom*, Australian and New Zealand Book Co., Sydney, 1974.

Horton, D. (gen. ed.), *The Encyclopaedia of Aboriginal Australia*, vols 1 and 2, Aboriginal Studies Press, Canberra, 1994.

Huggins, J., *Auntie Rita*, Aboriginal Studies Press, Canberra, 1994.

Jackomos, A. and Fowell, D. (eds), *Living Aboriginal History of Victoria: Stories in the Oral Tradition*, Cambridge University Press, Melbourne, 1991.

Janson, S. and Macintyre, S. (eds), *Through White Eyes*, Allen & Unwin, Sydney, 1990.

Jenkins, G., *Conquest of the Ngarrindjeri*, Rigby, Adelaide, 1985.

Langford, R., *Don't Take Your Love to Town*, Penguin, Ringwood, 1988.

Loos, N. A. *Invasion and Resistance*, ANU Press, Canberra, 1982.

Markus, A., *Governing Savages*, Allen & Unwin, Sydney, 1990.

Markus, A. (ed.), *Blood from a Stone: William Cooper and the Australian Aborigines' League*, Monash Publications in History, Melbourne, 1986.
Marshall, P. (ed.) *Raparapa: All right, now we go 'longside the river*, Magabala Books, Broome, 1988.
Mattingly, C. and Hampton, K. (eds), *Survival in our own land: 'Aboriginal' experiences in 'South Australia' since 1836*, Wakefield Press, Adelaide, 1988.
McGrath, A., *Born in the Cattle*, Allen & Unwin, Sydney, 1987.
May, D., *Aboriginal Labour and the Cattle Industry*, Cambridge, Oakleigh, 1994.
Meaney, N. (ed.), *Under New Heavens*, Heinemann, Sydney, 1989.
Morris, B., *Domesticating Resistance: The Dhan-gadi Aborigines and the Australian State*, Berg, 1990.
Mulvaney, D.J., *Encounters in Place*, University of Queensland Press, St Lucia, 1989.
Mulvaney, D.J. and White, J. Peter (eds), *Australians to 1788*, Fairfax, Syme, Weldon, Sydney, 1987.
Myers, F., *Pintupi Country, Pintupi Self*, AIAS and Smithsonian, Canberra, 1986.
Nannup, A., *When the Pelican Laughed*, Fremantle Arts Centre Press, Fremantle, 1992.
Pepper, P., *You Are What you Make Yourself to Be: The Story of a Victorian Aboriginal Family 1842–1980*, Hyland House, Melbourne, 1980.
Read, J. and Read, P., *Long Time Olden Time: Aboriginal Accounts of Northern Territory History*, CD-Rom, Firmware, 1993.
Read, P., *A Hundred Years War: The Wiradjuri and the State*, ANU Press, Canberra, 1988.
Reece, B. and Stannage, T. (eds), *European–Aboriginal Relations in Western Australian History*, University of Western Australia, Perth, 1984.
Reece, R.W., *Aborigines and Colonists: Aborigines and Colonial Society in New South Wales in the 1830s and 1840s*, Sydney University Press, Sydney, 1974.
Reynolds, H., *With the White People*, Penguin, Ringwood, 1990.
—— *The Law of the Land*, Penguin, Ringwood, 1989 and 1992.
—— *Frontier*, Allen & Unwin, Sydney, 1987.
—— *The Other Side of the Frontier*, Penguin, Ringwood, 1981.
Rose, D.B., *Hidden Histories*, Aboriginal Studies Press, Canberra, 1991.
Rosser, B., *Dreamtime Nightmares*, Australian Institute of Aboriginal Studies, Canberra, 1985.
Rowley, C.D., *The Destruction of Aboriginal Society*, Penguin, Ringwood, 1971.

—— *Outcasts in White Australia*, Penguin, Ringwood, 1971.
Ryan, L., *The Aboriginal Tasmanians*, University of Queensland Press, St Lucia, 1982.
Saunders, K. and Evans, R. (eds), *Gender Relations in Australia: Domination and Negotiation*, Harcourt Brace Jovanovich, Sydney, 1992.
Sommerville, M. and Cohen, P., *Ingelba and the Five Black Matriarchs*, Allen & Unwin, Sydney, 1990.
Swain, T., *A Place for Strangers*, Cambridge University Press, Cambridge, 1993.
Sykes, B. and Smith, S., *Mum Shirl*, Heinemann Education, Melbourne, 1981.
Sykes, R., *Black majority*, Hudson, Melbourne, 1989.
Sykes, R., *Murawina: Australian Women of High Achievement*, Doubleday, Sydney, 1993.
Toyne, P. and Vachon, D., *Growing up the country: The Pitjantjatjara struggle for their land*, McPhee Gribble/Penguin Books, Ringwood, Victoria, 1984.
Tucker, M., *If Everyone Cared*, Ure Smith, Sydney, 1977.
Ward, G., *Wandering Girl*, Magabala Books, Broome, 1987.
West, I., *Pride against Prejudice*, Aboriginal Studies Press, Canberra, 1984.
White, I., Barwick, D., Meehan, B. (eds), *Fighters and Singers*, George Allen & Unwin, Sydney, 1985.
Willmot, Eric, *Pemulwuy: The Rainbow Warrior*, Weldons, Sydney, 1987.

Index

Page numbers in italics denote illustrations.

Aboriginal/Aborigines: the term defined xix, 149, 199, 225–6, 280–1, 301–2n, 343–4, 361
Aboriginal Affairs Act, 1962 (SA) 232–3
Aboriginal Affairs Planning Authority (WA) 260–1
Aboriginal and Island Councils (Qld) 198, 200
Aboriginal Child Care Agency (WA) 262
Aboriginal Communities Act, 1979 (WA) 262
Aboriginal Councils and Courts Act, 1965 (Qld) 198
Aboriginal Cultural Heritage Unit, Museum of Victoria 155
Aboriginal Deaths in Custody, *see* deaths; Royal Commission
Aboriginal Heritage Act, 1972 (WA) 261, 262
Aboriginal Land Councils 112, 293, 297, 384
Aboriginal Land Fund Commission 329

Aboriginal Land Inquiry, 1983 (WA) 262–3
Aboriginal Land Rights (NT) Act, 1976 293
Aboriginal Lands Act, 1970 (Vic) 154
Aboriginal Lands Trust (SA) 234; (WA) 261
Aboriginal Lands Trust Act, 1966 (SA) 233
Aboriginal Legal Service (NSW) 110; (Tas) 329, 331; (WA) 262
Aboriginal Medical Benefits Fund (NT) 24
Aboriginal Medical Service (WA) 262
Aboriginal (NT) Ordinance, 1911 276
Aboriginal Protection Board (Victoria) 150–1, 158
Aboriginal Resource Centre, University of NSW 382
Aboriginal Studies 367, 375, 381–2, 385
Aboriginal–white relations, *see* relations; women, Aboriginal
Aboriginals (NT) Ordinance, 1933 279–80

INDEX

Aboriginals Protection and Restriction of the Sale of Opium Act, 1897 (Qld): implementation of 182–6, 189–93; exemptions from 192; *Amendment Act 1939* 193–5
Aborigines, dispossession of Chapter 1; *see also* colonisation/invasion
Aborigines, history of, *see* history
Aborigines, legal status of 234
Aborigines, perceptions of/beliefs about 286–7, 289, 339–40, 355–6 362; *see also* myths; by historians and anthropologists, *see* history
Aborigines Acts (Vic): *1869* 136; *1886* 139; *1910 Amendment* 140; *1915* 142; *1957* 150
Aborigines classified by colour (caste) 6, 138, 140, 142, 148, 149, 199, 225–6, 227, 247, 258, 286–7, 345, 346–7
Aborigines' Progressive Association (NSW) 87
Aborigines Protection Act, 1911 (SA) 210, 225–7, 228; *1939 Amendment* 230–1
Aborigines Protection Acts (WA): *1886* 249; *1905* 253, 254
Aborigines Protection Board, NSW (later Aborigines Welfare Board): policies 59–60, 73, 76–83, 84–6, 89–91, 103–5; demise of 107–8; *see also* Aborigines Welfare Board (NSW)
Aborigines Protection Board (SA) 211, 230
Aborigines Welfare Board (NSW) (previously A. Protection Board) 60, 88, 148
Aborigines Welfare Board (Vic) 150–2
activism/activists, Aboriginal/white 9, 80, 83, 87, 88, 99, 104, 106–7, 111, 146–8, 197–8, 306, 309, 372; *see also* civil rights; reformers; resistance; *see also by name*
Adnyamathanha people 210–12, 218, 235–6

alcohol 9, 31, 34, 44–5, 90, 101, 106, 143, 230, 233, 259, 286, *294*
Alice Springs 294–5
Angas, George French 213
anthropology, twentieth century 366–7
anti-slavery movement, *see* reformers/humanitarian
Armstrong, Francis 244
Arnold, John 389
arrest rate, Aboriginal 297, 305n; *see also* detention
Arthur, George 13, 317, 319–20, 321
Arthur's Proclamation of Demarcation, 1828 (Tas) 319–20
artists, Carrolup 255
assimilation policy 5, 31, 60, 89–91, 93–6, 105–6, 149–52, 220, 229–32, 257, 287, 328, 349, 350, 351–2
atomic tests, Maralinga and Emu 217
Attwood, Bain 344, 371–2, 385, 389, 390
Australia First Movement (NSW) 87–8
Australian Aboriginal Fellowship (NSW) 100, 104
Australian Aboriginal League (NSW) 87, 88
Australian Aboriginal Progressive Association (NSW) 83–4, 87
Australian Aborigines' League (Vic) 143, 147
Australian Institute of Aboriginal and Torres Strait Islander Studies 375
Australian Institute of Aboriginal Studies 367
Australian Investment Agency (NT) 277–8
Australian Natives Association (NSW) 5, 84
authors, Aboriginal 373–7, 380, 382; and ghostwriters/co-authors 386–9; *see also* history; *see also by name*
awards, literary 385, 397n

403

Awards, Pastoral Industry 259–60, 284, 295

Banggaiyerri 386
Barker, Jimmie 80–1, 373
Bartlam, Roy 197
Barwick, Diane 126, 136, 141, 149, 151, 152, 369
Bates, Daisy 217
Batman, John 125–6, 127
Beckett, J. 389
Behrendt, Paul 381, 382
Bell, Diane 296, 388–9
Bennelong 18, 63, 363
Benterrak, Krim 387
Berndt, C. 278
Berndt, R. 278
Bicentenary, 1988 9, 359
birthrate, attempts to reduce birthrate 77; *see also* infant mortality
Blackburn, Doris 154
Blainey, Geoffrey 379
Bleakley, J.W. 275, 277, 279, 280, 300n
Bleakley Report, 1929 277
Bob, Mount Serle 210
Bolte government 149
'bone rights' 330–1, 334
Bonwick, Charles 309, 315
Bonwick, J. 363
Bosun, Ted 195–6
Bourke, Richard 14, 125, 127
Boyoi, Waddi 40
Brennan, Frank 200
Brickell, Melissa 150, 151
Brindle, Ken 104
Briscoe, Gordon 374, 395n
Britten, Jack 260
Brock, Peggy xii, xxvii, 384
Bromby, Charles 326
Broome, Richard xii, xxvii, 340, 341, 370, 384
Bruny Island 322–3, *324*
Bruny Island Mission 323
Buckley, William 125
Bunerong people 127, 133, 134

Bungalow, the (NT) 280, 287
Burgmann, V. 372

Caldicott, A. 98
Cameron, Pelham 146
Campbell, Harry 269, 272
camps, fringe, *see* fringe dwellers
Canning, A.W. 245
Canning Stock Route 246, 254
Cape Barren Island reserve/community 325–8, 329, 345–51, 354; attempts to break up 351–2
Cape Barren Island Reserve Act, 1912 327–8; revoked 351
Carrolup Settlement 33, 255
cattle industry, *see* pastoral industry
census, Aborigines included in 108; *see also* citizenship
Central Australian Aboriginal Congress 295
Central Australian Aboriginal Legal Aid Service 110
Central Australian Aboriginal Media Association 297
Central Board of Aborigines (Vic) 135–6
Chewings, Charles 271, 299
Chi, Jimmy 264
child endowment payments 84
child mortality rates 141; *see also* infant mortality
children: in Aboriginal culture 11; controlled by Chief Protector 226; employment of 74, 76, 80, 315; expelled from schools 253–4; in foster care 90–1; in institutions 33, 189, 280, 275; *see also* Children's Homes; mixed descent
children removed from parents 2, 25, 77, 79, 80–1, 83, 84, 90, 136, 140–1, 150–1, 186, 195, 210, 250–1, 253, 255–6, 258, 266n, 315, 347, 350–1, 373, 384
Children's Homes/institutions 33, 77, 79, 80, 90, 141, 151, 280–1

INDEX

Christian attitudes 63, 87, 88, 95, 98, 101–2, 176; *see also* churches
Christianity taught 130, 135, 224, 247, 258
Christie, Michael 127–9
churches 73, 101–2; support for Aborigines 82, 98; *see also* white support
citizenship rights 256–7
civil rights demands/activism 46, 86–9, 107, 349
Clare, Monica 376
Clark, Glenn 331
Clark, Manning 365
Clarke family, Framlingham 146, *147*
Clay, Fred 195
Clint, Alf 102
Cochrane-Smith, Fanny 325, 353
Coe, Les 38
Cohen, P. 374
Collins, David 363
colonisation/invasion xxvii–xxviii; NSW 62–70; NT 273; Queensland 169–70; SA 208, 212–20, 235–6l; Tasmania 314–22, 338–41; Victoria 124–34; WA 243–8
colonisation/invasion, effects of 1–9, 40–7, 121; *see also* pastoral industry; resistance
colour bar in towns/residential areas 94–5, 107, 144, 150; *see also* racism; segregation
Coltheart, Lenore 362, 384
Community Services (Aborigines) Act, 1984 199
Community Services (Torres Strait) Act, 1984 199
concentration/re-education policies 85–6, 89, 92
Coniston Massacre 29, 277
convicts 22, 314
Cook, Cecil 41, 281
Cook, James 63, 124, 297
Coombs, H.C. 292
Cooper, Lynch 146

Cooper, William 45, 72, 87, 88, 98, 147–8
Coranderrk reserve 134, 136, 139, 140, 141, 142
Council for Aboriginal Affairs 292–3
Council for Aboriginal Rights (NSW) 99, 100; federal 291, 293
Council for Civil Liberties (NSW) 104
Council of Aboriginal Women of South Australia 233
Creaghe, Caroline 174–5
Creaghe, H.A. 175
cricket teams 137–8, 146
'crime', Aboriginal 27, 30–4; *see also* punishment
Croker, Len 197
Crowley, F.K. 372
cultural history/heritage, Aboriginal 9–12, 122–4, 242–3, 377–9, 384, 386–8; knowledge of 381; *see also* Dreaming; history
cultural/racial identity, Aboriginal 9, 83–4, 112, 113, 152–9, 330, 332, 345; denial of/questioning 339, 343–4, 346; recognition of 355; *see also* social structure
cultural museums 382
culture, Aboriginal 113, 152–3, 332; preserving 261, 347–8
Cumeragunja community 22, 45, 83, 87, 137, 140, 146–8, 154, 224; strikes 45, 88–9, 148
curfews 181, 276, 277
Curthoys, Ann 371
custody, *see* detention; deaths in custody

Dalrymple, Dolly 353
Danayirri, Hobbles 296–7
Daniels, Davis 291
Darwin 298–9
Darwinism, Social 15, 71, 139, 176–7, 247, 346, 363
Davey, Stan 154
Davey, Thomas 317, *319*

405

Davis, Jack 256, 264
Day of Mourning, 1938 88, 147–8
Daylight, Phyllis 396n
de Brune, A. 364
deaths: of children, *see* infant mortality; in custody 16, 39, 46, 110, 131, 156, 245, 263, 266n, 331; through early violence and/or disease 20–1, 64, 65–6, 124–5, 128–9, 130, 178, 214, 237n, 245, 314, 322, 323; on reserves 141; *see also* Royal Commission
Deleuze, G. 387
Department of Aboriginal Affairs 105, 152
Depression, 1890s 76, 140
Depression, 1930s 23, 59–60, 84–6, 144
desegregation policy, failure of 92–7
desert communities 294–5
detention, Aborigines in 6–7, 30–4, 232, 252, 297, 305n, 331; *see also* prisons
Deverell, Albert 328
Dharuk people 22, 61, 63, 64
Directorate of Aboriginal Affairs (NSW) 108–9
discrimination 6–7; economic 87; racial 29–30, 60, 110, 328, 331; wage 24; *see also* colour bar; racism; segregation; wages; welfare benefits, exclusion from
disease epidemics 85
diseases, introduced 20, 64, 124–5, 129, 141, 208, 212–13, 246, 248, 314; *see also* deaths
dispersal policy 76–83; Aboriginal resistance to 83–4; failure of 85; white resistance to 81–2
District Welfare Officers (NSW) 89–91
Dixon, Pharlap *378*
Dodson, Mick xxvii, 46, 298
Dodson, Pat xxiv, 46, 298
'Dog Act' 86, 88
'Dog Licences' (exemption certificates), *see* exemption certificates
dole, the, *see* unemployment benefits
Dreaming beliefs/stories 27, 242, 377–8, 381
Drew families 74, 78–9
Duffy, Gavin 134
Duguid, Charles 277, 291
Durack, M.P. 278

education 24–5, 43, 75, 96–7, 260; access to 113; *see also* schools; universities
Edwards, Coral xvi, 373, 377
Elkin, A.P. 366, 392n
Ellis, Viviene Rae 323
Elphick, Gladys 233
employment, Aboriginal, *see* labour
Eora peoples 17, 20, 22, 63, 124
equality: concept of 112; government recognition of 261; and loss of identity 152
Ernabella Mission 217
Europeans, first contact with 310–14; *see also* colonisation; Macassans
Evangelical Lutheran Church of Australia 228
Evans, Raymond 368, 384, 386
Everett, Jimmy 331, 333, 352
Everett, Ken 356
Everitt, Coral 354
exemption certificates 6, 89–90, 106, 199
exemption from government Acts 192, 211–12, 230–1, 253, 259
extinction myth 41, 177–8, 220, 252, 363

farms/farmers, Aboriginal 22–3, 64–5, 66, 72, 74, 77–8, 87, 92, 247–8
Federal Council for Aboriginal and Torres Strait Islander Advancement 46, 102, 198, 291, 292–3
Federal Government policies, post-1967 260–3

INDEX

Federal Pastoral Industry Award 259–60
Fels, Marie 127, 371, 385
Felton, H. 354
Ferguson, Bill 87
Fesl, Eve 385
First World War 23, 77, 257
Fitzroy, C.A. 66–7
Fletcher, J.J. 96
Flick, Barbara 99
Flinders Island 14, 356
Flinders Island Settlement/community 323, 326, 345, 352
Foley, Gary 359
food/rations 24, 73, 74, 76, 85, 179–80, 210, 222–3, 230, *258*, 259, 285, 300n; nutritional value of 285, 302n
football teams 146
Forrest, John 251–2
Forrest Commission (WA) 252
Forrest River massacre 29
fostering Aboriginal wards 90–1
Framlingham community/reserve 135, 142, 144, 146, 149, 154
Frances, Rae 384
Franklin Dam case, 1983 330
Fraser, Eliza 169
Fraser, Malcolm 293
Freedom Ride, 1965 34, 107
fringe dwellers/camps 145, 148–9, 180–1, 279–81, *290*, 294–5, 296
frontiersmen/settlers 17–19, 171; *see also* pastoralism
Furnell, L.C. 261

Ganai (Kurnai) people 153
Gandangara people 61, 64–5, 65
Garnet, F. 22
Geia, Albie 197
gender relations 43–4; *see also* women, Aboriginal
genocide: attempted 338–9, 342; the term 306–7
Gerrard, Alfie 247

Gibbs, Pearl 87, 99
gold rushes 68, 132, 170
Goodall, Heather xii, xvi, xxvii, 384, 388
Gordon, Arthur 174
Goss government 200
Goulburn Island 293
government policies 6–8; *see also* assimilation; concentration/re-education; dispersal; integration; multiculturalism; protectionism; segregation; self-determination; urbanisation
government policies, Aboriginal resistance to, *see* resistance
graduates, Aboriginal 374
Green, John 136, 139
Green, Lochy 257
Green, Morton Clare 347, *349*, *353*
Greenwood, Gordon 365
Grey, George 66–7
Gribble, J.B. 15, 246
Groves, Bert 87, 98, 99, 100
Guattari, F. 387
guilt, national 363
Gurindji people 39, 291, 292, 378; *see also* Wave Hill walk-offs

Haasts Bluff Reserve 277, 279, 292
Haebich, A. 248, 251
half-caste, *see* mixed descent; Aborigines classified
Hancock, W.K. 365
Hardwick, Fanny 313
Hasluck, Paul 149, 285
Hay, William 254
health, Aboriginal 98; *see also* deaths; diseases
Heiss, Anita *375*
Henty family 125
Hermannsburg Mission 275
Hippi, Albert 187–8
historical writing by Aborigines 373–7
histories, Australian 362–72; Aborigines excluded from 364–6;

Aborigines represented in 363–4, 368–72
history, Aboriginal 242–3, 272, 309–14, Chapter 10; who should write it? 379–86; *see also* cultural history/heritage
History Programme, Aboriginal (Vic) 155
homelands, return to traditional 293–6
Horsetailer, Peter 271, 299
hospitals, segregation in 94
housing, Aboriginal 92–7, 104–5, 108, 141, 144–5, 149, 150, 156, 159, 231, 258, 288, 328; fringe-dweller, *see* fringe dwellers
Housing Commission, NSW 104, 108, 109
Howitt, Alfred 137
Hudson, Jerry 186
Huggins, Jackie xxvi, 374, 381, 382, 388, 395n
Hughes, Robert 306
human rights, the United Nations and 284
humanitarian movement, *see* reformers

Identity magazine 155
imprisonment, *see* detention; prisons; deaths in custody
Industrial Workers of the World (IWW) 25
infant mortality rate 141, 278, 287–8; *see also* life expectancy
Inquiry into the Condition of Aborigines in the Northern Territory, 1928 277
institutions, *see* children; Children's Homes
integration policy 107–8, 220–1, 351
invasion of Australia, *see* colonisation/invasion
Jackson's Track fringe camp 145
James, Shadrach 149
James, Thomas 146–7
Jampijinpa, Kwementjaye 282
Jandamarra ('Pigeon') 249

Japangardi, Tim 282–3
Jay Creek reserve 279
Johnson, Colin 376
Johnson, Jill 155
Jose, Arthur 364
jury system 28, 29
justice system, Aboriginal, *see* law, Aboriginal
justice system, British/Australian: Aborigines and the 27–30, 37–40, 130–1, 289; on reserves 30–1, 195–6; *see also* law enforcement

Katter, Bob 199
Kaurna people 213–14, 220, 237n
Kennedy, Marnie 195, 373
Kickett, John 253
kidnapping of Aborigines 2, 18
Killalpannina Mission 223
Kinchela Boys' Home 79
Kinchela lands/reserve 78, 108
King, Philip 13
Kingstrands 288
Kociumbas, Jan 371, 372
Koonibba Mission 223, 228
Koori Club, Victoria 155
Koori Information Centre 155
Koori Oral History Programme 155
Kooris, the name xxix, 155, 361; *see also* cultural/racial identity
Kopperamanna Mission 223
Kulin people 14, 125, 126–7, 134
Kunoth-Monks, Rosalie 298
Kurnai people 137

La Grange Aboriginal community 384
labour/employment, Aboriginal 22–7, 68–70, 73–4, 91, 132–3, 137, 179–80, 181, 185–6, 210, 220, 247, 248, 273–5, 313; living/working conditions 180, 185, 277–8, 284–5, 288; *see also* wages
labour, convict 315
Lake Tyers reserve 43, 135, 137, 142–6, 146, 149, 152, 154

INDEX

Land Act, 1898 (WA) 247–8
Land Councils, see Aboriginal Land Councils
land ownership/use, Aboriginal 13–15, 22–3, 62, 66–8, 123, 178, 183–4, 215, 244–5, 293, 327; see also farms/farmers
land purchases, early European 125–6
land rights Acts 233–4, 293, 296, 297
land rights claims 8–9, 45–6, 71–4, 102–3, 134, 272, 293, 299n, 329, 384; supported by churches/reformers 46, 66–7, 71, 98, 172; government concessions to 72, 73, 111, 112, 154, 227, 233, 234, 325–6, 327, 328; 329; see also Mabo decision; Native Title Act, 1993
land rights inquiry (WA) 262–3
Lands Department, NSW 77
Lang, G.S. 170
Langford Ginibi, Ruby 32–3, 47, 373
Langton, Marcia xxvi, xxvii, 46, 374, 382, 388, 395n
language centres, Aboriginal 262
languages/language groups 61, 296, 299, 361, 310
Larbalestier, Jan 388–9
Laurie, Amy 16, 39, 376
Laverton Commission, 1976 (WA) 261
law, Aboriginal 27, 37, 242, 243–4, 276, 299–300n; and Native Courts 254–5
law, British/Australian, see justice system
law enforcement 171, 173–4; see also police; prisons
Lawford, Eric 249, 259
Lawrie, Margaret 233
Lee, J. 372
left-wing support for Aborigines 87, 88
legal services 110
Leslie, Patrick 170

life expectancy 159; see also infant mortality
Link-up 384
Lock Hospital Scheme (WA) 248
Long, Jeremy 290
Loos, Noel 219
Lumbia 254, 255
Lumholtz, Carl 177
Lyons, Joseph 148

McDaniel, Michael 381
McGinness, Jack 286–7
McGinness, Joe 197–8
McGrath, Ann xiii, xv, 274, 370
McLaren, Philip 376
McLean, Charles 149–50
McNab, Duncan 175
Macquarie, Lachlan 21–2
McQueen, Humphrey 365
McRae, Tommy 141
Mabo decision 4, 9, 13
Macassans, early Aboriginal contact with 12, 19, 168, 272
Maloga Mission 137, 140
Mansell, Michael 41, 306, 329
Maralinga atomic tests 217
Maralinga Tjarutja Land Rights Act, 1984 233
marriage in Aboriginal culture 153
marriages, mixed 225; broken up 287
martial law, Tasmania 320–21
Mathews, Janet 373
Matson-Green, Vicki (Maykutenner) xiii, xxv, xxvii, 333
May, Dawn xiii, xxvii, 384
Maykutenner, see Matson-Green
Maynard, Bernard 349
Maynard, Fred 83, 98
Maynard, Mary 352
Maynard, Vern 352
Melbourne Aborigines 149
Memmi, Albert 121
men, pressures upon Aboriginal 44–5
Meston, Archibald 19, 177, 179, 180, 181–2, 203n
Middleton, S.G. 257–8

409

Midnight Oil 309
migrations, *see* population movement
Milangga, Maggie 259
Milingimbi 294
military permits, World War II 256
military service, Aborigines on 23, 145, 257
Miller, Yari 228
mining industry 215, 261, 263, 292, 293; Aboriginal resistance to 261; royalties 293
Ministry for Aboriginal Affairs (Vic) 152
missionaries 2, 30, 73, 172, 176, 189, 222, 258, 275, 285, 326–7
missions 135, 137, 183, 188–9, 194, 211, 212, 218, 223–4, 227, 228, 244, 247, 255, 275, 323, 371; *see also* reserves
mixed descent, Aborigines of 225, 247, 248, 250–1, 255; attitude to/treatment of 139, 144, 193–4, 210, 220, 280–1; children 3, 247, 250–1, 253, 258, 279, 280–1; protection of 225–7; separated from 'full bloods' 210, 227, 286–7; *see also* Aborigines classified
Mollison, Bill 354
Moore, Russell (James Savage) 151
Moree 82–3, 89, 96, 104, 107
Moreton Bay Aborigines Friendship Society 172, 176
Morgan, Sally 47, 264, 373, 377
Morrell, James 169
Morris, B. 92
Morris, Ewan 291
mortality rates 141, 278; *see also* deaths
Moseley, H.D. 36, 254–5
Moseley Royal Commission, 1934 254–5
Mosely, Percy 77–8
Mosquito 316
Mount Serle station 210–11
Mountford, C.P. 211
Mudbura people 378
Mudrooroo 373, 381, 387

Muecke, S. 387
Mullagh, Johnny 138
Mullett, Albert 150
Mullett, Euphemia 145
multiculturalism 221
Mulvaney, D.J. 368
Munroe, James 313
murder/massacre, *see* violence
murder trials 29–30
Murray, George 307
Murray, John 140
Murray-Smith, S. 349
Murris 65, 82–3, 86, 103, 105; the term xxix, 361
myths: Captain Cook 378–9; 'extinction' 339, 350, 356, 363; of meek submission of Aborigines 338–9, 342; *see also* terra nullius

Namatjira, Albert 297–8
Nance, Beverley 128
Nannup, Alice 373
Native Administration Act, 1936 (WA) 255
Native (Citizenship Rights) Act 1944 (WA) 256
native courts 254
Native Police Force 170–1, 173–4, 175
Native Title Act, 1993 46, 385; WA oppposition to 263–4
Native Welfare Act, 1954 (WA) 258
Nauo people 215
Nelson, Topsy Napurrula 388
Nettheim, Garth 199
Neville, A.O. 254
New Norcia Mission 244, 247
New South Wales Chapter 2
Ngabidj, Grant 47, 374, 386–7
Nicholls, Doug 145–6, 148, 149, 154, 234–5, 291
Noble, Susie (Wilton) 210–11
Noonkanbah drama, 1980 261
Noonuccal, Oodgeroo (Kath Walker) 46, 367, 373
North Australian Workers Union 293

INDEX

Northern Territory Chapter 7
Northern Territory Land Rights Act, 1976 43, 234
Nyungar people 253–4

O'Donaghue, Lois 46
O'Shane, Gladys 197
Oenpelli 293
Onus, Bill 143
Oodnadatta *216*

Paakanti people 66
Pallawah (Tasmanian Aborigines) Chapter 9
Palm Island 187, 194–5; strike action 197
Papunya 290, 293
Parker, William 131
pastoral industry 273–5; effects of 65–6, 129–30, 169–70, 172, 183–4, 210, 214–15, 218, 220, 244–5, 278, 284–5, 314–16; *see also* frontiersmen; labour
Pastoral Industry Awards 259–60, 284, 295
Patches, Mary 354–5
paternalism, State 34, 182, 200; *see also* protectionist policies
Patten, Jack 87
Pearson, Noel xxvi, 46, 374, 380, *395, 396*
pensions, government 106; *see also* unemployment benefits; welfare benefits withheld
Pepper, Phillip 16, 145, 153, 373
Perkins, Charles 34, 47, 107, 280, 298, 299, 373
Peron, M. 311–12
Phillip, Arthur 63
Pike, Douglas 365
Pilbara strike, 1946 25, 259
Pink, Olive 367
Pintubi people 289–90
Pitjantjatjara Council 384
Pitjantjatjara Land Rights Act, 1981 233–4

Pitjantjatjara people 217, 236, 289–90
Point McLeay Mission 223
Point Pearce Mission 223
police, Aboriginal 170–1, 173–4, 175, 195
police, white 6, 16, 31, 33, 42, 73, 183, 249, 253; harassment/treatment by 82, 104, 110, 261–2, 331
Police Offences Act (SA) 231
political action by Aborigines 233–4; *see also* activism/activists
politics, Aborigines in 146–8, 234–5
Poonindie Mission 223–4
population, Aboriginal: attempts to reduce 77; NSW 80, 103–4; NT 294, 296; numbers reduced by disease/violence, *see* deaths; pre-invasion 10, 62; Queensland 171, 181, 193; Tasmania 306, 309, 315, 323–4, 329; Victoria 130, 135, 140, 141, 149, 153, 155–6, *157*; WA 263, 247
population, European 130, 171, 213, 214, 215
population movement/migration 217, 289–90, 293–5, 296
poverty 32–3, 72–3
prejudice, *see* colour bar; racism; White Australia Policy
prisons: Aborigines in, *see* detention; attitude of Aborigines to 35, 39–40, 45; escapes from 45; segregation in 35
protectionist policies 27, 33, 34, 38, 58, 59–60, 130, 132, 177, 182–3, 184–5, 221–2, 225–9, 249; *see also* Protectors
Protectors 182–3, 184–5, 191, 221–2, 226–7, 249, 253, 276, 280, 281
protests, Aboriginal 359–60; *see also* activism/activists; resistance
Punch, Jack 187
punishment 33; and the justice system 289; methods of 34–40

411

Queensland Chapter 4
Queensland State Council for the Advancement of Aborigines and Torres Strait Islanders 198

race relations, *see* relations
racial discrimination, *see* discrimination
racial superiority/inferiority 5, 15
racial violence, *see* violence
racism 43, 60, 81, 99, 144, 175–6, 295, 339, 345, 368
racist language/propaganda 339, 342–3
Randall, Bob 287
Ranger Uranium Project Area 293
rape cases 29
rations, *see* food/rations
Read, Peter xiii, xvi, xxvii, 92, 373, 377, 384
re-education policies, *see* concentration/re-education
Referendum, National (1967) 46, 108, 260
reformers/humanitarian pressure 63, 66, 71, 181, 246, 317, 319
relations between whites and Aborigines 43–4, 57–8, 125–9, 131, 179–80, 243, 310–14, 390
removal orders (Queensland) 186–8, 194–5
research on Aborigines 367; Aboriginal vs non-Aboriginal researchers 380–6
Reserve Act 1945 (Tas) 328
reserves/settlements 6, 30–1, 43; NSW 38–9, 67–8, 72, 73, 79, 104; NT 275, 276, 279, 290, 293–4; Queensland 43, 183, 184, 194–7, 199; SA 217, 222; Tasmania, *see* Cape Barren Island; Victoria 135–42; *see also* Cumeragunja; Framlingham, Lake Tyers
reserves/settlements revoked/closed 77–8, 102, 108, 142, 157–8
resettlement schemes, soldier 77
resistance, Aboriginal: to colonisation 40–7; in NSW 58–9, 71–2, 83–4, 86–9, 99–103, 127–9; in NT 291–2; in Queensland 197; in SA 214, 215; in Tasmania 316–17, 339–40, 341–2; in WA 248–51, 261; *see also* activism/activists; strikes; violence, Aboriginal
Revell, Mark 331
Reynolds, Henry xiv, xv, xxvii, 323, 342, 369, 372, 380, 384
Ridley, William 176
rights, equal 261; *see also* civil rights; land rights
Roach, Archy 151
Roberts, Frank Snr 98
Roberts, Hagar 275
Roberts, S.H. 364
Roberts families 82, 102
Robertson, Gilbert 320
Robinson, F. 368
Robinson, George Augustus 14, 130, 313, 314, 316, 317, 321, 322–5, 326
Roe, Paddy 374, 387
Roman Catholic Mission, New Norcia 244
Roper River Mission 275
Rose, Debbie 274
Rose, Lionel 145
Rosser, Bill 387–8
Roth, Walter 183, 185, 252–3
Roth Report 252–3
Roughsey, Dick 373
Roughsey, Elsie 373
Rowley, C.D. 28, 248, 285, 288, 367–8, 379–80
Rowse, Tim 371
Royal Commission into Aboriginal Deaths in Custody xxvi, 16, 110, 263, 266n, 331, 334, 384
Royal Commission on Aborigines 1913–16 (SA) 211, 227
Royal Commissions into the Condition of Aborigines (WA): 1883 252; 1904 252–3; 1927 254; 1934 254–5; 1974 261; 1976 261–2

INDEX

rural segregation, *see* segregation
Rusden, G.W. 363
Ryan, Lyndall 306, 370
Ryan, Tommy 195

sacred/ancient sites 329, 330
Saunders, Horace 100
Saunders, Kay 384, 386
Savage, James (Russell Moore) 151, 384
Scates, Bruce 384
schools 262; Aborigines expelled from 253–4; segregation in 75, 82–3, 96–7
schools/colleges, Koori 155
schools/universities, Aboriginal studies in 381–2, 385
Schürmann, Clamor 222
Scott, Evelyn 198
Sculthorpe, June 353
sealers and Aboriginal women 312–13
Seaman, Paul 262
Second World War, Aborigines in 23, 256, 257, 281–3; *see also* military service
segregation 30, 35, 38, 59–60, 85–6, 223, 319–20, 344–5, 346–7; Aboriginal perceptions of 97–9; of 'full-blood' and mixed-descent people, *see* mixed descent; in hospitals 35; in prisons 35; rural/residential 60, 94–7, 99–103, 104, 106–7, 108, 111; in schools 75, 82–3, 96–7; *see also* reserves
Select Committee on Aborigines (Tasmania) 308
self-determination policy 261
settlements, government, *see* missions; reserves
settlers, *see* pastoral industry
sexual relationships, *see* gender relations; women, Aboriginal
Shaw, A.G.L. 365
Shaw, Bruce 386–7
sheep/cattle farming, *see* pastoral industry

Shirl, Mum 26–7, 33
Simon, Ella 373
Skinner, Dickie 261
Skull Creek Royal Commission (WA) 261–2
Smoke Signals magazine 154
Social Darwinism, *see* Darwinism
social structure, Aboriginal 9–12, 61–2; *see also* cultural/racial identity
Sommerville, M. 374
song cycles 377
South Australia Chapter 5
South Australian Constitution Act 221–2
sovereignty, concept of 112
Spencer, Baldwin 144, 276, 277, 279
Spencer, Herbert 15
sports, Aborigines in 137–8, 145–6
Stannage, Tom 385
Stanner, W.E.H. 365
Stephens, Charles 327
Stephens, Edward 326–7
stereotyping Aborigines 339–40
Stevens, Frank 288, 368
Strehlow, T.G.H. 279, 295
Stretton, A.V. 37
strike action 25, 45, 88–9, 100, 197, 259, 291–2, *303*, 367
Strzelecki, P.E. de 325
Sturt, Charles 212
suicide 40
Suke 325
Sullivan, Jack 47
superiority philosophy, white, *see* Darwinism
surveillance policies (NSW) 30, 38–40, 41, 89–91
Swan River Colony 248
Sydney Aboriginal population 103–4

Tangentyere Town Council 297
Tasmania Chapters 8 and 9
Tasmanian Aboriginal Centre 329, 331
Tasmanian Aborigines xxiii, 4, 5, 10–11, 14, 20–1, 41, Chapter 9;

legal status of 355; *see also* Cape Barren Island reserve/community
Tatz, Colin 30, 152, 285, 288
Tench, Watkin 63, 363
terra nullius concept 1, 4, 5, 12–13, 71, 243, 288–9, 340
Thaiday, Willie 195
Thomas, Faith 233
Thomas, William 126, 129, 132–3, 134
Thompson, Barbara 169
Thorn, Ernest 175
Tongerie, Maude 233
Torres Strait Act, 1939 196–7
Torres Strait Islanders 168, 196–7; culture 10; population 155–6
Torres Strait Islands 43
Toussaint, Sandy xiv, xxvii
towns, Aborigines in 92–7; white resistance to 82, 89, 94–7, 104, 150, 253, 295, 296; *see also* curfews; urban Aborigines, urbanisation
towns, fringe camps outside, *see* fringe dwellers
Tozer, Horace 181
trade unions 100
Tranby Aboriginal Co-operative College 382, 384
treaty: absence of 13; Batman-Kulin (1835) 14
Trefoil Island 329
trials, murder 29–30
Truganini *308*, 309, 324–5, 330–1, 339, 354, 356
Tucker, Margaret 46, *47*, 80–1, 88, 373

unemployment 44, 84–5, 95, 156, 159
unemployment benefits 84–5, 87
United Aborigines Mission 211, 217
United Nations and human rights 284
universities, Aborigines in 374, 382
university Aboriginal Studies 381–2, 385

urban Aborigines, pressure on 109; *see also* towns
urbanisation policy 103–5, 108–9

Vesper, Alex 102
Victoria Chapter 3
Victorian Aboriginal Advancement League 154
Victorian Aboriginal Child Care Agency 151
violence against Aborigines 15–21, 29, 64–7, 127–9, 173–5, 178, 180, 203n, 214, 245–6, 254, 271, 277, 313, 314–15, 320–22, 323, 338, 363; *see also* children, removal; women, Aboriginal
violence against Europeans 19–20, 128, 172–3, 178, 316–17, 322; *see also* resistance
Vogan, A.J. 175
vote, Aborigines entitled to 259

wages of Aborigines 23–4, 254, 259–60, 284–5, 288, 292, 295; government control of 189–92; in rations 24, 74, 179–80, 259
Wakefield, Edward Gibbon 218
Walker, Frederick 171
Walker, Kath (Oodgeroo Noonuccal) 46, 367, 373
Wandin, Joseph 145
Ward, G. 373
Wards Employment Ordinance 288
Waste Lands Act, 1842 (SA) 222
Watson, James 35
Watson, John 244, 249, 250–1
Wave Hill pastoral lease 292
Wave Hill walkoffs, 1966 25, 291–2, 303n, 367
Wearne, Heather 194
Wedge, Patrick 104
welfare benefits, exclusion from 6, 24, 140, 144, 350; *see also* child endowment; unemployment benefits

INDEX

Welfare Board, *see* Aboriginal Welfare Board
welfare officers 89–91; *see also* Protectors
Welfare Ordinance, 1953 285–6
welfare policies 58, 60; *see also* protectionist policies
West, Alma *348*
West, Arthur *348*
West, Errol xxvi, xxvii, 332, 343, 346, 347, 349, 353–4, 384
West, Ida 47, 330, 332, 346, 373, 376
Western Aboriginal Legal Service (NSW) 384
Western Australia Chapter 6
Western Desert, migration from 289–90, 293–5, 296
Wheeler, Johnny 289
White Australia Policy 5, 340
white resistance to Aboriginal housing, *see* towns
white support for Aboriginal resistance/demands 87, 88, 100, 101–2, 104, 175, 177; *see also* activism
Whitlam Government 260, 293
wildlife, destruction of 244
Williams, Michael 380, 396n
Willmot, Eric 376
Wilson, Winifred 285
Wilton, Albert 210, 211
Wilton, Rufus 210–12
Wilton family and 'mixed descent' legislation 210–12, 235
Windjana Gorge Rebellion 249

Wiradjuri people 66, 104
Woiworung people 132, 134
women, Aboriginal: and Aboriginal men 313–14; employment of 70, 74, 77, *81*; and European men 3, 43–4, 131, 225, 248, 249–50, 253, 311–14, 341; and 'exempted' men 231; pressures upon 44–5; restrictions on 255; violence against 175, 312–14; *see also* labour; violence
women, early contacts between Aboriginal and white 63–4
women in Aboriginal social structure 11
Wood, George 254
Woomera Rocket Range 217
Wooraddy 324, 325
Worawa College 155
working conditions, *see* labour
writers, Aboriginal, *see* authors; history

Yangkunjatjara people 217
Yipirinya School 297
Yirrkala 293; land rights case 272, 299–300n
York, B. 368
Yorta-Yorta people 153
Yothu Yindi 298
Yuendumu 293
Yungnora people 261
Yunupingu, Galarrwuy xxx, 298, 299, 359, *360*,
Yunupingu, Mandawuy 298